Grass-Roots
Socialism

Grass-Roots Socialism

Socialism

Radical Movements in the Southwest

1895-1943

JAMES R. GREEN

LOUISIANA STATE UNIVERSITY PRESS

Baton Rouge and London

Design: Albert Crochet
Typeface: VIP Aster
Composition: Modern Typographers, Inc., Clearwater, Florida
Printing and binding: Kingsport Press, Kingsport, Tennessee

LIBRARY OF CONGRESS CATALOGING IN PUBLICATION DATA

Green, James R., 1944–
  Grass-roots socialism.

  Includes index.
  1. Socialist Party (U.S.) 2. Socialist Party (U.S.).

Oklahoma. 3. Socialism in the Old Southwest. I. Title.
JK2391.S6G73   329'.81'00979   77–28205
ISBN 0–8071–0367–5

To Carol

Contents

Illustrations

Preface

IN THE TURBULENT years before World War I the American Socialist party won its strongest grass-roots support in the area then known as the Southwest—Oklahoma, Texas, Louisiana, and Arkansas. Together these four states gave Socialist presidential candidate Eugene Debs over 80,000 votes in 1912, almost one-tenth of the party's national total. Oklahomans built the strongest Socialist state organization in the nation; their party claimed more dues-paying members than New York state and in 1914 the Sooner Socialists received 15,000 more votes than the Socialist party of the country's largest state. In the same year the Sooner Socialists reported twelve thousand dues-paying "red card members" in 961 locals and saw over one hundred of their comrades elected to county and township offices along with six to the state legislature. This remarkable political phenomenon extended to the other southwestern states as well, where Socialists built up grass-roots organizations modeled after the Oklahoma party.

Socialism in the Southwest was an educational as well as a political force. The Socialist party spread its message through fifty-five weekly newspapers and scores of summer encampments that drew thousands of farmers and workers to week-long radical revivals. Historians of the Socialist party in America have commented on the remarkable growth of socialism in the Southwest, but they have failed to analyze this political phenomenon or to connect it to the social and economic history of the New South in the West.

This is the story of the farmers and workers who joined together in the Socialist movement during the early twentieth century to resist the fate capitalism had in store for them. It tells of forgotten people—of indebted homesteaders, migratory tenant farmers, coal miners and railroad workers, "redbone" lumberjacks from the piney woods, preachers and schoolteachers from the sunbaked prairies, of village artisans and atheists, of the unknown people who created the strongest regional Socialist movement in United States history. These poor people have been forgotten because their political party was destroyed by vigilante and government repression during World War I and because the laboring classes who supported the movement have now disappeared from the region. Eroded cotton plantations and weather-beaten tenant shacks, depressed mining towns and broken tipples, cut-over forests and abandoned sawmills—these relics remain as traces of the people who worked in the great southwestern extractive industries. The working people who toiled in the cotton farming, coal mining, and lumbering industries, battling the powerful owners, have gone. Gone through the dust bowl to California. Gone to the City.

And so this study attempts to write an important missing chapter in the history of the American Socialist party. Previous histories of the Debsian movement have been preoccupied with the decline of socialism in the United States. This account explains the various disasters that befell the southwestern Socialists during and after World War I, and it carries their story through the 1930s when radicalism enjoyed an Indian summer. The focus, however, is not on the movement's decline, but on its remarkable growth in the years before the First World War, when, in a frontier farming region far removed from the urban centers of Marxist influence in the United States, an exceptional grass-roots strength developed.

Specifically, this study explores the relationship between populism and socialism, a relationship ignored in previous accounts, even by historians concerned with establishing the progressive nature of the People's party. This association was a particularly close one in the Southwest, especially during the early 1900s when radical Populists formed the Socialist cadre, as they most commonly did in Texas and the Oklahoma Territory. The southwestern case shows that many militant Populists refused to follow Texas leaders into the reform wing of the Democratic party or to take the reactionary course adopted by Georgia's Tom Watson, a hero to southern radicals on both sides of the Mississippi. However, it is not helpful to categorize southwestern socialism as a simple case of resurgent Populist agrarianism. Populism and socialism in the Southwest represented significantly different constituencies on the basis of rather different ideologies.

A regional analysis of southwestern socialism also provides an opportunity to test other generalizations offered in national histories of the Socialist party. If this grass-roots expression of radicalism cannot be categorized as a simple resurgence of Populist agrarianism, can it be analyzed in more general terms as the protest of insecure one-crop farmers, similar to those who created an agrarian Socialist movement in western Canada? If so, does southwestern socialism follow S. M. Lipset's proposition that the most successful Socialist movements in the United States have made their attack on capitalism "not in terms of the Marxian doctrine of class struggle, but as a continuation of the traditional struggle of farmers and workers against the 'vested interests' of . . . Wall Street"?

By evaluating precinct and county voting returns it is easy to test the generalization that agrarian socialism depended primarily upon the support of one-crop farmers; it is more difficult to analyze the impact made by Socialist propaganda. Contrary to Lipset's theories about agrarian socialism, the southwestern Socialist party did appeal to "a permanently exploited proletariat of workers and farmers" with a class-conscious ideology more radical than Populist reformism. Southwestern socialism clearly made more than a "little impression" upon the permanently exploited masses of the region, but it is difficult to know how the party's rank-and-file members interpreted the Socialist appeal.

Fortunately, a regional study of the Socialist party can provide a closer analysis of rank-and-file beliefs than can national studies that have tended to concentrate on the ideas and policies of the professionals and intellectuals from the North who dominated the party's leadership. In providing a statistical profile of the rank-and-file agitators who organized the southwestern Socialist movement on a grass-roots level, this study explores the fusion of nineteenth-century moralistic radicalism with modern "scientific socialism" as it occurred among largely self-educated farmers, workers, and villagers. Although in reconstructing the movement's history it is still necessary to rely heavily upon the evidence provided by party leaders, it is also possible to examine the ideas and activities of rank-and-file Socialists and to provide a look, from the bottom up, at the party's development. This view is especially important in the Southwest where the Socialist party was more democratic and less bureaucratic than it was in other sections. Without some appreciation of the efforts made by grass-roots agitators, it is impossible to understand the growth of southwestern socialism as a mass movement.

Given the southwestern Socialists' conscious use of religious rhetoric and revivalistic tactics, it is tempting to apply Daniel Bell's psychoreligious interpretation of Debsian Socialists as "chiliastic" utopians who were neither in nor of the real world of political "give and take." Socialism in the Southwest was filled with emotionalism and moralism, but it was quite nonsectarian in political terms; the party's electoral success depended largely upon its ability to organize methodically around pressing issues in the "real world" of regional and local politics. The southwestern Socialist appeal was more moralistic than materialistic, but the movement cannot be reduced to an expression of psychological or religious disturbance merely because of its religious content.

Although the popularity of southwestern socialism grew partly out of its firm attachment to the regional traditions of Populist agrarianism and religious revivalism, the movement transcended its provincial origins not only by attaching itself firmly to the Second International's principles of Marxian socialism, but by politicizing contemporary class struggles that could not be fully explained in the terms used by Populists or religious revivalists. The material basis of this radical movement cannot be understood through the rhetoric of the Socialists alone, though their analysis of regional class conflict provides a good starting point.

In order to understand the class basis of southwestern socialism it is necessary to examine the complicated social and economic history of this volatile region. Such an examination is lacking in all national histories of the Socialist party, their concentration being almost entirely on political history. A regional study of the Debsian Socialists provides an opportunity to describe the social and economic changes that created a setting for radical agitation and organization. It is not possible to include a comprehensive socioeconomic history of the southwestern region, but it is feasible to identify the causes of important class conflicts in this New South to the West.

This general examination of the setting opens up the possibility of analyzing in more detail the movement's socioeconomic composition—a necessary step in advancing beyond a political history of the Socialist party to a broader social history of a radical movement. Extensive voting analysis at the county and precinct level clearly reveals the class basis of Socialist support in the Southwest, but a more dynamic form of analysis is needed to demonstrate how profoundly regional class struggles affected the development of socialism. Class conflict between debtors and creditors, tenants and landlords, workers and industrialists was clearly documented by a federal commission in 1915, and it was clearly reflected in Socialist party voting support. But southwestern class struggles assumed many forms and affected many areas of life quite removed from the arena of electoral politics. Thus, in order to appreciate the effect of class conflict upon Socialist protest (in its many forms), it is important to move beyond voting analysis and the rather static, categorical definitions of class required in the study of election results.

This work does not employ a structural or categorical definition of class; it adopts the definition E. P. Thompson sets forth in his preface to *The Making of the English Working Class*. Class is an "historical phenomenon" with a "fluency that evades analysis if we attempt to stop it dead at any given moment and atomize its structure," writes Thompson. If history is stopped at any given point, at an election for example, "then there are not classes but simply a multitude of individuals" with various experiences. "But if we catch these men over an adequate period of social change, we observe patterns in their relationships, their ideas, and their institutions," Thompson observes. "Class is defined by men as they live their own history, and, in the end, that is its only definition."

The first phase of southwestern frontier development created a serious class conflict between indebted farmers and town creditors, soon reflected in the rapid development of the Texas Farmers' Alliance, the Arkansas Agricultural Wheel, and the Louisiana Farmers' Union. There were some connections between these developments in the late 1880s and the militant strikes conducted by the Knights of Labor against the railroad corporations—these corporations being viewed by most organized farmers as their main monopolistic oppressor. In 1886 a group of Alliancemen in Erath County, Texas, passed this resolution of sympathy with striking railroad workers: "Whereas combined capital by their unjust oppression of labor are casting gloom over our country and . . . . Whereas we see the unjust encroachments that the capitalists are making upon all the different departments of labor . . . we extend to the Knights of Labor our hearty sympathy in their manly struggle against monopolistic oppression." Farmers learned something about the politics of the Democratic party during the Great Southwest Strike of 1886. As Lawrence Goodwyn writes, "Democrats could not be the friends of railroad workers because the old party was dominated by the railroad corporations." Indeed, "Democrats, like Republicans, served the likes of Jay Gould [the railroad magnate], not the Knights of Labor or the Farmers Alliance." This discovery was reflected in the independent insurgency of the Arkansas Union Labor party, and later of the People's parties of Texas and Louisiana, but for various reasons Populist agrarianism failed to unite farmers and workers. It also failed to politicize the discontent of landless tenant farmers who joined the agrarian revolt without raising particularistic demands.

After the turn of the century and the decline of populism, the grievances of indebted farm owners remained unresolved whereas the problems of the tenants (who were oppressed as debtors as well as renters) remained unrecognized even by agricultural experts and neopopulist reformers in the Democratic party. Throughout the early 1900s, the countryside became more impoverished as cotton tenancy increased and the towns and cities grew prosperous, attracting wealthy farmers who, along with businessmen, speculators, and other absentee landlords, owned an increasing share of the land. The stage was set for a new kind of class struggle in the Southwest, a struggle that united the rural producers—indebted yeomen and landless tenants—against the "parasites" in the towns and cities. This was essentially an extension of the old town-country conflict politicized by the Populists in the 1890s, but it included a sharper class dimension as a result of the rapid growth of tenancy and absentee landlordism. In politicizing the southwestern "land question" in the 1910s, the Socialist party added political content and class consciousness to the rapid town-country polarization that occurred in this prosperous "progressive era." The party also relied heavily upon the activities of militant industrial unions, especially of miners and timber workers, to add a class-conscious content to their protest. Although southwestern tenants resisted proletarianization and insisted upon remaining on the land at all costs, they identified more readily with industrial workers than with the yeomen farmers who formed the backbone of the People's party. The possibility of a farmer-labor party in the Southwest diminished with the decline of the Knights of Labor in the late 1880s and disappeared after the defeats of the miners' strikes and the American Railway Union's Pullman boycott in 1894. But after the Socialist party's formation in 1901, militant industrial unionism grew in tandem with Socialist agrarianism until 1912. Although socialism continued its growth in Oklahoma after this date, it declined in the other southwestern states largely because of the increasingly violent nature of the region's class struggles, which provoked reactionary repression along with insurrectionary protest from frustrated Socialists.

In short, it is impossible to understand either the rise or the fall of southwestern socialism apart from the class struggles that punctuated the region's violent history. This study, however, does not portray southwestern socialism simply as the product of social and economic conflict. The Socialist movement did not arise spontaneously from unregulated frontier confrontations; it was painstakingly organized by scores of former Populists, militant miners, and blacklisted railroad workers, who were assisted by a remarkable cadre of professional agitators and educators and inspired by occasional visits from national figures like Eugene V. Debs and Mother Jones. In the decade following the Socialist party's founding in 1901, this core of organizers grew to include indigenous dissenters patiently converted to the Socialist gospel by party preachers. The expanded core depended increasingly upon a much larger group of amateur agitators who canvassed the region selling newspapers, forming reading groups, organizing locals, and making soapbox speeches.

Socialist party organizers acted as a cadre of professional agitators, but they could not have created a grass-roots movement in the Southwest without the support of amateur agitators. These "Jimmie Higginses" linked the party leadership to the rank and file, and they insisted that the party organize its campaigns around pressing local grievances. To a great extent, the Socialist parties in the Southwest were organized in response to issues raised at the grass-roots level. The party leadership helped to coordinate the activities of militants already at work: Populist farmers moving to the left after the decline of their party, miners struggling to build their own industrial union, leftist organizers mobilizing tenant farmers within the reformist Farmers' Union, women suffragists looking for partisan support, rebellious timber workers striking out against the lumber trust, and renegade preachers propagating a radical brand of Christian socialism. By sponsoring and organizing the activities of these indigenous militants the Socialist party could incorporate the leftist tendencies of other southwestern radical movements and could reach down to the grass-roots level. These indigenous radicals helped professional party organizers, editors, and lecturers establish something of an organic relationship with poor farmers and workers who, in many cases, had already developed a kind of natural rights socialism of their own.

The southwestern Socialists lacked "the kind of statewide cooperative infrastructure" which the Farmers' Alliance provided for the Populists, according to Lawrence Goodwyn's study, *Democratic Promise: The Populist Movement in America*. The Socialist party's organizers took advantage of the prior organization of the Farmers' Union and the United Mine Workers, but they could not build upon a class-conscious mass movement like the Farmers' Alliance. The Socialist movement did, however, provide its activists with a "schoolroom of ideology" and "a culture of self-respect" by borrowing many of the methods used by the earlier cooperative movement. This new movement also fulfilled the people's need to "see themselves" creating "new democratic forms" much in the way the Populist movement as described by Goodwyn did in its Texas and Kansas strongholds.

One of the most important objectives of this study is to describe the forgotten men and women who made the movement such a strong indigenous expression of socialism. This involves a description of the professionals—organizers, like "Red" Tom Hickey; popular Socialist philosophers and educators, like Oscar Ameringer and the "little professor," Walter T. Mills; revivalistic encampment orators like Kate Richards O'Hare; and publishers like Julius A. Wayland, the master propagandist of American socialism whose weekly, the *Appeal to Reason*, reached over sixty thousand readers in Texas and Oklahoma alone. They were colorful characters and they deserve further biographical study, especially as popularizers of Marxian socialism in the United States. However, this regional treatment also requires an examination of the amateur agitators who operated at the grass-roots level. Fortunately, a biographical "who's who" listing the leading salesmen-soldiers of J. A. Wayland's "army" of subscription hustlers provides the basis for an analysis of the unknown "Jimmie Higginses" of the movement—the rank-and-file Socialist activists.

A careful description of the agitational and organizational methods adopted by these southwestern Socialists may provide one key to understanding their party's extraordinary local strength, a strength that contributed significantly to the national party's rapid gains at the polls between 1904 and 1914. In this sense, it is more important to understand the role of the organizer-agitator than the role of the candidate, who generally articulated the immediate demands and philosophical principles already tested at local levels. The party's candidates also expressed well-developed political positions in which local and regional grievances were linked to the larger problems created by capitalist civilization. Southwestern Socialists clearly entered the "give and take" of the immediate political world by formulating demands to meet pressing problems ignored by the dominant political leaders.

In many respects, the southwestern Socialists did look back to the radical traditions of the nineteenth century, not just to Populist agrarianism, but further back to the natural rights philosophy articulated by Tom Paine and Thomas Jefferson. They looked beyond the cooperative industrial unionism of the Knights of Labor to the labor theory of value expounded by artisan radicals; behind Christian socialism they saw the millennial theology preached by the early radical revivalists. By relating their radicalism to these native traditions, the southwesterners enhanced the appeal of what they called "scientific" socialism. But unlike their nineteenth-century forerunners, the Debsian Socialists did not believe that the development of capitalism could be reversed or that the competitive system would fade away as soon as the ideal cooperative alternative had been articulated. Unlike the Populist agrarians and social gospelers, unlike Henry George's single taxers and Edward Bellamy's Nationalists, the Debsians saw "the whole history of mankind" as a "history of class struggle." And so they accepted the reality of class conflict in their own time and committed their considerable energies and abilities to the fight against the capitalist class. In the Southwest the reality of this conflict shaped Socialist politics as much as did Marxian theory.

The most difficult objective here is to describe the spirit of the southwestern Socialist movement, because the movement involved much more than just a political party with a particular program and philosophy. As a revivalistic crusade it created a kind of religious enthusiasm, a feeling produced partly by the colorful cast of characters who organized and vitalized the movement, ingeniously combining the demand for immediate change with the ultimate promise of a cooperative society. The feeling of immediacy and enthusiasm that so impressed Gene Debs when he traveled the southwestern encampment circuit was also a product of the desperate conditions faced by farmers and workers who had been attracted to a promising frontier only to find it despoiled and exploited by capitalist speculators and entrepreneurs. Consequently, the masses who were attracted to southwestern socialism brought to the movement a mood of anger and resentment that sometimes erupted into violent protest. The poor whites who joined the crusade for the Cooperative Commonwealth were motivated by bitterness, frustration, and even hatred, and though these feelings were common enough among members of their class throughout the South, what distinguished this group from other resentful, rebellious poor whites was their spirit of hopefulness.

In some cases the poor had this spirit of optimism when they came into the movement through religious millennialism or Populist agrarianism, and in other cases, it was the movement that gave them a sense of hope for their future and for their class. And so a combined feeling of anger and optimism characterized the leaders and members of the Socialist party in the southwest. The movement was motivated by conflicting feelings; it was both hateful and hopeful. The Socialists were terribly angry with the "parasites" who denied the "producers" the full reward for their honest toil, but they were also amazingly hopeful about the possibility of creating a new society in their own lifetimes, a society in which exploitation and competition would be banished. They truly believed that the Cooperative Commonwealth was within their grasp.

Acknowledgments

MANY PEOPLE HELPED me write this book. I would first like to thank C. Vann Woodward who has offered encouragement and enlightenment from the start. His own historical work has been an inspiration and a constant source of instruction. I am deeply indebted to my comrades Neil Basen, Paul Buhle, Garin Burbank, and James Weinstein who shared their ideas about American socialism and offered numerous thoughtful criticisms and helpful suggestions.

I am also grateful to the following people who helped me by reading parts of the manuscript or by providing me with important information: Sydney Ahlstrom, Ruth Allen, Ray Arsenault, Mari Jo Buhle, John Demos, Melvyn Dubofsky, Robert Dykstra, Paul Faler, Larry Goodwyn, Don Graham, Archie Green, Lewis Gould, Herbert Gutman, Jim Kendell, Morgan Kousser, Bruce Palmer, and John Womack, Jr. I have appreciated the encouraging advice I received along the way from Jim O'Brien and Ted Rosengarten, and the time, space, and congenial atmosphere provided by Royden Harrison and the staff of Warwick University's Centre for the Study of Social History, in Coventry, England, where I completed this work. I would also like to thank my excellent editor at LSU Press, Mary Jane Di Piero.

I could not have written this study without the assistance I received from the archival staffs at the following university libraries: Arkansas (Fayetteville), Duke, Indiana State (Terre Haute), Houston, Illinois (Champaign-Urbana), Kansas State (Pittsburg), Louisiana State (Baton Rouge), New York (Tamiment), Oklahoma, North Carolina, Texas (Austin and Arlington), Tulane, Wayne State, and Yale. I am also indebted to the staffs at the state historical society libraries in Missouri, Oklahoma, and Wisconsin, to Marietta Malzer of the Oklahoma State Library and to Dedsie Johnson of the Calcasieu Parish courthouse, Lake Charles, Louisiana.

Permission has been granted to reprint material that originally appeared in two journal articles: "The Brotherhood of Timber Workers, 1910–1913: A Radical Response to Industrial Capitalism in the Southern U.S.A.," *Past and Present*, No. 60, and "Tenant Farmer Discontent and Socialist Protest in Texas, 1901–1917," *Southwestern Historical Quarterly*, Vol. 81.

Finally, I would like to express my special appreciation to Freda Hogan Ameringer and H. L. Mitchell for sharing their memories with me and for letting me know that the spirit of the old movement lives on.

Grass-Roots
Socialism

Introduction
The Setting: A New South in the West

THE RICH DELTA flatlands and the fertile bottomlands of Louisiana, Arkansas, and East Texas had been settled by slaveowners before the Civil War, but most of the trans-Mississippi South remained a frontier region until after the Reconstruction period. In the middle seventies "refugees" from the Old South crossed the big river and homesteaded along the river bottoms of Louisiana, in the Arkansas Ozarks, and in the East Texas piney woods. Eventually those gaunt-faced men and women with bad cases of "Texas fever" pushed through the big thicket, out into the fertile black waxy prairie, and then onto the Great Plains, where they battled the cattle barons for the right to homestead beyond the ninety-eighth meridian.[1]

Those poor white refugees soon found that the homestead ideal had been "aborted by the land speculator and the monopolist." In the 1870s agents of northern and British capital acquired huge domains of rich timberland and ranchland, while the Democrats who had "redeemed" Texas from the Radical Republicans granted twelve railroad corporations 32 million acres of land from the public domain, an area larger in size than the state of Indiana.[2] Loui-

1. C. Vann Woodward, *Origins of the New South, 1877–1913* (Baton Rouge: Louisiana State University Press, 1951), 108–109; Walter Prescott Webb, *The Great Plains* (New York: Grosset and Dunlap, 1931), 205–55; Gilbert Fite, *The Farmers' Frontier, 1865–1900* (New York: Holt, Rinehart, and Winston, 1966), 193–214.

2. Henry Nash Smith, *Virgin Land: The American West as Symbol and Myth* (Cambridge, Mass.: Harvard University Press, 1950), 223; Woodward, *Origins of the New South*, 109–10.

siana and Texas were the picnic grounds for one of the juiciest barbecues of the Gilded Age.

The southwestern land struggle took a violent turn in 1883 when the "nesters" of central Texas battled the big ranchers in a remarkable fence-cutting war. When the cattle kings reluctantly fenced in their land, they provoked a kind of revolution which "bordered on civil war." Small farmers and stockmen started cutting the fences and forming night-riding groups like the Knights of the Knippers. "The fence cutting wars," remarked the Galeston *News*, "grew out of a dangerous policy of selling off the public domain and allowing the creation of principalities and baronates among a few capitalists." Land monopolies and enclosures had aroused a "spirit of agrarianism among the poorer classes." The fence cutters were soon suppressed by armed guards, who were bitterly labeled the "mounted Cassocks of the cattle barons," and by the Texas Rangers who also had killed Sam Bass, the "generous open hearted highwayman"—a kind of Robin Hood to the poorer classes.[3] The homesteaders lost the violent battle over the barbed-wire fences, but they eventually won a place for themselves on the fertile Texas plains.

The official opening of the Oklahoma Territory in 1889 enhanced the region's reputation as the most promising frontier in the United States. But the chaotic development of this western part of the Indian Territory soon revealed that "this celebrated 'last frontier' was an illusion," because homesteaders could not acquire enough free land to farm independently. During the 1890s share-tenancy spread like insect blight, as poor white migrants poured into the opened territory. "Land speculators and other grafters" had gained control of the best farm land belonging to the Five Civilized Tribes even before the eastern section was opened to settlement. This "perfect milieu for exploitation" also attracted the attention of

3. Webb, *The Great Plains*, 205–68, 313–15; R. D. Holt, "The Introduction of Barbed Wire into Texas and the Fence Cutting War," *West Texas Historical Association Yearbook*, VI (1930), 70–75. On Sam Bass, see Walter Prescott Webb, *The Texas Rangers: A Century of Frontier Defense* (Austin: University of Texas Press, 1965), 431–32.

railroad promoters, coal operators, and oil prospectors who leased or purchased "any kind of land they could get their hands on." By the turn of the century, many of these "grafters," especially the rich oilmen, had become gentlemen farmers whose land was worked by tenants. As a result of the corporate speculation sanctioned by the federal government, tenancy increased faster in the eastern Oklahoma Indian Territory than in any other section of the country. By 1900 tenants comprised about 64 percent of the farmers in the seven newly settled counties east of Oklahoma City.[4]

Some of these tenants were Indians who had been dispossessed of their tribal lands; others were Afro-Americans who had joined the exodus to Oklahoma in the 1890s when E. P. McCabe and his followers dreamed of making the territory an all-black state. By the end of the decade racist reaction had shattered this dream and blacks stopped coming to the Oklahoma territories. Many of those who remained banded together in separatist communities for self-defense and self-help. Consequently, blacks constituted about 8 percent of the population for another two decades after 1890.[5] The growing tenancy problem in eastern Oklahoma was thus largely a white problem. In Texas, white share-tenancy increased rapidly as a result of the depression of the nineties whereas the black proportion of the population (largely composed of sharecroppers and laborers) actually decreased from 22 percent in 1890 to less than a fifth by 1900.

The growth of a poor white class of renters was not publicly recognized until after the turn of the century, partly because the large black peasantry of sharecroppers in the delta regions of states like

4. Carey McWilliams, *Ill Fares the Land: Migrants and Migratory Labor in the United States* (Boston: Little Brown, 1941), 188; Angie Debo, *And the Still Waters Ran* (Princeton, N.J.: Princeton University Press, 1940), x, 95–125; Gerald Forbes, "Oklahoma Oil and Indian Land Tenure," *Agricultural History*, XV (1947), 189–94. Also see Fite, *Farmers' Frontier*, 201–14.

5. Mozell C. Hill, "The All-Negro Communities of Oklahoma: The Natural History of a Social Movement," *Journal of Negro History*, XXXI (1946), 257–59; Martin Dann, "E. P. McCabe and the Movement for Oklahoma Colonization," *Kansas Historical Quarterly*, XL (1974), 370–78; U.S. Department of Commerce, *Thirteenth Census of the United States, 1910: Population* (Washington, D.C.: Government Printing Office, 1913), III, 436.

Louisiana and Arkansas helped obscure the fact that tenancy in the Southwest was becoming a white folk's problem. Those who noticed the rise of white tenancy in the cotton states tended to dismiss the situation as temporary. The notion that a hard-working, thrifty, white tenant could easily work his way up an "agricultural ladder" to ownership was propounded by boosters of the New South in the West as an agrarian counterpart to the urban Horatio Alger mobility myth. But, as LaWanda Fenlason Cox explains, "tenancy in the post-Civil War cotton areas did not prove to be a rung on the agricultural ladder," because usurious interest rates and inflated land values kept most renters in permanent poverty.[6] The high cost of credit and land exacerbated the acute tenancy problem in the Indian Territory, though the problem had deeper roots. The federal government's land policy created so many opportunities for "speculation and land engrossment" that homesteaders in the territory and other parts of the West were "frequently forced to become tenants on the lands of speculators."[7]

State land policy in Texas was even more incongruous than the federal policy that aborted the Homestead Act in the Indian Territory. Under the Redeemer governments speculators and railroad corporations acquired the best lands, but the enormous Lone Star state still provided plenty of tracts for immigrant yeomen from the Old South. The disastrous depression of the mid-nineties, however, led to many foreclosures and to the creation of an enlarged class of white share-tenants. The boll weevil blight and the panic of 1907 swelled this class even further as did the continued immigration of poor whites to the north central counties above Abilene, where speculators inflated land values beyond the reach of ordinary settlers. In the early 1900s tenancy established itself firmly in this

6. LaWanda Fenlason Cox, "Tenancy in the United States, 1865–1900: A Reconsideration of the Agricultural Ladder Hypothesis," *Agricultural History*, XXII (1948), 98–100. For a discussion of the urban, middle-class "mobility myth" see Stephan Thernstrom, *Poverty and Progress: Social Mobility in a Nineteenth Century City* (Cambridge, Mass.: Harvard University Press, 1964), 57–79.

7. Paul W. Gates, "The Homestead Law in an Incongruous Land System," *American Historical Review*, XLI (1936), 672.

newly settled cotton-growing region and in the old black belt that ran from Dallas to San Antonio. In this black waxy prairie, the world's most fertile cotton-growing area, "there was a marked tendency for farm lands to be consolidated into the hands of fewer owners, many of them business and professional men who had foreclosed on mortgages or had invested their profits in farm lands." These "large landowners usually held their farm lands for a rise in value and rented them to immigrant farmers from the older Southern states."[8]

The renters soon found themselves caught in the credit web of the crop lien system, just as the black sharecroppers had been trapped in the older plantation sections of the South. This exploitative credit system "sprang out of the ruins of the old regime, and spread, like Jimson weed, a curse to the soil," holding black sharecroppers in a "state of helpless peonage," and preventing the white share-tenants from climbing the agricultural ladder to farm ownership. The oppressive crop lien system also perpetuated the one-crop economy by forcing farmers to raise cotton in order to secure credit.[9]

This produced an ironic situation in Texas and other cotton states: "New South editorialists enjoined the Southern farmer to end his poverty through thrift and crop diversification," writes Lawrence Goodwyn, while "furnishing merchants—themselves but intermediaries in a long chain of expensive credit . . . anchored in the nation's leading financial institutions—demanded that farmers plant one certain cash crop." As a result, the farmers who settled what was then known as the Southwest began to question the promise of opportunity and prosperity issued by boosters of the area. "Along the isolated pockets of the Southern plains . . . men and women labored in poverty year after year . . . coaxed another crop, absorbed another disappointment, and began to doubt,"

8. George W. Tyler, *A History of Bell County*, ed. Charles Ramsdell (San Antonio: Naylor Co., 1936), 329.

9. Woodward, *Origins of the New South*, 180; M. B. Hammond, *The Cotton Industry: An Essay in American Economic Development* (New York: Macmillan, 1897), 149.

Goodwyn explains. "Something was wrong, terribly wrong." This intuition, "haltingly articulated at first, was nevertheless deeply felt and therefore incipiently radical." The questioning of these pioneer farmers "went beyond their own situations, for they were aware that they had worked hard and had been thrifty as the tenets of the faith directed: their questions reached to the legendary covenant that had lured them to the West," and to the promoters of the New South who had promised them prosperity in the frontier beyond the Mississippi.[10]

New South ideology, which sang the praises of corporate capitalism, was largely eastern in origin. But the "agrarian resurgence eventually called forth in response . . . was definitely western in origin," says C. Vann Woodward. "It was from the southwestern and Gulf states of Texas, Louisiana, and Arkansas—especially from Texas—that agrarian radicalism, conducted by the Farmers' Alliance, was to electrify the eastern South."[11]

The Texas Farmers' Alliance originated in Lampasas County where a group of "nesters" formed the Knights of Reliance to defend themselves against the cattle kings. It linked up with the Arkansas Agricultural Wheel and the Louisiana Farmers' Union in 1886, united with the Colored Alliance formed in East Texas, and spread across the Red River into the Oklahoma territories. In its first years of growth the Farmers' Alliance supported the militant organizing activities of the Knights of Labor, who claimed 128 of their 906 locals in Texas and in 1885 struck victoriously against Jay Gould's southwestern railway system. The railroad corporations were the main enemies of the farmers' movement, and this victory over one of the most "hated" companies of the day may have produced a "chain reaction" that boosted the growth of the Alliance. The Knights declined rapidly after losing a second confrontation with Gould one year later, but many members of the order remained active in southwestern insurgent politics. In fact, Martin Irons, the militant leader of the railwaymen in the Great

10. Lawrence C. Goodwyn, "The Origins and Development of American Populism" (Ph.D. dissertation, University of Texas, Austin, 1971), 23.
11. Woodward, *Origins of the New South*, 188.

Southwestern Strike, at the turn of the century returned to the region as a Socialist agitator. And W. E. Farmer, another supporter of the Knights who lectured for the Alliance on the evils of class legislation, later became a founder of the Texas Socialist party.[12]

In 1886, Texas Alliance "missionaries," acting like "whirlwinds of zeal," took the farmers of the hard-pressed South by storm. They won thousands of converts to the ideas perfected by their brilliant chairman, C. W. Macune. Two especially popular reforms were the "Macune business system" of cooperative exchange, which promised to break the "serfdom of the lien system," and the "subtreasury plan," which committed the government to providing short-term, low-interest commodity credit to indebted farmers. The Alliance program appealed to tenants as well as landowners, both groups being hard hit by the crop lien credit system. "The Allianceman, like the Populist, was always more interest conscious than class conscious," Woodward notes. "There was much to be said for the contention that in a struggle between industrial capitalism and a colonial agrarianism, farmers big and little were in the same boat." Many poor renters cheered when Alliance organizers declared: "We are all mudsills." Other agitators, however, found "thousands of farmers" who thought all of their wage hands were against them. Still the land question, which threatened to divide landlords and tenants, remained a latent issue within the Farmers' Alliance.[13]

12. Robert Lee Hunt, *A History of Farmer Movements in the Southwest, 1873–1925* (College Station: Texas A & M Press, 1935), 21, 25–26; C. W. Macune, "The Farmers' Alliance" (MS in Barker Library, University of Texas, Austin); Theodore Saloutous, *Farmer Movements in the South, 1865–1933* (Berkeley: University of California Press, 1960), 60–68, 72–76; Goodwyn, "Origins and Development of American Populism," 89.

13. Woodward, *Origins of the New South*, 188–94; Lawrence Goodwyn, *Democratic Promise: The Populist Movement in America* (New York: Oxford, 1976), 80–81, 118–20, 632. Goodwyn rightly points out that both tenants and landowners were affected by the crop lien system in the 1890s. He may also be correct in arguing that the question of landownership was not "central" to members of the Alliance. It was certainly not as important in the Southwest during the eighties and early nineties as it was after 1907 when many landowners also became landlords, furnishing merchants, and creditors to white tenants. Finally, Goodwyn is surely right in saying that a

In 1887 C. W. Macune held the Texas Alliance together when a conflict developed between the nonpartisan moderates and the political militants. In 1888 the tension reappeared when "leftists," influenced by the Arkansas Union Labor party, decided to put up independent tickets in several counties, including Lampasas County, the Alliance birthplace. The militants gained an encouraging victory when they joined with the Knights of Labor in Tarrant County and succeeded in electing a radical mayor of Ft. Worth. The moderates beat back these independent party advocates in 1890 by supporting the successful gubernatorial campaign of Democratic reformer Jim Hogg, who endorsed several Alliance demands. However, discontent developed as a result of the governor's appointments to the railroad commission, and dissident Alliancemen, led by the leftists, formed a "Jeffersonian" Democratic caucus.[14] After their expulsion by the party regulars, the independents formed a new People's party that would become the most radical, uncompromising Populist movement in the nation.

The Texans were especially bold about recruiting black farmers into their People's party and they were intransigent about sticking to the Omaha platform of 1892, which included Macune's controversial subtreasury plan. In fact, the Texas Populists were militant antimonopolists who remained loyal to the movement's original

---

landowner threatened with indebtedness could be more radical than a tenant. However, Goodwyn, who calls for "precision" in the use of "class" categories, ignores the difference between landlords on the one hand and landowners and tenants who worked the land with their families on the other.

Goodwyn also shows that the Alliance was concerned with the land question; its 1886 land planks "demanded that all land held for speculative purposes be taxed," and that measures be taken to "prevent aliens from speculating in American land." In addition to foreign cattle syndicates, the Alliance condemned domestic railroad corporations and cattle companies for holding and enclosing public lands. The Alliance land policy may have been designed to end "capitalist activity," but it limited its policy to corporate capitalists. Individual landowners who hired tenants or wage hands apparently were not considered capitalists.

14. Goodwyn, *Democratic Promise*, 202–204, 238, 244; Ralph Smith, "The Farmers' Alliance in Texas, 1875–1900," *Southwestern Historical Quarterly*, XLVIII (1947), 360–61; Roscoe C. Martin, *The People's Party in Texas* (Austin: University of Texas Press, 1933), 39–44.

principles when other agrarians, including the left-leaning parties of Louisiana, Oklahoma, and Kansas, agreed to endorse the demand for free silver and to fuse with the Democrats when they nominated William Jennings Bryan as their 1896 presidential candidate. The huge militant Texas delegation led the resistance to fusion at the People's party's crucial St. Louis convention. The Texans' radical antimonopoly sentiments brought them into an alliance with Nationalists, Socialists, and other independent radicals in a vain effort to stop the Bryan fusion forces.[15]

Although the Louisiana Populists suffered from fraud and intimidation at the hands of the Bourbons, and the People's parties of Kansas and Oklahoma declined after their fusion with the Democrats, the Texas agrarians managed to conduct another independent campaign against the Democrats in 1898, polling over 100,000 votes—an impressive total at a time when the party had virtually dissolved in other southern states. Indeed, the interracial Populist movement retained control of some offices in East Texas until the turn of the century, when Democrats in places like Grimes County simply gunned down their agrarian opponents and proceeded to disfranchise blacks and to intimidate intransigent whites.[16] Many Texas Populists simply dropped out of politics rather than join their enemies' party when the Democrats turned to reformism in the early 1900s; a large number of antimonopoly radicals, however, veered to the left.

Some of these militant Populists decided that socialism, not reformism, was needed to end the oppression caused by monopoly capitalism. Others believed that a radical party had to create more unity between workers and farmers. The Populists, they believed, had been too concerned with sectional interests and not concerned enough with the class interests of the producers. A number of these

15. Woodward, *Origins of the New South*, 257, 286–89; C. Vann Woodward, *Tom Watson, Agrarian Rebel* (New York: Oxford University Press, 1963), 294–303. On Texas Populists and black voters, see Goodwyn, *Democratic Promise*, 404–406.

16. See Lawrence C. Goodwyn, "Populist Dreams and Negro Rights: East Texas as a Case Study," *American Historical Review*, LXXVI (1971), 1435–56.

class-conscious farmers also recognized that People's party leaders "chose to ignore" the increasing division between the landed and the landless in the cotton country. Even radical Populists like Tom Watson refused to recognize the growing importance of the land question, because, of course, "the trend toward tenancy was fraught with fatal implications for the ideology of populist agrarianism," which called for the unity of all farmers in the South and West against the plutocrats of the North and East.[17]

Thus, when prosperity returned for many southerners in the early 1900s, "the tenant farmer could well pose as the Forgotten Man," Woodward remarks. "He shared little of the new prosperity and continued a relic of the depressed nineties in the new century." The Populist parties "seemed for a time to offer the promise of effective agrarian leadership," writes one historian of the land problem, but because in most cases landowning farmers led these parties and spent most of their energy on a "will-o'-the-wisp search for a magic commodity price formula," the agrarians "offered no aid . . . to tenants struggling to retain their step on the ownership ladder."[18]

The small farm owners and larger planters who led the southwestern agrarian protests of the late nineteenth century could perhaps have sensed the divisive potential of the land question, but they could not have foreseen that in the second decade of the twentieth century a class struggle would develop between absentee landlords and tenant farmers.[19] The Populists warmly supported striking workers in the great industrial battles of 1894, but after the defeat of Eugene Debs's American Railway Union and of the Knights in the southwestern coal fields, the agrarian radicals must have thought that the labor movement was simply not ready for mass insurgent politics. Even the most class-conscious southwestern Populists could not have predicted that militant miners

17. Woodward, *Tom Watson*, 404–406.
18. Woodward, *Origins of the New South*, 407–408; Paul W. Gates, *Landlords and Tenants on the Prairie Frontier* (Ithaca, N.Y.: Cornell University Press, 1973), 324.
19. Charles W. Holman, "Probing the Causes of Unrest: The Tenant Farmer," *Survey*, XXXIV (April 17, 1916), 62.

and railroad workers, along with unorganized timber workers, would create a new labor movement in the next decade—an industrial union movement that would become the basis of a new political insurgency. And because the agrarians could not foresee the emergence of new class struggles between tenants and landlords, workers and industrialists, the pioneers of the old Populist movement were unable to predict that the New South in the West would produce the strongest grass-roots Socialist movement in American history.

I

From Populism to Socialism in the Southwest 1895-1907

CLEAR CONTINUITIES EXISTED between populism and socialism in the Southwest during the early 1900s. Radical Populists in the Oklahoma Territory formed Socialist clubs several years before the Socialist party was founded in 1901. Some of these clubs even affiliated with the New York-based Socialist Labor party, despite the contempt expressed for "petty-capitalist" farmers by Daniel DeLeon, the party's leader. The People's parties in the Southwest contained a small but proportionately significant number of socialistic Populists who identified strongly with the militant anti-monopoly bent taken by the Texans. In addition, many of these left-wing "Pops" had participated in the struggles of the Knights of Labor and other industrial unions; they tended to see the conflicts of the nineties more in terms of class than section. Others took a greater interest than most southern agrarians in the land question and in Henry George's single-tax plan; these were among the first to discuss the peculiar problems of the tenant farmer. The socialistic Populists looked to Julius A. Wayland's weekly *Appeal to Reason* for political guidance. After rejecting the People's party and DeLeon's Socialist Labor party, they waited impatiently through the turn of the century for a new kind of Socialist movement. When the Socialist Party of America formed in 1901, they became its leading southwestern agents.

Therefore, the Socialist party in Oklahoma and neighboring states contained a strong Populist flavor in its early years. The temptation, however, is to overemphasize the continuities between

12

populism and socialism, and it is important to remember that the key Populists in the new party had been dissidents in the old agrarian movement. They wanted to advance beyond populism. In addition, the early Socialist party contained important non-Populist elements, including tenant farmers, miners, and railroad workers from Arkansas and the Indian Territory where the Populists were weak and disorganized. This fact helps to explain the low correlation between Populist voting in the 1890s and Socialist voting in the early 1900s. Finally, the professional organizers in control of the Socialist party after 1907 tended to be Socialist labor organizers rather than Populist agrarians. They sharpened the ideological differences between their party and the neo-Populists in the Democratic party, and they heightened the organizational emphasis on recruiting a new constituency of tenant farmers and industrial workers to supplement the old cadre of former Populist farmers. Professionals like Tom Hickey, Kate Richards O'Hare, and Oscar Ameringer functioned not only as organizers, but as orators, educators, editors, and candidates; they played key roles in distinguishing the southwestern Socialist parties from the rapidly fading Populist movement and in criticizing the rising progressive reform movement within the Democratic party.

Socialistic Populists

In June of 1895 G. G. Halbrooks left his place on the Cherokee Strip in western Oklahoma and headed north along the dusty road that led to Kansas, where he had spent his youth. Just below the state line, he came to the little town of Medford in the wheat country of Grant County, Oklahoma Territory. Halbrooks headed straight for Mont Howard's newspaper office where a group of bearded, sunburned men awaited him. After a lengthy discussion with editor Howard and the assembled farmers, Halbrooks proposed that the men form a local of the Socialist Labor party. After several more hours of discussion, the group agreed.[1]

All of the men who attended that meeting in Medford were experienced radicals. Halbrooks, the oldest dissenter in the group,

1. *Appeal to Reason* (Girard, Kan.), September 5, 1903.

had lived for a time in Topolobampo, an ill-fated cooperative colony in Mexico. Others had participated in the cooperative stores and exchanges sponsored by the Grange and the Farmers' Alliance. Mont Howard, editor of Grant County's Populist paper, the *Mascot*, was interested in Edward Bellamy's nationalism and in the cooperative colony at Ruskin, Tennessee, founded by another Populist editor named Julius Wayland. Republicans in the Territory had already accused Howard and a few other Populist editors of having socialistic tendencies, but this did not trouble the Medford publisher. After printing the Socialist Labor party's Marxist program in 1894, he boldly declared: "There is absolutely nothing bad about or in Socialism." Unlike most Populists, Mont Howard focused on the land question. Having seen the effects of capitalist speculation on the Oklahoma frontier, he urged his readers to investigate Henry George's single-tax plan; it was a "wedge" that could break up large land holdings.[2]

Cooperation, communitarianism, nationalism, the single tax—all of these radical ideas attracted Mont Howard and the little group of free thinkers who formed the first Socialist local in Oklahoma. A year later Mont Howard wrote the Socialist Labor party's national secretary explaining that he could not form a "section" in the Oklahoma Territory "for the reason that there are very few mechanics and laborers." Unlike G. G. Halbrooks, a former printer who was a "true blue socialist," most of the "Pops" held back; they admit, Howard wrote, "that the Cooperative Commonwealth is the ultimate destination, but like the 'sinner' they are 'not quite ready yet'."[3] In 1896 the ideas espoused by Socialists like Howard and Halbrooks were still too advanced for the Populists in the Oklahoma Territory.

In Texas and Kansas, however, radical, antimonopoly populism was strong and socialistic Populists emerged more frequently. In

2. *Ibid.*, and Medford (Okla. Terr.) *Mascot*, February 9, March 2, September 7, 1894. For evidence of other Populist papers with socialistic sympathies see H. L. Meredith, "The Agrarian Reform Press in Oklahoma," *Chronicles of Oklahoma*, L (1972), 87–89.

3. H. L. Meredith, "Agrarian Socialism in Oklahoma" (Ph.D. dissertation, University of Oklahoma, 1969), 21–22. Also see O. M. Howard to Henry Kuhn, April 26, 1896, in Socialist Labor Party Papers, State Historical Society of Wisconsin, Madison. The author thanks Neil Basen for sharing this source.

the Jayhawk state, a number of important People's party leaders, including Governor Lorenzo Lewelling, and "the intellectual giant of Kansas Populism," Judge Frank Doster, "identified themselves as advocates of . . . evolutionary socialism," whereas a lesser number shared "Sockless" Jerry Simpson's interest in the single tax. Such leading campaigners as Governor Lewelling, G. C. Clemens ("Topeka's Mark Twain"), and Kansas Alliance leader John Willits converted to socialism because of their bitterness with the fusion, free-silver debacle of 1896. Others, like Annie Diggs and noted hell-raiser Mary Elizabeth Lease, declared their socialistic sympathies for other reasons.[4]

The Socialist sympathizers in the Texas People's party were not as well known, but they were relatively influential people. For example, G. W. Mendall, editor of the *People's Advocate* in Austin, proclaimed himself a Socialist in 1894, but never broke with the People's party. As party chairman of Travis County, he emphasized the more collectivist Populist demands for government ownership of railroads and a subtreasury system.[5] Other Texas "Pops" who shared Mendall's socialistic ideas were William Farmer, a noted leftist in the Knights of Labor; G. B. Harris, state secretary of the party; and the Rhodes brothers, Jake and Lee, two popular stump speakers. These radicals apparently retained their influence within the Texas People's party even though their socialistic ideas brought a "degree of odium" to the movement by opening it to new conservative attacks. The leftist tendencies among southwestern Populists also provoked some critical comments from Tom Watson, editor of the *People's Party Paper*, who perceived a clear conflict between socialism and individualism.[6]

Nonetheless, in the years after 1895 more and more southwestern Populists turned to the left toward socialism. Socialist ideas were

4. O. Gene Clanton, *Kansas Populism* (Lawrence: University of Kansas Press, 1969), 7, 146–47, 217–18, 223–36. Also see Michael J. Brodhead and O. Gene Clanton, "G. C. Clemens: The 'Sociable Socialist,'" *Kansas Historical Quarterly*, XL (1974), 475–502.

5. See *People's Advocate* (Austin), August 5, 26, 1894, for examples of anti-monopoly socialism. The author is indebted to Bruce Palmer for this source.

6. Roscoe C. Martin, *The People's Party in Texas* (Austin: University of Texas Press, 1933), 67–69; *People's Party Paper* (Atlanta), August 12, 1894, July 2, 16, August 13, September 25, November 1, 1895, January 17, 1896.

quite popular among East Texas Populists, wrote single taxer J. B. Wallace to Henry Demarest Lloyd in 1896: "To give you an idea of the trend of public opinion in this section toward advanced thought and liberality, I will say that I have been elected Secretary of the People's Party in Hardin County and could have been chairman if I would have accepted—all this in the face of my advanced views and the fact that my socialism is not hid under a basket."[7]

Wallace and other Texas delegates who attended the 1896 People's party convention at St. Louis joined with Lloyd and those radicals of "advanced views" in a futile effort to resist fusion with the Democrats under the banner of free silver. The "antimonopoly bloc" within the party, led by the Texans, came to "provisional terms with the Socialists on the basis of government ownership of all monopolies, which Henry D. Lloyd and the Nationalists supported" but, as C. M. Destler points out, the fusionists' "steamroller tactics" deprived this "powerful antimonopolist element of effective expression . . . and delivered the People's Party into the hands of the free silver Democracy."[8] After this event, which "precipitated the withdrawal of the labor and left wing elements from all association with Populists," a Texas radical expressed the feelings of many militant "mid-roaders" when he wrote to the Socialist Labor party's presidential candidate: "I am and have been a straight middle of the road Populist [*i.e.*, an antifusionist], but since the St. Louis convention am at sea without a rudder and would like to have a copy of your national platform with a view of voting your ticket in November." And, he added, "if there is no straight-out Populist ticket in the field, my vote will likely go to your party [and] there are others holding my views who could probably be induced to vot [*sic*] your ticket."[9]

There was, however, a straight Populist ticket running for state office in Texas, and it provided a rallying point for disaffected militants. Other southwestern Populists voted for the People's party

7. J. B. Wallace to Henry Demarest Lloyd, May 17, June 18, 1896, in Henry Demarest Lloyd Papers, Wisconsin State Historical Society, Madison.
8. Chester McArthur Destler, *American Radicalism, 1865–1901* (Chicago: Quadrangle, 1966), 30.
9. *Ibid.*, 30. Charles B. Kirkbride to Charles H. Matchett, August 27, 1896, in Daniel DeLeon Papers, Wisconsin State Historical Society, Madison.

presidential ticket, which included Tom Watson as Bryan's running mate. In any case, the Socialist Labor party did not conduct a real campaign in 1896, so it failed to mobilize protest votes from disaffected southwestern voters. Outside of Texas, Kansas, and northern Oklahoma, socialistic influence was rather limited within the southwestern Populist movements. W. S. Morgan, a leader of the Arkansas Wheel, became a Socialist after writing a history of the Alliance movement in which he warned that the condition of the Irish peasantry mirrored "the near future of the American farmer if land consolidation and landlordism" were not checked.[10] Veterans of the Union Labor party campaigns in Arkansas also moved in a Socialist direction during the nineties, especially in industrial counties like Sebastian and Pulaski. In Louisiana Socialist sympathizers cropped up mostly in New Orleans trade unions, especially among the German Brewery Workers. After allying itself with the People's party, the *Issue*, a radical port city labor paper, urged upland farmers to investigate socialism, "aye even Communism." Unlike most Populist papers, the *Issue*'s editors argued that class distinctions divided the farmers of the state and that planters who hired tenants or laborers should be excluded from the People's party. Needless to say, this kind of class-conscious appeal aroused little enthusiasm among the party's leadership, which included sugar and cotton planters.[11]

During the nineties Populist newspapers like the Medford *Mas-Cot*, *People's Advocate* of Austin, and the New Orleans *Issue* acquainted their readers with Socialist ideas, but these publications were not widely read. Few people in the Southwest had heard the Socialist appeal before Julius A. Wayland started publishing his *Appeal to Reason* in 1895.

Born at Versailles, Indiana, in 1854, Wayland made good as a young editor and publisher. His financial success extended into the 1880s when he moved to Colorado and began editing a small

10. W. S. Morgan, *History of the Wheel and Alliance and the Impending Revolution* (1891; facsimile New York: Burt Franklin, 1968), 661.

11. William Ivy Hair, *Bourbonism and Agrarian Protest: Louisiana Politics, 1877–1900* (Baton Rouge: Louisiana State University Press, 1969), 216, 227, 255; Melvin J. White, "Populism in Louisiana During the Nineties," *Louisiana Historical Quarterly*, V (1918–19), 14.

Populist-labor paper in Pueblo. In 1890 this hard-headed Republican businessman was converted to socialism by an English cobbler who supplied him with some provocative literature, notably Bellamy's *Looking Backward*. After participating in the Populist campaign of 1892 and trading editorial blows with Daniel DeLeon of the Socialist Labor party, Wayland returned to Indiana and started publishing a new weekly called the *Coming Nation*. It was a great success, eventually reaching a circulation of over fifty thousand. The *Coming Nation* combined utopian socialism (which Wayland absorbed from Bellamy and incorporated into his cooperative colony at Ruskin, Tennessee) with radical populism and "ill-digested scientific socialism" (which Wayland learned through Laurence Gronlund's *Cooperative Commonwealth*, a pioneering interpretation of German Marxism). Wayland's weekly attracted a wide variety of readers and a wide variety of critics, ranging from Tom Watson, who called the editor a Communist, to Daniel DeLeon, who branded him a "Salvation Army sentimentalist."[12]

After Wayland's communitarian experiment at Ruskin collapsed, the *Coming Nation* suspended publication, and Watson rejoiced. But the peripetetic "one hoss editor" was not quiet for long. In 1895, Wayland started his last and greatest radical weekly, the *Appeal to Reason*. After publishing for a few months in Kansas City, Missouri, the publisher moved his new paper to Girard, a little county seat town in the southeast Kansas coal fields. Laurence Gronlund suggested the location because he had learned that the farmers and miners of the region were disaffected from populism and "ripe for socialism."[13] This proved to be true, and Wayland attracted a good number of southwestern readers by launching an all-out attack on Bryan's fusion and free-silver campaign. After the election of 1896 the *Appeal to Reason*'s lead editorial declared: "The People's Party has run its course, performed its mission, and helped prepare the way for a party of scientific principles . . . the Socialist Party."[14] But, after burying the hatchet with DeLeon

12. Howard H. Quint, *The Forging of American Socialism* (Columbia: University of South Carolina Press, 1953), 175–95.

13. *Ibid.*, 195.

14. *Appeal to Reason* (Girard, Kan.), January 1, September 5, 1896.

during the 1896 campaign, Wayland found himself under increasing attack from the only Socialist party in existence. The Socialist Labor party's leaders could not accept the bold appeal Wayland made for the support of small farmers who were disgusted with populism. But the *Appeal* editor continued to pursue this course with even greater verve after he moved to Girard, and, as a result, the paper's circulation jumped to thirty-six thousand in the first year.[15]

Many of the new subscribers to Wayland's weekly were small farmers who were attracted to the *Appeal's* vision of a Cooperative Commonwealth in which monopolies would be owned and operated by the people and yeoman farmers would enjoy "fee-simple" title to land as long as they did not use it for speculation or the exploitation of wage labor. Having soured a bit on communitarianism, Wayland expressed little interest in the colonization plans revealed in 1897 by Eugene Debs and the founders of the Social Democracy movement. Battling with DeLeon on the left and with Watson on the right, the editor of the *Appeal to Reason* waited out the end of the nineteenth century, a Socialist without a party.[16] He was not alone.

Down in Texas, where Socialist Labor party influence was limited to a few city locals, William Farmer, a former Knight and leftist Allianceman, decided to wait no longer. Cutting his ties with the People's party in 1898, Farmer founded his own independent Socialist party in Bonham, where he published a newspaper called the *Social Economist*. Taking his cue from Wayland, "Battling Bill" used his paper to attack Daniel DeLeon, allegedly a "Grand Inquisitor" who controlled the Socialist Labor party with an absolute dictatorship. Farmer also turned his editorial pitchfork on Texas Populists like *Southern Mercury* editor Milton Park, who continued to vacillate between populism and socialism.[17]

15. Quint, *Forging of American Socialism*, 196.
16. *Ibid.*, 196, 200.
17. *Social Economist* (Bonham, Tex.), January 13, March, 1, 19, 1899. On Farmer's early activities, see A. L. Farmer to Ruth Allen, August 20, 1938, in Labor Movement in Texas Collection, Barker Library, University of Texas, Austin.

Shortly after the formation of the Social Democratic party in 1898, Wayland jumped on board and in the following year Farmer joined him. When Gene Debs passed through San Antonio in 1899 on an organizing tour for the new party, he met with Farmer and his comrades, convincing them to join the Social Democratic party and to abandon the plans they had for an independent Socialist Republic of Texas. Through Debs's influence the party recruited a number of blacklisted American Railway Union men around the Southwest, including a "good sprinkling" who had come into the Oklahoma Territory with the land rushes; these pioneers joined active Socialist locals formed by radical Populists in towns like El Reno, Medford, and Guthrie.[18] The Social Democratic party also attracted several leading socialistic Populists in Texas, notably G. B. Harris. This country doctor-turned-agitator took charge of organizing for the Social Democratic party in the Southwest and began by hiring a controversial figure from the region's radical past—Martin Irons, the man who had led the Knights in the "great" strike against Gould in 1886.[19] After speaking with the old man at Waco in 1899, Gene Debs had these sentimental words for the Scotsman whose militant leadership he emulated during the Pullman strike: "He bore the traces of poverty and broken health, but his spirit was as intrepid as it was when he struck the shield of Gould thirteen years before; and when he spoke of socialism, he seemed transformed and all the smouldering fires within him blazed once more from his sunken eyes." This notorious Knight of Labor was not as charismatic as Debs's memorial implied, but he did bring a number of southwestern farmers and railroad men into the Social Democratic party before he died in 1900. Just before his death, Irons issued this appeal to the old Knights and Alliancemen who built the People's party in Texas: "Populists are juniors; socialists are seniors. All Populists are not Socialists for it is impossible for juniors to be seniors, but all Socialists are Populists and

18. *Social Democratic Herald* (Chicago), June 3, 17, 1899; G. C. Clemens, "A Trip Through Oklahoma," *Western Socialist News* (Topeka), May, 1900.
19. Ruth A. Allen, *The Great Southwest Strike* (Austin: University of Texas Press, 1942), 145–53.

more."[20] This curious academic metaphor may have missed its mark with most people, but the new Socialist party won a respectful hearing from the Southwest's militant Populists through the advocacy of Irons and Debs, two great heroes of the western workingman.

In 1897 Dr. Harris and Martin Irons tried to politicize the first outbreaks of tenant discontent in the Texas cotton belt. When barn burnings and other forms of "night riding" erupted in over fifty counties, they organized a secret renters' union around Waco to fight landlords who were charging cash rents.[21] But they failed to channel these early outbursts into political organization.

The Social Democratic party exerted very little political influence in the Southwest because it was not well organized; it was, in the main, a way station for radical Populists passing through into the Socialist Party of America. When Debs made his first run for the presidency in 1900, J. A. Wayland made the *Appeal to Reason* "an all-out propaganda sheet" for the campaign, and helped to win a few thousand votes for the Social Democrats in the Southwest. Wayland's weekly, which had a remarkable list of 141,000 regular subscribers, included a special election edition that reached 927,000.[22] But despite the *Appeal*'s efforts, Tom Watson won more votes from southwesterners than did Gene Debs. In other words, at the turn of the century, populism still seemed more attractive than socialism to the region's voters.

But even the dedicated Populists who ran Watson's presidential campaign seemed to realize that socialism would soon eclipse their movement. In Texas Milton Park of the *Southern Mercury* and other leading "Pops" expressed an increasing interest in their new

20. Eugene V. Debs, "Memorial to Martin Irons" (MS in Eugene V. Debs Collection, Cunningham Library, Indiana State University, December 9, 1900); Allen, *Great Southwest Strike*, 145–53; G. B. Harris, "Martin Irons' Last Ideas in Regard to the Best Ways to Secure Socialism" (MS in Labor Movement in Texas Collection, Barker Library, University of Texas, January, 1899).

21. *Southern Farmer* (New Orleans), IV, December 25, 1897; Allen, *Great Southwest Strike*, 145–53.

22. Quint, *Forging of American Socialism*, 196–97. Wayland claimed that this was the largest single edition of a newspaper printed up to that time.

rival and actually veered toward socialism in the late nineties because they were disgusted with the "mental lethargy" of the state's so-called cattle reformers.[23] But Park and his supporters did not use their influence to win voters for the Social Democratic party or the Socialist Labor party. Instead, the *Southern Mercury's* editor helped form a new Allied People's party that campaigned for Tom Watson and endorsed a direct-legislation scheme proposed by the Fabian Socialists.[24] However, People's party loyalists continued to lose enthusiasm after the Socialist Party of America was formed at Indianapolis in 1901, unifying the various Socialist factions led by Gene Debs, Victor Berger of Milwaukee, Morris Hillquit of New York, and John Chase of Massachusetts.

A year later, Jo. A. Parker, Allied People's party chairman, wrote from Dallas: "Everything seems to be turning to Socialism. Everybody is talking about Socialism, and I much fear that we will be engulfed by the tide." The new Socialist movement, he feared, "has taken our place in the public mind." He posed this question to another veteran Populist: "Is it a better policy to patch up and come again or would it be better for all who are opposed to the merciless rule of the plutocracy to join the great Socialist movement, which is already world wide?" In 1903 Milton Park expressed the same sense of insecurity in the face of the new Socialist threat: "I want to serve the common people of Texas to the best of my ability and to do so I must have the advice and cooperation of the Old Guard. If the bulk of honest populists in Texas think it is best not to put out a ticket in 1904, I want to know it. Let's be honest to ourselves and then we cannot be untrue to our

23. Quoted in C. Vann Woodward, *Origins of the New South, 1877–1913* (Baton Rouge: Louisiana State University Press, 1951), 369–70.
24. *Southern Mercury* (Dallas), March 4, 1895, August 12, 1897, January 2, July 9, 1900, March 17, 1904; Quint, *Forging of American Socialism*, 319–88. Evidence of Populist activity in Texas during the early 1900s can be found in Watson's correspondence. Taylor McRae to Thomas E. Watson, June 11, 19, 1905, January 9, 1906, September 18, 1907, J. M. Mallett to Watson, November 6, 1906, H. L. Bentley, to Watson, September 7, October 6, 1907, all in Thomas E. Watson Papers, Southern Historical Collection, University of North Carolina, Chapel Hill.

constituents."[25] The Allied People's party did put out a ticket in 1904, but only Tom Watson, the presidential candidate, received noticeable support.[26] By this time, Park and the other party leaders who had "veered" toward socialism in the late nineties had decided to join progressives in the Democratic party and the newly organized Farmers' Union. Thus, migration to "the promised land of Socialism" was not always the course taken by the most dedicated populists.[27]

THE CONTINUITY OF POPULISM AND SOCIALISM

Populism was, to be sure, "a great training ground for Socialism." In fact, during the early 1900s most of the southwestern Socialist party leaders were former Populist militants. However, the strength of this continuity can be exaggerated. A survey of leading *Appeal to Reason* salesmen conducted in 1913 indicated that just over half of these leading agitators in Texas and Oklahoma (who converted to socialism before 1910) were former members of the People's party. Most Populist leaders were part of a political generation older than the one that spawned southwestern socialism. For example, only 20 of the 250 delegates at the 1896 Populist convention in the Oklahoma Territory were under thirty-five years of age.[28]

25. Jo. A. Parker to James W. Baird, December 5, 24, 1902, Milton Park to J. W. Mallett, October 24, 1903, both in James W. Baird Papers, Barker Library, University of Texas, Austin.

26. Martin, *People's Party in Texas*, 79. Watson received 8,062 votes in Texas in 1904 (3.4 percent). Most of his support came from the north central counties, especially the Western Cross Timbers area. *World Almanac, 1905*, 135.

27. Don K. Pickens, "Oklahoma Populism and Historical Interpretation," *Chronicles of Oklahoma*, XLV (1967), 281.

28. W. M. Coleman, "Socialism and Politics," *International Socialist Review* (Chicago), III (1903), 477–79; Martin, *People's Party in Texas*, 67, 79; Dallas *Laborer*, October 31, 1908; Oscar Ameringer, *If You Don't Weaken: The Autobiography of Oscar Ameringer* (New York: Henry Holt, 1940), 264; *Who's Who in Socialist America for 1914* (Girard, Kan.: Appeal to Reason, 1914). For a more general analysis see James R. Green, "The 'Salesmen-Soldiers' of the *Appeal* Army: A Profile of Rank-and-File Socialist Agitators," in Bruce Stave (ed.), *Socialism and the Cities* (Port Washington, N.Y.: Kennikat, 1975), 13–40; and T. P. Wilson, "The Demise of Populism in the Oklahoma Territory," *Chronicles of Oklahoma*, XLIII (1965), 286.

By the turn of the century, many important Populists had died or, disillusioned, had retired. H. S. P. "Stump" Ashby, one of Texas populism's greatest orators, expressed the exhaustion many veterans felt, when the Allied People's party asked him to take to the hustings again in 1900. "Stump" replied sadly that he had spent the "best years of his life in defense of the people," but, he continued: "Now I am old and poor. And I cannot take leave [from] my only hope of livelihood—that is my farm—and go out to make speeches. I am sorry that I am not younger and in better financial shape so that I might go out again on the free list, but I cannot."[29]

Of course, many old "Pops" found the energy to continue in a new crusade, and their leadership was crucial to the Socialist movement in its early years. However, by 1908, when the Socialist party achieved national recognition and regional influence, many of the old timers had given way to younger men and women who had earned their battle scars in trade union struggles rather than agrarian campaigns.

From the very start, the southwestern Socialist party showed a greater continuity with the People's party in leadership than in membership. In the first few elections, Socialist votes were concentrated in old Populist strongholds, like the northern Oklahoma Territory. The Oklahoma Socialist party's first state program contained agrarian demands attractive to former Populists. In 1902 a congressional candidate in the new party's first campaign received most of his support from "calamity howlers" in the northwestern counties, a "remnant of the Populist Party which refused to be swallowed up by the Democrats."[30] By 1906, however, Socialist electoral support had shifted from the old Populist strongholds in wheat-growing counties to the cotton-farming and coal-mining precincts in the southeast.[31] This shift showed up even

29. H. S. P. Ashby to Baird, July 14, 1900, in Baird Papers. Ashby did return to politics later, however. Like his fellow Populist orator, Thomas P. Gore, Ashby moved from Texas to the Oklahoma Territory and returned to the Democratic party as a progressive.

30. Meredith, "Agrarian Socialism in Oklahoma," 30, 32, 39–40.

31. The correlation coefficient between the Socialist party vote in 1906 and the independent Populist vote of 1892 was an insignificant +.21. Thus S. M. Lipset made a false generalization when he asserted that "virtually

more dramatically in the 1907 statehood elections when the Socialist party won its largest vote totals in tenant and coal-mining precincts in the old Indian Territory, which the People's party had not organized.[32]

A divergent pattern also developed in Texas. The Socialists received most of their early voting support from old Populist counties in the East Texas piney woods and the Western Cross Timbers section. In fact, in some of these counties the two parties polled most of their votes in the same precincts. In southeastern Texas this correlation also held when a German-American Populist leader, E. O. Meitzen, was elected judge of Lavaca County on a Socialist platform. After gaining the votes of white Populists in a special segregated primary, Meitzen easily won the 1904 general election with the assistance of his socialistic weekly the *New Era*, published in Hallettsville, the county seat. When Meitzen campaigned for reelection in 1906, he retained the support of many white Populist voters (black Populists were disfranchised) and of many immigrant voters, including the candidate's German-American friends and neighbors and the newer Czech settlers the judge had helped to naturalize. But in this campaign, the Democrats red-baited Meitzen and frightened Catholics by falsely accusing the judge of all sorts of "terrible things, such as anarchy, 'dividing up', taking away farms, negro equality and the abolishment of religion." Consequently, Lavaca County was polarized into hostile camps and Judge Meitzen failed in his 1906 reelection bid by only 100 votes out of the 2,000 cast, "an exceeding light turnout." The judge lost votes in the prosperous German farming precincts, some of his previous Populist supporters apparently having decided not to vote, and he picked up votes in the poor white tenant precincts. Class polarization in Lavaca County lessened the continuity between Populist and Socialist voting.[33]

---

all" of the Socialist party's Oklahoma vote "came from the wheat growing regions." Seymour Martin Lipset, *Agrarian Socialism* (Rev. ed.; Garden City, N.Y.: Doubleday Anchor, 1968), 27.

32. Meredith, "Agrarian Socialism in Oklahoma," 63.

33. Martin, *People's Party in Texas*, 80; Hallettsville (Tex.) *Herald*, July 14, 1904, September 20, November 8, 1906; for a more detailed analysis of

Although there are no statistics to determine whether or not these same changes operated at the state level, it is conceivable that the more prosperous Populist farmers returned to the Democratic party and the poorer "Pops" joined the younger tenants in the new Socialist party. It is clear that the disfranchisement of many poor farmers by the poll tax law of 1902, coupled with the significant demographic changes in the two decades after 1890, help to explain the lack of a significant statistical correlation between the county-level voting support of the People's party in 1896 and the Socialist party's support twelve years later.[34]

Many old "Pops," especially East Texas blacks, were violently harassed and intimidated by Democratic opponents in the late nineties. In Grimes County, Texas, for example, a white Populist sheriff and his black deputy remained in office until 1900, when vigilante Democrats gunned them down. Others were discouraged from voting by dishonest election officials or by the cumulative poll tax law, written by reform Democrats and enacted by referendum in 1902. Since only 41 percent of the state's adult males voted in this referendum, the poll tax law seemed merely to represent a "fait accompli," reflecting the fact that Texas Populists had already been discouraged and repressed. In 1904 only 33 percent of the adult males turned out to vote, causing the *Southern Mercury* to comment, "No one would have suspected that a presidential election was being held. Hundreds of prominent citizens did not vote at all. Negroes . . . abstained from voting entirely." Although the "Socialists developed unexpected strength" as Debs polled 2,787 votes, they lost potential support from poor farmers and workers who were discouraged from voting by the repression inflicted

---

political conflict in Lavaca County involving Meitzen's Socialist supporters and their opponents, see James R. Green, "Socialism and the Southwestern Class Struggle, 1898–1918: A Study of Radical Movements in Oklahoma, Texas, Louisiana, and Arkansas" (Ph.D. dissertation, Yale University, 1972), 17–20.

34. The correlation was +.20, virtually identical to the insignificant correlation between Populist and Socialist voting in Oklahoma during a similar period. Also see Raymond O. Arsenault, "From Populism to Progressivism in Selected Southern States: A Statistical Reinterpretation" (Senior thesis, Princeton University, 1969), 109–10, 115–19.

upon the Populists and by the residential and financial requirements of the new poll tax law.[35]

The disappearance of so many Populist voters after 1900 and the appearance of so many new voters, especially young tenants, created a somewhat new radical constituency for the southwestern Socialists. The Socialists took an increasing interest in the renters' problems, which had been slighted by those Populist leaders with "landowner leanings."[36] Whereas southern Populists, like Tom Watson, attempted to avoid stirring up conflict between landlords and tenants within that movement, the southwestern Socialists soon accepted the growing reality of this conflict.[37] Commenting on the evils of landlordism in the year of the Socialist party's birth, one Indian Territory Socialist wrote: "The renter is a slave. It makes no difference whether he is a subject of the Czar of Russia or an American citizen. His economic position is that of a slave. A large part of his life work is lost to him." This Socialist believed that the tenancy problem clearly resulted from Oklahoma's "orgy of exploitation." Socialist party pioneer, Mont Howard, wrote, "Under capitalism there is a constant tendency toward tenantry. The tenant farmer, above all others, ought to embrace Socialism."[38] It took Howard's comrades a few years to develop a special program

35. Lawrence C. Goodwyn, "Populist Dreams and Negro Rights: East Texas as a Case Study," *American Historical Review*, LXXVI (1971), 1435–56; V. O. Key, *Southern Politics* (New York: Random House, 1949), 535; *Southern Mercury* (Dallas), November 10, 1904; *Chicago Tribune Almanac, 1908*, 210. The Terrell election laws of 1903 and 1905 (named for a progressive reformer named Alexander Terrell) enhanced the power of the Democratic party by requiring nominating primaries that restricted the state's electorate even further by, in effect, removing "many Negroes, Mexicans and poor whites from the political process" through various stipulations designed to eliminate election abuses. Lewis L. Gould, *Progressives and Prohibitionists: Texas Democrats in the Wilson Era* (Austin: University of Texas Press, 1973), 6–7, 70.

36. As one Texas Populist wrote to Tom Watson, the younger men who were "sliding into the Socialist party . . . were mere lads when we were in the midst of our big fight"—that is, during the big Populist crusade of the early nineties. McRae to Watson, January 23, 1907, in Watson Papers.

37. C. Vann Woodward, *Tom Watson, Agrarian Rebel* (New York: Oxford University Press, 1963), 404.

38. *Social Economist* (Bonham, Tex.), June 6, 1901; *Challenge* (Medford, Okla. Terr.), September 12, 1904.

for tenants, but before the decade's end his prediction about the renters' radicalism proved correct.

Although the Socialists distinguished themselves from the Populists by calling for the public ownership of "all means of production, distribution, communication and exchange," the southwesterners did not demand the nationalization of all land.[39] Unlike DeLeon's Socialist Labor party, which called for immediate collectivization, the Socialist party followed the pioneering propaganda on the farmer question produced by J. A. Wayland's *Appeal to Reason*. Anxious to attract leftward-moving Populists, but nervous about Watson's charges that all Socialists favored the confiscation of small farms, Wayland assured the indebted family farmer that collectivization would only involve monopolistic landholdings used for speculation and the exploitation of agricultural wage labor. And, in order to escape the Socialist Labor party's charge that Wayland's socialism amounted to little more than warmed-over populism, writers like A. M. Simons, the *Appeal*'s farm expert, explained that the small family farm was doomed to extinction under capitalism. After studying with Frederick Jackson Turner in Wisconsin, Simons went on to write a book, *The American Farmer*, describing in Marxian terms the consequences of the frontier's closure.[40]

However, in the second edition of *The American Farmer* Simons argued that the 1900 census indicated an actual increase in the number of small farms. Adapting the revisionist theories of Karl Kautsky to the United States, the young agricultural "expert" called upon the 1904 Socialist party convention to adopt neo-Populist farm demands to appeal to small farmers who, as Kautsky wrote, were "by no means faced with extinction." Simons' "scientific" analysis of the agrarian question added credibility to the neo-Populist approach the southwestern Socialists had already adopted, but as a farm program it failed to win a national party

39. Pickens, "Oklahoma Populism and Historical Interpretation," 279.
40. *Appeal to Reason* (Girard, Kan.), February 8, 1896, August 14, 1897, June 30, 1900. For biographical information, see Kent and Gretchen Kreuter, *An American Dissenter: The Life of Algie Martin Simons, 1870–1950* (Lexington: University of Kentucky Press, 1969).

endorsement. Orthodox Socialists complained that Simons ignored the agricultural proletariat, which should be the party's only rural constituency. However, Simons also ignored the growing class of tenant farmers whose presence as small farmers in the 1900 census helped create the illusion that the family farm was a permanent institution. Although many southwestern Socialists had already recognized the tenancy problem, they were still not capable of articulating its political importance to the party as a whole. It took the southwesterners eight more years to convince the national party congress that they were advocating something more radical than warmed-over populism.[41]

PLANTING THE SEEDS OF GRASS-ROOTS SOCIALISM

Former radical Populists played an important role in building the early Socialist party locals, especially in the Oklahoma Territory, Texas, and northwestern Louisiana; they provided the new party with experienced organizers who readily grasped the poor farmers' long-standing grievances. But, again, these old "Pops" were less important in planting the grass-roots seeds of socialism in the Southwest than most historians believe. In fact, a disproportionate number of the pioneer organizers came to the Southwest from the labor movement rather than from the agrarian crusade. For example, the region's important *"Appeal* Army" contained more workers than farmers, and only one-fifth of the "salesmen-soldiers" in this army had been members of the Greenback or Populist parties.[42]

On an official 1903 organizing tour for the Socialist party, John Chase, the former Socialist mayor of Haverhill, Massachusetts, received his warmest responses from labor union locals. After speaking to friendly trade unionists in Del Rio and San Antonio, Texas, the party's paid organizer headed north to strike-torn coal

41. A. M. Simons, *The American Farmer* (Chicago: Charles Kerr, 1906); Karl Kautsky, "Socialist Agitation Among Farmers in America," *International Socialist Review*, III (1902), 152. Also see William A. Glazer, "Algie Martin Simons and Marxism in America," *Mississippi Valley Historical Review*, XLI (1954), 419–34.
42. Green, "The 'Salesmen-Soldiers' of the *Appeal* Army," 24–28.

fields. He spoke to a large crowd of militant miners at Thurber, Texas, one of the "worst slave dens in the U.S.," and then traveled up through the coal fields of the Choctaw Nation and into Sebastian County, Arkansas. National Secretary William Mailly had advised him to contact a radical Catholic priest named Thomas Hagerty, who was preaching Socialist gospel to workers in the Arkansas foothills. When the tired organizer arrived in the Hartford valley, he found that the striking Arkansas miners had already formed party locals in several camps, partly through the influence of Father Hagerty, who had had experience preaching socialism to miners in the Rocky Mountains, and of "Uncle Pat" O'Neill, an old miner. Both of these colorful agitators had reputations that went beyond the Ozarks, and in 1905 they played active roles at the founding convention of the Industrial Workers of the World (IWW).[43] If Judge Meitzen personified the influence of southern populism, Father Hagerty and "Uncle Pat" represented the proletarian influence in the early southwestern movement.

Eugene V. Debs, also present at the IWW's birth, established himself as the party's most popular proletarian figure. When he became the Socialist party's first presidential candidate in 1904, he was already a kind of working-class hero. His leadership of the threatening national railroad strike a decade before was still well remembered and his extensive tours for the Socialist Democratic party, the United Mine Workers (UMW), and then for the Socialist party had made him a well-known public speaker in most sections of the country, including the Southwest. Debs was due to turn forty-nine on election day, 1904. He was at the height of his powers. A tall, balding man with a friendly smile, a gangly walk, and a Hoosier wit, Debs made friends easily and inspired amazing adora-

43. William Mailly to E. B. Latham, March 19, 1903, Mailly to John C. Chase, March 13, 1903, Mailly to W. W. Freeman, March 28, 1903, all in Mailly Letterpress Book, Socialist Party Papers, Perkins Library, Duke University; Thomas J. Hagerty to A. M. Simons, August 25, 1902, in *International Socialist Review*, III (1902), 145. On the role played by Father Hagerty and "Uncle Pat" O'Neill see *Proceedings of the Founding Convention of the Industrial Workers of the World, 1905* (New York: Pathfinder, 1969), 132–33, 152–53, 351–55, 568–70, 590–94. On Hagerty's colorful career see Robert E. Doherty, "Thomas J. Hagerty, the Church and Socialism," *Labor History*, III (1962), 39–56.

tion from those who came regularly to hear him speak. He was the greatest orator American radicalism has ever known. Bending sharply at the waist, one hand on his hip, the other cutting the air to emphasize his points, Debs could hold a crowd of workers for hours. Ralph Chaplin, a young Socialist who heard him give a campaign speech in 1904, wrote: "I shall always remember the resonance, flexibility and volume of that voice. Debs was a speaker whose every gesture was full of simple eloquence. He spoke with great earnestness. You felt he really cared when he talked about the misery and injustice afflicting the world."[44]

Debs was at least as popular in the Southwest, especially among the miners and railroad workers, as he was in other sections. Prior to his 1904 campaign he conducted an organizing tour of the South and Southwest, using the occasion to speak out boldly on the race question. Following John Chase into San Antonio, where two Socialists had just been indicted for sabotage in a streetcar strike, Debs reaffirmed the Socialist party's original commitment to recruit black workers. After denouncing the white racists he encountered at a Texas train depot, he explained that the American Railway Union had made a big mistake a decade earlier when it "turned down the Negro." The leader of the Pullman strike called this error "one of the main factors in our defeat." These remarks probably had little effect on trade unionists, those, for example, in the strictly segregated railroad brotherhoods, but Debs continued to speak in this vein as he traveled through Louisiana and into the Deep South, refusing to address "lily-white" audiences in meetings sponsored by American Federation of Labor (AFL) locals. However, Debs failed to comment on the fact that at this time his Socialist comrades in Texas and Louisiana were also forming segregated party locals.[45]

44. Ray Ginger, *Eugene V. Debs: The Making of an American Radical* (New York: Colliers, 1966), 276–77; Ralph Chaplin, *Wobbly: The Rough-and-Tumble Story of an American Radical* (Chicago: University of Chicago Press, 1948), 84.
45. Eugene V. Debs, "The Negro and the Class Struggle," *International Socialist Review*, III (1903), 259; Ira Kipnis, *The American Socialist Movement, 1897–1912* (New York: Columbia University Press, 1952), 131–33; Ginger, *Eugene V. Debs*, 276–77.

Debs urged the union movement and the Socialist party to recruit black workers, but he did not argue for integration in union
and party locals. He seemed to agree with Wayland's *Appeal* that
"social equality" (the code word for miscegenation and integration) was undesirable to both blacks and whites. The Socialists
promised only economic and political equality in the Cooperative
Commonwealth. With these forms of equality assured, racial and
sexual oppression would disappear. With socialism, citizens would
be able to freely choose their own forms of association, including
segregated ones. Although Debs sometimes objected to segregation
in Socialist party and AFL locals because it inhibited the recruitment of black workers, he failed to change the segregated practices
within the party. In fact, he compromised his position on racial
discrimination by opposing any special appeals to minority groups
within the proletariat. For Debs, there was "no negro question
outside of the labor question"; the class struggle was colorless.[46]
As a result, Debs's support for the party's initial commitment to
recruit black workers failed to attract many blacks, since they
were suspicious of segregationists and various outspoken racists
within the Socialist party.

The few Afro-American Socialists in the Southwest were coal
miners recruited by UMW locals after they had been brought to
the region as strikebreakers in the 1890s. These union locals formed
class-conscious islands upon which the Socialists established their
strongest locals. When the United Mine Workers won a closed shop
in the Southwest in 1903, industrial unionism became an important force in the lives of more than twenty thousand coal miners
in the Indian Territory, eastern Kansas, western Arkansas, and
northern Texas. During the "long strike" that culminated in the
UMW's 1903 victory, the Socialists gained a foothold among the
region's militant miners and achieved their first signs of support
from black and immigrant workers.[47]

46. *Appeal to Reason* (Girard, Kan.), July 2, 1898; Debs, "The Negro and
the Class Struggle," 259.
47. *United Mine Workers Journal* (Indianapolis), March 30, 1899, September 17, 1903. Also see Gene Aldrich, "A History of the Coal Mining Industry
in Oklahoma" (Ph.D. dissertation, University of Oklahoma, 1952), 93–112.
Interview with Freda Hogan Ameringer, June 21, 1974.

For example, in coal-rich Sebastian County, Arkansas, Gene Debs outpolled Tom Watson by a 245 to 75 margin in the 1904 presidential election; this Socialist party tally represented 14 percent of Debs's Arkansas vote, even though Sebastian County included just 3 percent of the state's voters. In the next few years the party built upon this core of miner support in the Ozark foothills. Dan Hogan, the son of an Irish immigrant, joined the party shortly after setting up a law practice in Huntington, a leading Sebastian County coal town. He also edited a weekly that became the miners' voice during the last year of the "long strike." In 1906 the Arkansas Socialists nominated Hogan for governor, and though he polled a negligible vote in the statewide contest, he received a significant percentage of the vote in UMW strongholds like Jenny Lind and Hartford, and he carried his hometown of Huntington with 59 percent of the vote.[48]

The Oklahoma Socialist party achieved its first election victory in 1904 at Coalgate, a mining town in the Choctaw Nation, when the citizens elected John Ingram, a Welsh miner, as their mayor. Commenting on the victory, party organizer Frank O'Hare wrote: "The working class of Coalgate knows that . . . class war exists; knows which side of the fight it is on; and knows how to win the fight." After beating the coal trusts in the "long strike," these workers "found out how to prevent the idle, parasite ruling class" from keeping control of their town; "they are telling the world that they know this by electing a Socialist administration in Coalgate." However, these mine workers did not control their town for long. In 1905 John Ingram lost his bid for reelection when the two old parties fused to form a victorious "citizens' ticket."[49]

In the next few years the Socialists increased their activity in the southwestern mining camps. Socialist party organizers and editors, like Frank O'Hare in the Indian Territory, Dan Hogan in Sebastian County, and *Appeal to Reason* workers George and Grace

---

48. *World Almanac, 1906*, p. 453. Thanks to Ray Arsenault for the Sebastian County precinct voting returns.

49. *Appeal to Reason* (Girard, Kan.), April 16, 1904, April 15, 1905. Frank O'Hare's report in *American Labor Signal* (Butte, Mont.), II, April 21, 1904. The author would like to thank Neil Basen for sharing this source.

Brewer in Crawford County, Kansas, helped to expand miners' locals and to recruit militant unionists who would later play an important role. In 1906 "Mother" Mary Jones made a tour of the southwestern coal fields and packed UMW halls throughout the region. She had already earned herself a national reputation as a labor militant whose experience went back to the 1877 railroad strikes, the Haymarket affair, and the Pullman boycott. She began to win an adoring following among the nation's miners with her sensational activities in the 1902 anthracite strike and the violent 1903 battle at Cripple Creek, Colorado. Mother Jones was a real maverick, a motherly figure who ignored women's suffrage and spoke for the workingman, an outspoken agitator who went to jail for the UMW but regularly denounced John Mitchell and the union's big leaders, a Socialist by temperament, but an individualist who refused to submit to party discipline. In 1905 Jones had joined Debs, DeLeon, "Big Bill" Haywood of the Western Federation of Miners, and other militants (including Hagerty and O'Neill from Arkansas) in launching the Industrial Workers of the World. When she came to the Southwest in 1906, she contacted the UMW local in Pittsburg, Kansas (this local had sent a delegation to the IWW convention), spoke at a big farmer-labor convention in Shawnee, Oklahoma, and, according to Frank O'Hare, "made a big stir in the Indian Territory mining camps." Although she failed to adhere to the party line as closely as did Debs and other national organizers, Mother Jones converted more miners to socialism than most of the paid lecturers and agitators who invaded the troubled southwestern coal fields in the early 1900s.[50]

50. Mailly to Eugene Debs, July 21, 1906, in Mailly Letterpress Book. *Appeal to Reason* (Girard, Kan.), August 18, September 1, 8, 1906. After helping the United Mine Workers with their big West Virginia organizing drive in 1901, Mother Jones was imprisoned a year later for her role in the national anthracite strike of 1902. After this, she became a paid organizer for the Socialist party (at three dollars a day) and joined Gene Debs in criticizing John Mitchell's leadership of the miners' union. Mailly to Mother Jones, April 15, 1903, *ibid.* For O'Hare's comments see *Appeal to Reason* (Girard, Kan.), September 1, 8, 1906. See also Mary Field Parton (ed.), *Autobiography of Mother Jones* (Chicago: Charles Kerr, 1925), and Dale Featherling, *Mother Jones: The Miners' Angel* (Carbondale: Southern Illinois University Press, 1974), esp. 28–78.

Although UMW militants provided the Socialist party with its strongest locals in the early days, at that time trade unionists in large cities also showed some interest in the new party. An active local of Sicilian Socialists formed in Houston during the 1890s and provided Debs with some of the 175 votes he polled there in his 1900 campaign as presidential candidate from the Socialist Democratic party. Two years later a local ticket of Socialist workingmen received 600 votes, causing one of the city's dailies to comment on the "marked growth of socialism among many of our most progressive and worthy people." In Dallas the Central Labor Council decided to adopt the *Laborer* as its official organ even though its editor, George C. Edwards, was an outspoken Socialist. And in Oklahoma City in 1902, the Socialist party actually won the endorsement of the state's AFL newspaper, the *Labor Signal*.[51]

New Orleans, the region's largest, most cosmopolitan city, contained a colorful Socialist colony of Bavarian brewers, former Populists from the uplands, Mexican exiles from the tyranny of Diaz, Italian dockers, and sailors from various European ports of call. In 1907 another general strike paralyzed the city when the independent Brewery Workers, a socialist-led industrial union, struck in a jurisdictional dispute with AFL craft union locals. The telegraphers, telephone workers, and dockers (including many blacks) responded with a sympathy strike blocking the port of New Orleans for nearly three weeks. Socialists actively participated in this conflict. Indeed, they had been agitating in labor circles since the general strike of 1892, but they had made little political progress because the Democratic bosses retained control of working-class wards. The corrupt Choctaw machine oiled its own gears a bit in 1899 by pushing through a restrictive primary law that kept Socialists off the ballot.[52]

51. Malcolm Sylvers, "Sicilian Socialists in Houston, Texas," *Labor History*, XI (1970), 77–81; *Southern Mercury* (Dallas), February 27, 1902; Houston *Post*, April 24, 1902; J. C. Kennedy, "Socialist Tendencies in American Trade Unions," *International Socialist Review*, VIII (1907), 242; *Labor Signal* (Oklahoma City), October 24, 1902.
52. Philip Foner, *History of the Labor Movement in the United States* (4 vols.; New York: International, 1964), III, 250–53; Ameringer, *If You Don't Weaken*, 193–213; George M. Reynolds, *Machine Politics in New Orleans, 1897–1926* (New York: Columbia University Press, 1936), 91.

During the tumultuous events of 1907, two Socialists distinguished themselves, especially in their efforts to preserve solidarity during the long struggle. Covington Hall, a dapper young poet from Mississippi, worked tirelessly to help weld the "white and black dock slaves of New Orleans into a solid body." For his trouble, the United Sons of Confederate Veterans forced him to resign as their adjutant general. "Covy" was the "handsomest, best-dressed young man in all New Orleans," recalled Oscar Ameringer, a friendly rival in union politics and in a contest for the affections of a "beautiful Louisiana lady." Hall's experience in the 1907 strike permanently alienated him from the AFL and the German "gradualists" who dominated the Socialist party in New Orleans. His increasing radicalism and poetic romanticism led the Mississippi Marxist into the Industrial Workers of the World, and he finally found his cause later in 1907 when the timberworkers of Louisiana's piney woods launched their own general strike to restore wage cuts made during the "panic."[53]

Hall's rival in politics and romance, Oscar Ameringer, was sent to New Orleans in 1907 by the Socialist leaders of the Brewery Workers' Union; they wanted him to do liaison work with dockworkers, many of whom were blacks. As an editor of the Brewers' newspaper, *Labor World*, Ameringer advocated interracial unionism and wrote some scathing pieces about his AFL rivals, including a classic satire "Union Scabs and Others." Although he was an enemy of Sam Gompers' "business unionism" and a supporter of industrial unionism, Ameringer did not join his friend Covington Hall in the IWW. He was a Bavarian social democrat on good terms with the Germans who controlled the Socialist party in parts of the Midwest, and he followed the party line of "boring from

53. Ameringer, *If You Don't Weaken*, 209; Covington Hall, "Labor Struggles in the Deep South" (Typescript in Howard-Tilton Library, Tulane University), 54–55, 89–120. Hall was involved in a conflict between his fellow left-wing Reds and the right-wing Yellows over an invitation extended to Daniel DeLeon, a founder of the IWW. A split resulted over this issue in 1906. The right wing remained in control of the New Orleans local and the Reds went north to the piney woods to organize for the IWW among the lumberjacks. Grady McWhiney, "Louisiana Socialists in the Early Twentieth Century: A Study of Rustic Radicalism," *Journal of Southern History*, XX (1954), 321.

within" the AFL instead of forming a rival union. But during the 1907 strike Oscar made a lot of enemies in New Orleans with his organizational and editorial militancy. When the struggle ended and the Brewers made peace with the AFL craft unions, Ameringer became a thorn in the side of the city's labor leadership.[54]

After he was forced out of his job in the port city, the German Socialist took a position as a "field organizer" for the Jeans Foundation, which contributed some millions of dollars to "uplifting the poor whites and Negroes of the South." Working for an institution "tangled up with such shining exploiters as steel king Carnegie, and Charles Taft, the corporation bonanza farmer, grated on my proletarian consciousness," Oscar recalled in his entertaining autobiography. But he took the post anyway and headed west to Oklahoma where he mistakenly thought there was "less resistance to black and white uplift than in the deep South." He chose to work in the new Sooner state because it had sprouted a lively Socialist movement, "a fact," Ameringer noted, "which indicated a high degree of intelligence on the part of its population." At first, this self-styled troubadour of socialism followed the pattern of most outside organizers and worked with the city trade unions, specifically the unions of the rapidly growing construction trades in Oklahoma's booming capital city. But before long Ameringer discovered the discontented tenant farmers of the old Indian Territory. In 1906, territorial organizer Frank O'Hare reported that these rack-rented farmers "were not far behind" the miners in their zeal for socialism. A few renters in the Choctaw Nation might actually have been influenced by the growth of socialism in the UMW, which seemed like an invincible organization in the early 1900s. But most Indian Territory tenants had little contact with the miners. And since few of them had been Populists, Ameringer believed that their miserable condition naturally dis-

---

54. Ameringer, *If You Don't Weaken*, 182–83, 189–97. The Brewery Workers' fight with the AFL in New Orleans involved a dispute with various craft unions, notably the Teamsters who were raiding the industrial union's membership. The Brewers were at that time expelled from the AFL. See Hermann Schlueter, *The Brewing Industry and the Brewery Workers' Movement* (Cincinnati: United Brewery Workmen, 1910), 206; Foner, *History of the Labor Movement*, III, 313.

posed them to radicalism. The Socialists were simply the first political group to take up the cause of these "forgotten men."[55]

Unlike the Indian Territory and western Arkansas, most of the Oklahoma Territory and western Texas had been swept by populism in the 1890s. Therefore the Socialists relied heavily upon former Populist organizers in building their new party. Indeed, some of these socialistic Populists, like Mont Howard and Bill Farmer, formed Socialist clubs and locals as early as 1898.[56] After the Socialist party moved into the area in 1902 and 1903, it gladly accepted the services of experienced Populist organizers like Uncle Sam Hampton, E. O. Meitzen, and the Rhodes brothers of Texas who were doubling as organizers for the Farmers' Union, founded in 1902. These veteran "stump speakers" were the first organizers to bring large numbers of poor farmers into Socialist party locals, but their individualistic tactics and "crackerbarrel" Socialist philosophies gave the state headquarters fits.

"It is always preferable to have a resident of the state act as organizer," wrote William Mailly, the national secretary, to his Texas lieutenant, "but it is still more preferable to have a man experienced in party routine and organizational work to go first into unorganized territory to get things started right." These directives from party headquarters looked good on paper, but they were not always carried out. The Socialist party simply did not have enough experienced organizers to cover the vast reaches of the Southwest, and so state leaders had to depend on old "Pops," renegade preachers, and suspicious salesmen like Comrade Stephenson, a drummer who toured the Cherokee Strip in a little wagon filled with Socialist literature and equipped with a telescope and a gramophone to help draw the crowds.[57]

55. Ameringer, *If You Don't Weaken*, 222–23; *Appeal to Reason* (Girard, Kan.), September 1, 8, 1906.

56. For examples of rural locals that formed, if not spontaneously, at least without any assistance from national party headquarters, see *Alva Review* (Okla. Terr.), November 2, 1899; El Reno *News* (Okla. Terr.), May 24, 1900; Stillwater *Gazetteer* (Okla. Terr.), January 10, 1901.

57. Mailly to John Kerrigan, July 24, 1903, in Mailly Letterpress Book; *Appeal to Reason* (Girard, Kan.), February 13, April 15, 1904, September 15, 1906.

In 1906 Otto Branstetter was appointed party secretary for Oklahoma to introduce what his enemies would later call "the German form of organization." This really amounted to coordinating operations more carefully through the state office and keeping in closer contact with the national office on questions of policy; it also meant bringing some of the old "Pops" under party discipline. Branstetter established close contact with the National Executive Committee and with Berger's successful Milwaukee organization, but he could not have established a German "oligarchy" in Oklahoma if he had tried. Branstetter had had trade union experience in Kansas City, but he had also homesteaded in the Cherokee Strip. He knew Oklahoma radicals well and had no illusions about imposing centralized party authority on the movement. In fact, Branstetter and the other professional state secretaries appointed at this time realized the continuing importance of indigenous radicals; there were simply not enough official Socialist party organizers and lecturers to cover the length and breadth of the United States.

In fact, during these early years the state party offices had to lean quite heavily on the substantial resources of the *Appeal to Reason* and its large staff based in the Crawford County seat of Girard, Kansas, just at the northern edge of the southwestern organizational field. Before the local party press started blossoming in 1910, Wayland's weekly was the only point of contact many rural Socialists maintained with the movement. By 1907 the *Appeal* attained a national circulation of over three hundred thousand, making it one of the largest weekly periodicals in the country. Southwestern readers purchased nearly one-sixth of this total. Wayland's editors paid particular attention to the region's problems and to the growth of the party in the surrounding states. The *Appeal's* inventive managing editor, Fred Warren, joined with Grace Brewer in forming a remarkable national "army" of volunteer subscription salesmen who continually boosted the paper's sales. The southwestern subscription armies generally won the yearly subscription contests. In 1907 the Oklahoma "army" claimed the largest corps. Consequently, the Sooner state led the nation in

Appeal subscriptions, with 22,276. As a reward to the banner state, in 1908 Wayland and Warren announced the publication of a special Oklahoma City edition of the *Appeal*. In addition to hustling thousands of *Appeal* subscriptions, these salesmen-soldiers started discussion groups and, despite the objections of the national party secretary, organized Socialist party locals. Although the *Appeal* Army received its orders from Wayland and Warren in Girard rather than from the National Executive Committee in Chicago, its services were welcomed by southwestern party officials whose paid organizers had far too much ground to cover.[58]

Besides the *Appeal* Army, the southwestern Socialists of the early 1900s depended tremendously on an old Populist institution, the summer encampment. A cross between an American religious revival and a European political carnival, these camp meetings allowed the party's orators, agitators, and educators to reach rural poor people the traveling organizers never touched. In 1904 Lee Rhodes, veteran of several Populist camp meetings, organized the first Socialist summer encampment in a shady grove of the Grand Saline area of Van Zandt County, a marginal farming section in northeast Texas between the black waxy and the piney woods. This week-long event drew over four thousand people from the Red River to Port Arthur, reported the Socialist *Vanguard*, and they manifested genuine enthusiasm for the speeches of Frank O'Hare, Lee Rhodes, M. A. Smith and others, even though these "lectures" lasted for several hours. "Go into the Grand Saline country," the editor declared, "and see erstwhile democrats . . . preaching Socialism as earnestly as did the Pentecostals preach the New Gospel and you will perhaps have a clearer conception of what the encampment accomplished."[59]

Two years later the Grand Saline encampment drew even more people, despite heavy rainfall, because Mother Jones agreed to

58. Quint, *Forging of American Socialism*, 196–97; David Shannon, *The Socialist Party of America, A History* (New York: Macmillan, 1955), 29; Mailly to A. W. Ricker, March 23, 1903, in Mailly Letterpress Book; *Appeal to Reason* (Girard, Kan.), April 6, 1907, January 18, July 18, 1908.

59. *Vanguard* (Alba, Tex.), August 19, 1904. Also Frank P. O'Hare to Lucy Henschel, September 13, 1945, in Frank P. O'Hare Papers, Missouri Historical Society, St. Louis.

speak. After witnessing the original encampment, Frank O'Hare encouraged Oklahoma Socialists to bring the idea across the Red River. They did, and the camp meeting became an even more successful organizing device there than it was in Texas. Eventually, teams of encampment speakers, headlined by Jones, Debs, and others toured Texas and Oklahoma speaking in sites well prepared by the local comrades. By 1908 a few camp meetings attracted as many as ten thousand people. The Socialists had discovered that they could reach poor people in the remote southwestern backlands by pulling them off their isolated farms into a collective meeting place where they could socialize with each other, listen to speeches by Gene Debs, Mother Jones, and other noted orators, and attend "educationals" offered by Socialist teachers like Walter Thomas Mills, who published his own textbook on "scientific socialism" in 1904.[60]

A distinguished-looking little man who "stood 5'3" on a soapbox," Mills had come to Kansas as a minister educated in the best Ohio Quaker schools. After joining the radical Kansas People's party, he departed in disgust following the fusion debacle of 1896. He then gravitated toward Wayland's *Appeal to Reason* in Girard, where in 1902 he set up the School of Social Economy for Socialists. If Farmer, Meitzen, and the other Texas agrarians represented the radical influence of southwestern populism, Mills personified the more moderate midwestern brand. Along with G. C. Clemens and other Kansas Populists, "the little professor" was quite popular with the pioneer farmers in the Oklahoma Territory. Dressed like a Victorian minister with a neatly trimmed beard, he brought respectability to the Socialist encampments through his impressive lectures.[61]

His textbook, *The Struggle for Existence*, allegedly sold half a million copies; it was reprinted many times and widely used in encampment educationals. The book contained an encyclopedic

60. O'Hare to Henschel, September 13, 1945, in O'Hare Papers; *Appeal to Reason* (Girard, Kan.), July 21, September 1, 1906, July 25, August 29, 1908. Also see Ameringer, *If You Don't Weaken*, 263–67.
61. Ameringer, *If You Don't Weaken*, 263–67; *Appeal to Reason* (Girard, Kan.), September 5, 1903; "The International School of Social Economy," *Comrade*, I (July, 1902), 218–19.

approach to the science of society, harkening back to the early Owenite belief that education was the main road to socialism—that the laboring classes would control the world as soon as they understood it. Combining contradictory strains of Darwinian, Spencerian, and Marxian social science with an enlightened form of Christian idealism, Mills reflected the intellectual tension in Debsian Socialists who adopted both a materialistic and a moralistic view of capitalism. Like many former Populists, Mills came under attack by party leaders who disapproved of his organizational opportunism and his homespun version of scientific socialism. Yet even after the "professor" left the Southwest, his textbook remained popular because it was written like an old-fashioned primer with clear summaries and review questions, and because it presented a view of socialism congenial to former Populists. It was not surprising that Walter Mills returned to the southwestern encampment circuit in 1912 and became its "little giant." Like his popular textbook, his lectures and seminars effectively encouraged self-education among farmers and workers. And as Debs later pointed out, Socialist self-education was the most direct road to effective self-organization and grass-roots party growth. Like the Populist movement which, according to Lawrence Goodwyn, provided people with the "instruments of self-education," the Socialist movement gave poor people "hope—a shared hope—that they were not impersonal victims of a gigantic industrial engine ruled by others but that they were, instead, people who could perform specific political acts of self-determination."[62]

The work of party organizers, *Appeal* Army agitators, and encampment promoters began to bear fruit by 1906, at which point Texas and Oklahoma Socialists had formed two hundred locals with an average membership of ten persons per cell. Although some of these new locals proved unstable, they represented the Socialist party's deepest level of organization outside of a few cities like Milwaukee. Even at this early date the Oklahoma and

62. Walter Thomas Mills, *The Struggle for Existence* (Chicago: International School of Social Economy, 1904); Lawrence Goodwyn, *Democratic Promise: The Populist Movement in America* (New York: Oxford, 1976), 196.

Texas parties showed signs of local organizational strength. The ratio of dues-paying members to voters in Oklahoma was 1:3, and in Texas it was 1:5, as compared to 1:16 in Massachusetts (where the Socialist party had been strongest at the turn of the century), 1:9 over the entire United States, and 1:7 in Germany.[63] Although the southwestern Socialists were as guilty of fixing their gaze on vote-getting as their comrades in the rest of the country, they did not neglect organization on the grass-roots level where the seeds of socialism had to be planted and nurtured.

In the early 1900s the growth of southwestern socialism depended upon its local leaders: radical Populists in the marginal farming counties, old American Railway Union strikers and Knights of Labor in the railroad centers, brewers and typographers in the bigger cities, and UMW militants in the coal camps. However, as the party grew more rapidly after 1904, the national and regional leadership hired more professionals to help consolidate the movement's initial gains. State secretaries like Otto Branstetter in Oklahoma, W. J. Bell in Texas, Dan Hogan in Arkansas, and Walter Dietz in Louisiana improved party organization throughout the Southwest after they took their positions in 1906, but the young movement needed more than administrative efficiency and organizational energy. In the years when Populists still controlled many rural locals and party organizers doubled as lecturers for the reformist Farmers' Union, the Socialists needed inspirational leadership that could distinguish radicalism and socialism from reformism and populism, leadership that could give the rank and file a strong sense of the nationwide class struggles and the international principles their party supported. Eugene V. Debs and Mother Jones were leaders who could inspire great commitment to socialism as a cause, but their time was divided between countless party locals throughout the country and numerous industrial battles in which workers requested their presence.

63. *International Socialist Review*, IX (1908), 309. Other figures on voter-membership ratio from Henry F. Bedford, *Socialism and the Workers in Massachusetts, 1886–1912* (Amherst: University of Massachusetts Press, 1966), 64, 290; Peter Gay, *The Dilemma of Democratic Socialism* (New York: Collier, 1963), 117.

Around 1906 or 1907 three Socialists appeared in the Southwest who helped provide the movement with the kind of inspirational direction it had lacked. All three characters were experienced labor organizers who depended on the militancy of industrial unionism as a guide for the organization of rural radicalism. They appreciated the radical potential of populism but were willing to abandon some of the old agrarian appeal to the yeomanry in order to take up the new problems of the tenantry. Two of the three were "outside agitators" but they mastered the regional idiom quickly and soon came to rival the popularity of Gene Debs and Mother Jones on the encampment circuit. These three radicals were not only outstanding orators and organizers, they were also talented editors, writers, and educators, who insisted that a commitment to socialism required serious thought as well as organized action. Oscar Ameringer, Thomas Hickey, and Kate Richards O'Hare did almost everything for the party and did it better than anyone else.

When Oscar Ameringer arrived at Oklahoma City in 1907, he had already earned a certain reputation for himself as a labor organizer, editor and, more importantly, as a radical satirist.[64] He promptly told Branstetter, the state secretary, that it was foolish to try building a Socialist party on the bent backs of farmers who were, after all, petty capitalists and exploiters of wage labor. "The secretary confessed that there wasn't much of a proletariat in Oklahoma to build a proletarian revolution on," Ameringer recalled. There was a "fine fighting bunch" of coal miners in the Indian Territory "and a good number of them were members of the Party," but the organized construction workers in the larger towns were pretty conservative. Yes, Branstetter argued, if there was going to be a Sooner Socialist movement, it would have to win the support of farmers. But, he asked Ameringer, was he so sure that all Oklahoma farmers owned their land and hired wage labor?

64. For a review of Ameringer's career see James Green, "The Mark Twain of American Socialism," *Nation*, September 21, 1974, 245–47. Ameringer was not the only well-known humorist the southwestern Socialist movement produced. G. C. Clemens, who converted from populism to socialism, was known as "Topeka's Mark Twain" not only because of his name and his remarkable resemblance to Samuel L. Clemens, but because of his political wit. See Brodhead and Clanton, "G. C. Clemens," 475–502.

Complaining about the "idiocy of rural life," Ameringer embarked on his first speaking tour in rural Oklahoma toward the end of 1907. Having come west with the knowledge of country people he had gained from Bavarian peasants and Ohio dairy farmers, he was shocked by the audience he faced in his first schoolhouse meeting. "This indescribable aggregation of moisture, steam, dirt, rags, unshaven men, slatternly women, and fretting children were farmers!" Oscar exclaimed. "I had come upon a new America!" These poor people were indeed farmers but they were neither fat nor conservative, as Ameringer had expected, nor did they own their own farms or take on hired hands. "These people," he gasped, "occupied an even lower level of existence than the black and white 'water rats' of New Orleans."[65]

Oscar Ameringer's ability to depict both the tragedy and the irony of the poor whites' dilemma in Oklahoma made him an extremely popular writer, pamphleteer, and, despite his heavy German accent, a popular campaigner and encampment speaker. The art of telling funny stories (*fabulieren*), developed during his boyhood in Bavarian beer halls, stood him in good stead with the workers and farmers of the region. His family brass quartet also helped to attract crowds. Ultimately, Ameringer's sense of humor won him the title, the "Mark Twain of American Socialism," and earned him a niche in that remarkable comic tradition called "southwestern humor." Oscar's personality matched his politics. He was impressed by the German Social Democrats and maintained close ties with Victor Berger and his comrade countrymen in Milwaukee, but he had been converted to socialism by reading Henry George and Edward Bellamy, not Marx or Lassalle. Although Ameringer was as militant as many party left-wingers, especially on important issues like racism and industrial unionism, he was fundamentally a "gradualist" or evolutionary Socialist, not a revolutionary.

Thomas Alyoysius Hickey was Oscar's opposite in many respects. Shortly after Ameringer came to Oklahoma City, Hickey appeared in Texas where he soon became the most charismatic figure in the

65. Ameringer, *If You Don't Weaken*, 228–29.

state's Socialist movement. He claimed to have been born in 1869 under the shadow of Dean Jonathan Swift's Dublin cathedral where he grew up loving the Molly Maguires and hating the British landlords who ground down the tenants of Ireland. He found a perfect outlet for those feelings in the Texas land struggle, which erupted into open conflict a few years after his arrival in the state. Through his popular newspaper, the *Rebel*, and his energetic organizing efforts, Hickey helped to make the land question the paramount issue in Texas politics by 1914.[66]

Like Ameringer, Hickey joined the Knights of Labor soon after he arrived in the United States. But unlike the German humorist, who modeled his gradualist approach to socialism on that espoused by Victor Berger, the Irish revolutionist initially embraced the Marxism propounded by Daniel DeLeon. A defender of Bill Haywood's Wobblies and the rebellious bands of Villa and Zapata, "Red" Tom emerged as the southwestern leader of the Socialist party's left-wing, especially in supporting the IWW and attacking the bureaucratic control of the party's right-wing National Executive Committee. This hot-blooded, hard-drinking Irishman was called "Red" because of political views, but he had a rebel temper and a ruddy complexion to match. Hickey, who was proud of his nickname and the politics it represented, had the disturbing habit of calling his right-wing opponents "yellows." In advertising for his newspaper, the *Rebel*, Hickey boasted that his weekly had "no saffron tint"; it was "red to the core."[67]

Both Tom Hickey and Oscar Ameringer were "outside agitators" in the Southwest, but they were experienced labor organizers who worked easily with the old Knights and former Populists who had initiated the movement. Hickey always sounded like a "Harp" and Ameringer like a "Dutchman," but their accents did not prevent them from adopting the region's revivalistic rhetoric of protest. And, although they were experienced in the labor movement rather

---

66. *Rebel* (Hallettsville, Tex.), November 12, 1914. In describing Hickey's career, I have benefited greatly from Ruth A. Allen's typescript, in her possession, entitled "Thomas A. Hickey and the *Rebel*."
67. *International Socialist Review*, XIII (October, 1912), 91.

than in the Populist crusade, they did not ignore the Southwest's troubled farmers in favor of unionized workers. Like most professional organizers who came into the Southwest after 1906, they started with working-class contacts, but Hickey and Ameringer made rapid strides toward reaching the region's rural poor people. In fact, these two "outsiders" grasped the importance of the tenancy issue before many old "Pops" in the movement, and, in less than three years after they arrived, each was instrumental in founding a renters' union based on the industrial model. For, despite their disagreement over the IWW, Hickey and Ameringer agreed on the futility of craft unionism and on the necessity of organizing the workers of each industry into one big union. There were, however, many other issues that divided these two Socialist leaders and the political tendencies they represented.[68]

Oscar Ameringer's experience with the interracial industrial unions of New Orleans led him to take an important, progressive role in defending black voting rights, whereas Hickey, who had worked exclusively with whites when he organized for the Western Federation of Miners, adopted regional racial prejudices without even questioning them. In fact, he sometimes descended to the level of his racist opponents by trying to "outnigger" Democrats who accused the Socialists of race mixing. When the IWW actually started organizing across race lines in the Louisiana piney woods, Hickey supported the Wobblies, but he failed to argue for an integrated strategy within the Texas Socialist party.[69]

And while Ameringer defended the National Executive Committee in its efforts to increase party discipline and decrease local and regional deviation from the party line, Hickey tried to create a "decentralization movement" against the national executive leadership which, in his view, was dominated by northern "yellows" who favored the German centralized form of organization. "Red" Tom's leftism on this issue was, of course, related to his desire to defend

68. Green, "Socialism and the Southwestern Class Struggle," 43–46.
69. Donald R. Graham, "Red, White, and Black: An Interpretation of Ethnic and Racial Attitudes of Agrarian Radicals in Texas and Oklahoma, 1880–1920" (M.A. thesis, University of Saskatchewan, 1973), 147–53.

the Texas Socialists' freedom to adopt their own positions on the controversial questions of recruiting small farm owners and black workers.

However, Hickey joined Ameringer and other southwesterners in fighting for a national farmers' program for the Socialist party. Furthermore, the differences between the two on the issues of organization and black recruitment did not harden into factional struggles that seriously weakened the movement. In this sense, the political differences symbolized by Oscar Ameringer and Tom Hickey really represented tendencies that exerted a constant tension rather than an actual division in the party. Ameringer, protégé of Victor Berger and admirer of Henry George and Edward Bellamy, emerged as the leading advocate of "evolutionary" socialism in the Southwest. Hickey, protégé of Daniel DeLeon and defender of "Big Bill" Haywood and Pancho Villa, became the region's foremost apostle of insurrectionary socialism. The "yellow" and the "red," the "Dutchman" and the "Irishman," they came to personify the ideological and emotional tensions within southwestern socialism.

Kate Richards O'Hare, the third important leader who helped inspire the growth of southwestern socialism, was an agitator who bridged the tensions in a way that symbolized the unity and strength of the region's radical movement. Unlike Ameringer and Hickey, Kate Richards was a native of the area, born to a central Kansas farmer and his wife who had been wiped out in the terrible drought of 1887. This disaster had forced her father to move to Kansas City where he got a job as a machinist. Kate never forgot her first season in the city. "The sordid, grinding, pinching poverty of the workless workers and the frightful, stinging, piercing cold in the winter" of 1888 made a lasting impression on this "child woman." In response to the human suffering she witnessed, Kate Richards devoted herself to religious and temperance work in the years when the radical ideas of the Knights and the Alliance swept through Kansas. Before long this sensitive young woman came to feel that "prayers" would not fill an empty stomach or prevent a panic and that "intemperance and vice did not cause poverty." The time had come to "fight the cause and not the effects." Although she never lost her evangelical frame of reference, Richards turned away from religious and temperance work in the early nineties toward a kind of agitation inspired by the antimonopoly writings of Henry George and Henry Demarest Lloyd.

When Kate took a job as a machinist in her father's shop (one of the first women of her time to do so), she became a trade unionist and, shortly thereafter, a Socialist. She converted to socialism when she heard Mother Jones speak at the annual Cigar Makers' Ball in Kansas City. After the speech, the young working-woman "hastily sought out 'Mother' and asked her to tell what Socialism was." Mary Jones readily complied and Kate Richards began her remarkable career as a "socialist agitator."[70] Under the guiding influence of *Appeal to Reason* publisher J. A. Wayland, Kate read the Socialist classics and shed her loyalties to populism, prohibition, and organized Christian evangelism. In 1899 she joined the Socialist Labor party in Kansas City. In this company she met two sister Socialists who later agitated with her throughout the Southwest; they were Caroline Lowe, an idealistic school teacher, and Winnie Shirley, who would soon homestead on the Cherokee Strip with her husband, Otto Branstetter. Richards joined the Socialist Party of America as soon as it was founded in 1901. Like her mentor, Julius Wayland, Kate had no love for Daniel DeLeon or his organization. The next year she enrolled in the International School of Social Economy at Girard where she learned skills of Socialist agitation from "Professor" Walter Thomas Mills and met her husband-to-be, Frank P. O'Hare of St. Louis. After "graduating" from Mills's agitational academy, Kate and Frank spent two years barnstorming around the country before they settled in the Oklahoma Territory where they helped organize the early Sooner Socialist movement. In 1905 the O'Hares moved to a small farm near Vinita in the Indian Territory where, in the next few years, Frank organized among the tenants and miners while Kate gave birth to a daughter and to twin boys, Gene and Vic, both named

70. Kate Richards O'Hare, "How I Became a Socialist Agitator," *Socialist Woman*, II (1908), 4–5.

for the Socialist party's popular leader. Like Mother Jones, Debs
was a kind of parental figure to young party workers such as Kate.

In 1909 the O'Hares moved back up to Kansas City. Although
most of their efforts in the next few years were devoted to the Socialist party in Kansas and to a St. Louis monthly called the *National Rip-Saw*, the couple frequently returned to Oklahoma and
the other states to the south to speak at the big summer encampments. Frank had a hand in organizing the first camp meetings in
Oklahoma, but it was Kate who distinguished herself on the platforms of these unusual gatherings.[71] Unlike her city-bred husband,
she shared the experiences of her encampment audiences. "I loved
the Midwest and Southwest crowds and my work there," she later
wrote, "because I am one of them; I know what pioneering means."
She saw the tragedy that befell the post-Civil War homesteaders
from both sides of the Mason-Dixon line. And she knew that for
these people, effective Socialist propaganda had to be "expounded
in King James Bible words and quotations" and explained in the
"language of Populism."[72] Ameringer and Hickey knew this too,
but it did not come naturally to them.

Kate Richards O'Hare, who adored Gene Debs, ultimately came
to rival the great Socialist orator's popularity at the southwestern
encampments. She was one of the few Socialists from the region
who attained a national reputation and the only one who attained
a bit of international recognition. Like Oscar Ameringer, she was
a pragmatic Socialist who followed the party line, but she frequently joined the "decentralizers" in criticizing party bureaucrats
who laid down the line without understanding the "American psy-
chology."

Like Hickey, Kate accepted the segregated nature of the party in
the South, and unlike her hero, Gene Debs, she expressed no mis-

71. I am indebted for much of this information to Neil Basen's typescript,
in his possession, on Kate Richards O'Hare. Also see David Shannon's portrait in *Notable American Women* (Cambridge, Mass.: Harvard University
Press, 1974), I, 419–20.
72. Kate Richards O'Hare to Samuel Castleton, September 16, 1945, in
Eugene V. Debs Collection, Castleton Papers, Tamiment Institute, New
York.

givings about lecturing before deliberately segregated audiences. In 1916 the party's most important female leader responded to the criticism of her St. Louis comrades and moved toward the more progressive position many Socialists were adopting on the race question. But for most of her career in the Southwest, Kate Richards O'Hare maintained that little or nothing could be done for black rights until the working-class struggle had been resolved in the Cooperative Commonwealth.

This belief in the primacy of the class struggle also affected her attitude toward the woman question. Like Debs and most other party leaders, Kate argued that the Socialists should support female suffrage, but she did not believe that the oppression of women was distinct from the general exploitation of the working class. She was a zealous advocate of certain women's rights, notably suffrage, but she was not a "rampant feminist." One of the few southwestern Socialists to point out that the exploited tenants of the region oppressed their wives, she nevertheless did not push this insight to its logical conclusion. To do so would have been to disrupt the movement by injecting feminist issues. Kate was not only a party loyalist who believed in the primacy of class struggle, she was also a family sentimentalist who believed that woman's "natural station" was in the home, not in the factory or the field.[73]

As a proud, intelligent woman who had witnessed the militant suffragist demonstrations in London, Kate was more sensitive to feminist issues than anyone else in the southwestern movement. This may help explain why she took a more progressive approach to the race question after 1916 than did her segregationist comrades. Her sensitivity must have been cultivated further by her position as a national party leader who did not limit her political concerns to the Southwest. When William Allen White wrote "What's the Matter with Kansas" in 1896, he was describing the cantankerous milieu in which Kate Richards had been raised, but a decade or so later this daughter of the sunbaked Kansas plains was no longer a provincial Populist. Two decades later, in fact, she

73. Mari Jo Buhle, "Feminism and Socialism in the U.S., 1820–1920" (Ph.D. dissertation, University of Wisconsin, 1974), 369.

was an internationally recognized Socialist leader. But even after
the attention she received as an antiwar leader and a controversial
federal prisoner during World War I, Kate Richards O'Hare remained most gratified by the recognition she won as the best orator
on the southwestern encampment circuit. After the Second World
War she wrote lovingly about those crowds of poverty-stricken people who responded to her as a fellow pioneer able to tell the world
about their troubles. In 1945 Kate was still proud that the much-
admired French Socialist, Jean Jaurès, who knew about the southwestern encampments, asked her for advice on how to reach the
stolid French peasantry. Jaurès paid Kate and the southwestern
movement a compliment because he sensed the kind of socialism
she personified.[74] Kate Richards O'Hare was not much of a theorist;
indeed, some of the positions she took conflicted with Marxist
principles. But her militant enthusiasm truly personified the grass-
roots strength of American socialism.

74. O'Hare to Castleton, September 16, 1945, in Debs Collection.

II

Southwestern Progressivism and Agrarian Socialism 1908-1911

ALTHOUGH THE REMNANTS of the People's party had finally disappeared by 1908, Populist ideas remained very much alive in southwestern politics. The Socialists' immediate demands were of course rooted in that Populist tradition, but so were most of the reforms advocated by progressive Democrats. And so it became necessary for the radical party to distinguish its program from that of the reformers in the Democratic party, an easier task after 1910 when regional Democrats turned away from Bryanism back toward conservatism. The radical movement grew rapidly in the 1910s, especially in tenant-farming districts, but agrarian Socialists still could not convince their comrades in other sections to support a national farm program. The debates over the farmer question, which pitted southwestern pragmatists against more orthodox Socialists, revealed the theoretical difficulties involved in blending Marxism with populism. However, the contradictions in agrarian socialism troubling orthodox Marxists did not vex the southwesterners who were finally beginning to politicize the rural class struggle and to mobilize large sections of the Democrats' lethargic farm constituency.

SOCIALISM VERSUS PROGRESSIVISM

In 1902 Newton Gresham and a small group of dirt farmers gathered at a one-room schoolhouse in Rains County, Texas, a marginal farming area just west of the "big thicket," and there they formed the Farmers' Educational and Cooperative Union. Disillusioned with the failure of the People's party, Gresham and his neighbors wanted to return to the nonpartisan principles and cooperative practices of the original Texas Farmers' Alliance. Prosperity of a sort had returned to the southwestern cotton country, but times were still hard for indebted dirt farmers and share tenants; "cawn n' cotton" paid more on the market, but the merchants and landlords demanded more in interest and rents. The old-timers who had seen the first Alliance dissolve joined the hard-pressed newcomers, largely tenants, in seeking some kind of protection against their creditors. Like the small landholders, the renters continued to worry largely about their problems as borrowers, producers, and consumers in a market economy that allowed small farmers little control over credit, commodity, or consumer prices. Tenants protested briefly and violently against rent charged by some Texas landlords in the late 1890s, but these protests quickly faded away.[1]

Consequently, the Farmers' Union easily revived the cooperative coalition of small farmers and tenants originated by the Texas Alliance twenty years before. Adopting the programs and tactics perfected by the original Alliancemen, the organizers recruited 30,000 members in Oklahoma and 100,000 in Texas within three years, and by 1905 the Farmers' Union was an important political power in both states.[2]

As the Farmers' Union gained strength, it attracted the attention of aspiring Democratic politicians, like lawyer William H. Murray, who owned land in the Chickasaw Nation and after joining the union used it to build a powerful constituency in Oklahoma politics. The Union was composed primarily of small farmers and tenants but, unlike the original Alliance, it also contained a number of lawyers and landlords and a few merchants. The organization's "business unionism" thrived in Texas during the boll weevil scourge of the early 1900s when farmers, merchants, and bankers were forced to cooperate to combat total economic ruin. And in

1. Robert Lee Hunt, *A History of Farmer Movements in the Southwest, 1873–1925* (College Station: Texas A & M Press, 1935), 55–60.
2. Theodore Saloutous, *Farmer Movements in the South, 1865–1933* (Berkeley: University of California Press, 1960), 184–212.

the Indian Territory "representative farmers embracing a large portion of the best and most substantial planters" joined the Farmers' Union and solicited the "friendship and cooperation" of local merchants and bankers.[3] In any case, the Farmers' Union lacked the militancy of the old Alliance, which had had very little to do with businessmen of the towns and cities.[4]

At the 1905 Farmers' Educational and Cooperative Union convention in Waco, Texas, the "actual farmers" who had started the movement rose up in anger and purged the politicians and businessmen who merely "disguised themselves as farmers" in order to use the Union to advance their own interests. The revolt led to a more critical posture toward the political and economic status quo, but it did not result in real gains for the group's poorest members.[5] Even after 1905 the Farmers' Union was controlled by landed farmers; thus, the growing problems of tenants and croppers remained unrecognized and unresolved.

Furthermore, the purge of the "politicos" in 1905 did not return the Union to nonpartisan control, as aggressive "pols" remained active in the organization on a local level. Partisan union leaders included progressive Democrats like Bill Murray of the Indian Territory and J. Y. Callahan, a Methodist minister elected to Congress from the Oklahoma Territory on a Populist-Democratic fusion ticket in 1896, as well as a number of outspoken Socialist party members, like Lee Rhodes and Sam Hampton of Texas. Despite their "radical tendencies," Rhodes and Hampton "were permitted to act as organizers because of their persuasive powers . . . and because of their previous experience" in the Alliance. The reformist leaders of the Farmers' Union were confident that any "radicalism could be detected at the home office and rooted up as it appeared."[6]

The Socialists knew they were being used, but they went along for the ride, because, as the founder and first state secretary of the Oklahoma Socialist party declared, the Farmers' Union was a hope-

3. Madill (Okla.) *News*, November 14, December 23, 1904, May 28, 1907.
4. C. Vann Woodward, *Origins of the New South, 1877–1913* (Baton Rouge: Louisiana State University Press, 1951), 413.
5. Hunt, *Farmer Movements in the Southwest*, 41–79.
6. *Ibid.*, 61.

ful sign of renewed radicalism among the rural poor. Furthermore, party members knew they could use the Union to "make Socialists." This was especially important in Texas where the Rhodes brothers and other "red carders" used their influence within the Union to recruit important figures like Clarence Nugent, one of the organization's founders and son of the great Populist leader, and E. O. Meitzen of Lavaca County, the most important German-American leader in the People's party.[7] In any case, since both radicals and reformers made good use of the Union in the early 1900s, the Socialists refrained from attacking the leaders' "business unionism" and the Democrats refrained from red-baiting the organizers who were "hot for Socialism."

Nevertheless, progressive Democrats benefited more than the agrarian Socialists from the growth of the Farmers' Alliance in the Southwest. In fact, the reform politicians elected to the Texas statehouse in 1906 and those sent to the new Oklahoma state capital in 1907 had captured their Democratic primaries and defeated their Republican opponents largely through the efforts of the Farmers' Union and the coalition it formed with American Federation of Labor affiliates.

In 1906 Texas voters elected a reform governor named Thomas Campbell. Like his mentor, James Hogg, Campbell ran on a platform that assailed big business. With the continuing support of the big Texas Farmers' Union and a small, but influential State Federation of Labor, Governor Campbell and his legislative supporters enacted an "unprecedented number of laws regulating business and morals."[8] The Socialists clearly suffered from this competition; they polled only three thousand votes in 1906, their first election contest with the progressives. However, party leaders refused to admit that Campbell and his reformers were stealing their thunder. The state secretary, W. J. Bell, blamed the Socialists' weak performance on the lack of stable organization at the local

7. *Appeal to Reason* (Girard, Kan.), September 5, 1903; *Rebel* (Hallettsville, Tex.), August 23, 1913.
8. James A. Tinsley, "The Progressive Movement in Texas" (Ph.D. dissertation, University of Wisconsin, 1953), 63–67.

level. Bell was a precise, methodical man, a piano tuner by trade, and he suffered some anguish over the atrophy of many locals organized in 1904 and 1905. Ignoring the problem presented by the appeal of progressivism in the Democratic party, the state secretary ordered his comrades to sow only deep-seeded "Johnson weed" locals if they wanted to keep pace with the rapidly growing Socialist party in Oklahoma.[9]

In the Oklahoma territories, a much stronger farmer-labor coalition met at Shawnee in 1906 in order to push the Democratic party in a more progressive direction. The factionalized Oklahoma Farmers' Union was not as powerful as the parent body in Texas, but the Twin Territories Labor Federation exercised far more clout than its counterpart below the Red River. In fact, the AFL claimed over twenty thousand members in its Oklahoma affiliates, including seven thousand from the militant United Mine Workers' union. After listening to a fiery speech by Mother Jones, who was on tour for the Socialist party at the time, the Shawnee delegates passed a Socialist resolution affirming the innocence of William D. Haywood and two other "kidnapped" Western Federation of Miners officials on trial for the murder of the former governor of Idaho. The representatives of the territorial unions of farmers and workers also issued twenty-six demands to be written into the new state constitution or enacted by the first legislature. These "Shawnee demands" included many populist and progressive proposals, notably initiative, referendum and recall, and the abolition of child and convict labor. The farmer-labor convention also ratified a Socialist demand that declared: "the state shall not be denied the right to engage in any occupation or business."[10]

Impressed by the potential power of the Shawnee coalition, seventy-three of the Democratic candidates to the Constitutional Convention endorsed the farmer-labor demands. The Socialist candi-

9. *World Almanac, 1907*, 72–73; also see *Appeal to Reason* (Girard, Kan.), September 7, 1907.
10. Shawnee (Okla.) *Herald*, August 21, 1906; *Appeal to Reason* (Girard, Kan.), February 2, 1907. Also see James B. Scales, "Political History of Oklahoma, 1907–1949" (Ph.D. dissertation, University of Oklahoma, 1949), 32, 42–43.

dates refrained from offering a full endorsement and leveled radical criticism at some of the more reformist proposals. The Democrats' support for the Shawnee program helped sixty-seven of their candidates win seats at the Constitutional Convention; the Socialists, who were becoming more critical of the kind of progressivism represented by the Farmers' Union, lost every seat they contested.[11]

However, some of the victorious Democratic candidates discovered that the Socialists were winning some converts at the grassroots level. Running for the Constitutional Convention as a strong supporter of the Shawnee demands, William "Alfalfa Bill" Murray "made a special effort to get the goodwill of the Socialists" in his meetings with the Farmers' Union in his south central Oklahoma district. Murray figured that by 1906 there were already about 750 "red carders" in the Chickasaw Nation, including a number of his own tenant farmers; he claimed that at least 600 of these Socialists supported him in his campaign to become a constitution maker.[12]

When the big convention opened at Guthrie, William Murray was elected speaker. He quickly formed an alliance with two other popular politicians, Robert L. Williams of Durant, another lawyer-landlord, and Charles N. Haskell, a Muskogee railroad promoter. These three, whose success stories symbolized the business history of the Indian Territory, exercised great power during the convention. All campaigned as supporters of the Shawnee demands, but in the heat of events at the Guthrie meetings they sabotaged some of the most important planks in the farmer-labor platform. They eviscerated the initiative and referendum proposals and helped to defeat the woman's suffrage amendment by red-baiting its sponsors. Speaker Murray enraged "social justice" progressives, led by Kate Barnard, when he blocked the proposal to outlaw child labor. He also outfoxed the Socialists by amending their demand for state freedom to engage in any business enterprise so that agriculture was excluded from public control. And like the other landlords at

11. Keith L. Bryant, Jr., "Labor in Politics: The Oklahoma State Federation of Labor During the Age of Reform," *Labor History*, XI (1970), 167.
12. William H. Murray, *Memoirs of Governor Murray and True History of Oklahoma* (2 vols.; Boston: Meador Publishing, 1945), I, 324.

Lecturers on the Oklahoma encampment circuit, 1908. Standing, Oscar Ameringer (left) and Walter Thomas Mills. Seated, Caroline Lowe and Eugene V. Debs.

Courtesy Freda Hogan Ameringer

Julius A. Wayland, publisher and "one hoss editor" of the *Appeal to Reason.*

SOCIALISTIC POPULISTS FROM KANSAS

Governor Lorenzo Lewelling

Annie L. Diggs

Mary Elizabeth Lease

G. C. Clemens

Courtesy Kansas State Historical Society

Oklahoma Socialist party secretary, Otto Branstetter (left), with J. T. Cumbie and Ida Hayman Callery, 1910.
Courtesy Pittsburg State University

Thomas A. Hickey, 1911.
Courtesy Wayne State University

Kate Richards O'Hare, Frank P. O'Hare and "all the short hares."
Courtesy Duke University

the Constitutional Convention, this young politician from Tisho-mingo rejected the Socialists' charge that private landlords treated their tenants unjustly.[13]

Although they worked behind the scenes to scuttle the most radical Shawnee demands, the Murray-Williams-Haskell triumvirate emerged from the Guthrie convention with strong progressive credentials. Indeed, in some quarters "Alfalfa Bill" Murray was considered an agrarian radical because he supported a graduated land tax. Unlike R. L. Williams and other landlords of the old school, Murray recognized the problems caused by land monopoly. He hoped that a mildly progressive tax on idle land would eliminate speculative holdings "without recourse to socialism."[14] Charles Haskell, who won the Democratic party's gubernatorial primary, was not as daring as "Alfalfa Bill," but he did campaign as a progressive, having won the hearty endorsement of the "Great Commoner" himself, William Jennings Bryan. In 1907 even rather moderate Democrats like Haskell seemed to be advanced reformers because they were campaigning on a platform that supported the Oklahoma constitution, a document one newspaper called the "most radical organic law ever adopted in the Union." But even though Samuel Gompers of the AFL called the Oklahoma constitution the "most progressive" in existence and Charles Beard praised the document for its "fierce opposition to monopolies," the Sooner Socialists attacked it for not being radical enough.[15]

During the 1907 election the Democrats claimed to be worried that the "reds," who usually obeyed "the mandate of their party," were joining the conservatives in voting against the constitution.

13. *Ibid.*, II, 7–9. Also see Keith L. Bryant, Jr., *Alfalfa Bill Murray* (Norman: University of Oklahoma Press, 1968); and Edward Everett Dale and James D. Morrison, *Pioneer Judge: The Life of Robert L. Williams* (Cedar Rapids, Iowa: Torch Press, 1958), 163. On Kate Barnard, see Keith L. Bryant, Jr., "Kate Barnard, Organized Labor and Social Justice in Oklahoma During the Progressive Era," *Journal of Southern History*, XXXV (1969), 145–64.

14. Bryant, *Alfalfa Bill Murray*, 53–54.

15. *Oklahoma State Capital* (Oklahoma City), July 5, 1908; *Washington Post*, November 17, 1907; *Oklahoma State Labor News* (Oklahoma City), August 16, 1907. See also Charles Beard, "The Constitution of the State of Oklahoma," *Political Science Quarterly*, XXXIV (1909), 95–114.

But the Socialists knew that the Democrats and their progressive constitution would attract widespread support. In fact, the leaders of the new party expected to lose a large number of votes by taking a principled stand against the "phoney progressivism" embodied in the constitution and the Democratic platform. "The Oklahoma constitution," declared J. A. Wayland's *Appeal to Reason*, was but an instrument designed "for the purpose of heading off the Socialist movement."[16]

Of course, this charge was ill founded. The progressivism of the Oklahoma constitution was the product of class-conscious political pressure applied by farmers' and workers' organizations; it was not a ploy concocted by a Democratic conspiracy to stunt the Socialist party's growth. In fact, the reform campaign of 1907 did not take many votes away from the radicals. Much to the surprise of Socialist party leaders, their candidates polled almost 10,000 votes in Oklahoma's first official statewide election. The compromises many Democrats made on the Shawnee demands alienated some farmers and workers who were disillusioned with the duplicity of politicians like Murray, Haskell, and Williams. Furthermore, the Socialists' bold attack on progressivism cut the party loose from reform organizations like the Farmers' Union and forced its leaders to define their politics, to distinguish radicalism from reformism. Out on their own, with their backs to the wall, the Socialists worked like fanatics against their powerful opponents. They improved their grass-roots organization and expanded their propaganda operation. The *Appeal to Reason*, which claimed 22,276 paid subscribers in Oklahoma (the largest number of subscribers to the publication in the nation), assured the Socialists of a sizeable audience for their attacks on the progressive Democrats.[17]

But, despite the party's surprising showing at the polls in 1907, the fastest-growing Socialist organization in the country had problems. According to State Secretary Branstetter, "many comrades

16. Shawnee (Okla.) *Daily Herald*, April 3, 1907; *Appeal to Reason* (Girard, Kan.), July 6, 1907.
17. *Appeal to Reason* (Girard, Kan.), November 6, 1907.

failed to vote" in various sections because they were too busy, were "careless and came to the polls late," or had failed to register. He was even more disturbed to note that some "alleged Socialists are nothing but populistic reformers who are possessed of the 'good man' hallucination, the belief that honest and moral men can relieve the working class and at the same time maintain the system that is exploiting them."[18] The state secretary might have been referring to the Socialists who had helped elect William Murray to the Constitutional Convention on his populistic platform. These people definitely posed a problem, but the "red carders" who failed to show up at the polls at all were a greater problem.

The growth of the Farmers' Union and reformism within the Democratic party probably limited the Socialist party's growth between 1902 and 1905. However, after the "actual farmers" revolt of 1905, the Socialists won more converts within the Farmers' Union, and after the panic of 1907 they recruited many more farmers who were disillusioned with the Union's cooperative reforms. Furthermore, the expectation of change created by southwestern reformers benefited the radicals. A wide variety of Oklahoma and Texas progressives, including Hogg Democrats like Bill Murray and Tom Campbell, former Populists like Thomas P. Gore, "social justice" advocates like Kate Barnard, and ardent prohibitionists like Morris Sheppard, raised questions about the rights of the people versus the "interests." These Democratic reformers posed queries about the social, economic, and political order to which the Socialists could offer their own radical solutions. This was also the case in Arkansas, where Governor Jeff Davis launched an all-out attack on the national trusts and the state's Bourbon "upper crust," and to a lesser extent in Louisiana where governors Newton Blanchard and Jared Y. Sanders campaigned as "good government" reformers. Racism was an organic part of progressive reformism throughout the Southwest, but it was strongest in Louisiana where the Democrats had violently repressed interracial populism; therefore, tol-

18. *Ibid.*, November 28, 1907.

erance for dissent was weaker there than in the southwestern states with smaller black populations.[19]

The assassination of President McKinley in 1901 by an "anarchist" produced an antiradical hysteria that lasted for about five years. "It is astonishing, an almost unbelievable thing, this growth and tolerance of Socialism," wrote the editor of a Dallas Socialist-labor paper in 1908, "when one considers that only a few years ago Socialism and anarchism were identical in the minds of the people." Indeed, after around 1905, this generous spirit of the early 1900s even extended to real anarchists. When Emma Goldman, the notorious advocate of freedom and feminism, came to speak at Houston in 1908, she was surprised by an invitation from reform mayor Baldwin Rice to talk at city hall. A consistent anarchist like Goldman could not accept, because she did not believe in government, but she warmly thanked the mayor for Houston's "astonishing courtesy."[20]

However, it was not the confusion of socialism with anarchism that caused the new party its greatest worries in the Southwest. The Socialists naturally feared that the violent repression suffered by the Populists would turn upon them. But since they did not threaten the racial status quo as seriously as had the Populists, the agrarian radicals of the early 1900s did not suffer the intimidation and political assassination that had victimized their predecessors in East Texas and other sections during the late nineties. There were a few incidents however. When Laura B. Payne spoke to a Socialist schoolhouse meeting in Rains County, Texas, during the summer of 1906, "a gang of armed toughs," reportedly "functionaries of the Democratic Party," threatened to break up the

19. Descriptions of the southwestern progressive Democrats can be found in Woodward, *Origins of the New South*, 376–77, 387–88; and George B. Tindall, *The Emergence of the New South, 1913–1945* (Baton Rouge: Louisiana State University Press, 1967), 6–16. For a revealing case study see Lewis L. Gould, *Progressives and Prohibitionists: Texas Democrats and the Wilson Era* (Austin: University of Texas Press, 1973).

20. Dallas *Laborer*, August 29, 1908; and Frank Putnam's column of recollections, Houston *Post*, August 11, 1943. See also W. S. Morgan, "The Respectability of Socialism," *National Rip-Saw* (St. Louis), November, 1911, p. 1.

gathering, but some rifle-bearing comrades from nearby Grand Saline came to the rescue. And in the fall of the same year, H. L. A. Holman, one of the Socialist party's leading speakers, was "pulled from his box" in Galveston "because his doctrines were allegedly too radical for the people to hear." The Socialists had to be careful.[21]

The "reds" worried about increasing denunciations from the pulpits of many southwestern churches. Socialist agitators actually met with increased competition in the field after 1906, notably from the "holiness" preachers who came into the area to revive the flagging spirit of fundamentalist religion. Socialist party leaders, who were experimenting with their own kind of political revivals, detected nefarious motives in the new influx of evangelists. "We do not know whether these religious revival meetings were started for the purpose of depriving our speakers of a place to speak or to draw crowds away from our meetings," wrote the state secretary of the Texas party in 1907, "but we know that it is sometimes done for that sole purpose."[22]

On the whole, however, the southwestern Socialists suffered from relatively little repression or harassment in the first decade of the twentieth century. "Armed toughs" and red-baiting preachers became a far more serious problem in the second decade when the Socialist party presented a real political threat to the Democratic party and the men who controlled it. When the "progressive impulse was fresh and young," John Higham remarks, "people with great expectations of building a better society could perhaps afford a certain nonchalance toward radical critics of the present one." But after 1910 antiradicalism increased significantly as "the ferment of reform revived the anxieties it had initially helped to repress."[23] This was certainly true in the Southwest. Reformism

21. *Appeal to Reason* (Girard, Kan.), July 12, 1906, October 20, 1906, July 25, 1908.

22. *Ibid.*, September 27, 1907. On the coming of the "holiness" sects to the Southwest in 1906–1907 see Nils Bloch-Hoell, *The Pentecostal Movement* (Oslo, Norway: Universitets Character, 1964), 11–20, 62.

23. John Higham, *Strangers in the Land: Patterns of American Nativism, 1860–1925* (New York, Atheneum, 1966), 175–77.

opened the door for radicalism in the early 1900s, but as protest grew more strident in the 1910s, Democratic party leaders tried to close that door, since "the ferment of reform" seemed to be arousing the minds of the poorer classes without satisfying their needs.

But although the southwestern Socialists benefited indirectly from the climate of political tolerance and rising expectations created by the progressives, they gained in very concrete terms from the decline of reformism between 1907 and 1910. The panic of 1907 hurt the progressive Democrats in the Southwest because it crippled the Farmers' Union, the biggest grass-roots reform organization in the region. The Union had been experiencing internal difficulties resulting from political opportunism and corruption. Many of the newer members, especially the forgotten tenant farmers, were disgusted with the reformist leadership and attracted to the Socialists. As one Farmers' Union editor from Ft. Worth wrote to Tom Watson in 1907: "The old Populists are all right, but it is the young ones that need looking after; they are sliding into the Socialist Party."[24] Indeed, the "old Populist formula of agrarian solidarity to which the Farmers' Union appealed was put under increasing strain by the burden of rising tenancy," according to C. Vann Woodward. The organization occasionally passed a resolution of sympathy for the tenants, but the dominant landowning farmers failed to understand the significance of the tenancy problem. Like the Alliancemen and Populists, the leaders of this newer agrarian "fraternity" refused to acknowledge the growing signs of "conflict between the landed and the landless."[25] Significantly, the economic crisis of 1907 led to the demise of the *Southern Mercury*, the powerful voice of Texas populism in the nineties and the official organ of the Farmers' Educational and Cooperative Union in the early 1900s. The death of the *Mercury* seemed to symbolize the failure of neo-Populist reformism in the Southwest.

24. *Southern Mercury United with Farmers Union Password* (Dallas), February 1, March 29, 1906; Tinsley, "Progressive Movement in Texas," 164; McRae to Watson, January 23, 1907, in Thomas E. Watson Papers, Southern Historical Collection, University of North Carolina, Chapel Hill.
25. Woodward, *Origins of the New South*, 415.

The decline of the Farmers' Union itself resulted when the depression of 1907 shattered the members' confidence in their leaders' marketing schemes. The Union's failure to reduce crop production and to withold cotton from the market caused a drastic decline in membership; between 1905 and 1907 it dropped from 120,000 to 11,000 in Texas and from 30,000 to 13,000 in the Oklahoma territories. The Socialists undoubtedly gained members among the union men disgusted with the leadership of agrarian reformers who tried to battle rural poverty by cooperating with business and manipulating the commodity market.[26]

During the depressing months following the 1907 panic, many frustrated cotton farmers took to night riding to force up the prices for their crops. Farmers' Union president, Charles Barrett, joined his friend, President Theodore Roosevelt, in denouncing these "white cappers" as "anarchistic and un-American," while Socialists praised southern farmers for abandoning reformism and declaring their own "Ku Klux War on the trusts."[27] Lee Rhodes, a Socialist working within the Farmers' Union, tried to bring together night-riding tenant farmers in a secret cotton growers' union, and he was joined by "Uncle Sam" Hampton, another Union organizer. There were biblical precedents, "Uncle Sam" insisted, for staying underground. "God almighty advanced the first idea of unionism. Jesus Christ was a member of the first union, and it had one scab in it. But you say it was not a secret union. Yes, it was. The last meeting was held down in Jerusalem, and Jesus sent two of his disciples out to find a secret place in an upper chamber."[28] But despite these sacred precedents and secret precautions, Rhodes and Hampton were no more successful in unionizing frustrated tenant farmers than Dr. Harris and Martin Irons had been a decade earlier.

26. Tinsley, "Progressive Movement in Texas," 164; Robert L. Tontz, "Membership in General Farmers' Organizations in the U.S., 1874–1960," *Agricultural History*, XXXVIII (1964), 155.
27. Tontz, "Membership in General Farmers' Organizations," 169; *Southern Mercury* (Dallas), March 14, 1907; Dallas *News*, October 22, 1908; *Appeal to Reason* (Girard, Kan.), January 9, 1907.
28. Quoted in Hunt, *Farmer Movements in the Southwest*, 85.

The panic of 1907 not only ruined many small farmers and crippled their Educational and Cooperative Union; it also forced more indebted yeomen into tenancy or wage labor. A poll of 450 Texas cotton growers taken during the height of the panic revealed a sizeable minority working at wage-earning jobs, cutting railroad ties, picking cotton, or sawing timber in the lumber mills because they could not even find a place to farm "on the shares." In the newly settled counties of West Texas thousands of homesteaders sold their farms and could not buy them back later because speculators forced the price of land up beyond their reach. "Land is getting high; lots of it is being sold and advancing fast in price," wrote one angry Panhandle farmer. "If we could just keep the capitalists out of the country, it would be good," he declared. "They buy up the land and hold it in large tracts at high prices." The same marked tendency toward land monopolization occurred in the heart of the Texas black prairie. In Bell County, for example, creditors in the towns foreclosed on indebted farmers, held the land for a speculative increase in value, and then rented it to poor white refugees who continued to pour into Texas from the Old South.[29]

And so, while the depression proletarianized small farmers and aggrandized their creditors, agricultural experts, including the new business-oriented leaders of the dying Farmers' Union, preached the virtues of crop diversification and efficient management, and various regional boosters propounded their rural version of the Horatio Alger myth even more vigorously. Like the proponents of the urban mobility ideology, the Southwest prophets of progress urged the poor to work hard and save their money in order to

29. Poll taken by Dallas *News* reprinted in Madill (Okla.) *News*, July 12, 1907; J. F. Connor to editor, May 28, 1907, in Hallettsville (Tex.) *New Era*, June 14, 1907; George W. Tyler, *A History of Bell County*, ed. Charles Ramsdell (San Antonio: Naylor Co., 1936), 329. For further information on the growth of tenancy in north central Texas and the Panhandle region, see W. E. Leonard and E. B. Naugle, "The Recent Increase in Tenancy, Its Causes and Some Suggestions as to Remedies," in L. H. Haney (ed.), *Studies in the Land Problem in Texas*, University of Texas Bulletin No. 39 (Austin, 1915).

climb the "agricultural ladder" to farm ownership.[30] The bankers, who were taking over more and more of the lucrative credit market from the supply merchants, were understandably anxious to encourage thrift. For example, in Marshall County, Oklahoma, which suffered from one of the highest tenancy rates in the region, the county seat bank ran the following advertisement in the Madill *News*: "Some people are always poor, because they never save any proportion of what they earn; it just melts away . . . . A savings account at this bank will put you in the OTHER Class."[31]

Although many poor farmers in the Southwest still believed in the promise of mobility, others were beginning to question the validity of the agricultural ladder theory; they did not understand how they were supposed to save money and advance when they could not make any money in the first place. After the depression of 1907, the ownership of a nice family farm, the respectable status that went with being in that "other class," seemed more remote than ever for thousands of rural poor people.

John R. Commons was partially correct in 1908 when he observed no "appreciable class conflict" between the landed and the landless, because tenants were "the sons of farmers destined to pass into their fathers' places." The agricultural ladder was working in some areas of the Midwest, but in the Southwest the rungs were broken. In the Southwest of 1908 obvious signs of deteriorating landlord-tenant relations appeared with the resurgence of violent night riding, but the signs of rising class tensions among whites could be seen elsewhere. Class conflict, as is often the case, reflected itself in cultural as well as economic affairs. The "play

30. On the creation of the agricultural ladder theory in the Southwest, see Shu-Chung Lee, "The Theory of the Agricultural Ladder," *Agricultural History*, XXI (1947), 53; and Henry L. Taylor, *Agricultural Economics* (New York: Charles Scribner's Sons, 1905), 240, 243. Taylor developed the ladder concept at Texas A & M. For a discussion of the urban Horatio Alger myth see Stephan Thernstrom, *Poverty and Progress: Social Mobility in a Nineteenth Century City* (Cambridge, Mass.: Harvard University Press, 1964); and J. W. Tebble, *From Rags to Riches: Horatio Alger and the American Dream* (New York: Macmillan, 1963).
31. Madill (Okla.) *News*, October 11, 1907.

party" of the frontier days provides a good example. B. A. Botkin, in his study of the Oklahoma play party, describes it as "a rural American social gathering for playing games" and singing songs, "distinguished by the manner in which it was 'got up'." It was not an "invitation only" affair, "but was open to the whole country-side." Fundamentalist church restrictions against dancing made the play party a popular alternative form of entertainment on the Oklahoma frontier. But "church repression" was "simply a sec-ondary, negative . . . factor," writes Botkin; the "primary, posi-tive" cause for the play party's growth was "cultural isolation." W. L. Wilkerson, an Ozark native raised in the relatively pros-perous country south of Oklahoma City, told Botkin that in the years before statehood "the church's attitude was against dancing" but he did not believe there was any "connection between church prejudice" and the popularity of the play party. "We were all farmers and we had to make our own entertainment. We couldn't get canned entertainment like now [1929]. It was not only self-made but vigorous." Wilkerson said that the people where he grew up were landowners "as a rule," but that "some of the best citi-zens we had were tenant farmers." In fact, "there were no class distinctions; everyone was on an equal basis in the community there if considered respectable." But, as Botkin explains, in poorer communities not everyone was considered respectable and "both dances and parties were kept alive by stealth or open defiance and, like drinking, were referred to under the breath." In some com-munities "there were class distinctions" in the early 1900s. "Since people who went to dances were social outcasts, dances came to be restricted largely to the homes of the lower classes—that is, the 'tenants' as distinct from the 'settlers'—who had no caste to lose. The social line was likewise drawn at revivals, which each church held during the summer and at which the better-educated folk did not go in for the extremes of shouting and singing" favored by the poor. As the frontier days passed and Oklahoma's poverty grew, the better classes condemned "the drunkeness, fighting, love-mak-ing and card playing" that followed dancing and play parties. Indeed, as Botkin remarks, "sometimes, among the rougher ele-ment" rowdiness extended to "breaking up the parties and socials of the better families" who no longer invited everyone in the countryside.[32]

In the early 1900s, this anger lacked direction, especially during the boll weevil blight when everyone seemed to suffer. But tenant discontent became more focused after the depression of 1907 when absentee landlordism increased. As urban creditors foreclosed on farms and the most prosperous planters moved to town to become gentlemen farmers, the absentee landlords became part of that "other class" of businessmen and boosters, promoters and politicians who made the false promises about prosperity and mobility for the honest workingman. As the second decade of the twentieth century approached, more and more poor folk began to believe that the progress of the speculators, creditors, and absentee landholders caused the poverty of the "actual cultivators." The agricultural ladder hypothesis proved false in the experience of thousands of southwestern tenants. The older tenants in the southwestern cotton states were not moving on up the ladder to farm ownership; in Texas and Oklahoma there were twice as many tenants over the age of fifty-five and three times as many renters over the age of sixty-five as there were in the United States as a whole.[33] In other words, even grandfathers were stuck in the south-

32. John R. Commons, "Is Class Conflict in America Growing and Is It Inevitable?" *American Journal of Sociology*, XIII (1908), 763; B. A. Botkin, *The American Play Party Song* (New York: Ungar, 1963), 16, 19, 20–23.

33. "Age of Farmers," in U.S. Department of Commerce, *Thirteenth Census of the United States, 1910: Abstract* (Washington, D.C.: Government Printing Office, 1913), 9, 19. For an academic study that attempts to verify the agricultural ladder theory in the Texas cotton country, see J. T. Sanders, *Farm Ownership and Tenancy in the Black Prairie of Texas*, in U.S. Department of Agriculture Bulletin No. 1068 (Washington, D.C.: Government Printing Office, 1922). This study maintained that the average number of years required to attain farm ownership had actually decreased during the first decades of the twentieth century. The ladder really measured the progress of the best "accumulators"—that is, those farmers with superior wealth-saving and wealth-using ability. This report did indicate that some renters were still able to acquire their own farms, but it was not a convincing verification of the ladder theory because the study was admittedly based on an insufficient sample and was only based upon those tenants who succeeded in becoming owners; it excluded those who died or quit farming. See G. H. Von Tunglen, "Some Observations of the So-Called Agricultural Ladder," *Journal of Farm Economics*, IX (1927), 99–100.

western tenant system. And the young men of the early 1900s who
remained on the land were destined to become the Grandpa Joads
of the 1930s. Many small farmers' sons could not even stay on the
land by farming the shares; hundreds were forced to take jobs
with the black and brown gangs of wage hands who picked cotton,
cut lumber, and repaired railroad track.

During the first decade of the twentieth century the number of
tenant farms increased in the Southwest at twice the national rate.
By 1910, 54 percent of the region's farms were operated by tenants.[34] The growth of this discontented tenant class affected the
development of socialism profoundly, but the impact did not register immediately. Some indigenous southwestern Socialists quickly
recognized the political potential of the tenancy problem. Indeed,
the leaders of the Oklahoma party wrote a radical land plank into
their 1902 platform, just one year after the national organization
was founded. But, as former Populists flooded into the party and
professional organizers demanded a tested program that appealed
to politically experienced farmers, the southwestern Socialists concentrated on the problems of indebted yeomen, the most consistently radical class of people in the South and West.

However, when the panic of 1907 provoked actual tenant militancy, the southwestern Socialists discovered the "forgotten man"
of the southern "progressive era." In 1908 the Oklahoma Socialist
party recognized the potential of tenant protest by including several "land planks" in its program, and the party's candidates in
the cotton country reaped a gratifying reward from these efforts.
Riding on the coattails of Gene Debs's whistle-stop presidential
campaign aboard the "Red Special," Socialists made substantial
gains at the polls in high tenancy counties. For example, in Marshall and Johnston counties of south central Oklahoma, where
tenancy rates averaged 80 percent (the highest in the country),
Debs and his running mates received a surprising 24 percent of the

---

34. E. A. Goldenweiser and Leon E. Truesdell, *Farm Tenancy in the United
States, Census Monograph IV* (Washington, D.C.: Government Printing Office, 1924), Table 53, pp. 148–49.

vote total, despite the anti-Socialist campaigns of local progressive Democrats.[35]

However, the Socialists' new appeal to tenants only partially accounted for the electoral gains of 1908; the decline of progressivism also helped Debs and his party. For example, in the Sooner state the disintegration of the Farmers' Union opened many farmers to the increasing organizational pull of the Socialist party. And Governor Charles Haskell, elected on a program of Bryanism, ran into trouble with the powerful State Federation of Labor after only one year in office. Although the Democratic state legislature passed most of the Shawnee farmer-labor demands in its 1908 session, Governor Haskell vetoed the bill abolishing child labor in Oklahoma, provoking a sharp attack from trade unionists and "social justice" progressives, notably Kate Barnard, the charities commissioner. The outspoken commissioner also expressed indignation at another progressive Democrat, House Speaker Murray, because he sabotaged important labor legislation and allegedly acted with "duplicity" regarding proposed land-tax and antiusury statutes. In July of 1908 the State Federation of Labor endorsed a resolution authored by Kate Barnard branding Murray a "representative of class interests" and pledging to work for his defeat in future elections. In a concluding slap at the Democrats, the resolution declared any party that "boosted Wm. H. Murray . . . an enemy of the masses."[36]

35. On Debs's "Red Special" campaign of 1908, see Ray Ginger, *Eugene V. Debs: The Making of an American Radical* (New York: Colliers, 1966), 279–302. Also see Frank P. O'Hare, "The Oklahoma Vote," *International Socialist Review*, IX (1908), 519.

36. Bryant, *Alfalfa Bill Murray*, 81–82. At about the same time, officers of the Oklahoma Federation of Labor, J. Harvey Lynch and J. Luther Langston (who later became a Socialist), started agitating for a labor party because of their disappointment with the old parties. The Oklahoma insurgents generated considerable interest among other state federations until AFL President Samuel Gompers' opposition to independent political action overwhelmed Lynch, who was just a poor plasterer "trying to push a cause." The failure of this Oklahoma labor party initiative in 1908 may have opened more southwestern AFL members to Socialist party appeals. Philip S. Foner, *Policies and Practices of the AFL, 1900–1909* (New York: International, 1964), 347–48.

While he was being attacked in Oklahoma, "Alfalfa Bill" led his state delegation to the Democratic party's convention in Denver where he came on like an agrarian radical and threatened to "queer" William Jennings Bryan's play for conservative eastern delegates. Bryan easily won the nomination, despite the antics of Murray and his "long haired outfit" from Oklahoma, and the "Great Commoner" went on to carry the southwestern states by significant margins in the November election.[37] But Bryan, no longer the "boy orator" of the Platte River country, did not conduct the kind of energetic campaign he had waged in the "Battle of the Standards" and the antiimperialist crusade of 1900. By contrast, Debs was at the height of his career as a Socialist orator, and in 1908 the young Socialist movement went to extraordinary lengths to advance its leader's cause. The campaign was especially vigorous in Texas and Oklahoma where the progressives seemed to be on the defensive on many state and local issues. As a build up for the election, twenty full-time speakers were in the Oklahoma field at all times. And although some isolated points around the state still had not been visited by an official party representative, the popular *Appeal to Reason* (which published a special Sooner edition in 1908) kept many of them in touch with the campaign. Others came into direct contact with the traveling Socialist bandwagon by packing up their families and heading for one of the summer encampments sponsored by the party. The biggest camp meeting, at Konowa in July, attracted ten thousand people in a week-long political and social affair that featured many Socialist candidates, including Gene himself. The Texans, who first adapted the camp meeting for Socialist purposes in 1904, attracted even more country folk to the big field in Grand Saline where Debs appeared along with the notorious radical labor leader, William D. "Big Bill" Haywood, recently cleared of a murder charge in a sen-

---

37. Murray, *Memoirs*, I, 122; Denver *Post*, July 5, 9, 1908. Election returns are from Oliver Benson, *et al.*, *Oklahoma Votes, 1907–1962* (Norman: University of Oklahoma Press, 1964).

sational trial won by Clarence Darrow.[38] Thus, both the decline of progressivism on a state level and the increased organizational and educational work, especially among tenants, contributed to the 1908 gains made by the Texas and Oklahoma Socialists. The reformers' loss was not necessarily the radicals' gain. The Socialists had to take advantage of the opportunities before them.

Although the Socialist party was still not a serious threat to the ruling Democrats, its leaders were heartened by the big advances their candidates made at the polls, and the Democrats were beginning to worry.[39] In Oklahoma Gene Debs won 21,425 votes (8.4 percent of the total), twice the number the party had received in the state's first election just one year before. In Texas the increase was less dramatic, but significant nonetheless, the Socialists polling nearly 8,000 votes, almost three times the number they had gained in 1904. In that earlier election Tom Watson, running on the People's party ticket, had outpolled Debs by a margin of about three to one; in 1908 the old Georgia Populist obtained only about one-tenth the votes of his Socialist rival.[40] Watson's poor showing, combined with the decline of the Farmers' Union and the demise of the *Southern Mercury*, eliminated populism as an organized alternative to socialism in the Southwest.

Of course, many of the new Socialist voters were former Populists, but by 1908 the correlation between the voting support of the People's party and the Socialist party had decreased significantly. For example, in Texas a 75 percent population increase and

38. O'Hare, "The Oklahoma Vote," 519; *Appeal to Reason* (Girard, Kan.), September 5, December 12, 1908; *Daily Oklahoman* (Oklahoma City), July 21, 1908; Ginger, *Eugene V. Debs*, 287; Dallas *Laborer*, September, 1908.

39. The Socialist party, even in the Sooner state, was not a serious threat to Democratic hegemony, but leaders of the predominant party in Oklahoma were concerned about the very rapid rise of socialism. "The time is at hand to be up and doing something if we are to maintain a Democratic state government," said one circular of the incumbent party a year after the election of 1908. "The Socialists are making inroads in our ranks, especially in the central and southern counties, and it will take persistent work to counter this enemy." *Weekly Chieftan* (Vinita, Okla.), October 29, 1909.

40. Benson, *Oklahoma Votes*, 62; and *World Almanac, 1904* and *1908*.

a 25 percent tenancy increase altered the demographic and economic nature of the electorate and helped reduce the correlation between Socialist and Populist voting to an insignificant level (+.05).[41] Some precincts in old Populist strongholds like the piney woods and the "big thicket" turned out relatively high Socialist totals, but Debs and his radical running mates had also politicized a new constituency in areas where the People's party had been very weak, notably in the high-tenancy counties of the black prairie and new cotton country around Abilene.

Socialist party leaders in Texas blamed weak local organization for their inability to keep pace with the Oklahoma party, but other factors entered in as well. Populism had been repressed more violently in Texas than in Oklahoma and disfranchisement had been accomplished more thoroughly. By 1908 the voter turnout in Texas dropped to 33 percent (from 61 percent a decade earlier), whereas in Oklahoma voter participation remained relatively high (63 percent of the adult males, including blacks, who were not excluded until 1910).

The same factors that limited the growth of socialism in Texas slowed the party's progress in Arkansas and Louisiana, where disfranchisement excluded poor whites as well as blacks. Despite these problems and despite the Socialists' lack of organizational resources in these two states, party candidates made noticeable gains in 1908. In fact, the Socialist party in the Razorback state made greater strides proportionately than it did anywhere in the Southwest. Led by Debs and gubernatorial candidate J. Sam Jones, the Arkansas party polled 5,842 votes in 1908 (4 percent of the total), three times the number garnered in 1904. In Louisiana the Socialists received only 2,500 votes, but this represented an encouraging increase over the 990 they had polled in 1904.[42]

41. Raymond O. Arsenault, "From Populism to Progressivism in Selected Southern States: A Statistical Reinterpretation" (Senior thesis, Princeton University, 1969), 109–10.

42. *World Almanac, 1906*, p. 468, and *1910*, p. 654. *Report of the Secretary of State to His Excellency the Governor of Louisiana* (Baton Rouge: State of Louisiana, 1905), xvi, and 1910 *Report*, p. 147.

The Arkansas Socialists registered noticeable support in some of the rural strongholds of the Union Labor party, like Polk and Scott counties in the Ouachita Mountains, whereas the Louisiana Socialists ran well in old Populist bastions like Winn Parish, where they polled 36 percent of the votes and elected half of the parish officials despite the efforts of a young anti-Socialist debater named Huey Long.[43] Gene Debs and his comrades also won significant support in the industrial sections of Arkansas and Louisiana, Debs recording his largest Arkansas vote total in coal-rich Sebastian County, a UMW stronghold hard on the Oklahoma border, and his highest Louisiana tally in Orleans Parish which included most of the state's trade union voters. The Louisiana Socialists also won significant totals (over 200 votes) in three piney woods parishes on the Sabine River to the west, where timber workers had launched their general strike in 1907. These parishes had returned quite a few Populist votes in the nineties, but this agrarian support came more from the farmers than the lumber workers. In 1908 Debs received the votes of both the diehard Populist "peckerwoods" and the timber workers, though he failed to win the support of disfranchised black mill hands.[44]

Like their comrades in Oklahoma, the Socialists in other southwestern states benefited in varying degrees from the waning of progressive reform in the region's Democratic parties. Governor Thomas Campbell ran successfully for reelection in Texas, though he lacked the support of a strong farmer-labor coalition and therefore campaigned not as a dedicated foe of big business, but as a reliable incumbent who tried to please everyone. Although farmers supplied the driving force behind progressivism in the Lone Star

43. *Report of the Secretary of State*, 1910; and T. Harry Williams, *Huey Long: A Biography* (New York: Knopf, 1970), 43–44.

44. In addition to the Socialist strength in Arkansas coal-mining towns, precinct voting returns show support for Debs in railroad maintenance centers, like Argenta outside Little Rock, and Van Buren, which accounted for 34 of the 102 Socialist votes recorded in Crawford County for the 1908 election. On Socialist strength in Louisiana see Grady McWhiney, "Louisiana Socialists in the Early Twentieth Century: A Study of Rustic Radicalism," *Journal of Southern History*, XX (1954), 320–22.

state, they received few tangible benefits from the reform administration. "Warehouse laws . . . gave some relief to Texas cotton farmers," but, as one historian of Texas progressivism notes, "bankers, merchants, and commercial warehousemen" profited more from these laws. In Arkansas, Governor Jeff Davis, a Democratic demagogue who appealed to the hill folk by attacking the rich, went off to the United States Senate in 1907 and left the state party without a popular spokesman for the poor.[45] In Louisiana the "good government" administration of Newton Blanchard passed without noticeable gains for farmers and workers, and 1908 brought the election of J. Y. Sanders, a more demagogic Democratic governor who claimed to be a progressive, but pushed racism much harder than reformism.[46] Under these circumstances, socialism made significant gains in contesting progressive reformism.

The 1908 election proved that the Socialist parties in the Southwest could attract more support from trade unionists in indus-

45. Tinsley, "Progressive Movement in Texas," 150; and Arsenault, "From Populism to Progressivism," 153–54. For example, in Washington County, Arkansas, a rich agricultural area in the northwestern corner of the state, the Socialists polled 105 votes in the 1904 Democratic primary while Jeff Davis carried the county handily with about 60 percent of the vote. In 1908, after Davis left for Washington, D.C., Gene Debs and Sam Jones polled 208 votes, twice the party's 1904 total, whereas Davis' successor polled only half of the proportion of the vote his mentor had achieved four years earlier.

In 1908 the Socialists polled their highest totals in the poorest farming precincts, notably in Cove Creek and Crawford where they won 20 and 27 percent of the vote respectively. Davis had swept both precincts in 1904, polling over two thirds the total vote; in 1908 his successor ran poorly in these rural areas. In Prairie Grove, a rich precinct with twice the per capita assessed valuation as Cove Creek and Crawford (measured in terms of taxable property per person), the Socialists polled only 1.6 percent. Another measure of the difference in these precincts lies in the fact that Prairie Grove (which contained a small marketing town and about the same total population as Cove Creek and Crawford) contained ninety-seven citizens with gold or silver watches whereas only twenty-five people in the two poorer rural districts owned valuable timepieces.

The author would like to thank Raymond O. Arsenault for sharing this statistical information, which he gleaned from the Washington County records at Fayetteville and Little Rock.

46. Perry H. Howard, *Political Tendencies in Louisiana, 1812–1952* (Baton Rouge: Louisiana State University Press, 1957), 211–21.

trial centers and from former Populists in the Farmers' Union, as well as from tenant farmers who had had little experience with the old unions and political parties. The Oklahoma state platform had taken the first steps toward offering a Socialist solution to the tenancy problem, but much remained to be said and done before the Socialist party could claim the last word on the land question.

THE FARMER QUESTION

For Socialists in other sections of the country, the "land question" remained inextricably confused with a larger and more complex "farmer question." At the 1908 party congress southwestern delegates encountered strong resistance when they tried to win a national convention endorsement for their immediate farm demands. A majority of the delegates, including a number of farmers from outside the Southwest, rejected the Oklahoma farm platform because its planks were too populistic. John M. Work of Iowa led the fight for a national farm program by arguing that the Socialists should nationalize only those trusts that denied the laborer the full product of his toil. Cleverly adapting the labor theory of value to American conditions, the Iowa "lecturer" maintained that small farms and businesses were not really capitalistic if they were owned and operated by producers who performed useful labor; therefore, these concerns would not have to be nationalized under socialism. A. M. Simons bolstered Work's argument by reiterating his revisionist theory that small farmers and businessmen were not disappearing under capitalism. In fact, contrary to Marx's prediction, in many sections of the United States this class seemed to be growing. It was a discontented class suffering oppression at the hands of the trusts, and according to Simons, it was open to the Socialist appeal.[47]

With the exception of Stanley Clark, a self-proclaimed "revolutionist" from Texas who insisted on "the collective ownership of the entire earth," the southwesterners strongly supported the re-

47. *Socialist Party Weekly Bulletin* (Chicago), January 18, 1908; and *Socialist Party, Proceedings of the First National Convention, 1908* (Chicago: Socialist Party of America, 1908), 13–16, 168, 178–86.

visionist arguments advanced by Work and Simons, because these arguments provided a political rationale for a farm program. Even delegates like Kate Richards O'Hare, who opposed middle-class proposals to save small businessmen, closed ranks with the revisionists, agreeing on the necessity for a national endorsement of the southwestern farm demands. Southwestern Socialists agreed with John Work's theory that small farmers were not capitalists, but rather members of the exploited "producing classes."[48]

Patrick S. Nagle, a shrewd Socialist lawyer from Kingfisher, Oklahoma, pointed out in 1908 that although the farmer, unlike the wageworker, was not exploited in the labor market, he suffered in the credit market as a borrower, in the consumer market as a buyer, and in the commodity market as a seller. According to Nagle, this provided ample grounds for a unified movement of the producing classes against the "parasites" who controlled all the markets. This neo-Populist philosophy was echoed by other articulate spokesmen for agrarian socialism, notably by the skilled propagandist Oscar Ameringer who was then creating a synthesis of the various positions marshaled on behalf of the Oklahoma farm program.[49]

In 1908 the southwesterners, including Ameringer, still relied upon the leadership of Work and Simons, whose revisionism alienated orthodox Socialists of the left and center. The southwesterners had not yet injected the issue of tenancy into the national debate, and in their defense of the small-farming class they appeared to be opportunistic vote-getters. Their farm program of 1908, which was rejected by the national convention, did in fact contain a large number of old Populist planks and to a majority of the party's representatives seemed more agrarian than Socialist.[50]

Undeterred, in 1909 the Oklahoma Socialists drafted a new farm platform which went far beyond anything the Populists had ad-

48. *Proceedings of First National Convention, 1908*, 13–16, 168, 178–86.
49. Patrick S. Nagle, *The Man on the Section Line* (Kingfisher, Okla.: n.p., 1908), 19–25. See H. L. Meredith, "Oscar Ameringer and the Concept of Agrarian Socialism," *Chronicles of Oklahoma*, XLV (1967), 78–80.
50. See criticisms of the Socialist farm bloc in *International Socialist Review*, VIII (1908), 731–32; and in *Proceedings of First National Convention*, 15, 20–21.

vocated in respect to the land question. This "Farmers' Programme" included three key demands designed to reduce the suffering of this "exploited class" and to induce support for the Socialist party. A "radical" new land plank demanded that the public domain be expanded for tenant use, graduated land taxes provided a means of eliminating the profit in speculative landholding, and the proposed state-sponsored cooperatives would serve not only for exchange but for new forms of collective production. Other planks in the 1909 platform called for government ownership of transportation, marketing, and manufacturing facilities, free agricultural education, a state-owned farm insurance program, and tax exemptions for farms with property (excluding land) valued at less than ten thousand dollars.[51]

After formulating a program that appealed directly to the landless tenant as well as to the indebted small farmer, the Oklahoma Socialists supported the organization of a labor union for land renters. Founded in September, 1909, by Sam and Luke Spencer of McClain County, the Oklahoma Renters' Union dedicated itself to the emancipation of farmers and workers through "united class conscious organization." The Union's preamble, written with the help of the ubiquitous Oscar Ameringer, insisted that farmers would reap the full fruit of their labor only when they followed the route taken by their brothers in the shops and mines. "In the union there is strength," the founders declared. "If we renters organize, we can stop the competition among ourselves for the land; we can not only keep the rent from rising, we can force it down." The formation of this Union, which Ameringer called the economic arm of Oklahoma socialism, not only marked the party's first tangible effort to organize its growing tenant support, it also provided Ameringer and other southwestern Socialists with evidence for their argument that the small farmer was not part of the capitalist class.[52]

51. "Farmers' Programme, 1909," in Oklahoma State File, Socialist Party Papers, Perkins Library, Duke University.
52. *Oklahoma Pioneer* (Oklahoma City), February 2, March 2, 1910. "Declaration of Principles of the Oklahoma Renters' Union," in Socialist Party Collection, Bureau of Government, University of Oklahoma. See also Stuart Jamieson, *Labor Unionism in American Agriculture*, Bureau of Labor Statis-

In 1910 the Oklahoma Socialists strengthened their demands for the "retention and constant enlargement of the public domain" for tenant use, and after the Texas party endorsed the new farmers' program the southwestern delegates proposed it to the national convention. Supported by Oscar Ameringer, Kate Richards O'Hare, and others, A. M. Simons tried for a fourth time to convince his comrades that the party needed a national platform for the farmer. Rejecting the demands of the "immpossiblists" (who succeeded in passing a resolution for the immediate collectivization of all land in 1908), the party "farm expert" marshaled an impressive array of quotes from European Socialist leaders opposed to the nationalization of small farm holdings.[53]

Most of the southwestern delegates limited their remarks to a practical plea for a program that would win even more votes from discontented farmers. This sounded quite self-serving, if not downright unprincipled, especially when it came from the likes of J. Tad Cumbie, the party's candidate for governor of Oklahoma.[54] Curiously, the Sooner Socialists failed to emphasize the party's new turn toward propertyless tenant farmers. Ameringer, Simons, and other leading spokesmen hauled out essentially the same arguments they had used to support neo-Populist platforms at the previous two conventions.

Caroline Lowe, a Kansas City schoolteacher who was popular on the Southwest encampment circuit, tried in vain to shift the debate away from the small-farm owner to the landless tenant farmer. Lowe explained that many Socialists who had no contact with farmers dismissed them all as part of the capitalist employing class. But those who worked in the Southwest and the Midwest realized that these rural producers were being exploited. The comrades who called all farmers petty capitalists had never seen a

---

tics Bulletin No. 836 (Washington, D.C.: Government Printing Office, 1945), 262.

53. *State Platform of the Texas Socialist Party, 1910*, in Socialist Party Papers, Duke; *Socialist Party, Proceedings of the First National Congress, 1910* (Chicago: H. G. Adair, 1910), 212–35.

54. *Proceedings of First National Congress, 1910*, 212–35.

"tenant serf, enslaved with his wife and children, bound hand and foot to the money lender and the land owner."[55] However, Lowe made her important comments out of context and failed to push the debate over the farmer question into a discussion of the land question and the tenancy problem.

Once again the southwestern delegates and their midwestern supporters failed to win a national endorsement for their farm program. They could take little solace in the fact that orthodox Socialists now criticized their demands as "state socialistic" rather than populistic. Victor Berger, the powerful Milwaukee Socialist who had actually supported earlier farm programs, moved to table (and, in effect, to kill) the 1910 platform because it took "a long step toward permanent private property" by guaranteeing tenants the right to public land in perpetuity. This fee-simple form of "state socialism," Berger warned, would play right into the hands of collectivist reformers whose New Nationalism sought to revive capitalism through government action.[56]

And so on a national level the farmer question remained unresolved in 1910. At the regional level it was clearly resolved. The southwestern parties refused to abandon their popular neo-Populist planks, their confiscatory taxation schemes borrowed from Henry George, or their ambitious plans for state-controlled farms for landless tenants. The Socialists of Oklahoma and neighboring states knew that "their strength lay in their immediate demands on state issues."[57]

Although the southwesterners had shed some of their neo-Populist demands in 1910 and moved away from the yeoman farmer toward the tenant, most of their demands were anchored firmly in the Populist tradition. In the Midwest and some other rural sections, populism left a bitter legacy of frustrated reformism; in the Southwest it represented a tradition of *defeated* radicalism, a tra-

---

55. *Ibid.*, 224.
56. *Ibid.*, 228–29, 235. Also see William English Walling, *Socialism As It Is* (New York: Henry Holt, 1912), 318–20.
57. David Shannon, *The Socialist Party of America, A History* (New York: Macmillan, 1955), 36.

dition that had, in itself, produced an indigenous agrarian Socialist movement. Although the southwestern Socialists battled
Populist rivals for over a decade, they were not as reluctant as
comrades in other sections to renew the unfulfilled demands of the
People's party. They were also unafraid to popularize Henry
George's attack on land monopoly. For although they rejected the
single tax as a panacea, the southwestern Socialists recognized the
importance of confiscatory taxes as a popular means of attacking
land speculators. It was an obvious solution to a problem that had
been sidestepped by the old parties and the People's parties alike.
The Oklahomans were also willing to risk co-optation of their fee-
simple brand of socialism by collectivist reformers who favored
state capitalism. Unlike Victor Berger and other northern Socialists who competed with Theodore Roosevelt's New Nationalism,
the southwesterners battled individualistic reformers in the Bryan
tradition who opposed any serious state involvement in land taxation or land ownership.

Oscar Ameringer understood these things. As a single taxer who
appreciated the importance of the region's radical populism,
Ameringer consciously drew on old traditions of rural protest. His
close reading of United States history convinced him of the importance of the "natural rights" tradition and of the significance
of the abortive Homestead Act, which promised land to the people
and granted it to the corporations. Through A. M. Simons and the
German revisionists, Ameringer learned that the small-farmer class
was not disappearing and decided that the party had to appeal to
these indebted yeomen on a neo-Populist platform. He also developed the notion that the small farmer was, if not a proletarian,
at least a producer who was part of the exploited class rather than
the employing class. Skillfully adopting the terminology of the
Knights of Labor and the Farmers' Alliance, Ameringer applied
Marxian class analysis to the Southwest and urged farmers to join
their natural allies, the workers, in a struggle against the parasitic
"exploiter class." As editor of the *Oklahoma Pioneer*, one of the
best southwestern party papers, he blended agrarian socialism with

the traditional proletarian brand he had learned in the Knights and the Brewery Workers' Union.[58]

When Ameringer turned his talents as a labor organizer toward the Renters' Union, he also began to direct his writing away from the old yeoman class of farmers toward the rising class of tenants he discovered on his encampment tours. But Ameringer never abandoned his belief that in the Cooperative Commonwealth all hard-working, productive farmers deserved the "use and occupancy" of the land. This became the central tenet of southwestern agrarian socialism, and no one articulated it better than Ameringer, whose most notable statement of that belief appeared in his popular pamphlet, "Socialism for the Farmer Who Farms the Farm." If socialism guaranteed the worker the full product of his labor, then, he argued, it also owed the farm producer the full product of his toil. In fact, Ameringer maintained that the small farmer, as well as the tenant and farm laborer, had a "natural right" to the use and occupancy of the land as long as it was utilized for productive and not exploitative purposes. This natural right was documented in common law by Blackstone and in scriptural law in Leviticus, but it was denied to the farmer by the capitalists. The Socialists would restore that precious right.[59]

Ameringer's propaganda appealed to a wide range of farming people throughout the Southwest. It emphasized the superiority of cooperative production over monopoly capitalism without demanding the immediate collectivization of all land. Through confiscatory land taxes, state subsidies, and the expansion of the public domain for tenant use, Socialists could relieve the sufferings of the small farmers and prevent them from being reduced to the level of "feudal serfs." At the same time, they could "open the way for the development of cooperative farming and the gradual na-

---

58. Oscar Ameringer, *If You Don't Weaken: The Autobiography of Oscar Ameringer* (New York: Henry Holt, 1940), 175–280. Also see Meredith, "Oscar Ameringer and Agrarian Socialism," 75–82.

59. Oscar Ameringer, *Socialism for the Farmer Who Farms the Farm*, in *National Rip-Saw* Series No. 15 (St. Louis: Rip-Saw Publishing, 1912).

tionalization of the land."[60] Ameringer was convinced that small farmers would see the superiority of cooperative production in the Cooperative Commonwealth, but it was politically insane to demand the immediate collectivization of all land. This persuasive brand of gradual socialism was bolstered by the growing electoral successes of the southwestern parties. This fact, coupled with the discovery of the tenancy problem, set the stage for a national party endorsement of the Oklahoma farm program in 1912. Oscar Ameringer was not solely responsible for synthesizing the various traditions that ran through agrarian socialism in the Southwest, but in his inimitably witty but convincing style he was largely responsible for popularizing the movement's approach to the farmer question.

Ameringer's agrarian Socialist propaganda expressed the southwestern Socialist party's confident solution to the farmer question. The answer they provided was still unacceptable to many orthodox Socialists in other sections, but, as the appeal of the southwestern farm program grew, the opposition to a national party endorsement declined. In any case, the agrarian Socialists were more concerned about competing with their Democratic rivals in the Southwest than they were with convincing their factional rivals in other sections. The reform Democrats, despite their neo-Populist rhetoric, had failed to meet the needs of the small farmer and had virtually ignored the needs of the growing class of discontented tenants who were beginning to make political trouble. The Socialists' answer to the land question gave them a wedge to drive into the Democrats' poorest constituency in the cotton country.

60. *Ibid.*

III

Troublesome
Questions

BY 1910 THE southwestern Socialists had resolved the farmer question for themselves by blending Populist reforms with immediate demands oriented to the land question and they were on the verge of winning a national party endorsement for their agrarian variant of "constructive" socialism. Needless to say, theoretical questions remained unresolved in this southwestern formulation, though these became less problematic as grass-roots socialism began to grow faster in Oklahoma and Texas than anywhere else in the country. It was clear that tenants and small indebted farmers would play a key role in the party's development west of the Mississippi, where the prewar Socialist party was strongest.

On a superficial level, it seemed even easier to resolve the woman question and the race question; the party would agitate for female and black voting rights as it had done quite militantly in Kansas and Oklahoma, but the inequalities could not be fully resolved until the Cooperative Commonwealth arrived. Then, political and economic equality between the races and sexes would dispel troublesome questions about the social equality of men and women, whites and blacks. Although the party's vote-getting electoral strategy reduced the significance of the disfranchised blacks and women, the southwestern Socialists involved working-class women and blacks more extensively in party work than their comrades in most other sections, because of the significant contact established through militant industrial unions like the United Mine Workers and the Brotherhood of Timber Workers. This contact strength-

ened the spirited campaigns launched on behalf of black and female voting rights, but the women and blacks who participated in
the party did not directly challenge the problems caused by male
supremacy and white supremacy within the organization.

As a result, debates over educational and organizational problems actually seemed more important than the question of social
equality for women and blacks. The southwestern Socialists looked
ahead of their times in many ways, especially with regard to crucial economic problems like the growth of tenancy and absentee
landlordism. And they took more advanced positions than their
political rivals in defending black and female voting rights; in fact,
they advanced beyond their comrades in most other sections in
this fight for political equality. But they were not so forward
thinking when the issue of social equality confronted them with
so many troublesome questions.

THE WOMAN QUESTION

In its 1901 constitution the American Socialist party pledged itself
to struggle for "perfect equality of women with men in political
and social matters." However, as Mari Jo Buhle shows, equal relations between the sexes did not prevail within the party. The
men who dominated the southwestern Socialist movement did not
confront the issues raised by the real feminists in the party, though
they did strongly support the campaign for women's suffrage—the
issue considered by many of their female comrades as the key
aspect of the woman question. They also encouraged women to
participate in many levels of party work.[1] Southwestern women,
who probably would have been active even without the encouragement of male leaders, actually involved themselves more deeply in
organizational activity than their sister Socialists in most other
states.

The leading female agitators in the movement included several
remarkably talented, resourceful women. Laura B. Payne, a noted

1. Mari Jo Buhle, "Women and the Socialist Party, 1910–1914," *Radical
America*, IV (1970), 36–57. Also see Bruce Dancis, "Socialism and Women in
the United States, 1901–1917," *Socialist Revolution*, No. 27 (1976), 81–144.

grass-roots Texas organizer, ran for statewide office in 1910 as did Winnie Branstetter, who had settled on the Cherokee Strip after working for wages in Kansas City. Ida Hayman Callery, raised on an Oklahoma tenant farm, came over to Arkansas to work for the party in 1908 and was elected state secretary a few years later, an unusual distinction for a Socialist woman. Ida had been a teacher of Creek Indian boys at the federal school in Wetumpka, Oklahoma, before joining the Socialist party. After working at the Oklahoma state headquarters, she took over at the Arkansas office in July, 1911. She received a good deal of publicity in the party press and received most of the credit for increasing the Arkansas party's membership from 400 to 2,376 by February of 1912. "To increase the membership of a state socialist party six times within six months is no small task," wrote one admiring sister Socialist. Freda Hogan, who worked on her father's Socialist newspaper in Huntington, Arkansas, a small coal-mining town, succeeded Ida as party secretary, even though she was in her early twenties. May Beals published a newspaper called the *Red Flag* in Abbeville, Louisiana, during the early 1900s and May Wood-Simons coedited the *Coming Nation* with her husband in Girard, Kansas. Grace Brewer worked as an assistant editor of the *Appeal* and of the *Workers' Chronicle* at Pittsburg, Kansas, in the heart of the coal fields. She also served as an administrative officer of the *Appeal* Army. With the help of Kate Richards O'Hare and Caroline Lowe, two peripatetic workingwomen from Kansas City, May and Grace worked among the miners' wives in southeast Kansas to create one of the strongest Socialist organizations of working-class women in the country. O'Hare and Lowe developed popular followings around the Southwest as a result of their encampment speaking tours, and eventually they became known throughout the country. The influence of southwestern women within the Socialist party was reflected in the fact that Branstetter, Lowe, and Simons were all elected to the National Women's Committee in 1911, and Freda Hogan was elected a few years later.[2]

2. *Oklahoma Pioneer* (Oklahoma City), October 29, 1910; *Rebel* (Hallettsville, Tex.), March 2, 1912; *Appeal to Reason* (Girard, Kan.), December 25,

All of these Socialists played an important role in the female suffrage movement with the exception of Laura Payne, the Texas organizer who boldly refused to join the suffragettes because they were part of a middle-class women's reform movement that would do nothing to "educate the people as to class consciousness." Kate Richards O'Hare responded to this point of view at the 1910 national congress, arguing that it was not at all "impossible for a Socialist to . . . take an active part in the women's suffrage movement without sacrificing her Socialist principles in the slightest degree."[3]

Most active southwestern Socialists agreed with O'Hare's position; they did not believe that women's rights campaigns took precedence over the party's main goal of winning an electoral majority, but the two seemed perfectly compatible because enfranchisement would qualify far more workingwomen than middle-class women. Few Socialists took the side of Laura Payne and other critics of suffragism who complained that the vote for women would play into the hands of bourgeois reformers. Since the Southwest lacked a strong independent women's suffrage movement, the Socialists were able to take the lead in the Oklahoma and Kansas campaigns for political equality. With the exception of Kate Barnard, Oklahoma's charities and corrections commissioner, the old parties lacked female leaders to compete with the likes of Kate Richards O'Hare, who used the suffrage movement as a platform for recruiting women to the party.

In fact, Kate joined with her sister Socialists and other suffragists in forcing a referendum on woman's suffrage onto the 1910 ballot in Oklahoma. Having voted in their own party referendum to support "unrestricted suffrage," the Sooner Socialists faced a

1909 and April 17, 1917; *Socialist Party Monthly Bulletin*, VIII (September-October, 1911); May Wood-Simons, "A Socialist Woman's Work," *Coming Nation* (Girard, Kan.), May 11, 1912; interview with Freda Hogan Ameringer, June 21, 1974.

3. *Socialist Party, Proceedings of the First National Convention, 1908* (Chicago: Socialist Party of America, 1908), 302–305, and *Socialist Party, Proceedings of the First National Congress, 1910* (Chicago: H. G. Adair, 1910), 185.

difficult two-sided struggle in the summer of 1910—to defend the franchise for black men and to win it for women. Allying with black political leaders and a few progressives and suffragists in the old parties, the Oklahoma Socialist party waged a spirited propaganda campaign for political equality, but it lost on both counts, though the party took some satisfaction in the support it mustered among poor white farmers and workers. In 1912 Kansas voters passed a women's suffrage amendment and again Socialists played a leading role in the agitation. The amendment carried in all but one of the twenty-two counties where the party polled more than 10 percent of the vote. Women's suffrage passed overwhelmingly in the Socialist strongholds of Crawford and Cherokee counties.[4]

The campaigns for women's suffrage, combined with the organization of women's clubs and branches under the forceful leadership of O'Hare, Lowe, Branstetter, and Brewer attracted more poor women into Socialist party activity in Kansas and Oklahoma than in most states. Since southwestern Socialist women had not been active in the battles over the question of women's autonomy in the years before 1908, they were not regarded as threatening feminists, and they thus received strong support in their organizational work from the party's male leaders.[5]

Coal miners' wives, especially in southeastern Kansas, participated actively in party affairs, particularly during and after the 1910 strike in which they played a militant part. Socialist women also played a role in a "strong union" organized by female domestics of several Oklahoma cities in 1911. Farmers' wives seemed

4. In Marshall County, Oklahoma, a Socialist stronghold, the 1910 women's suffrage amendment carried in all of the precincts (all rural) won by the party's candidates and lost in all of the precincts (mainly towns) carried by the Democrats. *Marshall County News-Democrat* (Madill, Okla.), November 9, 1910. The strong Socialist counties in southeast Kansas also contributed big majorities for women's suffrage in 1912. May Wood-Simons, "Suffrage and Socialism in Kansas," *Christian Socialist* (February 1, 1913). The author would like to thank Jim Kendell for making available his unpublished paper on Kansas socialism, from which some of this information on women's suffrage is drawn.

5. See Dancis, "Socialism and Women," 103–17 on the early battles over the woman question and autonomy.

less involved in local party activity, perhaps because they were widely separated from one another, but they did join enthusiastically in summer encampments, which were always billed as family affairs. And although rural women participated to a limited degree in the Socialist party, some female farmers were influenced by radical propaganda and began to speak out about the class nature of their oppression. "Our young girls' and women's health is ruined from dragging big, heavy sacks up and down cotton rows," said one Oklahoma farm woman. The tenant's wife toiled "like a slave," because she had to work in the fields, keep house, tend the garden, and raise the children all at once. "The main cause of it all," she concluded, "is that the majority of us are landless people, renters and homeless, therefore a discontented and enslaved people." This angry woman ended her statement by endorsing the party's demand for a confiscatory tax on all land held for speculation and for a statute declaring that "use and occupancy be the only title to the land."[6]

Another female Socialist who failed to escape the druggery of farm life described her oppression this way: "It is not the lack of cosmetics that ages women of the farm before our time. It is the treadmill, the life of hard, incessant labor without reward. The wife has no definite share of the husband's income. She is the stewardess of riches, the actual possessor of none. Moneyless, she can project nothing. She gives up, loses her individuality, grows dull." Her woman's solution to this oppressive situation was an unusual one: every farmer's wife should receive wages for housework and other chores, just like a hired girl. If one could not achieve emancipation without being a member of the proletariat then one should become a proletarian by earning wages at some level; it was a logical conclusion for a female Socialist to draw,

6. See *Appeal to Reason* (Girard, Kan.), February 17, 24, March 4, 1912, on the organization of Socialist women. Quotation from "Social and Labor Needs of Farm Women," U.S. Department of Agriculture, *Report No. 103* (Washington, D.C.: Government Printing Office, 1915), 52–53. On the Oklahoma domestics' union see letter from Jane Street of Workers' Industrial Union, 1917, reprinted in *Labor History*, XVII (1976), 103–104.

given that her oppression was viewed simply as a part of the general oppression of the working class.[7]

Southwestern female Socialists like Kate Richards O'Hare naturally understood the special oppression of farm women, because they had experienced it themselves or had perceived it at close range. In fact, Kate once pointed out boldly that farmers exploited their wives and children even when they did not exploit wage-earning field hands; but she did not pursue this point because, like most of her sister Socialists who were not involved in the initial conflict over the woman question within the party, she did not believe in special demands for women in either the social or the economic realm. Kate Richards O'Hare, a militant suffragist but not a feminist, believed that a woman's place was in the home. Socialism would make monogamous marriage a viable, healthy institution by eliminating the poverty that forced poor women to suffer from abortion, prostitution, and domestic oppression. Like her comrade, Winnie Branstetter, O'Hare refused to separate the "sex struggle" from the class struggle;[8] these women were party loyalists who would not jeopardize the Socialist appeal to farmers and workers by injecting the feminist issue of women's special oppression in the home. In fact, most Debsian Socialists were unwilling or unable to distinguish the "specific oppression of women and children from the general oppression of the working class," because they excluded the "family from their concept of capitalist production."[9]

The talent and determination of southwestern Socialist women and the ambitious nature of the party's work drew an unusual

7. *Economic Needs of Farm Women*, U.S. Department of Agriculture, Report No. 106 (Washington, D.C.: Government Printing Office, 1915), 49.

8. See Kate Richards O'Hare's writings in *National Rip-Saw* (St. Louis), August, 1912, p. 3 and March, 1913, pp. 18–20; and Winnie Branstetter, "The Sex Struggle," *Oklahoma Pioneer* (Oklahoma City), March 10, 1910. O'Hare's comment on the exploitation of farm women is in *Proceedings of First National Congress, 1910*, 233, and on marriage see Kate Richards O'Hare, *The Sorrows of Cupid* (St. Louis: Rip-Saw Publishing, 1912), 186.

9. Eli Zaretsky, "Capitalism, the Family and Personal Life," *Socialist Revolution*, No. 15 (1973), 22.

number of females into the movement, especially in Kansas and Oklahoma, but this did not lead to a satisfactory resolution of the woman question within the organization. Male supremacy prevented the question from being confronted in a determined, principled manner, and the Socialist party's emphasis on vote-getting encouraged radicals to avoid the special problems of disfranchised women.

THE RACE QUESTION

Although southwestern Socialists actively organized indebted yeomen and tenant farmers without the official endorsement of the party congress, they all but ignored the "unambiguous invitation" the Socialist party had extended to blacks at its Unity Convention in 1901.[10] Oklahoma Socialists defended black voting rights more courageously than any political party in the country, but their comrades throughout the Southwest generally avoided recruiting blacks. They could not avoid the race question, however, because their enemies constantly accused them of favoring race mixing and social equality. The southwestern Socialists always denied these charges and sometimes responded by turning the tables and race-baiting the Democrats. Most often, however, they simply stated that their party favored political and economic equality for blacks, but not "social equality."[11]

Some Socialists stood behind the 1901 invitation in which the party's founders asked the "negro worker" to join the "world movement for economic emancipation" and equal liberty. In his tours through the South and the Southwest in 1903 Eugene Debs denounced racial discrimination with characteristic militancy and called upon black workers to oppose those who preached meekness and humility in the face of oppression.[12] His appeal, however,

10. R. Laurence Moore, "Flawed Fraternity: American Socialist Response to the Negro, 1901–1912," *The Historian*, XXXII (1969), 1–2.
11. See Donald Graham, "Red, White, and Black: An Interpretation of Ethnic and Racial Attitudes of Agrarian Radicals in Texas and Oklahoma, 1880–1920" (M.A. thesis, University of Saskatechewan, 1973).
12. Moore, "Flawed Fraternity," 2; Ira Kipnis, *The American Socialist Movement, 1897–1912* (New York: Columbia University Press, 1952), 133;

failed to advance the recruitment of blacks by southern Socialists or to alter the segregated policies of those locals that included blacks. The Louisiana Socialists, for example, endorsed segregation in their founding convention in the same year Debs made his southern tour. Although the party's National Executive Committee (which still stood by the 1901 invitation to black workers) forced the Louisiana party to withdraw its segregation clause, the leaders of this southern organization vowed to continue practicing *de facto* segregation on a local level.[13]

Some southwestern Socialists, like E. A. Brenholtz of Texas, opposed local segregation and called upon southern comrades to fight racial prejudice.[14] But these equalitarians were regarded as dangerous adventurers by southern party leaders, who, like Texas State Secretary John Kerrigan, preferred to keep the race question submerged. Kerrigan, a member of the National Executive Committee, voted to hold up the Louisiana party charter until the segregation clause was deleted, but this did not mean that he favored a campaign against segregation. Far from it. "We have never touched upon it [the race question]," he told a New Orleans party leader, because, "when a man became a well-informed Socialist, he would settle the question himself." In addition, he cautioned, "We should not place a weapon in the hands of the enemy when we can avoid it." Like many southwestern Socialists, Kerrigan supported the *Appeal to Reason* position of "economic but not social equality" for blacks. Socialists should not call for "the mixture of races"; this would only play into the hands of their Democratic enemies who would use the fear of "race mixing" as a cover to destroy the

---

Ray Ginger, *Eugene V. Debs: The Making of An American Radical* (New York: Colliers, 1966), 276–77.

13. Ginger, *Eugene V. Debs*, 130–31. Details of the controversy can be found in correspondence carried by *Worker* (Chicago), October 16, 20, November 8, 15, December 27, 1903. Also see Eraste Vidrine, "Negro Locals," *International Socialist Review*, V (1905), 389, a defense of segregation by a New Orleans Socialist who argued that Negro locals were as legitimate as Slavic locals or foreign language federations.

14. E. A. Brenholtz to editor, *Socialist* (Seattle), January 17, 1904.

Socialist party in the same way they had destroyed the Texas Populist party.[15]

Party leaders, like the *Appeal* editors, hastened to separate themselves from the racist Democrats, for although they opposed race mixing, as Socialists they were not to "assume that the negro is inferior." At the same time, they refrained from criticizing comrades who responded in kind to the Democrats' race-baiting attacks. Thus, Kerrigan opposed official segregation in the Louisiana party charter but ignored the racism of E. O. Meitzen, a prominent member of his own party who had endorsed the idea of "negro inferiority" after winning the nomination as a candidate for Lavaca County judge. After Meitzen failed to be reelected judge in 1906 he retreated from the race question, but when he began publishing his weekly *Rebel* in 1911, he joined editor Tom Hickey in race-baiting Democratic opponents. Since the *Rebel* became the official organ of the Texas Socialist party, it tinted this state's movement with racism and drew the criticism of northern egalitarian Socialists like Mary Ovington White. By 1914 the Texas Socialists had actually started to organize black and brown tenant farmers, but these interracial organizing efforts were undoubtedly weakened by the overtly racist strain added to the movement by leaders like Hickey and Meitzen.[16]

The Oklahoma Socialists took a far more progressive position on the race question than their comrades in Texas and in most other states as well. Most leaders of the state organization refrained from engaging in racist rhetoric and from endorsing segregation, and they refused to write off the possibility of recruiting black support. Of course, Sooner Socialists had more to gain by taking these positions. Although blacks accounted for only about 10 percent of the state's electorate, they held the balance of power in many territorial elections and remained a force to be reckoned with until most were disfranchised by the grandfather clause in

15. Kerrigan to P. Aloysius Molyneaux, October 29, 1903, in *Social Democratic Herald* (Milwaukee), November 21, 1903; *Appeal to Reason* (Girard, Kan.), April 25, 1903.

16. *Appeal to Reason* (Girard, Kan.), April 25, 1903; Graham, "Red, White, and Black," 114–21.

NEGROES FAVOR SOCIALIST PARTY

PREAMBLE.

The Negro was seized in Africa and brought to this country for mercenary purposes by white men whose conscience was so elastic as to be stretched to cover the legitimate accretion of honest labor, and for nearly three centuries he was placed upon the auction block by the side of dumb brutes and sold to the highest bidder, thus serving the government as a source of revenue. The civil strife through God's will came to his rescue. Two hundred thousand negroes fought, and fifty thousand were slain. The ground is holy where they fought, holy where they lie, thanks be to God, that by their blood their liberty was bought. December 18th, 1865, freedom was declared July 28th, 1868, citizenship was granted and on the 30th day of March, 1870, the mantle of suffrage was thrown over him.

These blessed amendments were God sent. They make us joint heirs to American citizenship and the history of this government justifies us in demanding protection and rights to the fullest extent of the law.

We are Americans to the manner born. Our blood was the first to be used to cement the cornerstone of this Republic, and we cannot sit still while our rights are being denied. Our citizenship withheld and our immunities abridged. Discriminatory laws are made against us, and today we are disfranchised in Oklahoma, virtually we are not part of the state government and cannot be a factor in its functions.

The negro has always voted the Republican ticket in a solid phalanx, thus engendering the enmity of other parties, and yet, the very party to which we have contributed our life and support have not been loyal to us, they have not protected our franchise in the way it should, consequently our condition politically, however honorably to contemplate, is due to the tardiness of the very party that should have been first in making of the laws by which this new state was to be governed.

Realizing the crisis under which we are now going is the most critical one of our life, we hereby meet in mass and pass the following resolutions, to-wit:

We denounce the action of the two great parties of said state for the part they have taken in the nefarious legislation that robs us of ourrights, jeopardizes our future and curbs the ambition of our future posterity and do hereby agree to support the party that stands for the fatherhood of God and Brotherhood of Man and which really believes in political privileges to all men.

We declare ourselves in sympathy with female suffrage and hereby agree to lend our support to the end that such will come to pass and that women will be our helpmate in life for which God created and ordained her.

We demand that in case the Supreme Court upholds the constitutionality of the Grandfather Clause that the Congressional Representation from this State of Oklahoma be reduced in accordance with the number of qualified voters so disfranchised by reason of race, color or prejudice, and that the Negroes who are not allowed to vote be exempted from paying any poll or personal taxes.

Be It Further Resolved, We do therefore recommend that the Third, Fourth and Fifth Congressional Districts be thoroughly organized, and that said organization do hereby co-operate with the State Constitutional League and all moneys raised be held by the local treasurer and disposed of by its members when necessity demands; and further,

Whereas, The Colored Race of Oklahoma, consisting of about 15 or 20 per cent of the entire population of this State, have loyally supported the Republican Party and its principles, and with the exception of the Hon. Joe McNeal and the Hon. Bird McGuire, have never received any social or political recognition from the Republicans, and,

Whereas, The Socialist Party has invited us to affiliate with them for the reason that the Socialist Party believes in Social Equality of all races; and,

Whereas, The Colored Race of Oklahoma believes with the Socialists that all men are born free and equal in every sense of the word;

Therefore, Be It Resolved, That we hereby endorse the platforms put out by our Socialist brothers and recommend that all the colored people of Oklahoma vote the Socialist ticket and allign themselves with our Socialistic brethren of Oklahoma. Respectfully submitted,

(Signed) J. A. ROPER,
Of the Third Congressional District, Chairman of Committee of Resolutions.

W. M. HUTTON,
Of the Second Congressional District, Secretary of the Resolutions Committee.

REV. J. A. JOHNSON,
Fifth Congressional District, Chairman of the Convention.

W. T. MORTON,
Of the First Congressional District.

T. W. GILES,
Of the Fourth Congressional District.

PRINTERS PUBLISHING CO. OKLAHOMA CITY, OKLA.

1910. Oklahoma blacks not only comprised an important voting bloc in the early 1900s; they were poor people increasingly discontented with the Republican politicians who claimed to represent their interests. Unlike the black voters of Arkansas, Louisiana, and Texas who were disfranchised and discouraged, the Afro-Americans of Oklahoma continued to wage an increasingly militant and overtly political struggle against racial oppression and economic degradation. The egalitarian leaders in the Oklahoma Socialist party could not ignore the blacks' impressive legacy of protest.

During Reconstruction, free blacks in the Indian Territory had protested vigorously against the mistreatment they suffered at the hands of their old Indian masters; they also launched bold petition campaigns to secure full tribal rights in the Five Civilized Tribes. In the late eighties and early nineties other former slaves from the Old South (sometimes called "exodusters") moved into the Nations and began to nourish the dream of making Oklahoma a black-controlled state. When the continuing influx of white "intruders" destroyed this dream, some disillusioned black folks in the Indian Territory turned to Bishop Henry Turner's nationalist "back-to-Africa" philosophy. Others began withdrawing into all-black towns like Boley, where the citizens erected a sign that said: "White man, don't let the sun set on your back in this town." By 1905 separatists had founded several racial communities in both the Oklahoma and Indian territories based upon Booker T. Washington's self-help ideas and instinctive forms of grass-roots black nationalism. The citizens of Oklahoma's all-black communities hoped to use their towns as bases of political power, but dishonest Democratic election officials often frustrated their electoral efforts.[17]

17. Parthena L. James, "Reconstruction in the Chickasaw Nation: The Freedman Problem," *Chronicles of Oklahoma*, XLV (1967), 44–57; Edwin S. Redkey, *Black Exodus: Black Nationalist and Back-to-Africa Movements, 1890–1910* (New Haven, Conn.: Yale University Press, 1969), 99–107, 250; Mozell C. Hill, "The All-Negro Communities of Oklahoma: The Natural History of a Social Movement," *Journal of Negro History*, XXXI (1946), 254–68; and William L. Biddle and Gilbert Geis, "Racial Self-Fulfillment and the Rise of an All-Negro Community in Oklahoma," *Phylon*, XVIII (1957), 247–60.

The high level of frustration among Oklahoma's blacks led to violent confrontation in March, 1907, when a "secret organization of negroes" called the United Socialists fought a gun battle with police and federal officers in Muskogee, a city with a large Afro-American population. The battle, during which two officers and three blacks were killed, began when authorities tried to evict the United Socialists from their "clubhouse." According to the press, this "organization of negro anarchists" claimed a number of members in other black communities of the Indian Territory and believed it could literally expropriate private property because, as a United Socialist leader put it, "their authority was higher than that of the United States." It is difficult to explain why the group chose to call itself Socialist; it certainly had no direct connection with the Socialist party. The political goals of the United Socialists in Muskogee remain obscure, but their shootout with the police indicated clearly that some Oklahoma blacks were turning toward armed self-defense in response to the growth of racist repression.[18]

As statehood approached, Oklahoma blacks fought harder to protect their rights. In 1906 they successfully urged President Roosevelt to prevent discriminatory laws from being written into the state constitution. However, when Oklahoma attained statehood, black protest failed to prevent the Democrats from enacting Jim Crow laws in the first legislature. And although Afro-American voters gave the Republicans a margin of victory in several territorial elections, they saw their loyalty go unrewarded as many GOP legislators joined their Democratic rivals in "roaring approval" of discriminatory statutes. The state's first legislature attained considerable notoriety for progressive reform, but progressivism in Oklahoma, like other states, was for whites only.[19]

In 1908 there was extensive and at times violent resistance to Jim Crow laws in several of Oklahoma's black communities. In

18. Shawnee (Okla.) *Daily Herald*, March 27, 29, 1907, and Muskogee (Okla.) *Daily Phoenix*, March 27, 1907.
19. James B. Scales, "Political History of Oklahoma, 1907–1949" (Ph.D. dissertation, University of Oklahoma, 1949), 47, 91–92. Also see C. Vann Woodward, *Origins of the New South, 1877–1913* (Baton Rouge: Louisiana State University Press, 1951), Chap. XIV.

contrast to the legal boycotts and "conservative protests" against segregation in other southern cities, Oklahoma's Afro-Americans launched militant actions.[20] In Muskogee, for example, the street-car company "failed to enforce the jim crow law" as "negroes ignored the moveable signs placed in the cars" and employees "made no successful effort to enforce the segregation of the races." Segregation was particularly difficult in eastern Oklahoma where conductors had trouble distinguishing Indians, who were allowed to ride with whites, from blacks who were of mixed blood. While black lawyers brought the Jim Crow laws to court and clergymen convened a big antisegregation convention at Wagoner, other angry blacks took more forceful actions. The strongest resistance surfaced in all-black towns like Tullahasse, where a crowd broke nearly all the windows in the white cars of a passing train, and Taft, where another crowd burned the new Negro waiting room to the ground. Indignant blacks also threatened the lives of the lieutenant governor and the sheriff of Lincoln County. Unrest continued in Oklahoma's black communities for several years, but most of the state's Afro-Americans were discouraged by the futility of their protests against the "selfish and coldblooded white man" who, according to one black newspaper, "stole the labor of the Negro and the land of the Indian under the protection of the law."[21] During the furor the Socialist party of Oklahoma remained conspicuous in its silence. Socialist leaders did not endorse segregation like their counterparts in Texas and Louisiana, but they did not join the black militants in protesting the arrival of Jim Crow.

In August of 1910 a grandfather clause was amended to the state constitution, and Socialists did join in attacking a law that made

20. Boley (Okla.) *Progress,* October 5, 1906. Also see *Southern Mercury* (Dallas), December 18, 1902, for a report of a peaceful protest against Jim Crow streetcars in Houston. For an overview, see August Meier and Elliott Rudwick, "The Boycott Movement Against Jim Crow Street Cars in the South, 1900–1906," *Journal of American History,* LV (1969), 756–75, which stops short of describing the Oklahoma protests.
21. Madill (Okla.) *News,* February 20, 1908; Harthshorne (Okla.) *Sun,* February 20, 1908; Muskogee (Okla.) *Daily Phoenix,* February 18, 1908; Mc-

it almost impossible for black men to vote. Democratic lawmakers designed the clause to disfranchise "illiterate" black men, but not white or red men, by requiring a literacy test that excepted those citizens and their descendants who had registered before 1866 (thus excluding all slaves and their heirs). The act also excluded those citizens and their descendants who were born in foreign nations (including Indian "nations" but not African tribes). In other words, the grandfather clause exempted every male voter from the literacy test except the black man.[22]

Oklahoma Socialist party secretary, Otto Branstetter, denounced this "nefarious law" as soon as the Democrats officially proposed it as a referendum measure. In June of 1910 he formed a protest committee consisting of Oscar Ameringer and Jack Hagel of the *Oklahoma Pioneer*, and Pat Nagle and W. L. Reynolds, two Socialist lawyers. Nagle, an experienced attorney and a former United States marshal, filed a suit against the clause on behalf of three old slaves, in an effort to prevent the measure from appearing as a referendum question in August.[23] He also demanded a hearing before the secretary of state to show that the proposed referendum clearly violated the state and federal constitutions. In a dramatic cross-examination of the Democratic party's state chairman, Nagle insisted on public admission of the fact that the clause was designed to "disfranchise voters of African descent." The secretary of state, however, sustained the objections of Democratic lawyers who did not want their state chairman to admit that the grandfather clause conflicted blatantly with a replica of the Fifteenth Amendment included in Oklahoma's progressive constitution. The secretary of state even refused to allow Nagle to subpoena the secret record of the "extraordinary" legislative session in which both Democrats and Republicans had revealed their intention to

Alester (Okla.) *Daily Capital*, April 10, 1908, *Weekly Chieftan* (Vinita, Okla.), August 14, 1908. Quote in Boley (Okla.) *Progress*, November 8, 1909.

22. "The Grandfather Clause in Oklahoma," *Outlook*, XCV, August 20, 1910, 853–54.

23. *Daily Oklahoman* (Oklahoma City), June 2, 20, August 7, 1910; *Appeal to Reason* (Girard, Kan.), April 16, 1910; *Oklahoma Pioneer* (Oklahoma City), June 1, 1910.

disfranchise black voters.[24] Through these legal challenges Nagle embarrassed Democratic officials, but he failed to prevent their disfranchisement law from appearing on the August ballot.

While the Republicans made "half-hearted efforts" to oppose the grandfather clause, the Socialists in Oklahoma City spoke out forcefully against it, especially in their official paper, the *Pioneer*. In fact, Oscar Ameringer, the paper's editor, wrote the official statement against the amendment circulated to voters as part of the referendum process.[25] In arguing against black disfranchisement, Ameringer and Nagle appealed for justice on behalf of the black voter. "The negro is entitled to equal opportunity for access to the means of life and to the full social value of his own labor," they wrote. "And he should not be deprived of the ballot, because the ballot is an instrument with which he can fight his way to industrial freedom." In an effort to cut down the "bloody flag" the Democrats had been waving since Reconstruction, the Socialists contended that the black man had not always voted wrong. "He has voted right more often than the white section of the working class—he has unswervingly voted against those who murdered his father, outraged his mother, and raped his sister."[26]

Nagle and Ameringer also appealed to the class interests of white workers in Oklahoma: "The negro belongs to the working class, and the working class must stand by the negro. If the white section of the working class abandons the negro, he will become a scab and a strikebreaker on the industrial fields and, in times of unrest, the armed and uniformed mercenary of the ruling class." Finally, and most importantly, the Socialist opponents of the grandfather clause appealed to the political self-interest of white

24. "Transcript of Exhibits Presented to Secretary of State of Oklahoma and a Record of Hearing Before the Secretary," June 6, 1910, in Oklahoma State Library, Oklahoma City. The author would like to thank Marietta Malzer for making this source available.

25. Scales, "Political History of Oklahoma," 128–29; and Oscar Ameringer, *If You Don't Weaken: The Autobiography of Oscar Ameringer* (New York: Henry Holt, 1940), 279.

26. "A Word to the Working Class," submitted by Otto Branstetter, Jack Hagel, Oscar Ameringer, W. L. Reynolds, and P. S. Nagle in "Transcript to Secretary of State," 7.

workers and farmers. They explained that poor whites suffered in states that disfranchised blacks and concentrated control over elections in the hands of Democratic governors. The Socialists were equally opposed to the Senate bill that included the grandfather clause and the House bill that gave the governor complete control over election machinery. Under the second statute, framed "along the lines of the Taylor and Goebel election laws . . . the people are entirely excluded from any participation in conducting the election" because no one, except the governor's appointees, would be permitted to have any knowledge of election results. The Socialists legitimately feared the implications of this law for their future at the polls. But in trying to present their argument against the Democratic election laws in a nonpartisan fashion, they insisted that the poor white voter would suffer from these so-called election reforms along with the poor black voter. The grandfather clause represented an "entering wedge" to split the working class; it would lead to the same disfranchisement of all poor voters that had already occurred in Louisiana, Arkansas, and other southern states. A vote against the grandfather clause was not a vote for "social equality," as the Democrats argued; it was, the Socialists maintained, a vote for political equality for all people without which economic equality could never be attained. These appeals to class interest and self-interest, and perhaps even to political justice, had some effect within the Socialist party, for in the spring of 1910 the "red card" rank and file voted by referendum to include a demand for "unrestricted suffrage" in their party platform.[27]

As the heated debate over disfranchisement continued through the summer of 1910, Socialists began to question their party's official defense of black voting rights. This opposition was especially significant in the "Little Dixie" section of eastern Oklahoma where dissident local leaders criticized Ameringer, Branstetter, and other state officials for sacrificing potential Socialist votes from discontented southern Democrats in order to wage a hopeless campaign

27. H. L. Meredith, "Agrarian Socialism in Oklahoma" (Ph.D. dissertation, University of Oklahoma, 1969), 95–96. Also see *Appeal to Reason* (Girard, Kan.), April 16, 1910.

against the grandfather clause. Although most of the Socialists in "Little Dixie" shared the racial prejudices common to other whites in the region, they remained relatively silent on the race question until the Democrats put them on the defensive with their race-baiting attacks on the party and its leaders, notably striking at Oscar Ameringer, whom they called a "nigger loving Dutchman." In response, some Socialists tried to "outnigger" their Democratic critics.[28]

But Ameringer, Branstetter, Nagle, and other opponents of disfranchisement won significant support for their struggle against the grandfather clause, especially in the northwestern counties where blacks and southern Democrats were scarce and in the coal towns of the old Choctaw Nation where the Socialist party had built on the interracial solidarity achieved by the United Mine Workers and had actually recruited a few black miners.[29] The defenders of black voting rights also won the support of proletarian Socialists like John G. Wills, a blacklisted member of Eugene Debs's American Railway Union who had settled in Oklahoma when the Cherokee Strip opened. Like his leader Debs, Wills believed that the Railway Union had made a great mistake when it excluded black workers. He hoped the Socialist party would not make the same mistake. His experience in the industrial union movement had convinced him that "when treated right," the black worker's "fidelity to labor was of the highest order," and he boldly insisted that the party had to organize blacks. At the close of his campaign as the Socialist candidate for lieutenant governor in 1910, J. G. Wills called upon his comrades to organize blacks in

28. Meredith, "Agrarian Socialism in Oklahoma," 97. For a lurid example of how Oklahoma Democrats used race baiting against the Socialists, see Purcell (Okla.) *Register*, September 1, 1910. For an example of a racist Socialist response to an attack by Tom Watson see *Industrial Democrat* (Oklahoma City), March 12, 1910.

29. For example, in one coal town black miners voted Socialist "almost to a man" in the August, 1910, primary and referendum, but the ballots they cast for Socialist candidates and against disfranchisement were frequently discounted by Democratic election officials. J. L. Gibson to editor, *Appeal to Reason* (Girard, Kan.), August 13, 1910. Freda Hogan also remembered black Socialist miners in her Huntington, Arkansas, local. Interview with Freda Hogan Ameringer, June 21, 1974.

the area that had not yet been "Jim Crowed," the mines, the mills, the cotton fields, and "other avenues of industrial life."[30]

Wills's call for an interracial party organization was never answered, but the more limited appeal Socialist leaders made on behalf of Oklahoma's threatened black voters elicited a rather gratifying response from white farmers and workers. The grandfather clause was amended to the constitution in the referendum of August, 1910, but it carried by an unimpressive margin of 30,000 votes. Despite the efforts the Democrats made to slander and defraud voters who opposed the clause, a total of 106,222 men cast their ballots against disfranchisement. Since the Republican party, which campaigned weakly against the clause, brought out only 84,158 voters in the GOP primary it held concurrently with the referendum, other voters obviously declared themselves in opposition to the Democrats' election reforms.[31] These additional votes probably did not come from Democratic partisans, since their leaders at all levels were militantly in favor of excluding black voters. Rather, they must have been cast by the Socialists who had supported their leaders' demand for "unrestricted suffrage" in a party referendum conducted only a few months before the state-wide referendum.

A voting analysis of the 1910 referendum confirms this view, since a significant positive correlation existed between the level of opposition to disfranchisement and the level of Socialist support in the general election of 1910 (especially in predominantly white counties). Thus, statistical evidence supports the conclusion that "most Socialists honored their commitment to the 'black section' of the working class."[32]

Some Socialist party members voted for disfranchisement because they succumbed to what Oscar Ameringer called "the bitter race hatred that has been a nightmare to every clear-seeing Socialist working man in the South." This happened most frequently

30. *Oklahoma Pioneer* (Oklahoma City), November 5, 1910.
31. W. R. Richards (comp.), *Oklahoma Red Book, II* (Oklahoma City: Tulsa *Daily Democrat* Press, 1912), 307.
32. Graham, "Red, White, and Black," 288–90.

in eastern counties with large black populations. But a majority of members probably voted against disfranchisement. They did so not because they "loved the negro" but because their own political rights and class interests were threatened by black disfranchisement. In western Oklahoma there is evidence that Socialist voters opposed the grandfather clause more strongly than partisans of the Republican party, an organization that had gained a great deal from black support in territorial days.[33] For example, in Major County, a GOP stronghold, the disfranchisement amendment was "buried" in West Dane, the Socialists' banner precinct in 1910, where 94 percent of the voters opposed black disfranchisement. The only precinct in which a majority favored disfranchisement was a Republican area where the Socialist party polled just 8.5 percent of the vote.

Although Socialists argued about how many white votes they would lose in the fall of 1910 as a result of their summer campaign against disfranchisement, there was very little talk about winning black support. Throughout the struggle only a few blacks defected from the Republican party, despite that party's lukewarm opposition to the grandfather clause. Therefore, the Socialists were surprised when a black political convention met at Chickasaw and proceeded to condemn the Republicans for their lackadaisical campaign against the amendment and to praise the Socialists for their support. One of the angriest black delegates declared: "The negro voter sold his political birthright to the party of Lincoln after the Civil War for a mess of pottage." Now he was "tired of being a tool of republican bosses" and was in favor of "a nationwide revolution in politics." The delegate concluded, "The negro must turn to the only true friend he has ever had, the socialist party." This black militant joined other delegates in endorsing a resolution that boosted the Socialist party as strongly as it attacked the two old parties. The black delegates at the Chickasaw convention recommended that "all the colored people of Oklahoma vote the Socialist

33. *Oklahoma Pioneer* (Oklahoma City), June 1, October 22, 1910; and Graham, "Red, White, and Black," 288–90.

ticket" and "align themselves with our socialistic brethren" who "believed in the Social Equality of all races."[34]

This remarkable resolution (which surprised the Socialists almost as much as the Republicans) indicated that in the wake of disfranchisement important leaders of the black community in Oklahoma were ready to reject their traditional allies and to turn toward new, radical "brethren." However, the Chickasaw resolution, adopted in a time of anger and confusion, misrepresented the Socialist party's commitment to "social equality" and therefore lacked credibility with most blacks. In fact, after passing a militant resolution in favor of socialism, the convention reconvened in the afternoon, packed with loyal Republicans, and passed a countermeasure supporting the GOP. In any case, the first Chickasaw resolution represented only rhetorical support for the Socialists. There would be no shift of black votes to the new, third party because most Afro-American voters in Oklahoma lost the franchise as a result of the new literacy test required by the grandfather clause. Those blacks who did vote in 1910 were able to do so only in the strongest Republican precincts where defections to the Socialists were least likely.[35]

After surveying the effects of the antidisfranchisement campaign, Oscar Ameringer observed that years of protest attested to the race consciousness of Oklahoma's black people, but he concluded that the "transition to class consciousness" would not be easy.[36] Although the spirited attack Ameringer and other Socialists had led against the grandfather clause won the admiration of many militant blacks, the party's leaders failed to follow up their bold initiative by actually recruiting Afro-Americans into their organization. This resulted mainly from their unwillingness to raise the

34. "Negroes Favor Socialist Party," undated broadside in Socialist Party Papers, Perkins Library, Duke University. Most of the document is reprinted along with an interview with one of the militant black delegates in *Marshall County News-Democrat* (Madill, Okla.), October 21, 1910.
35. *Oklahoma Pioneer* (Oklahoma City), October 22, 1910; Boley (Okla.) *Progress*, July 28, November 3, 1910.
36. *Oklahoma Pioneer* (Oklahoma City), October 22, 1910.

race question in its largest sense within party circles and to seriously attempt to alter the race prejudice that existed within those circles. Thus, the difficulty Oklahoma blacks experienced in making the "transition to class consciousness" stemmed not only from their own race consciousness but also from the rather narrow class consciousness of white supremacists within the Socialist party.

Some Oklahoma party leaders, like Ameringer, J. G. Wills, and Pat Nagle, continued in the 1910s to argue for interracial organization. Nagle hoped the newly formed Renters' Union would act as an "economic arm" of the Socialist party that would recruit black sharecroppers as well as white share tenants. He urged his comrades to follow the example of the United Mine Workers, an organization that had achieved interracial solidarity in its southwestern locals, rather than the example of the "lily white" Farmers' Union, which had floundered when "colored farmers" (who were excluded from the Union) refused to cooperate with its crop-withholding campaigns after the panic of 1907.[37]

But Ameringer, Nagle, and other party leaders who favored interracial organization had very little influence within the Renters' Union. They could not convince tenant union organizers to include black sharecroppers in a movement dominated by southern-born poor whites who feared and often hated their "colored competitors." In any case, black sharecroppers probably reacted with great suspicion to tenant union organizers who promised them relief through an organization controlled by a class of poor white farmers who generally expressed violent antiblack prejudices. In fact, the local leaders of the Renters' Union in Oklahoma's southern cotton counties had opposed the defense of black voting rights launched by the state office in 1910. One of the most important of these leaders was J. Tad Cumbie, a Confederate veteran from Texas who had run as the Socialist party's candidate for governor in 1910 when it was widely believed that the ticket lost thousands of votes because the state leaders insisted on opposing disfranchisement. Unlike his running mate J. G. Wills, whose experience as an in-

37. *Ibid.*, June 1, 1910.

dustrial unionist had taught him the value of interracial organization, J. T. Cumbie adhered to the old Farmers' Alliance model and accepted the need for separate renters' unions for white tenants and black croppers. Like Tom Hickey of Texas, this so-called "gray Horse of the Prairie" proudly proclaimed himself a Red and attacked the moderates or Yellows who controlled the party's National Executive Committee. Because Ameringer, Otto Branstetter, and other state leaders were close to moderates like Victor Berger on the executive committee, Cumbie and his allies began to turn their fire on the centralized party headquarters in Oklahoma City. But although the state's top party officials were not as radical as Cumbie and the Reds on certain issues, they were far more progressive on the race question.[38]

While the Oklahoma Socialists were waging their campaign against black disfranchisement, they also made some overtures to the state's Indian population, but these recruitment efforts were no more successful than those aimed toward Afro-Americans. Oscar Ameringer reported on one hilarious organizing foray he made into the Kiamichi Mountains to agitate among the Choctaw tribesmen, but he noted only one instance in which the Indians showed much interest in his Socialist ideas. In 1909 Chitto Harjo (called Crazy Snake) led a militant band of full-blood Creeks and angry black men in an armed uprising to stop government allotment of lands originally deeded the tribes by treaty. It was the last forceful opposition of the Oklahoma Indians to the theft of their lands. The old parties ignored injustices committed against the Indian Nations, but in 1910 the Socialist party denounced the corrupt "guardianship laws" through which lawyers, speculators, and oil prospectors expropriated tribal lands under legal cover.[39]

38. Graham, "Red, White, and Black," 219–28; and Meredith, "Agrarian Socialism in Oklahoma," 95–100.
39. Ameringer, *If You Don't Weaken*, 234–40. Reports on Crazy Snake's rebellion can be found in the Kingfisher (Okla.) *Weekly Star*, April 1, 1909, and in the Harthshorne (Okla.) *Sun*, April 9, 1909. Also see Angie Debo, *And the Still Waters Ran* (Princeton, N.J.: Princeton University Press, 1940), 186; and Charles W. Holman, "Indian Landlords in Oklahoma," *Farm and Ranch*, XXI (January 27, 1912).

However, in the election of 1910 the Socialists did not poll many votes in the counties with large Indian populations. In fact, the party found it difficult to make a convincing appeal to Oklahoma's poor Indians, even though some of them were locked in the last stage of a militant land struggle which the Socialists admired. But whereas the poor whites' struggle for the land was just beginning, the poor red man's struggle was coming to an end. Crazy Snake's rebellion was the last battle in a tragic war the Five Civilized Tribes had been losing since they were removed to the territory along the "trail of tears." By the 1910s the Indians of Oklahoma were poor prospects for the Socialist party, because few were interested in partisan politics outside of tribal circles, and they were also poor prospects for the Renters' Union because those who did farm usually worked the land differently than the white tenant. Furthermore, poor white renters were almost as hostile to the Indians as they were to the blacks, not because the red men were economic competitors but because there were a number of unscrupulous landlords in the tribal hierarchy.

When the Texas Socialists formed their own Land Renters' Union in 1911, prompted by organizer Tom Hickey and other Reds, they embraced the IWW's industrial union strategy. But unlike the Wobblies, they restricted their membership to whites. Over 100 delegates from 42 counties gathered at the founding convention and declared that "use and occupancy" was the "only genuine title to the land" and that a "confiscatory tax should be placed on all land held out of cultivation for speculative purposes." They had learned from their experiences in the Farmers' Educational and Cooperative Union that landowners, lawyers, and other businessmen worked against the interests of landless farmers, and so they excluded these bourgeois elements. One Texas tenant explained that many Socialists were "made" within the Farmers' Union, but as a poor renter he was convinced that he had been "in with the wrong crowd." All of those businessmen and rich farmers in the Union had taught him some lessons; the experience "made him fit for a class conscious organization."[40]

40. *Rebel* (Hallettsville, Tex.), August 26, October 7, November 11, 1911; Thomas A. Hickey, "The Land Renters' Union in Texas," *International So-*

The Texas Land Renters' Union was a class-conscious organization, but only in a limited sense.[41] Tom Hickey argued that tenants shared a common identity because they were bound to the "slave chain" of rent, but unlike Pat Nagle, his fellow Irish land leaguer from Oklahoma, he did not at first urge the Renters' Union to organize black farmers who paid rent.[42] "Red Tom" and the other Texas Socialists accepted the limits of share tenants' class consciousness. Most white tenants pitted themselves against landlords and businessmen on the one hand, and against black sharecroppers and brown migrants on the other. Their exploiters and their competitors seemed to form an unholy alliance dedicated to pushing the poor whites off the land. In this sense, the consciousness of Texas tenant farmers was similar to that of unskilled workers in California and other states who supported the radical but racist leadership of trade unionists and politicians who promised to protect the workingman's interests against the money-hungry employer and his compliant "coolie" laborers.[43]

In 1910 party lecturer Mary O'Reilly reported on the dangerous racial situation in the Texas black waxy:

cialist Review, XIII (1912), 239–44; Dallas *Laborer*, November 8, 1911; and *Farm and Ranch*, XXX (October 28, 1911).

41. After examining the causes of the "deeply-rooted and widely spread discontent" produced by the southwestern land struggle, the chief investigator for the United States Commission on Industrial Relations concluded in 1915 that the growing "discontent of the producing classes" in the region "changed into a class conscious movement in 1911 when the Renters' Union of America was founded." Charles W. Holman, "Probing the Causes of Unrest: The Tenant Farmer," *Survey*, XXXIV (April 17, 1916), 63.

42. *Rebel* (Hallettsville, Tex.), October 7, 1911.

43. In California most labor leaders, including some "class-conscious" Socialists, decided to compromise their principles and "sail under the flag of anti-coolieism." This was to serve merely as a tactic, "a means of uniting and educating the working class," but, Saxton notes, "tactics have a way of becoming habits" and so, instead of raising the "strategic flag of working class unity," California labor leaders continued to sail under the tactical flag of Asian exclusion. The parallels between the activities of Frank Roney, California Socialist leader, and Tom Hickey of Texas are striking. See Alexander Saxton, *The Indispensable Enemy: Labor and the Anti-Chinese Movement in California* (Berkeley: University of California Press, 1971). In fact, the *Appeal* opposed Asian immigration vociferously. *Appeal to Reason* (Girard, Kan.), July 8, 1905.

There is nothing like this "black belt" in more ways than one. With the increasing value of land the economic struggle grows more tense. Great plantations are controlled by one man and, in many cases, conditions are terrible. The landlords are autocratic. Around here they are renting on the "halves" to get the negroes into debt and hold them in peonage. Landlords are gradually putting negroes in the place of whites, because they are more helpless. It will bring on a race riot.[44]

The threat posed by "negro peons" in the minds of poor whites did not bring on a race riot in the Texas black belt, but it did foreclose any plans tenant organizers might have had for recruiting across race lines. G. W. Walston, a white renter from East Texas, wrote to Union leaders expressing the racial fears that were welling up along with antilandlord feelings:

> I see that you want to organize the renters. The landlords have gotten hard on us. They tell us if we don't do like they say that they will rent to negroes. Times are hard here. I don't know what we will do. I do believe we will have to raise up in arms. The union may do good. I don't know but I believe the landlords will get the negroes to work the land and tell us to go to hell.
>
> Well I am so tired now I can't hardly write, so excuse the bad hand writing. I will write again if I live, because I love you and the great fight you are making for us slaves. May God Bless You.[45]

Because they were trying to recruit desperate white men like Walston, the Socialist leaders of the Texas Land Renters' Union refused to take on the difficult "task of arousing the unorganized negro tenant" at the start of their movement. One of the early organizers reported that blacks liked his message but were "afraid to talk Socialism . . . for fear the White Dems would mob them."[46] There was some basis for this fear, especially among black Populists, but the Socialist party did not make the effort the People's party had made to organize Afro-Americans.

As the influence of the IWW increased in Texas, the Land Renters' Union began to organize black and brown tenants in special

---

44. *Appeal to Reason* (Girard, Kan.), August 13, 1910.
45. *Rebel* (Hallettsville, Tex.), October 7, 1911.
46. *Ibid.*, August 5, 1911.

locals, but the militant interracial struggle of the Brotherhood of Timber Workers in the piney woods of East Texas and western Louisiana did not impress tenant organizers enough to cause them to change the fundamental direction of their movement. Tom Hickey supported the Wobblies' efforts to organize black 'and white timber workers in the woods, and in 1912 he supported the separate organization of nonwhite tenants, but he did not use his influence to push for full-scale interracial organization in the cotton fields.[47] Despite his revolutionary rhetoric, "Red Tom" was fairly yellow when it came to facing the challenges posed by the race question.

In fact, Hickey and his publisher, E. O. Meitzen, sometimes indulged in racist rhetoric in dealing with their race-baiting Democratic opponents. In his first months as editor of the *Rebel*, Hickey reaffirmed the Socialist party's commitment to economic but not social equality and accused the Democratic party of fostering race mixing. He maintained that by recruiting black votes in northern cities and by supporting a capitalist system that forced black and white workers to toil side by side, the hypocritical Democrats created a kind of crude "social equality that would not be possible under Socialism." But this accusation was not enough. For a belligerent polemicist like Hickey, it was always important to turn the tables on an enemy. Since the whites who had fathered the thousands of mulatto children throughout the South were undoubtedly Democrats, Hickey outraged his critics by accusing them of privately fostering race mixing while publically condemning the Socialists for the same actions. Needless to say, these editorial antics did nothing to win the confidence of blacks. Indeed, the editors of the *Rebel* were trying to win the confidence of poor whites not only by race-baiting the Democrats but also by appealing to the regional prejudices of poor whites with thinly veiled racist references to the glories of the Old South and the myths of the Lost Cause. On one occasion, the *Rebel* called upon its readers to be-

47. *Ibid.*, August 26, 1911. For a discussion of the problems posed by Anglo prejudice in Socialist politics toward Texas Mexicans, see Emilio Zamora, Jr., "Chicano Socialist Labor Activity in Texas, 1900–1920," *Aztlán*, VI (1975), 226–30.

come the "New Rebels of the South" and to fight for their "sacred rights" like the "out-gunned, out-capitalized" Confederates of old.[48]

Although local Socialist editors in Oklahoma also engaged in racist apologetics of this sort, the party members north of the Red River adopted a much more progressive approach to the race question than their comrades in Texas. Indeed, the struggle the Sooner Socialists waged against black disfranchisement was probably the most determined defense of minority civil rights made by any political party, north or south, in an era when progressive movements often turned their backs on the race question. It is tempting to attribute the more advanced racial policy of the Oklahoma Socialist party to its "outside" leaders, notably Nagle, Branstetter, and Ameringer, who came to the Southwest from the Midwest. But racial prejudices in the Midwest were just as severe and German immigrants were not immune to Negrophobia. In fact, Oscar Ameringer's famous mentor, Victor Berger of Milwaukee, was a raving racist, even though he had almost no contact with blacks.[49]

Ameringer, the "outside agitator" was much less prejudiced than E. O. Meitzen, a descendant of German forty-eighters, who had worked with blacks in the Populist movement and then abandoned interracial tactics. But Tom Hickey who had spent his early years in the North was much more prejudiced than his fellow Irishman, Dan Hogan, a southern-born lawyer who was the most important Socialist editor in Arkansas. Walter Deitz, state secretary of the Louisiana Socialist party, was a native of Debs's Indiana, but he did not share the party leader's willingness to organize across racial lines. While Dietz was agreeing with right-wing leaders that the time had not come "to try to organize negroes," southern-born Reds like J. W. Barnes and Covington Hall were bringing Louisiana's black mill hands into the Brotherhood of Timber Workers. Thus, if the Socialists who supported a progressive race policy in the Southwest held anything in common, it was not their regional

48. Graham, "Red, White, and Black," 146–59.
49. David Shannon, *The Socialist Party of America, A History* (New York: Macmillan, 1955), 50. Also see Sally M. Miller, "The Socialist Party and the Negro," *Journal of Negro History*, LVI (1971), 220–22.

background but their experience in the industrial union movement.[50] This was particularly true of Oscar Ameringer, a gradualist from Germany, and Covington Hall, a revolutionary from Mississippi. After their experience in the interracial New Orleans strike of 1907, these two labor organizers became the most outspoken advocates of interracial organization in the Southwest. Industrial unions like the UMW and the IWW proved that black and white workers could be organized in the South, and this made a big impression on the egalitarians in the party.[51] But those progressives on the race question did not have enough influence in the Southwest to effectively open the party to blacks or to turn the renters' unions toward the "arduous task" of recruiting sharecroppers as well as white share tenants.

ORGANIZATIONAL QUESTIONS

The voting power of white yeomen and tenants made it relatively easy for Socialist parties of the Southwest to provide solutions for the land question and to avoid the troublesome problems raised by the question of the farmer's class position. On the other hand, the fact that black sharecroppers, brown migratory laborers, and red subsistence farmers were all but excluded from the electoral process made it relatively easy to avoid the serious political problems raised by the race question. Consequently, in the heyday of southwestern socialism certain organizational problems aroused

50. W. F. Dietz to Carl D. Thompson, May 26, 1913, in Socialist Party Papers, Duke. For Covington Hall's vision of a "red day" when "three Clans of Toil"—"the Anglo-Americans, the Afro-Americans, and the Mexican Americans"—put away superstition and "arose together," see *Rebel* (Hallettsville, Tex.), December 21, 1912. J. W. Barnes, a Red delegate from western Louisiana who supported the IWW, issued the most forthright statement made at the party's 1910 national convention in support of interracial organization. See *International Socialist Review*, X (1910), 1128. For discussion of how industrial unionism favored interracial solidarity in the South, see Paul B. Worthman and James R. Green, "Black Workers in the New South, 1865–1915," in N. I. Huggins, *et al.* (eds.), *Key Issues in the Afro-American Experience* (2 vols.; New York: Harcourt Brace, 1972), II, 62–68.
51. Ameringer, *If You Don't Weaken*, 193–213; Covington Hall, "Labor Struggles in the Deep South" (Typescript in Howard-Tilton Library, Tulane University), 98–120.

much more furor within party circles than the profound questions of class and race.

Essentially, the organizational problems of the southwestern Socialist parties between 1908 and 1912 revolved around one general question: Should state organizations adopt the centralized form of administration favored by the National Executive Committee (dominated by right wingers and moderates) or should the states be allowed to encourage local autonomy and political diversity through a decentralized form of administration? But beyond this bureaucratic debate the organizational disputes that occurred in Texas, Oklahoma and, to a lesser extent, in the other southwestern states involved personal feuds, factional power plays, and serious ideological struggles.

In the early stages, those who favored centralized state administrations generally identified with the gradualistic politics of the National Executive Committee, and especially in Oklahoma this tended to mean that supporters of the national office favored tight party discipline and commitment to party policy, including the controversial positions the organization had taken in favor of black recruitment and in opposition to the dual unionism represented by the Industrial Workers of the World. Those southwestern Socialists who favored decentralized party administration with maximum local autonomy resented the power and politics of the National Committee. Although they denounced the reformism of the national administration, the southwestern dissidents, led by Hickey, Meitzen, and their Texas allies, favored neo-Populist reforms to attract small farmers and opposed any bold effort to recruit blacks on an equal basis. But the militancy of these Reds was not entirely rhetorical. The decentralizers were sincere foes of party bureaucrats who often exerted undemocratic control over the movement and they were sincere friends of the IWW which opposed the national party policy of "boring from within" AFL unions. These southwestern Reds identified themselves with the radical wing of the party, but in practice their politics often deviated from "orthodox" left-wing positions.

The debate over centralization began in the Southwest during the late nineties when J. A. Wayland of the *Appeal* and Bill Farmer of the *Social Economist* attacked Daniel DeLeon and the Socialist Labor party for practicing a "military" form of organization. The issue appeared again in 1908 when W. J. Bell, the Texas state secretary, antagonized various leaders by revoking the charters of important locals and "rerouting" popular speakers like Stanley Clark, an outspoken lawyer who refused to cooperate with the state office. In 1909 dissident Socialists gathered at Grand Saline, Texas, the scene of the big summer encampments, and demanded Bell's resignation after accusing him of bossism and corruption. Eventually the rebels set up their own headquarters at Grand Saline while Bell held down the official state office at Tyler. This imbroglio continued for several months until a mass meeting of Socialists voted to suspend Bell and appoint an acting state secretary. Left-wing gadfly Tommy Morgan of Chicago came to Bell's defense and charged that he was a victim of a conspiracy of Texas preachers and professional organizers allied with the National Executive Committee. There was some truth to Morgan's comments about the backgrounds of Bell's critics, but opposition to the state secretary's high-handed bureaucratic procedures was too widespread for the conspiracy charge to hold. A believer in tight party discipline and centralized state administration, W. J. Bell was a victim of his own bureaucratic zeal.[52]

In any case, the National Executive Committee refused to investigate Bell's suspension, thereby ratifying his ouster. Organizer Tom Hickey, a veteran of party battles with the arch-centralist DeLeon, came forward with a new, decentralized organizational plan for the Texas Socialist party, and in January of 1911 the party rank and file adopted most of Hickey's proposals by endorsing a revised constitution with provisions for more internal democracy

52. Dallas *Laborer*, December 7, 1908, January 14, February 13, 27, March 5, August 7, 1909. Also *Socialist Party Official Bulletin*, V, No. 12, August, 1909. For Tommy Morgan's defense of Bell, see "Who's Who and What's What in the Socialist Party," *Provoker* (Chicago), January, 1911.

and local autonomy. Party members also elected E. O. Meitzen state secretary to replace Bell and to administer the new decentralized plan. In the following year "Judge" Meitzen claimed that the so-called Texas "programme" had doubled the party's membership and added fifty new locals, since Socialists in remote sections of the state could now form their own locals instead of waiting for state headquarters to send out an organizer.[53] Meitzen's claims for decentralization were somewhat extravagant. Texas Socialists also strengthened their state organization by expanding the encampments, forming a renters' union, founding a newspaper, and hiring Tom Hickey as state organizer.

In Oklahoma the state office continued to operate in a relatively centralized manner throughout the Texas upheaval but State Secretary Branstetter was in a much stronger position than his Texas counterpart, W. J. Bell. He had recruited a number of skilled organizers, including outsiders like Ameringer, who helped to build one of the fastest-growing state parties in the country. It was hard to argue with success, even though it came through disciplined organizational tactics that tended to diminish local autonomy.

When Ameringer, Branstetter, and Nagle tried to push for a stronger party commitment to racial equality, they encountered some resistance from local leaders in "Little Dixie," and these protestors then linked up with the Texas decentralizers. Stanley Clark, who had moved to "Little Dixie" to become the editor of a rapidly growing weekly called *New Century*, published at Sulphur, attacked the "silk stocking contingent" in Oklahoma City, attempting to turn the party's country members against its city leaders. In addition to criticizing the Ameringer-Branstetter position on the race question, the dissidents exposed the state office's close connection with right-wing centralizers on the National Executive Committee. When Ameringer decided to run for mayor of Oklahoma City in the spring of 1911, "Little Dixie" dissenters warned that the German editor would introduce Victor Berger's Milwaukee "machine" into their state capital. Stanley Clark maintained contact with

53. Nat Hardy, "The Texas Programme," *International Socialist Review*, XI (April, 1911), 622–23; and *Rebel* (Hallettsville, Tex.), September 30, 1911.

Hickey, Meitzen, and the Texas decentralizers, but at the same time he joined forces with J. Tad Cumbie, the party's 1910 gubernatorial nominee, who shared the editor's distaste for the party's northern leadership and the kind of discipline it demanded.[54]

Both of these southern-born Socialists were popular stump speakers who used Red rhetoric with great effect in Oklahoma's "Little Dixie." Tad Cumbie was an imposing figure with a flowing white beard, and his folksy manner and bombastic radicalism made him one of the movement's best campaigners. Stanley Clark, the radical revivalist, used his good looks and powerful voice to win over audiences in well-publicized debates with professional Socialist haters. Both of these charismatic characters would end up in Ft. Leavenworth for their violent opposition to World War I, but nonetheless they were not always as revolutionary as they sounded. Clark eventually abandoned his uncompromising demand for immediate collectivization of all farms and joined Cumbie in adopting a more pragmatic solution to the land question and in assuming leadership of the growing Renters' Union in southeastern Oklahoma. They followed the segregated organizational approach originally adapted by the Texans rather than the integrated approach advocated by Ameringer, Nagle, and Wills. Drawing their support from undisciplined but deeply discontented poor white party members, "Dad" Cumbie and "Preacher" Clark pushed for a more militant tenant organization to take direct action against landlords and usurers. They were also preparing to make more trouble for state leaders like Ameringer who were outsiders with close ties to the German centralizers in Milwaukee.

THE RISING TIDE OF SOCIALISM

Internal problems undoubtedly limited the growth of socialism in Texas and Oklahoma, but the parties in these two states still made respectable showings at the polls in 1910. The continuing decline

---

54. Graham, "Red, White, and Black," 237–38. *Oklahoma Pioneer* (Oklahoma City), April 27, June 1, September 3, August 27, 1910; *Industrial Democrat* (Oklahoma City), May 7, July 23, 30, 1910; and Meredith, "Agrarian Socialism in Oklahoma," 78–79, 81–82, 112–13, 118.

of the Farmers' Union all but eliminated the progressive influence of farmer-labor coalitions. By 1909 the weakened Union had fallen into the hands of business leaders who "stressed that the farmer, the merchant, the manufacturer, and the railroad were members of the same team in the same struggle for economic progress." These boosters failed to convince old Populist dirt farmers and angry young tenants to ally with big capitalists in a "fight to smother the demagogue" who played upon rural discontent. Progressive spokesmen for the Farmers' Union and mercantile associations praised high commodity prices but ignored the tenant's chronic problems. When the *Buyers' Banner* compared the relatively high price of cotton in 1910 to the situation in the depressed nineties and remarked that "surely the farmer of today doesn't realize how well off he is compared with his position twelve or thirteen years ago," it was telling the truth.[55] Cotton prices were up again, but many farmers had fallen into permanent indebtedness and migratory tenancy.

Under these conditions, the Socialists' new farm program began to win more and more rural converts, including many dedicated Democrats who were fed up with their party's broken promises. Tom Hickey, the kind of "demagogue" businessmen wanted to "smother," predicted that the Socialist party in Texas would make great gains in the 1910 elections. His prediction gained force when Oscar Branch Colquitt, a conservative railroad commissioner, won the Democratic gubernatorial nomination by defeating the forces of progressivism and prohibition in the primary. Now the Democratic party would be less inclined to make alluring promises to poor farmers and workers. To oppose Colquitt, the Texas Socialists nominated a respectable-looking candidate named Reddin Andrews who had been a Confederate officer and the president of a small Baptist college. Sporting a stetson hat and a neatly trimmed vandyke beard, Andrews looked more like a southern planter than a

55. James A. Tinsley, "The Progressive Movement in Texas" (Ph.D. dissertation, University of Wisconsin, 1953), 160; Ft. Worth *Record*, July 31, 1909; *Buyers' Banner* quoted in *Marshall County News-Democrat* (Madill, Okla.), September 23, 1910.

Socialist standard-bearer. But the former Populist was a good campaigner and an articulate advocate of the party's new farm program. Stumping the extensive encampment circuit, Andrews polled 11,538 votes in 1910 and helped the Texas Socialist party increase its vote by 30 percent.[56] This tally fell far short of the impressive vote Hickey and other Socialist party leaders had predicted, but it was a measure of steady progress. And like their comrades around the country, the Texas Socialists were encouraged by even the smallest gains at the polls.

In Oklahoma the growing conservatism of the Democratic party was even more beneficial to the Socialists. With the decline of the Farmers' Union, business and railroad interests rapidly occupied the political vacuum which had been partially filled by the Shawnee farmer-labor coalition in the 1906–1908 period. Discontented with the growing conservatism of the Haskell administration, House Speaker William H. Murray decided to run for governor in 1910 as the true "exponent and leader of the militant progressive Democracy of Oklahoma." Murray won a warm endorsement from Populist hero Tom Watson, who had returned to the Democratic party as an advocate of economic reform and social reaction. But "Alfalfa Bill" failed to match the racist support for disfranchisement expressed by his primary opponent Lee Cruce, a conservative banker from Ardmore who advocated moral reform instead of economic reform. "Outniggered" by his opponent, deprived of the strong support he had once enjoyed from the Farmers' Union, and again branded as enemy of the wage-earning masses by organized labor, Bill Murray, the leader of progressive Democracy, went down to defeat.[57]

However, the "sage of Tishomingo" returned to the fray shortly after he lost the gubernatorial nomination, for he was more con-

---

56. *International Socialist Review*, X (October, 1909), 376–77; Tinsley, "Progressive Movement in Texas," 270, 295; *World Almanac, 1910*, pp. 58–61; *Rebel* (Hallettsville, Tex.), July 10, 1909; "State Ticket and Platform of the Socialist Party of Texas," 1910, in Socialist Party Papers, Duke.

57. Keith L. Bryant, Jr., *Alfalfa Bill Murray* (Norman: University of Oklahoma Press, 1968), 63–64, 91–98.

cerned than Cruce about the rising Socialist sentiment in the cotton country. Since it was doubtful that poor white voters would respond to Cruce's crusade against bootlegging, prizefighting, horseracing, and other moral problems, Murray took the field to campaign against the Socialists on economic grounds. Like Tom Watson, who turned to intensive anti-Socialist activity in 1910, "Alfalfa Bill" warned farmers that the Reds would take away their land and reduce them to the level of "nigger field hands" on giant farm collectives. This propaganda about the Socialists' leveling tendencies, combined with the rabid race-baiting of party leaders who opposed black disfranchisement, no doubt interferred with the Socialists' showing at the polls in the 1910 election.[58]

But a balanced ticket headed by J. Tad Cumbie as a segregationist from the Indian Territory and John G. Wills as an integrationist from the Cherokee Strip in the west, gained 6,000 more votes than the 1908 ticket headed by presidential candidate Debs. The Oklahoma Socialists polled 28,000 votes in 1910 (11.2 percent of the total), running especially well in the southeastern congressional district where discontented tenants and militant coal miners gave them 14 percent of the vote. Cumbie and Wills polled 17 percent of the vote in strike-torn Coal County, and carried the UMW strongholds of Krebs and Coalgate where the citizens elected "red" miners as mayors the following spring. The Socialists also polled over 20 percent of the vote in several cotton-growing counties where the tenancy rates ranged from 66 to 84 percent. But the Cumbie-Wills ticket polled only 6 percent of the vote in the north central congressional district of Oklahoma, a stronghold of populism and the early Socialist movement. Thus the party's strength continued to shift away from the old Populist sections in the north to the southern counties with large populations of cotton tenants and coal miners. In his analysis of the "rising tide of socialism" within the farming class of plains states like Oklahoma, Robert Hoxie noted the continuity of the agrarian demands advocated by the Populists and the Socialists, but he did not find any strong

58. *Ibid.*, 98.

causal connection between the electoral support achieved by the two radical movements.[59]

By 1910 the Oklahoma Socialists had created a much stronger organization than their comrades in other southwestern states, even though their organizational problems remained unresolved. The "centralization" issue smoldered, important leaders and newspaper editors still disagreed over the party's defense of black voting rights, the Renters' Union maintained an all-white membership and remained rather undisciplined with regard to the party, and there were "transient renters and laboring men" in remote sections who sometimes voted Socialist but "neglected to take out party cards."[60] Nevertheless, the Oklahoma party organization dwarfed its nearby competitors, and by 1910 was on its way to becoming the strongest grass-roots movement in the country. Despite the problems raised by the antidisfranchisement campaign, the Sooner Socialists easily outpolled party candidates from other southwestern states in 1910.

The Texas Socialist party, troubled by factional strife, polled less than half the total Oklahoma Socialist vote. The Louisiana party was also divided between the Reds who controlled the upland locals of dirt farmers and timber workers and the right-wing Yellows who still held onto the state office in New Orleans. This polarized party ran a weak campaign in 1910, polling only a tiny fraction of the Oklahoma vote.[61] The Arkansas Socialists did not suffer from internal problems, but they still failed to achieve more

59. Oliver Benson, *et al.*, *Oklahoma Votes, 1907–1962* (Norman: University of Oklahoma Press, 1964), 73, 77, 143; *Daily Oklahoman* (Oklahoma City), August 14, 1910; *Industrial Democrat* (Oklahoma City), August 20, 1910; Harthshorne (Okla.) *Sun*, November 3, 1910; Meredith, "Agrarian Socialism in Oklahoma," 109–10; and Robert F. Hoxie, "The Rising Tide of Socialism," *Journal of Political Economy*, XIX (October, 1911), 621.

60. Quote from W. L. Crawford, a former president of the Farmers' Union, who had "been voting Socialist for years," but like the comrades who lived in his "neck of the woods" he had not taken out a party card or participated in a local. *Oklahoma Pioneer* (Oklahoma City), June 20, 1911.

61. Grady McWhiney, "Louisiana Socialists in the Early Twentieth Century: A Study of Rustic Radicalism," *Journal of Southern History*, XX (1954), 323.

than a small portion of the votes garnered by the Oklahomans, despite the efforts of their gubernatorial candidate, G. E. Mikel, an important UMW leader from Jenny Lind.

The Oklahoma Socialists probably benefited a great deal from the expectations falsely raised by reformers like Murray who were forced to support a rather conservative Democratic ticket in 1910. In a long-term sense, they also gained enormously from the fact that fewer poor whites were disfranchised in Oklahoma than anywhere else in the South, which of course meant that the Sooner Socialists could fish for discontented Democratic supporters in a much larger pool of poor white voters. These factors help to account for the Oklahoma Socialist party's surprising electoral gains in an off-year election held just after party officials had led a very unpopular campaign to defend black voting rights. But of course the Socialist organizers and campaigners themselves deserve most of the credit for the advances made under such unfavorable conditions.

The rising tide of socialism measured at the polls in 1910 was ultimately the product of the Oklahoma party's remarkable grass-roots organization. In 1910 the party's dues-paying "red-card" membership was not only the largest in the Southwest, it was the largest in the nation, registering 5,482 official members, exactly 800 more than the giant state of New York in second place. As a result, the Oklahoma organization paid more dues to the national office ($3,800) than any other state and enjoyed an unusually large war chest with which to finance its candidates.[62]

The Oklahoma Socialists not only took advantage of the progressives' decline and of the relatively high level of poor white voting participation, they also "made hay" from tenant and worker discontent (especially among the miners who had just concluded a bitter six-month strike) by making practical demands that spoke to the unmet needs of the laboring classes. As David Shannon notes, the strength of Oklahoma socialism was rooted in its popular immediate demands on state issues like tenancy. Orthodox So-

62. J. Mahlon Barnes, Secretary's Report, January 4, 1911, in Labor Collection, Political Parties, Wisconsin State Historical Society, Madison.

cialists opposed the formulation of these demands as "conservative and in the long run self-defeating" whereas decentralizers opposed the implementation of the tightly controlled "Milwaukee system of organization" on a state-wide basis as undemocratic; but the linking of practical policy with efficient organizational strategy created a strong movement in Oklahoma. "Furthermore, the spirit of the Oklahoma movement" evoked by "the tub thumping of the Socialist encampments and the red ink of the *Appeal*" reflected, writes Shannon, a "class consciousness and militancy that was pregnant with the promise of social change."[63]

There was of course more involved in the Oklahoma Socialist story than the formulation of popular demands and the organization of strong locals, because more than being just a political party Sooner socialism was also a social movement that depended upon education and inspiration as well as on organization. The organizers and the candidates won most of the credit for the party's growth, but they were ably assisted by the teachers and preachers who spread the Socialist gospel.

63. Shannon, *Socialist Party of America*, 35–36.

IV

Propagating the Socialist Gospel

COLORFUL STUMP SPEAKERS like J. Tad Cumbie and respectable standard-bearers like Reddin Andrews enhanced the electoral appeal of the Socialist party's 1910 program. Like their comrades in Wisconsin and other well-organized states, the southwestern Socialists were very much involved in the give and take of regional and local politics. Indeed, they were overly concerned with political candidates and campaign issues, because vote-getting was their first priority, their clearest barometer of success. After the 1910 election Eugene Debs criticized party members who were so concerned about vote-getting that they made "representations not at all compatible with the . . . uncompromising principles of a revolutionary party," and he warned: "An inflated vote secured by compromising methods can only be hurtful to the movement." Debs may have been criticizing the southwestern movement for compromising on the land question in order to get the votes of small farmers and tenants; he was undoubtedly objecting to those elements of the movement, especially in Texas and Louisiana, that refused to honor the party's 1901 commitment to black workers. In any case, the Socialists' titular head obviously had the southwestern parties in mind when he said: "I yield to no one in my desire to see the party grow and the vote increase, but in my zeal I do not lose sight of the fact that healthy growth and a substantial vote depend on efficient organization, the self-education and the self-discipline of the membership."[1] In order to get votes the

1. Eugene V. Debs, "Danger Ahead," *International Socialist Review*, XI (1911), 413.

Socialists of the Southwest may have compromised Marxian principles with regard to the farmer question and the race question, but they certainly did not sacrifice "efficient organization" in favor of vote-getting campaigns or one-shot agitational efforts. In the years before World War I broke out, the southwesterners combined organization with coordinated approaches to education and agitation.

Although the region's Socialist leaders could not always create satisfactory self-discipline among party members, especially those in the newer rural locals, they did promote an unusual level of self-organization and self-education among the poor working people who joined the movement. In fact, the grass-roots strength of the Socialist party in the Southwest typified the growth of Debsian socialism in its first decade when, as Paul Buhle notes, the movement effectively blended agitation, education, and organization on a local level.[2] Professional party intellectuals like A. M. Simons, who appeared as a farm expert in the press and at conventions, played an insignificant role in the actual growth of Socialist strength, but propagandists like J. A. Wayland, Kate Richards O'Hare, Oscar Ameringer, Tom Hickey, and Walter Thomas Mills explained socialism in traditional terms and acted as "organic intellectuals" who, in Antonio Gramsci's terms, were committed to educating the masses rather than serving the dominant class.[3] The role of these outstanding Socialist educators cannot be underestimated, but in the early years the southwestern parties also depended upon the services of indigenous agitators who were less cosmopolitan. These self-taught radicals included experienced Populists and Alliancemen, small town artisans and merchants who

2. Paul Buhle, "Marxism in the United States," in Bert Grahl and Paul Piccone (eds.), *Towards a New Marxism* (St. Louis: Telos Press, 1973), 196–200; and Paul Buhle, "Marxism in America" (Ph.D. dissertation, University of Wisconsin, 1975), Chap. 1.
3. On Gramsci's concept of the "organic intellectual," see the explanation in John M. Cammett, *Antonio Gramsci and the Origins of Italian Communism* (Stanford: Stanford University Press, 1967), 201–203. It is important to note that Gramsci's concept referred largely to intellectuals who advanced the hegemony of the capitalist class. It was the task of socialism to create new organic (as opposed to traditional) intellectuals for the working class.

had commerce with poor country people, as well as old railroad workers and coal miners like J. G. Wills and "Mike McGraw" who homesteaded in Oklahoma's Cherokee Strip and spread the Socialist gospel to their neighbors.[4]

Many of these grass-roots agitators joined the *Appeal to Reason*'s subscription army, whose members not only hawked Wayland's weekly but also organized locals, spoke at schoolhouse meetings, conducted evening educationals, circulated radical literature, and campaigned for Socialist candidates. No propagandist enlisted more grass-roots support than Wayland, who started spreading "common sense" through the prairies and piney woods in 1895. Borrowing his style and the title of his weekly from Tom Paine, the master propagandist of the American Revolution, Wayland boosted the *Appeal*'s circulation to over three quarters of a million by 1913, more than any other weekly periodical in the United States, including the *Saturday Evening Post*. Since the region's party press was still rather undeveloped in 1910, Wayland's weekly assumed the burden of the movement's propaganda work in the Southwest, especially in Oklahoma and Texas where the largest *Appeal* "armies" in the country were located.[5]

THE SALESMEN-SOLDIERS OF THE APPEAL ARMY

By 1912 *Appeal* managing editor Fred Warren had joined with another key editor, Grace D. Brewer, in supervising the work of over sixty thousand salesmen-soldiers who "hustled subs" for the Girard weekly. Louis Klamroth, a particularly energetic hustler, bicycled all over the Midwest selling Socialist literature, and, despite being

4. On John G. Wills see *Otter Valley Socialist* (Snyder, Okla.), September 1, 1915. Mike McGraw was a semifictionalized coal miner from the Indian Nation who settled around Guthrie after the land rush and started doing "missionary work among his neighbors." After selling *Appeal* subscriptions to his neighbors for years, McGraw started a party local among his fellow farmers in 1907. Angie Debo, *Prairie City: The Story of an American Community* (New York: Knopf, 1944), 131.

5. *Appeal to Reason* (Girard, Kan.), January 18, July 18, 1908, January 22, 1910, January 22, March 2, 1912. Also see Howard H. Quint, "Julius Wayland, Pioneer Socialist Propagandist," *Mississippi Valley Historical Review*, XXXV (1949), 585–605.

"rotten-egged, knocked down and clubbed, drenched with fire hose and water bucket, arrested and deported," he sold over 100,000 subscriptions and countless pamphlets. At the start of 1912 over six thousand *Appeal* volunteers were walking, bicycling, and driving buggys through Oklahoma and Texas spreading the Socialist gospel according to Wayland. The *Appeal* reported gleefully that its agents were "constantly devising methods of reaching new territory." Wayland exaggerated when he called the *Appeal* Army the "backbone of the Socialist Party in America," but in the Southwest where the Kansas weekly enjoyed its largest readership, this group of enthusiastic agitators was extremely important.[6]

In 1914 Wayland's Girard staff published a valuable *Who's Who in Socialist America* containing biographical information about "the lives of Socialists who . . . helped to make the *Appeal* and the movement it stands for a menace to capitalism."[7] This unusual directory offers the only extensive picture available of the Socialist party's rank-and-file organizers and agitators. It also provides an opportunity to compare southwestern party activists with those in the rest of the country.[8]

Of the ninety-seven Socialists from the Southwest appearing in *Who's Who* only three were women. This may reflect the fact that women who sold the paper had less time to volunteer, or it may mean that in the 1910s traveling sales work was mainly a male job. Many women read the *Appeal to Reason* and participated in other phases of party activity (in fact, Grace Brewer was a co-commander of Wayland's "army") but they were not among the *Appeal*'s leading corps of traveling salesmen.

Of the ninety-four southwestern men appearing in the *Appeal* Army's *Who's Who* of 1914, nearly half (forty-one) were middle-

6. *Appeal to Reason* (Girard, Kan.), January 22, 1910, January 22, 1912.
7. *Who's Who in Socialist America for 1914* (Girard, Kan.: *Appeal to Reason*, 1914), title page.
8. For a more general discussion of the composition of the *Appeal* Army on a national level, see James R. Green, "The 'Salesmen-Soldiers' of the *Appeal* Army: A Profile of Rank-and-File Socialist Agitators," in Bruce Stave (ed.), *Socialism and the Cities* (Port Washington, N.Y.: Kennikat, 1975), 13–40.

aged (between the ages of forty-five and sixty). There were only thirty old soldiers over sixty years involved in this energetic work and only twenty-three younger men. Most were born in the Midwest (thirty-eight) or the South (thirty-two, including those in Texas and Oklahoma), and only 10 percent were foreign born (just half the proportion of immigrants in the national sample). Like the foreigners in the *Appeal* armies of other states, the southwestern immigrants were largely natives of northern and western European countries, notably England, Ireland, Austria, and Germany.

The top *Appeal* salesmen from this section were mainly self-employed, self-educated members of the "producing classes" who hailed from small towns (57 percent) or farms (34 percent). Only 10 percent resided in the few larger cities of the Southwest. The national roster of award-winning newspaper hawkers contained a larger percentage of big-city dwellers (23 percent), about the same proportion of small-town residents, and a smaller proportion of rural residents (20 percent). A clear majority of Wayland's southwestern salesmen-soldiers, then, were small-towners—the artisans, shopkeepers, and railroad maintenance workers who played such a key role in spreading Socialist propaganda through the Midwest and Southwest.

Only one of the top southwestern soldiers actually worked for a living as a traveling salesman, but all of these men, including some of the farmers, moved around quite a bit. Some were "tramping artisans"—shoemakers, building tradesmen, and the like—who followed their jobs from place to place; others were tenant farmers who migrated throughout the Southwest trying to find a better place to "make a crop." Few were prosperous as a result of their work, but few were desperately poor or totally uneducated either.

This southwestern contingent included only six professionals and ten businessmen, mainly barbers, druggists, and real estate agents. These men, along with many of the farmers and artisans, were respectable members of their communities; they made good salesmen because, for the most part, they were known and trusted in their localities. For example, J. V. Kolachny, a druggist from Ft.

Cobb, Oklahoma, converted from Bryanism to socialism in 1900 when he heard Eugene V. Debs attack the "Great Commoner" during the presidential campaign. When the Socialist Party of America was formed in 1901, this small-town pharmacist joined up, became an avid reader of the *Appeal,* and enlisted in Wayland's subscription army. Over the next few years he became an important Socialist leader and editor in northern Oklahoma, and after his election to the town council, he asserted that "he never lost any business on account of Socialism."

Over 80 percent of the southwesterners in the highest ranks of the *Appeal* Army were farmers (thirty-three in number) or workers (forty-six in all). This large proportion of wage earners (42 percent) is smaller than the proportion on a national level (56 percent), but it is nonetheless surprising because the region's population was overwhelmingly rural. Over half of the workers who sold record numbers of *Appeal* "subs" in the Southwest were skilled craftsmen who were part of a highly articulate artisan culture that thrived in native "Middletowns" around the country as well as in immigrant cities like Milwaukee.[9] The skilled workers who led the *Appeal* Army were the kind of self-educated, self-disciplined party workers Debs so often praised. They were also self-reliant craftsmen and active trade unionists who inherited the critical view of industrial capitalism their artisan forbearers first articulated in the early nineteenth century.

If southwestern coal miners are included with the skilled workers (as they usually were in the early 1900s), then craftsmen represented 70 percent of all the wage earners in Wayland's largest army. Mine workers comprised 17 percent of the Southwest troop as compared to 6 percent of the national sample. The miners' class consciousness developed in a more violent but no less cultured milieu than that of the small-town craftsmen. Like the self-taught village artisan, the coal miner loved to prop his feet up after work,

9. For a revealing analysis of the "radical culture" among skilled workers in the towns and small cities of the Midwest at the turn of the century see Robert and Helen Lynd, *Middletown* (New York: Harvest, 1956), 77–79, 296, 300–301.

light up a pipe, and argue about the political questions of the day. Most of the leading *Appeal* salesmen in the southwestern mining camps were older workers who had emigrated from the British Isles (and in a few cases from France or Belgium) to work in the Pennsylvania anthracite fields or the Illinois bituminous fields, where most had been involved in strikes and union organizing drives in the late nineteenth century. When they came to the southwestern fields, many of these militant miners of "old English stock" acted as organizers for the Knights of Labor and then for the United Mine Workers, who started their long struggle for recognition in, 1898. They created the "class conscious type of socialism" Hoxie discovered in coal mining communities throughout the Midwest and the Southwest in 1910.[10]

Significantly, only 21 percent of the Jimmie Higginses had belonged to earlier radical political parties. A larger percentage of the southwestern soldiers belonged to the Greenback or People's parties than their counterparts in other sections, but over half of the crack *Appeal* salesmen came to socialism directly from the Democratic party and one quarter came from the Republican party. Although radical third parties were unusually strong in the Southwest, most of the *Appeal* Army's members had not been activists, since over half joined the Socialist party in the years after 1907, long after the Greenback and Populist parties had disappeared as organized political forces.

Only a few of the salesmen-soldiers who joined the Socialist party after the turn of the century converted because of dramatic events like the Haywood murder trial in Idaho or by listening to charismatic speakers like Debs and Mother Jones. A few noted that they became Socialists simply by observing and experiencing conditions of life and labor in capitalist America. Common sense told them there had to be a better way. The overwhelming majority of the people listed in the *Who's Who* from the Southwest (88 percent) joined the party after reading Socialist literature, especially books like Bellamy's *Looking Backward*, George's *Progress and*

10. Robert Hoxie, "The Rising Tide of Socialism," *Journal of Political Economy*, XIX (October, 1911), 624.

Poverty, and Blatchford's *Merrie England.* The final convincing push came through reading the *Appeal to Reason,* which may seem a bit suspicious since these people were part of Wayland's organization. In fact, the influence of the *Appeal* was probably exaggerated a good deal by its leading salesmen, but its importance as a medium of conversion should not be underestimated, especially in the Southwest where it was the only significant Socialist publication available before 1910. It was literally the only contact with socialism experienced by many people in the first decade of the century, and it was particularly important in converting younger farmers and workers who had not been part of agrarian radicalism or industrial unionism in the late nineteenth century.

Nevertheless, the somewhat exaggerated influence of the *Appeal* in this survey also presented a skewed picture of the importance of reading as a means of converting ordinary farmers and workers. Although almost 90 percent of the southwestern salesmen-soldiers attributed their conversions to Socialist literature (significantly higher than the 74 percent average for the national *Appeal* Army), just 52 percent of the party rank and file questioned in the national survey of 1908 said that they discovered socialism through reading. In any case, the literate path of socialism was very common, especially in rural regions like the Southwest where poor people were often too far removed to be reached by political speakers and organizers. And reading obviously played an unusually important role in the conversions of the articulate agitators of the *Appeal* Army, who chose to take their ideas out into the world and use their wits to sell them to skeptical Democrats and Republicans. These men were truly "organic intellectuals," committed to using their knowledge to benefit the interests of the laboring classes. The fact that so many of the Socialist party's most dedicated agitators (along with a majority of its rank and file) converted to the cause through a rational experience like reading casts doubt upon the view that Debsian socialism was essentially an emotional, "chiliastic" experience.[11]

11. For the chiliastic interpretation of Socialists, see Daniel Bell, *Marxian Socialism in the United States* (Princeton, N.J.: Princeton University Press, 1967), 5–7.

The "soldiers" undoubtedly loved to read the *Appeal*'s exposés of capitalist hypocrisy and immorality, but they also appreciated the paper's scientific critiques of the economy, its timely reports on strikes and revolts from around the world, and its detailed accounts of party building from Socialists in the Southwest and other parts of the country. "Besides sensationalism, Wayland wanted articles in which the economics of socialism would be seriously and scientifically presented by writers prominent in the socialist movement," recalled George Shoaf, a Texan who was one of the *Appeal*'s best reporters. And so the weekly printed fiery columns by Debs, who served as an associate editor for many years, economic analyses by farm expert A. M. Simons, and translations of Marx, Engels, Lassalle, Kautsky, and even Luxemburg. But most readers probably found the works of German Socialists more difficult to understand than the *Appeal*'s regular excerpts from the writings of Anglo-American "Socialists" like Blatchford, Shaw, Ruskin (a favorite of Wayland's), William Morris, and the Webbs, as well as Bellamy, George, Henry Demarest Lloyd, and the master of "common sense," Tom Paine. This engaging literature of discontent made the *Appeal* more than a newspaper; it was a school for Socialists. In fact, the editors eventually set up an ambitious correspondence course prepared by Walter Thomas Mills for the paper's readers. This was later linked to a larger Socialist effort known as the People's College, a correspondence school centered in Ft. Scott, Kansas, offering courses in United States history, political economy, and law.[12]

The agitators who hawked the *Appeal to Reason* not only liked to read, they liked to discuss what they read with anyone who would listen. They had to be patient, well mannered, and well informed, as well as being extremely confident of their convictions. This they were. Time was on their side, and so, said the gospel according to Wayland, was history and morality. Given this confidence in the truth of scientific socialism, determination and con-

12. See W. J. Ghent, "The 'Appeal' and Its Influence," *Survey*, XXVI (April 1, 1911), 24–28; George Shoaf, "Debs and the *Appeal to Reason*," *American Socialist*, II (1955), 10–16; and *Appeal to Reason* (Girard, Kan.), June 2, 1901, October 3, 1903, October 9, 1915, March 3, 1917.

viction easily followed. The anti-Socialist editor of an Oklahoma commercial weekly aptly described a dedicated agitator: "The average democrat or republican can state his political views in the briefest manner and let it go at that . . . but it takes the socialist nine hours just to get started and when he gets hold of the victim, he never turns loose. If the socialists would devote half as much time to personal affairs . . . they would become immensely rich."[13]

Of course, these salesmen-soldiers were convinced that they would never become rich no matter how much time and energy they expended: they were committed to creating a Cooperative Commonwealth in which no one would be rich, but everyone would have enough to live a decent life. And so they were willing to devote their time and effort to making Wayland's newspaper the most popular weekly in the country. Through the efforts of the subscription armies and an excellent Girard staff, headed by the "Fighting Editor" Fred Warren and Grace Brewer, the *Appeal* doubled its circulation between 1908 and 1912, the period of greatest Socialist growth at the polls. By 1913 the paper was very influential in the Southwest, with over sixty thousand subscribers in Texas and Oklahoma alone. These two banner states boasted the largest subscription armies in the country, which not only helped boost circulation, but also helped build up a grass-roots Socialist movement. In early 1912 new Arkansas State Secretary Ida Hayman Callery credited the six-fold increase of members within a six-month period to the efforts of *Appeal* workers. However, the *Appeal to Reason*'s success should not be attributed only to the subscription armies, to its managing editor Fred Warren, or to crack reporters like Grace Brewer, George Shoaf, and John Kenneth Turner (who sent in the first on-the-spot reports about the Mexican Revolution). Most of the credit belongs to Julius Wayland himself. Tom Paine would have been proud of his student. The folksy "one hoss" editor was, in the words of an adoring comrade, "one of the greatest Socialist-makers this world of woe ever produced."[14]

13. Hollis (Okla.) *Post-Herald*, May 30, 1912.
14. Ghent, "The 'Appeal' and Its Influence," 25–27; May Wood-Simons, "A Socialist Woman's Work," *Coming Nation* (Girard, Kan.), May 11, 1912; *Appeal to Reason* (Girard, Kan.), January 22, 1912. On John Kenneth Tur-

THE SOUTHWESTERN SOCIALIST PRESS

After standing alone for almost fifteen years as a Socialist propaganda source in the Southwest, in 1910 the *Appeal* started to receive some journalistic assistance from several quarters. Oscar
Ameringer and Kate O'Hare joined Gene Debs as associate editors
of a monthly called the *National Rip-Saw*. In 1904 "Colonel" Dick
Maple had started publishing the lively magazine in St. Louis and
three years later he decided to "run up the red flag of the working
class and nail it to the mast." When Phil Wagner took over as editor and publisher, the *Rip-Saw* became one of the party's most
popular periodicals; it reached a circulation of 150,000 by 1913.
Writers like Frank and Kate O'Hare, Oscar Ameringer, and W. S.
Morgan, the old Arkansas Populist, gave the *Rip-Saw* a colorful
southwestern flavor. Emulating the *Appeal*'s combination of sensational and educational journalism, the *Rip-Saw* sold well among
the farmers and workers of the Southwest. Its rural popularity was
enhanced by a successful encampment tour Wagner organized to
feature his orator-editors, Ameringer, Debs, and the O'Hares. The
Missouri monthly also lived up to its name by winning a loyal
readership among the rebellious timber workers of the Louisiana
piney woods whose struggles attracted the journalistic attention of
Rip-Saw reporters Kate O'Hare and H. G. Creel.[15]

With more sophisticated intentions, Algie and May Simons
started a similar publication, the *Coming Nation*, at Girard in 1910.
Initially seen as an artistic supplement to the *Appeal*, this polished
weekly attracted a far-flung readership and came to be known as
the "country cousin" of the New York City *Masses* magazine. Like

---

ner's role in the Mexican Revolution, see William W. Anderson, "The Nature
of the Mexican Revolution as Viewed from the United States" (Ph.D. dissertation, University of Texas, 1967), 34; quote about Wayland is by Frederick Heath in Quint, "Julius Wayland," 602. Also see Julius A. Wayland,
Leaves of Life: A Story of Twenty Years of Socialist Agitation (Girard,
Kan.: *Appeal to Reason*, 1912).

15. *National Rip-Saw* (St. Louis), August, 1911, p. 1; on the timber workers, see issues of February, 1913, p. 14, and March, 1913, p. 32. Kate Richards
O'Hare to Castleton, September 16, 1945, in Eugene V. Debs Collection, Castleton Papers, Tamiment Institute, New York. Also see James Weinstein,
"The Socialist Party: Its Roots and Its Strength," *Studies on the Left*, I
(1960), 24 for circulation figures.

its city cousin, the new *Coming Nation* promoted the use of illustrations and cartoons in radical journalism, but it failed to solicit exciting literary contributions. Both editors wrote some excellent reports on the land question in the Southwest that resembled the later exposés by John Steinbeck and Carey McWilliams, but these two outsiders never became an organic part of the southwestern movement. Unlike other city slickers from the Midwest who came to know and love the region's poor folk, Algie and May Simons, who were part of Chicago's Socialist community, regarded their brief editorship of the *Coming Nation* as their "Kansas exile."[16]

After the ambitious Oklahoma *Daily Socialist* ceased publication at Newkirk in the movement's early years, the Sooner Socialists had to depend largely upon the *Appeal*, especially after Wayland started publishing a special Oklahoma City edition in 1908. In 1910 C. H. Armstrong hired Oscar Ameringer to edit a new paper, the *Industrial Democrat*, in the capital city, but within a short time the German journalist fell out with his publisher and fellow editor Marvin Brown, a former *Appeal* staffer, over the question of supporting a referendum favored by the railroad brotherhoods. Ameringer quickly started his own weekly, the Oklahoma *Pioneer*, and accused his former employer of accepting money from a railroad lobbyist. This provoked a bitter feud between the two papers, which ended in a complete victory for Ameringer when the State Executive Committee expelled Armstrong, Brown, and a controversial *Industrial Democrat* columnist named "Pap" Davis, and then recognized the *Pioneer* as the party's official publication. Ameringer's paper was in fact far superior to its rival, but the feud that brought it into existence continued to smolder. Stanley Clark, a writer for the *Industrial Democrat*, later wrote for the *Social Democrat* and the Sulphur *New Century*, two newspapers that carried a grudge against Ameringer and others of the so-called "silk stocking contingent" who controlled the state office.[17]

---

16. See Kent and Gretchen Kreuter, *An American Dissenter: The Life of Algie Martin Simons, 1870–1950* (Lexington: University of Kentucky Press, 1969), 116–28.

17. H. L. Meredith, "Agrarian Socialism in Oklahoma" (Ph.D. dissertation, University of Oklahoma, 1969), 112–14.

With the exception of the *Appeal* and the Dallas *Laborer*, edited by George Clifton Edwards, a Harvard-educated high school teacher fired for his radicalism, the Texas Socialist party lacked a significant journal until 1911 when E. O. Meitzen founded the *Rebel*, merging his small Hallettsville weekly with J. L. Hicks's Abilene *Farmers' Journal*. Within a year this new Socialist weekly had gained thousands of subscribers, mostly Texans, and much of the credit for this rapid success belonged to the *Rebel*'s colorful editor, Tom Hickey. Just a few months after the *Rebel* started publication the Houston *Chronicle* observed: "T. A. Hickey has a larger personal acquaintance with Socialists throughout Texas than any other man—an acquaintance formed during the years when he served as state organizer. He is a remarkably effective stump speaker and has scored a striking success with his weekly paper *The Rebel*, established about six months ago. It now has a circulation of over 18,000."[18]

Like J. A. Wayland, Hickey advanced his newspaper's circulation with sensational exposés, hard-hitting editorials on regional as well as national problems, and aggressive subscription drives promoted by volunteer hustlers known as *Rebel* "scouts." Hickey borrowed his folksy style and provocative approach from a notorious Texas "muckracker" named W. C. Brann, a self-styled iconoclast who was shot in the back ("where his suspenders crossed") by an irate victim of some journalistic probe. The *Rebel*'s editorial politics resembled those of Wayland's popular weekly. Hickey, an experienced industrial unionist, continued to report on workers' struggles, but he devoted his weekly largely to recruiting former Populists and to winning over tenant farmers by publicizing the evils of their plight. He also shared Wayland's virulent Anglophobia and anti-Catholicism as well as his outspoken advocacy of racial segregation. But since the Hallettsville weekly appealed largely to a Texas audience, it lacked a national readership, like the *Appeal*'s, to temper comments on the race question which sometimes

---

18. On the Dallas *Laborer*, see Nat L. Hardy to Thompson, June 10, 1913, in Socialist Party Papers, Perkins Library, Duke University. Quote from Houston *Chronicle*, February 12, 1912.

amounted to racist rhetoric. Its parochial focus also encouraged an unusually strong editorial evangelicalism designed to appeal to readers who still saw the world more in moral than political terms. The *Appeal* contained moralistic condemnations of capitalist evils and millennial predictions about the "coming nation," but it lacked the Bible-thumping of the Reverend M. A. Smith's "Five Minute Sermons" or of Hickey's own exegetical columns which held up the conduct of landlords, bankers, and politicians to the piercing light of the "good book." The "Bible socialism" preached by the *Rebel* had a much more fundamentalist tone than the Christian socialism propounded by urban preachers and other social gospelers; it was rooted in the religious rhetoric of the Texas Populists who had recruited a large number of Campbellites and preachers from other revivalist groups. The *Rebel*'s firm commitment to publishing in the region's religious idiom and to attacking pressing regional problems (notably tenancy) paid big dividends: within a year, the Hallettsville weekly's circulation jumped to 22,000.[19] Unlike Oscar Ameringer's *Oklahoma Pioneer*, which aspired to this kind of popularity, the *Rebel* became a real statewide Socialist party organ. Whereas the *Pioneer* suffered from its role in the *Industrial Democrat* purge and the fight against the grandfather clause, Tom Hickey's more opportunistic publication became a real rallying point for Texas Socialists. And like the *Appeal*, it served as an educational and organizational tool as well as a source of information and propaganda.

In Oklahoma, another Socialist weekly attempted to reach the state's discontented renters without resorting to the biblical moralism and polemical racism of the *Rebel*. The *Tenant Farmer*, edited by Patrick S. Nagle, approached the land question more scientifically than the Texas weekly. Nagle was no less indignant than Hickey in denouncing landlordism, as he, too, was a militant Irish Republican who loved the Land League and its violent attacks on English landlords. But instead of using biblical standards to judge

19. Ruth A. Allen, "Thomas A. Hickey and the *Rebel*," typescript in her possession. *Rebel* (Hallettsville, Tex.), June 29, July 8, 1911, August 1, 22, 1914.

the behavior of planters and merchants, Nagle used his historical and legal knowledge of Oklahoma's development to reveal the interlocking connections between big land owners, businessmen, bankers, and Democratic politicians.[20]

Building upon the legacy of Alliance and Populist hostility toward town creditors, the *Tenant Farmer*'s editor constructed a class analysis of southwestern society which explained how the "interlocked parasites of the electric light towns" exploited the "producers" in the countryside. The parasitic class included old Populist villans like the credit merchants and cotton factors, as well as exploiters who became more prominent in Oklahoma after the turn of the century—the landlords and bankers. Pat Nagle documented the exploitation of the tenant class so thoroughly (right down to the kind of "crooked clause" in each contract that "put a diamond ring on the finger of the landlord's daughter") that the *Tenant Farmer* came to be known by Socialists and by their opponents as the most authoritative voice in the region on the land question.[21] Needless to say, Nagle's practical and legal knowledge of landlord-tenant relations made his newspaper extremely valuable to insurgent renters who were organizing against the "interlocked parasites."

By 1913 southwestern Socialists had created an impressive, grassroots press to supplement the propaganda work of bigger regional papers like the *Appeal* and the *Rebel*. At that point Socialists edited and published fifty-five weeklies in Oklahoma, Texas, Louisiana, and Arkansas, including rural papers like the *Tenant Farmer* oriented toward the Renters' Union and the *Constructive Socialist* of Alva, Oklahoma, which still maintained ties with the Farmers'

20. Nagle reviewed his career before federal investigators in 1915. See U.S. Commission on Industrial Relations, *Final Report and Testimony* (Washington, D.C.: Government Printing Office, 1916), X, 9059. Also see *Tenant Farmer* (Kingfisher, Okla.), May, 1915.

21. *Tenant Farmer* (Kingfisher, Okla.), September, 1915. Oklahoma's leading progressive journal declared that the *Tenant Farmer*'s first issue was "perhaps the most powerful political document that has appeared in the state." *Harlow's Weekly* (Oklahoma City), September 25, 1915.

Union.[22] The proletarian papers ranged from the Dallas *Laborer*, a moderate union-sponsored weekly that favored "boring from within" the AFL, to Covington Hall's revolutionary *Lumberjack*, the voice of the IWW in the Louisiana piney woods. Whereas the labor papers frequently identified with the party's left-wing and took a militant stand on the race question, small-town weeklies in the cotton country, like Oklahoma's *Otter Valley Socialist* in Snyder and the Okemah *Sledge Hammer*, took conservative positions on farm questions, generally reflecting regional prejudices. These smaller weeklies received a good deal of their copy from the *Appeal* office or from the Socialist Cooperative Press in Iola, Kansas, and they tended to be less radical than the city and labor papers because they had to depend upon local advertising for support. Small-town newspapers financed solely by the party took more militant stands on the issues, but, according to Arkansas State Secretary Ida Callery, they frequently "left the locals financially busted."[23]

In sum, by 1913 the bulk of the southwestern party propaganda work was assumed by the Kansas and Oklahoma editions of the *Appeal* and the Texas *Rebel* which, according to proceedings from the Oklahoma Socialist party convention of 1914, "contributed in large measure to the growth and class consciousness of the movement."[24] In 1913 over 100,000 subscribers in the Southwest received one or more of these three weeklies; the overall readership of the party press was certainly much larger. In fact, even if circulation figures were available for the smaller newspapers, it would not provide an accurate indication of the numbers of people who read radical periodicals. Subscription figures did not include the numbers of copies sold at Socialist locals or in the big summer en-

22. Weinstein, "The Socialist Party," 24–25; W. F. Wiltze to Thompson, June 4, 1913, in Socialist Party Papers, Duke. Neil Basen has discovered seventy-five Socialist publications in the Southwest between 1901 and 1920.
23. Ida Hayman Callery to Thompson, June 5, 1913, in Socialist Party Papers, Duke.
24. *Oklahoma Socialist Party, Convention Proceedings*, December 29–31, 1914, p. 23, in Oklahoma Historical Society, Oklahoma City.

campments (like the 32-day western Oklahoma swing of 1914 which netted the *National Rip-Saw*, the tour sponsor, over 10,000 new subscribers). Socialists also passed their literature around among comrades too poor to spend the few pennies it cost to buy a paper or magazine. After speaking and selling Socialist newspapers to the striking timber workers of western Louisiana in 1911, Kate O'Hare remarked: "The *Rip-Saws* and *Appeals* we left were passed around from hand to hand, hidden under sweat-stained jumpers in tatters."[25]

But how many people who were moved by the Socialist gospel were actually able to read the party press? The southwestern Socialists worked with a relatively literate population, especially in Oklahoma where illiteracy rates were reported below the national average, yet Socialist journalists were trying to reach the poorest, least-educated sectors of the populace.[26] Poor folk who had trouble reading could sometimes obtain assistance from more skillful comrades. The idea of having someone read to people at work was unique to cigarmakers and a few other groups of artisans, but the tradition of evening readings on the porch or before the fireplace was quite common in rural America during the early part of this century. In Louisiana, where illiteracy rates were notoriously high

25. *National Rip-Saw*, September, 1914, p. 16; October, 1911, p. 3.
26. The statistics on school attendance and literacy are:

State or Section	Percent Attending School, 7–13 Years of Age, 1920	Percent Illiterate 1910
Oklahoma	85.8	5.6
Texas	83.7	9.9
Louisiana	75.9	29.9
East South Central States	83.6	17.4
South Atlantic States	85.6	16.0
U.S.A.	90.6	7.7

The difference in these illiteracy rates is partly due to the smaller proportion of blacks in the southwestern states of Texas and Oklahoma. But illiteracy rates among Negroes were lower there too—12.4 percent in Oklahoma and 17.8 percent in Texas as compared to 27.9 in the East South Central states and 25.2 in the South Atlantic states. U.S. Department of Commerce, *Fourteenth Census of the United States, 1920: Population* (Washington, D.C.: Government Printing Office, 1922), III, 34, 38.

among whites as well as blacks, the perceptive propagandist Kate O'Hare found that the "unlettered listened to the more fortunate read the newspapers and pamphlets we left behind."[27] Illiterate prisoners have been known to teach themselves to read and to master whole disciplines. The rural poor of the Southwest, who were also very isolated, searched in a remarkably determined way for information that would explain their desperate condition and lead them to liberation.

The southwestern Socialists experienced less difficulty with illiteracy than their comrades in the Deep South and less difficulty with foreign languages than their northern comrades, but they did not underestimate the problems of spreading the printed word to poor folk who lacked formal education; they made every effort to clarify Socialist literature. Newspaper editors and pamphleteers wrote in simple, direct prose punctuated with homespun metaphors and frontier humor. As satirist Oscar Ameringer said of his encampment audiences: "Humor appealed to them immensely, for they belonged to the tribe from which America's great humorists—from Mark Twain down to Oklahoma's own Will Rogers—have derived their inspiration." Ameringer was one of the best of the southwestern Socialist propagandists, because he listened to the people and spoke to them in their idiom, even though he spoke through a heavy German accent.[28]

THE SOUTHWESTERN SOCIALIST APPEAL

The history of political class consciousness in North America "has been largely a story of agrarian upheavals," Seymour Martin Lipset writes in his study, *Agrarian Socialism*. It is significant, he contends, "that the most successful socialist or semisocialist parties in the United States," including the Oklahoma Socialist party, "based their attack on the capitalist economic structure, not in terms of the Marxian doctrine of class struggle, but as a continua-

27. *National Rip-Saw*, October, 1911, p. 3.
28. Oscar Ameringer, *If You Don't Weaken: The Autobiography of Oscar Ameringer* (New York: Henry Holt, 1940), 262–63; Kate O'Hare to Castleton, September 16, 1945, in Debs Collection.

tion of the traditional struggle of farmers and workers against the 'vested interests' of eastern bankers and Wall Street." Indeed, "propaganda designed to appeal to a permanently exploited proletariat of workers and landless or mortgaged farmers has made little impression." This description may apply to populism, but it does not help to explain agrarian socialism in the Southwest. Radicals in Oklahoma and neighboring states did in fact propound an ideology based upon the "Marxian doctrine of class struggle" and they did make a significant impression upon a "permanently exploited" class of landless and mortgaged farmers. Lipset goes on to argue that "a successful socialist movement on this continent must basically be one that does not attempt to destroy the American creed," because of the "extent to which the values of the creed of American equality, of freedom of opportunity, of democratic classlessness, have permeated every aspect of the culture."[29] However, the success of the Socialist party in the Southwest depended precisely upon its ability to expose this American creed as a myth created by the ruling class. And since this creed did not actually "permeate" the culture of southwestern poor whites, the Socialists could convince many discontented farmers and workers that the reality of permanent poverty conflicted with beliefs in the ideology of "democratic classlessness" and "freedom of opportunity."

Other values imbedded themselves more deeply in the mentality of impoverished country people—beliefs in white supremacy, the natural right to the use and occupancy of the land, and the truths revealed in the Bible. Indeed, many regional Socialist leaders shared these values with their followers. Radical educators and agitators attempted to show that the ruling class used racism, respect for private property, and religious resignation to oppress the poor, but they did not convert their comrades to pure equalitarianism, communism, or atheism. In fact, they never tried. However, since economic changes had already eroded the poor whites' beliefs in the American "creed" of opportunity and equality, the southwestern Socialists effectively challenged rural versions of the Hora-

29. Seymour Martin Lipset, *Agrarian Socialism* (Rev. ed.; Garden City, N.Y.: Doubleday Anchor, 1968), 190.

tio Alger myth and exposed the nature of class society on the frontier, a society in which there was opportunity for the capitalist entrepreneur but only insecurity for the honest farmer.

In their campaign to make the land question the paramount issue in southwestern politics, the agrarian Socialists received valuable assistance from several experienced farm journalists, including former Farmers' Union journalists like E. O. Meitzen, J. D. Hicks, Taylor McRae of the *Rebel*, and H. H. Stallard of the Oklahoma *Constructive Socialist*, as well as younger agricultural reporters, notably Nat L. Hardy who was "born in a rented shack on a Texas cotton plantation" and hired by a progressive farm journal in Dallas. After quitting this job Hardy wrote numerous exposés of the Texas tenant's condition for the regional radical press and for national left-wing magazines like the *Masses*.[30]

The *Rebel* was always in the vanguard of the fight against landlordism. In the paper's first issue, Hickey and Meitzen issued a militant call to action appealing to the "manhood" of tenants whose families were exploited and degraded by greedy landlords. The theory of the agricultural ladder was a cruel myth. "The tenants," they declared, "have been going steadily downhill and they will be dumped in the ditch of despair if they don't watch out." Exploiting the growing alarm over the rising rate of tenancy revealed in the 1910 census, the *Rebel* reprinted an editorial from a conservative Galveston newspaper questioning the conventional notion that the tenant could "accumulate a small amount of money" and "inevitably be able to buy a place of his own and leave the landlord." The editorial admitted that new farmland was no longer readily available and that "nine out of ten tenants today (probably 19 out of 20) are destined to remain tenants." Clearly, the *Rebel* continued, a permanent tenant class existed in Texas under conditions that "even the tenants of poor old Ireland scorned 100 years ago."[31]

30. Dallas *Laborer*, June 17, 1911, and *Rebel* (Hallettsville, Tex.), June 6, 29, July 6, 1912.
31. *Rebel* (Hallettsville, Tex.), July 15, 1912.

What would the renters of the Lone Star state do about these conditions? The landlords, bankers, and merchants still counted on their docility. These "exploiters" simply wanted the "tenant to be a nice, subservient menial who will meet the landlord cap in hand and confer with him as to how much of his hide will be taken and under what conditions the skinning shall be accomplished." How much longer, Hickey asked, "will Texans submit to the European conditions of life long tenantry?"[32] "Red Tom," who frequently resorted to insurrectionary rhetoric, pointed out that, like the Irish tenants who rose up against their English landlords, Texas farmers had risen up in the past against the Yankees who were carpetbagger capitalists. The "New Rebels of the New South" would rise again—this time against oppressors who came from their own state but acted like "galvanized" Yankees.

In addition to attacking the landlords as a class the *Rebel* lashed out at the publicists, pundits, and preachers who reproached tenants for their "shiftlessness" and their failure to do the "things that 'thrifty', 'patriotic', 'home loving' people should do." Publications of the "landlord class," like the *Progressive Farmer*, not to mention the pious small-town weeklies, ignored the honest, hardworking, thrifty renters who were still tied to the "slave chain" of debt peonage. As Monroe Jones pointed out in his "Short Talks to Renters" column: "How often we hear the expression: 'He is poor but honest.' Had you ever thought that poverty and honesty are nearly always linked under the present system?"[33]

Oscar Ameringer exposed the absurdity of the rural mobility myth and the bourgeois work ethic in the following parody of a self-righteous small-town editor:

> The trouble with you tenant farmers of the South is that you spend your money foolishly. Take your table for instance. What's the use to squander good money on such luxuries as baking powder, biscuits, cone pone, and salted swine's bosom?
>
> There are all kinds of mussels in the nearby creek that are mighty good eating when taken out of their shells. Grasshoppers are plenti-

32. *Ibid.*, November 8, 1911.
33. *Ibid.*, February 1, 1913, December 26, 1914.

ful too . . . and if you bite off their heads, they won't kick in your stomach. John the Baptist became a great man on a grasshopper diet.

It's extravagance that's ailing you. You raise a crop and give one third to your landlord who is kind enough to furnish you with an opportunity to work. You give another third to your mules. But you have no right to squander a whole third on yourself. You should save that . . . so your children will have a place to rent when they grow up.

Everybody can have a farm that way if they only save hard enough.[34]

If advancement through hard work and savings was impossible under capitalism, the "shiftless" tenant was naturally inclined to move further west. What would he find? Certainly not opportunity, the Socialist replied, because, as Frederick Jackson Turner had demonstrated, the frontier was officially closed in the 1890s. Turner did not elaborate extensively on the consequences of the frontier's closure, but his Socialist student, A. M. Simons, capably demonstrated that class conflict increased as western opportunity declined.[35]

As May Wood-Simons pointed out, Oklahoma settlers, the last of the southwestern pioneers, saw land speculators extort land from the Indians and rent it out to poor whites who remained indebted. In 1913 she estimated, land speculators, mainly bankers, controlled 79 percent of the land in eastern and central Oklahoma, where it had become "practically impossible for a poor man to secure and retain title to the land." Most tenant farmers had given up hope in the frontier, but they were forced to keep on moving. "They move in from Arkansas and Texas in covered wagons," Simons reported, "and they are continuously on the move from one county to another in a vain hope that they can better their condition." Tenancy was, of course, a vicious circle from which there was "no hope of escape."[36]

Some Socialists also tried to convince white tenants that their poverty could not be blamed on their black and brown competitors

34. *Sword of Truth* (Sentinel, Okla.), January 1, 1913.
35. See A. M. Simons, *The American Farmer* (Chicago: Charles Kerr, 1906). On Simons and Frederick Jackson Turner, see Kent and Gretchen Kreuter, *An American Dissenter*, 7, 74.
36. *Coming Nation* (Girard, Kan.), May 29, 1913.

who toiled as sharecroppers and hired hands. Nat Hardy sought to calm the fears of those who scapegoated the "niggers and greasers" by describing living and working conditions that were "a disgrace to capitalist civilization" in an East Texas cotton county where only four nonwhite tenants lived. However, Socialist editors like Tom Hickey weakened these efforts by printing letters from white tenants who worried about being displaced by Afro and Mexican Americans and implied that their competitors were as much to blame as their oppressors. Oklahoma editors Vernon Rhodyback of the *Otter Valley Socialist* and J. Fleming Jones of the Okemah *Sledge Hammer* attacked Democratic landlords for displacing white tenants with black labor, but they also blamed the desperate sharecroppers who were being used by planter bosses to replace troublesome "red" renters.[37]

A few white tenants responded favorably to the warnings against racial scapegoating issued by Socialists like Nat Hardy. For example, a renter from Leon County, Texas, wrote to the *Rebel* explaining that his landlord sold out to a northern capitalist who then replaced the whites with blacks. "Away went our school and our church that we loved so dearly," he mourned. But he added: "Mr. Negro, we don't hate you. We ask you in the name of our homes and our churches not to under-rent the white man and we will not under-rent you." A black renter explained that only a tenant union for "colored people could put a stop to 'throat-cutting' between renters, both white and black." In its 1912 convention the Texas Renters' Union removed its "white only" clause and urged black renters to form their own parallel unions, along the lines of the old Colored Farmers' Alliance. However, mutual suspicions hampered the growth of such parallel organizations among both Afro-American and Mexican American renters.[38]

37. Nat L. Hardy, "Tenantry in the South," *Appeal to Reason* (Girard, Kan.), August 31, 1912. Also see *Oklahoma Pioneer* (Oklahoma City), August 27, 1910; and Donald Graham, "Red, White, and Black: An Interpretation of Ethnic and Racial Attitudes of Agrarian Radicals in Texas and Oklahoma, 1880–1920" (M.A. thesis, University of Saskatchewan, 1973), 154–58, 235–37.
38. *Rebel* (Hallettsville, Tex.), February 20, 1913; and *Farm and Ranch*, XXXI (November 16, 1912).

The Socialists opposed racial scapegoating far less than they attacked the capitalist exploitation of poor whites. At first southwestern party propagandists accepted A. M. Simons' revisionist views on the permanency of the small-farmer class, but after 1910 the spread of tenancy and the renters' growing discontent convinced most agrarian Socialists that Marx's theory of land concentration was correct after all. The rising proportion of mortgaged land combined with increasing tenancy rates indicated that most small farmers would be dispossessed before capitalism ran its disastrous course. As one Socialist tenant complained, "We are living under capitalism and under it farmers are losing their lands and they are gradually passing into the hands of the capitalist class to be farmed in larger tracts until the small farmer can no longer compete." Mortgaged freeholders were "travelling an open road that leads to tenantry," Pat Nagle declared. Once the homesteader's promised land, western Oklahoma now witnessed hundreds of foreclosures and sheriffs' sales, this desperate situation indicating to Nagle that the "pioneer farmer was becoming extinct." He would become a transient tenant farmer and then move to the city or continue to roam the countryside as a "hobo harvest hand."[39]

The corporation farm was the "wave of the future." Giant farms like the Taft family ranch on the Texas Gulf Coast signaled the coming of advanced capitalist agriculture. Scientifically managed by a Texas A & M professor who utilized the latest farm machinery and the cheapest Mexican wage laborers, the Taft Ranch was a convenient propaganda symbol for Socialists like Nat Hardy who called it "one of the most perfect instruments of exploitation" he had ever seen. "The time is not far distant," he wrote, "when we shall see all of the land gobbled up by a few great land syndicates with the present small farmers and tenants employed on these immense farms . . . more abjectly enslaved than the peons of Mexico."[40]

39. *Constructive Socialist* (Alva, Okla.), September 15, 1912; *Tenant Farmer* (Kingfisher, Okla.), May, 1915.
40. *Rebel* (Hallettsville, Tex.), December 15, 1912. Also see A. Ray Stephens, *The Taft Ranch: A Texas Principality* (Austin: University of Texas Press, 1965).

This was powerful propaganda for poor white farmers haunted by the twin spectres of losing their land and being forced down to the level of Negro sharecroppers and Mexican migrants. Many of the rural people faced with displacement were "seething with discontent," Hardy reported; they were ready to adopt "revolutionary measures to secure relief," but there was still resistance to the complete socialization of all means of production because the "ideal of owning an individual farm" was still "deeply implanted" in their consciousness.[41] The Socialist party's immediate demands defended their natural right to remain on the land they used productively, but at the same time, the party's leaders warned that capitalism would displace many small farmers before the Cooperative Commonwealth arrived.

One farmer, J. N. Price of Granfield, Oklahoma, spoke for others who saw the logic of this analysis. Like the small businessman, the small farmer would be crushed by big capitalists who would "install the most powerful, up-to-date machinery on such a large scale" that the little producer would be unable to compete. "Farmers, if we don't wake up it will soon be too late," he exclaimed. "The only possible way to escape is through the collective ownership and democratic management of all industries upon which the people depend." The southwestern Socialists promised those small farmers who survived capitalism the use and occupancy of their land in perpetuity, but, they insisted, little producers who held out would see the superiority of cooperative production.[42]

In the meantime, said the *Coming Nation*, the growth of big tenant plantations and "bonanza farms" like the Taft Ranch broke down old paternalistic relations between landlords and tenants and brought out "the class struggle clear and plain." Such large-scale farming intensified the exploitation of farm labor, Nat Hardy observed, and it sheared the farmer's mind of the "middle class ideas" to which he clung so persistently.[43] The southwestern class

41. *Coming Nation* (Girard, Kan.), June 1, 1912.
42. *Rebel* (Hallettsville, Tex.), September 2, 1911; Oscar Ameringer, *Socialism for the Farmer Who Farms the Farm*, in *National Rip-Saw* Series No. 15 (St. Louis: Rip-Saw Publishing, 1912).
43. *Coming Nation* (Girard, Kan.), June 11, 1912.

struggle necessarily undermined some ideas about "democratic classlessness" and "freedom of opportunity."

As Pat Nagle pointed out, the class struggle was clearly established between tenants in the countryside and exploiters in the towns. But there was more to it than this. While these local "parasites" joined with "eastern deposit banks, trusts, and other big capitalist interests in defense of the right to exploit," the tenants were "drawn into reciprocal solidarity with the wage workers" in various industries.[44] Propagandists like Nagle and Hickey easily documented the first part of this equation, but it was more difficult to convince isolated rural tenants to identify with industrial workers. For although this proved quite easy in certain sections, like the Louisiana piney woods where tenants and mill hands were related, in general the southwestern Socialists had to depend upon renters' unions and the strike reports in the party press to instill a sense of solidarity between rural and industrial sections of the "exploited class."

By analyzing the political economy of agricultural capitalism, the southwestern Socialists could explain the plight of the small farmer and, by bringing their class analysis down to the local level, they could identify his class enemy, but this "scientific" approach to propaganda was not enough to move poor people to radical action. A people accustomed to seeing the world in moral rather than empirical terms would respond more readily to a biblical approach to socialism which brought their oppressors to a premature judgment day.

RADICAL REVIVALISM

Preachers like M. A. Smith, who wrote the *Rebel*'s "Five Minute Sermon" column, quoted chapter and verse to prove that those who monopolized the earth and its fruits were sinners of the highest magnitude. "Hear Him speak through his prophets," wrote Smith: "The land shall not be sold forever; for the land is mine;

---

44. Patrick S. Nagle, *The Interlocked Parasites*, Bulletin No. 1 (Oklahoma City: Oklahoma Socialist Party, 1914). Also see *Rebel* (Hallettsville, Tex.), October 24, 1914.

for ye are strangers and sojourners with me. Leviticus (25:23)." He then asked what could be clearer than Ecclesiastes', "Moreover the Profit of the Earth is for all." The Texas Socialists were especially active in sending preachers into the field to speak on the "Socialism of the Bible" and to "prove that capitalist rent, interest, and profit [were] condemned by the word of God."[45]

Those agitators who used scripture to condemn landlords and usurers also quoted biblical "laws" to justify the farmer's natural right to the use and occupancy of the land. They combined the condemnation of greedy private ownership in Leviticus with Tom Paine's radical interpretation of Lockean natural rights theory. The southwestern Socialists also followed Paine's *Agrarian Justice* in insisting that "the earth, in its natural uncultivated state was, and ever would have continued to be, *the common property of the human race.*"[46] Human rights came before property rights. The Bible said so, but so did the patron saint of American agrarianism, Thomas Jefferson. Cooperation could clearly be justified through biblical passages like Acts 2:44, 45, which showed how God's children "were together and had all things in common." According to the Reverend Smith, the "architect of the universe" stated that "when men cooperate instead of competing in a jungle-like fight," there will be "laughter instead of tears, joy instead of sorrow, health instead of pain" because "with the 'rod and staff' of cooperation for comfort, we can fear no evil."[47]

The Socialist preachers' revivalistic style was nearly as important as the subversive content of their biblical exegesis. They had learned from the Populists that an urgent atmosphere created the context for radical education and inspiration. The Socialists usually attempted to place the southwestern class struggle in nationwide and even worldwide context, a task that was comparatively easy during the "age of industrial violence" between 1910 and 1915,

45. *Rebel* (Hallettsville, Tex.), July 1, 29, August 1, 1911; *Social Democrat* (Oklahoma City), December 17, 1913.
46. See Staughton Lynd, *Intellectual Origins of American Radicalism* (New York: Pantheon, 1968), 75–76.
47. *Rebel* (Hallettsville, Tex.), August 26, 1911, and *Beckham County Agitator* (Sayre, Okla.), July 9, 1914.

especially since a land revolution had erupted just below the Rio Grande. Furthermore, party preachers and teachers in the Southwest tried to tie the necessity of the Cooperative Commonwealth to the urgent need for change expressed by the working people themselves. As Ameringer recalled of the indebted Oklahoma dirt farmers who attended the encampments:

> After the night meetings, discussions around the glowing campfire continued on into the small hours. For these people radicalism was not an intellectual plaything. Pressure was upon them. Many of their homesteads were already under mortgage. Some had already been lost by foreclosure. They were looking for delivery from the eastern monster whose lair they saw in Wall Street. They took to their socialism like a new religion. And they fought and sacrificed for the spreading of the new faith like the martyrs of other faiths.[48]

These summer encampments gave the southwestern Socialists an unusual collective forum through which they could appeal to a generally captive audience of largely isolated farmers and workers. The most important weapon in the party's "propaganda arsenal," the "protracted" camp meeting offered entertainment and recreation which could draw whole families from great distances, and it provided an ideal context for educational and inspirational lectures.

Grand Saline, the first and foremost summer encampment, took place annually for thirteen summers after its founding in 1904, attracting thousands of East Texas farmers from the big thicket to the piney woods. Smaller camp meetings were also organized throughout the Southwest, 125 in Texas alone during the depressed summer of 1914. After touring the Lone Star state's Socialist party encampment circuit in this torrid summer, Eugene Debs wrote enthusiastically about the "Socialist spirit" of the sunburned tenant farmers whose wagons rolled into the camp sites off the dusty prairies, their red flags flapping in the breeze.[49]

Debs's presence at these camp meetings was important; it underlined the party's recognition of the southwestern movement's sig-

---

48. Ameringer, *If You Don't Weaken*, 265–67.
49. Eugene V. Debs, "Revolutionary Encampments," *National Rip-Saw* (St. Louis), September, 1914, p. 12.

nificance. Extraordinarily skilled at speaking to massed audiences, Debs thrilled the southwesterners with his indignant attacks on the capitalist oppressors and their political agents. More important, the party's standard-bearer could convince the poor and the disinherited that the Cooperative Commonwealth was within their grasp. He could identify with their problems but he could also make them feel their collective power. Like William Cobbett and other successful radical prophets, Debs could enter into a "dialectic with the people." He never spoke at them; he spoke for them. Poor people believed him when he said: "I don't want to rise through the ranks of labor; I want to rise with them."

Debs was more than a great orator, Ameringer observed. "He was a great soul," a "dreamer, poet and prophet of the weary and heavy-laden. People loved him because he loved the people."[50] Debs was not only a powerful speaker; he was a natural educator, a popular writer, and a tireless campaigner. He was the "fountain of enthusiasm." Kate Richards O'Hare, Debs's only rival for popularity at the southwestern encampments, drank deeply from this fountain, and she, too, found herself in a messianic frame of mind when she spoke to enthusiastic rural masses assembled at the party's summer conclaves. Many years later, she wrote: "Gene was at his best in these camp meetings. We often traveled together to cover them and as I watched him and the response of the crowds, Oklahoma faded and we were Jesus of Nazareth and Martha, burdened with many cares, speaking to the harried Jews in Palestine. I don't think anyone could have known Gene well, lived and worked with him, watched his power over the masses and not known the Carpenter of Nazareth intimately."[51]

Of course, successful encampments involved organization as well as inspiration. Richey Alexander, an enterprising insurance salesman from Grand Saline, administered the booming Texas encampment business quite effectively. He set down some basic rules for other promoters to follow: book in the best speakers, set up ap-

50. Ameringer, *If You Don't Weaken*, 267.
51. Kate Richards O'Hare to Castleton, September 16, 1945, in Debs Collection, Tamiment.

MAMMOTH TENTH ANNUAL
Socialist
ENCAMPMENT

—————————— AT ——————————

GRAND SALINE, TEXAS
AUGUST 18 TO 23, 1913

Excursion Rates Will Be Secured Over All the Principal Railroads of Texas for this Gigantic Gathering.

THREE ADDRESSES DAILY by different orators who know and will tell the
real truth. They will prove that Socialism will give every man an equal
opportunity to labor, with hand or brain, and receive the full product of his
toil undiminished by legalized robbery. The only way to get the facts
about Socialism is to read and hear what representative Socialists themselves say it is.

GROUNDS IN PICTURESQUE PROGRESS PARK one mile west of the T. & P. station where there is an abundance of pure, limpid water for all purposes and
plenty of dense shade. Bring all the folks, camp on the grounds and have
a solid week of instructive and entertaining pleasure. Meals and supplies
on grounds at regular rates.

MANY PROMINENT SPEAKERS—Many of the brainiest and ablest speakers in
America will positively attend. The following is only a partial list of the
speakers expected: Eugene V. Debs, Dick Maple, A. W. Ricker, Associate editor Appeal to Reason; A. M. Simons, editor Coming Nation; Senator Winfield R. Gaylord, Samuel W. Ball of Chicago, Stanley J. Clark, Mrs.
Kate O'Hare, Phil Callery of Okla., Hon. Lee L. Rhodes, Clinton Simon-
ton of Iowa, Oscar Ameringer, Wm. A. Ward of St. Louis, Rev. M. A.
Smith, J. C. Thompson, editor Texarkana Socialist; Hon. Dan Hogan,
editor Southern Worker; Rev. W. T. Woodrow, Hon. J. C. Rhodes. Geo. C.
Edwards, editor Dallas Laborer; Richey Alexander, W. S. Noble, Rev. John
A. Currrie, Tom Cross, D. B. Carter, J. L. Scoggin, Rev. D. D. Richardson, P. G. Zimmerman and Rev. Reddin Andrews. Watch for advertisements and announcements giving further particulars.

PRIVILEGES FOR SALE—For stands, shows, Ferris wheel and all kinds of
attractions that make an enjoyable and festive occasion. For information
address Richey Alexander.

Grand Saline is the place. August 18 to 23 the dates. Everybody Invited. Tell Everybody. Come Join the Mammoth
Merry Throng and Have Your Part of the Fun.

Advertising Committee—Richey Alexander, D. B. Carter and Will Anders.

JOURNAL PRINT, GRAND SALINE

pealing concessions to keep the kids happy, send out newspaper advertisements and print up handbills far in advance, and be sure to find a spot with plenty of shade and water. Alexander's Oklahoma counterpart, Oles Stofer, added that it was important to "employ some comrade well fitted to conduct a school of instruction each day," because the most important point of an encampment was "educating our own comrades." He also issued a few warnings: "Don't hire a brass band, unless you have money to waste. Better spend the money for literature. Don't allow the concession stand or the merry-go-round to be too near the speakers' stand. And don't believe the hard luck stories of the professional privilege man." In short, the successful encampment resulted from only "10% inspiration and 90% perspiration."[52]

In addition to Oles Stofer's camp meetings, Oklahoma socialism benefited from the big tour sponsored by the *National Rip-Saw*, featuring such top speakers as Oscar Ameringer, Kate and Frank O'Hare, and sometimes Debs himself. These tour meetings were especially popular in western Oklahoma where the *Rip-Saw* troop was featured with a rodeo and carnival, all under the "stars and stripes and the red flag of international socialism." Oscar Ameringer recalled that the camp meetings drew such large crowds the local merchants helped sponsor them because they appreciated all the business the Socialists brought to their small towns. Frank O'Hare later described a typical encampment on the *Rip-Saw* tour's western swing through Snyder, Oklahoma, a tiny village of 250 people flooded by thousands of Socialists in the course of a week-long radical revival. The crowds were big this time because Gene Debs and Mother Jones were speaking. Hundreds of wool-hatted farmers and their sunburned wives listened attentively for hours while the movement's greatest orators told them about the evils of capitalism and the coming of the Cooperative Common-

---

52. *Rebel* (Hallettsville, Tex.), March 25, 1912, August 1, 1913; Richey Alexander, "The Socialist Encampment," *National Rip-Saw* (St. Louis), April-May, 1913, July, 1914, p. 7, and September, 1914, p. 16; Oles Stofer, "Conducting a Socialist Encampment," *International Socialist Review*, X (1909–10), 278–79.

wealth. The scene was a bit like a "holiness" revival except that it featured "Socialist speakers instead of religious evangelists."[53]

Debs, O'Hare, Mother Jones, "Red Tom" Hickey, and other popular radicals who spoke at the encampments often borrowed their oratorical techniques from the revivalists, but their message was much less spiritual than the gospel presented by preachers in the party. There were teachers as well as preachers at the summer camp meetings, and the former were perhaps more important than the latter. Socialist educators like Oscar Ameringer, Walter Thomas Mills, and Caroline Lowe were really the most effective "socialist makers" on the encampment circuit. They were more concerned with offering systematic education than with injecting "emotional doses of agitation." Ameringer, a skilled encampment instructor, described the evening "educationals" this way: After a day of listening to speeches, picnicking, and socializing with old friends and new comrades, the campers sang "Socialist songs, usually of Populist origin" using familiar melodies like "Onward Christian Soldiers." The most popular number was the "Red Flag" to the tune of "Maryland, My Maryland" with the chorus: "Then raise the scarlet standard high; Within its shade we'll live and die. Though cowards flinch and traitors sneer, We'll keep the red flag flying here." Following the inspirational singing, the Ameringer family brass quartet would add a cultured refrain to the evening with music by the German masters.[54]

The more dedicated Socialists stayed up after the music to attend informal lessons in history and economics which began when the "instructor planted himself in the chair or store box on a raised platform and then urged the audience on the ground or pine planks to ask questions." More formal educational lectures were also arranged in which "Professor" Mills expounded on his text, *The Struggle for Existence*, A. M. Simons adapted the theories of Fred-

53. *National Rip-Saw* (St. Louis), July, 1914, p. 7, September, 1914, p. 16; *Oklahoma Pioneer* (Oklahoma City), October 4, 1911; Ameringer, *If You Don't Weaken*, 264; and Frank P. O'Hare to Henschel, September 13, 1942, in Frank P. O'Hare Papers, Missouri Historical Society, St. Louis.

54. Ameringer, *If You Don't Weaken*, 265–69; David Shannon, *The Socialist Party of America, A History* (New York: Macmillan, 1955), 27.

erick Jackson Turner and Charles Beard to his Socialist version of United States history, and Ameringer educated by entertaining through his witty pamphlet, "The Life and Deeds of Uncle Sam, A Little History for Big Children," which sold half a million copies before the war.[55]

These noted Socialist lecturers, along with lesser pedagogical propagandists, contributed as much to the growth of the southwestern movement and to its spiritual intensity as did the charismatic orators, candidates, and preachers. The educators committed themselves to raising consciousness; others could raise tempers.

How successful were party propagandists in teaching Socialist principles and practices to the poor, uneducated people of the Southwest? Unfortunately, it is as difficult to measure the effects of the teachers as it is those of the preachers. Ameringer, speaking from his "long experience of riling up the people, including class conscious immigrant workers in several cities," insisted that the southwestern frontier people were his "most satisfactory audience." They had "more than average intelligence," he believed, and "they followed the main arguments easily and even caught the more subtle points quickly." Since they had been deprived of a formal education and were "grateful for anything that broke the monotony of their lonesome lives," the rural poor listened enthusiastically. Eugene Debs, who experienced more audiences than any other Socialist speaker, tried to explain the "genuine ardor and enthusiasm" he discovered at the southwestern encampments by emphasizing that these poor people desperately needed a message of hope. Once they heard the gospel from the party's best preachers, they could "wend their way homeward . . . feeling that they had refreshed themselves at a fountain of enthusiasm." They could then go out among their neighbors and "deliver to them the glad tidings of the coming day."[56]

55. Shannon, *Socialist Party of America*, 269; *Appeal to Reason* (Girard, Kan.), January 29, 1916; *Rebel* (Hallettsville, Tex.), December 12, 1913, February 26, 1914. Also see *Appeal to Reason*, July 8, 1911, and *Harlow's Weekly*, (Oklahoma City), September 25, 1915.

56. Ameringer, *If You Don't Weaken*, 262; Debs, "Revolutionary Encampments," 12; Kate Richards O'Hare, "How Oklahoma Talks Socialism to the Farmer," Chicago *Daily Socialist*, September 16, 1910.

Kate Richards O'Hare surrounded by the *National Rip-Saw* editorial board, St. Louis, 1912. Frank P. O'Hare, standing right; Oscar Ameringer, seated right.
Courtesy Freda Hogan Ameringer

George D. Brewer, associate editor of the *Appeal*, and Grace Brewer, co-commander of the Appeal "Army," 1904.
Courtesy Wayne State University

Fred D. Warren, editor of the *Appeal to Reason.*

Staff of the *Appeal to Reason*, Girard, Kansas, 1905.
Courtesy Pittsburg State University

Oklahoma cotton tenant family, 1913.

Photo by Lewis Hine
Courtesy Edward L. Bafford Photography
Collection University of Maryland
Baltimore County Library

Gene Debs speaking on one of his southern
campaign tours.

Courtesy Indiana State University

Five-year-old cotton picker in Oklahoma,
1916.

Photo by Lewis Hine
Courtesy Edward L. Bafford Photography
Collection University of Maryland
Baltimore County Library

The southwestern Socialist encampments worked because they drew upon the collective traditions of the frontier and added political significance to common experiences. Unlike the industrial workers who were divided by craft, nationality, and religion, the poor white farmers were, Ameringer emphasized, united by language, culture, and to some extent by common work routines and social traditions. The pioneer farmers of the Southwest could not afford to rely solely upon rugged individualism; they cooperated in building houses and barns, harvesting crops, coping with plagues and natural disasters, and in celebrating holidays and special events with "play parties" and other forms of entertainment.

Following his successful tour of the Socialist camp meetings in 1914, Debs remarked: "The most class conscious industrial workers in the cities are not more keenly alive to the social revolution nor more loyal to its principles . . . than these farmers in Texas and Oklahoma."[57] Allowing for Debs's overly optimistic revolutionary rhetoric, this assessment of the southwestern movement, derived from the encampments, is persuasive. Debs did not say that the farmers were more class conscious than the workers in the party, but he did say that they were more enthusiastic about socialism and more loyal to the party that promised to bring the Cooperative Commonwealth into existence. Arguing solely from the party's grass-roots strength in Oklahoma and Texas, it is difficult to dispute this point. The frontier farmer's isolation and his feelings of "possessive individualism" toward the land prevented the development of proletarian class consciousness.[58] The Socialists created small tenant unions based upon the proletarian model in order to arouse the renters' sympathy toward industrial unionists' struggles, but the party's rural masses still expressed a consciousness that was more petty bourgeois than proletarian.

However, in the 1910s this did not mean that the tenant farmers' opposition to corporate capitalism was less radical than that of

57. Debs, "Revolutionary Encampments," 12.
58. See Garin Burbank, *When Farmers Voted Red: The Gospel of Socialism in the Oklahoma Countryside, 1910–1924* (Westport, Conn.: Greenwood, 1976), 44–66.

Socialist workers or that their enthusiasm for the movement was less intense. On the contrary, Debs was right in stating that no regional grouping within the Socialist party was more alive to its possibilities or more loyal to its principles. Unlike most of the workers in the party, the farmers' socialism was not mediated by trade-union consciousness; their organizational loyalties were relatively undivided. Unlike city people or rural folk in more settled sections, the frontier people of the Southwest were not as exposed to what Ameringer called "the propaganda of their betters" regarding the blessings of capitalism and the evils of socialism. And unlike immigrant workers who were exposed to the antiradical teachings of the Catholic church, the poor whites of the Southwest were increasingly divorced from established Protestant churches, as a result of a general polarizing process that was separating rich and poor. Under these conditions, the rural mobility myth lost credibility among the poor. The economic changes that created the southwestern class struggle also began to undermine some of the consensual beliefs that held rural society together in the early twentieth century. Socialist propaganda subverted these beliefs even further and sometimes destroyed them altogether, yet the enthusiasm aroused by the party's appeal was derived more from its vision of socialism than from its critique of capitalism. Socialist preachers and teachers offered desperate, disillusioned poor people a remarkably tangible picture of a new society based on the kind of cooperation that they knew human beings were capable of producing. This is why Ameringer said the encampment audiences "took to their Socialism like a new religion."

THE SOCIALIST MILLENNIUM

Oscar Ameringer, Frank and Kate O'Hare, Caroline Lowe, and the other agitators and educators who worked the Oklahoma encampments often used a revivalistic approach to sway their audiences, but they were primarily secular Socialists who attacked capitalism more from a materialistic than a moralistic point of view. The most popular preachers on the western Oklahoma circuit, like Walter Thomas Mills, were really teachers rather than fundamentalist ministers. The Texas Socialists, however, were not tied as closely to the national organization or to the international principles of socialism and so their propaganda was much more explicitly religious. Tom Hickey and other propagandists cultivated the style of the old Populist preachers. And though in reality he was more attached to the bottle than the Bible, "Red Tom" came on like a "fire and brimstone" revivalist. An experienced stump speaker, the *Rebel* editor excelled at the summer encampments where he set the millennial tone of the impatient Texas movement. Preaching before an "immense gathering" at the Ellison Springs encampment in 1912, Hickey trumpeted the main chorus of the southwestern radical revivalists: "Be Ye of good cheer, ye disinherited of the earth, for the day is coming when, with the spirit of the Lord in your hearts and with your footsteps lighted with the lamp of Socialism . . . we will, with that old prophet Nehemiah, say to the rulers of the nation: 'Restore, I pray you, even to this day, their land, their vineyards, and their houses.' And they shall be restored."[59]

Like the Owenite Socialists a century before, the Debsian Socialists tried to secularize millennialism. The *Appeal*'s serialization of Upton Sinclair's novel, *The Millennium*, symbolized their effort. But this use of millennialism was represented most clearly in the rhetoric of Texas evangelists like Hickey who described the "coming nation" in prophetic terms.[60] The "ideology of millennialism" which helped transmit Robert Owen's ideas from Britain to the United States in the early nineteenth century also helped translate Karl Marx's ideas in the Southwest during the early twentieth century. Owenite millennialism was "first and foremost an ideology of change which was sudden, total and irrevocable." In this sense, it was a revolutionary ideology, J. F. C. Harrison explains. "The change envisaged was not an improvement of the present, but an utter rejection and replacement of it by something perfect."[61]

59. *Rebel* (Hallettsville, Tex.), August 10, 1912.
60. *Appeal to Reason* (Girard, Kan.), June 1, 1912; *Rebel* (Hallettsville, Tex.), October 7, 1911.
61. John F. C. Harrison, *Quest for the New Moral World: Robert Owen and the Owenites in Britain and America* (New York: Scribner, 1969), 101.

Social democrats like Oscar Ameringer, Otto Branstetter, and Pat Nagle gave the Oklahoma party a gradualist direction emphasizing the evolutionary path to socialism, whereas Texas militants like Tom Hickey, E. O. Meitzen, and M. A. Smith offered their followers a millennial vision of socialism including the prophecy of an apocalyptic, if not revolutionary, birth of the Cooperative Commonwealth. But both groups of southwestern Socialists shared the Owenites' postmillennial perspective—"believing that the millennium was simply a more perfect state of society, which could with equal propriety be called 'the Rational State of Human Existence' or . . . 'the Brotherhood of the Human Race'." Still, postmillennialists did not "empty the concept . . . of all theological content" by "leaving it simply and essentially a description of a state of society in which the new system prevailed."[62] The Cooperative Commonwealth was clearly a state in which fundamental Christian values would finally reign supreme.

In the very earliest days of the southwestern movement farmers and workers saw socialism in postmillennial terms. For example, in 1901, the year the party was founded, a Texas worker wrote:

> I am only a common, hard working, dollar-a-day (often less) wage slave, but I have read after the Nazarene a little, and he told of a Golden Happy Day that was coming on earth. Those eighteen hundred years have rolled by without its realization. But now, today, unworthy though we may be, we are brought face to face with what generations have longed, hoped, prayed, yes, even died for: the Brotherhood of Man, which means the fulfillment of the Nazarene's promise—the Millennium.[63]

Thirteen years later such radical revivalists as the Reverend Ham reportedly had a great effect upon encampment audiences when he explained that "socialism was the next step in civilization after capitalism"; it was "the idealistic stage of the millennium." At about the same time A. B. Cox, a renter from Jewitt, Texas, spoke

62. *Ibid.*, 133–34. *Rebel* (Hallettsville, Tex.), July 29, September 9, and concerning the editor's effort to start a Socialist preachers' organization, October 11, 1911.
63. H. B. Cochran to Sam Hampton, *Social Economist* (Bonham, Tex.), June 6, 1901.

for those fundamentalists in the party who took the millennial metaphor for socialism literally: "I am a Socialist from the Bible standpoint and also the political standpoint," he declared. "And I fully believe that the Socialist movement is the forerunner of the second coming of Jesus Christ." Socialist millennialism generally lacked the vengeful, cataclysmic quality of holiness religion, as preached by sects like the Pentecostals, but an apocalyptic, premillennial tone frequently crept in. Poor people who had been victimized by capitalists expected the "coming nation" to bring punishment for the parasites as well as justice for the honest producers. As J. H. Haden, a railroad worker from Yoakum, Texas, wrote to the *Rebel*: "Capitalism has been weighed in the balance and found wanting. As sure as God reigns, Babylon is falling to rise no more. The international socialist commonwealth—God's Kingdom—shall rise on the wreck and ruin of the world's present ruling powers."[64] But this was not the "chiliasm of despair" calling for God's vengence against all sinners, rich and poor, nor was it the expression of a hope that society could be "transformed in a cataclysmic flash."[65] Even the most emotional millennialists in the Socialist movement believed that capitalism would be transformed only through methodical agitation, education, and organization.

The religious orientation of southwestern socialism did not prevent party members from being branded as infidels, free lovers, and even anti-Christs. The Socialists responded to these dangerous charges in several ways. First, they argued that they, not the defenders of capitalism, were true Christians, because Jesus, the son of a carpenter, had preached a radical gospel that condemned the wealthy. The Nazarene had spoken clearly when he said to his disciples: "It is easier for a camel to pass through the eye of a needle, than for a rich man to enter the kingdom of heaven" (Matthew 20 : 24). W. S. Noble, who started out as a Campbellite preacher and then turned to organizing for the Farmers' Alliance

64. *Rebel* (Hallettsville, Tex.), June 6, 1914, June 10, 1916, February 21, 1914.
65. E. P. Thompson, *The Making of the English Working Class* (New York: Pantheon, 1963), 375 ff; and Bell, *Marxian Socialism in the United States*, 7.

and the Renters' Union, explained the political significance of this carpenter's son: "Jesus denounced the ruling classes, and they in turn denounced Him as an agitator who stirreth up the people by teaching the poor that they should inherit the earth."[66]

The Socialists also insisted that their party did not officially oppose religion. In 1914 the Oklahoma state secretary repeated the official line: "The Socialist Party has nothing to do with religion"; it "has no fight with the Roman Catholic Church or any other church." As "a movement for things material" it had "no part in things spiritual." Thus, the party official concluded, "A man can believe anything he wishes as to things beyond." Each person should "let the religion of the other man alone. Even under Socialism there will be those who entertain spiritual beliefs contrary to the beliefs of others." However, these official declarations did not put a stop to religious controversy over the "question of Socialist morals."[67] Nor did they end the hard-hitting attacks made by agitators against the hypocrisy of organized religion and its established clergy.

The radical revivalists of the Southwest distinguished between wealthy Protestant churches with their "holier than thou" ministers and two-faced congregations, and poor people's churches. But they made few distinctions when it came to the Roman Catholic church. This institution seemed monolithic, even though poor Catholic parishes often shared social values quite different from those of the Vatican. In any case, there were very few Catholics in the Southwest outside of South Texas and the Louisiana Cajun country, so the Socialists did not worry about offending the faithful. It was, of course, easier for a propagandist to convince his audience that Catholic priests and bishops represented the forces of secrecy and oligarchy than it was in the case of Protestant ministers (generally Americans) who used the language of democracy. Such muck-

66. *Rebel* (Hallettsville, Tex.), August 1, 1914. See also A. W. Ricker, *The Political Economy of Jesus*, *Rip-Saw* Series No. 12 (St. Louis: Rip-Saw Publishing, 1912).

67. *Rebel* (Hallettsville, Tex.), August 1, 1914. Also see *Social Democrat* (Oklahoma City), November 13, 1913; "Socialism vs Religion," *Laborer's Free Press* (Lake Charles, La.), 1914.

rakers as Oscar Ameringer limited their attacks to Catholic groups like the Militia of Christ, a conservative labor organization that actively opposed socialism. But other editors—Tom Hickey, for example—believed in a papal conspiracy against democracy and resorted to classical Know-Nothing attacks on Catholicism. Hickey's publisher E. O. Meitzen blamed the church for defeating him in his effort to be elected judge of Lavaca County in 1906, and so his paper the *Rebel* featured a number of anti-Catholic articles and exposés, including an extensive report on the notorious Father Schmidt, an accused murderer who also happened to be an anti-Socialist lecturer. Hickey, who was raised as a Catholic, tried to restrict his attacks to the hierarchy, remarking that the *Rebel* "had no fight with the pure men and women who make up the rank and file of the Catholic church." But sometimes this distinction did not make a great difference. For example, in Val Verde County, Texas, the party's only stronghold in the Rio Grande valley, the Socialist club regularly purchased and distributed one hundred copies of the *Menace*, a sensational anti-Catholic newspaper which resorted to traditional nativist attacks on the church's immigrant membership. And although the Socialists in Val Verde directed their criticism at the Catholic hierarchy, they undoubtedly furthered the divisions between the county's white workers in Del Rio and the Mexican wage hands (a majority of the population) who depended on the church for many reasons, including protection from racist Anglos. However, nativism and racism were probably greater obstacles to Socialist cooperation between Anglos and Chicanos than was anti-Catholicism, which, on the whole, played a rather small role in party propaganda.[68]

68. *Oklahoma Pioneer* (Oklahoma City), September 23, 1911; *Rebel* (Hallettsville, Tex.), December 27, 1913, January 9, 1915; *Social Democrat* (Oklahoma City), April 16, 1913. The *Rebel* attacked the *Menace* on several occasions, including July 8, 22, 1911, January 25, 1913. Also see Graham, "Red, White, and Black," 182–95. Emilio Zamora, Jr., "Chicano Socialist Labor Activity in Texas, 1900–1920," *Aztlán*, VI (1975), 226–30, discusses the effects of Anglo prejudice upon Socialist recruitment of Chicanos in Texas. In addition to the party's failure to publish a Spanish newspaper, Zamora cites the publication of racist letters by Anglo party members; it is likely that some of the letters also contained anti-Catholic prejudice, though Zamora does not mention this.

The southwestern Socialists' anti-Catholicism was related less to anti-immigrant sentiment than to an old radical tradition of anti-papism in which the Roman pope and his clergy stood for aristocracy, secrecy, and hypocritical morality. There was also talk of a papal conspiracy with big business, but this was in no way essential to the Socialists' critique of capitalism. Like the Populists, many Socialists believed that there was an international financial conspiracy, but this octopus was not controlled by either Catholics or Jews. In fact, there was no significant evidence of anti-Semitism in the agrarian Socialist press. Indeed, when "anti-Semitism rose to a fever pitch in the South" between the time Mary Phagan was murdered and Leo Frank was lynched, the Socialists remained calm. After Frank's murder, the *Rebel* "hotly denounced the atrocity," and editor Hickey used the occasion to renew his attack on Tom Watson, the "renegade Populist," whose lurid Jew-baiting contributed to the tragedy. Hickey did, however, adopt the stereotype of Jews as moneymen in charging that Frank was lynched by "envious gentile businessmen" who found "Semitic competitors menacing to their financial stability." But there was "no evidence of pervasive anti-Semitism" in the *Rebel*—"the kind which identifies Jews as agents of conspiratorial plots." In fact, the only time "Red Tom" ever praised the German Social Democrats was when he noted their principled opposition to anti-Semites in the Reichstag.[69]

The Socialists also distinguished between the clergy and the religious rank and file when they criticized established Protestant denominations. There were Christian believers, and there were organized churches. "Christianity is one thing," they asserted, "churchianity another."[70] Secular party preachers like Stanley Clark emphasized this dichotomy in well-publicized debates with clerical "socialist slayers" sent out by certain churches. After defending the Socialist party against charges that it favored atheism,

69. Graham, "Red, White, and Black," 177. This study also found no references in the Oklahoma party press, urban or rural, that betrayed any anti-Semitism.
70. *Rebel* (Hallettsville, Tex.), July 22, June 1, 1912.

adultery, and free love, Clark and other debaters attacked their opponents for hypocritically defending the morality of evil capitalists. And since the *Appeal* or some other muckraking party journal supplied weekly reports on the private lives of big businessmen and politicians, the radicals were armed with a full case of ammunition. These small-town debates between anti-Socialist ministers and defenders of the party faith generally attracted a good deal of attention. The party press rarely produced any evidence to prove the claim that its debaters "annihilated" or "vanquished" their opponents in every single encounter, but there is evidence that some noncommitted members of the audience were converted to socialism through these debates.

Indeed, Stanley Clark, the sharp-tongued attorney who had reportedly met "scores of the strongest debaters" and had sent them down in "crushing defeat," actually converted one of his adversaries. In 1911 the Reverend G. G. Hamilton, a Methodist minister from Crowell, Texas, conducted several heated debates with Clark in southern Oklahoma. After a spirited confrontation at Hollis, Hamilton took up his opponent's challenge to read *Christianity and the Social Crisis* by Walter Rauschenbusch. Shortly thereafter, the noted red-baiter dramatically announced his conversion to socialism. He was especially impressed with Rauschenbusch's interpretation of Isaiah as an argument for the collective, as opposed to the individual, nature of evil. Small wonder, Hamilton noted, that those ministers who were "at ease in Zion" condemned Socialists as "calamity howlers" for attacking the pervasive evil produced by the capitalist system.[71]

The influence of Rauschenbusch's sophisticated brand of Christian socialism was actually quite limited in the Southwest. The violent rhetoric and evangelistic style adopted by Stanley Clark and the radical Texas revivalists would have shocked such middle-

71. *Social Democrat* (Oklahoma City), March 12, 1913; *Rebel* (Hallettsville, Tex.), September 9, 1911. A year earlier a sheriff was needed to restore order when W. L. Thurman, a Socialist lecturer, took on the Reverend Hamilton in a series of four debates in the latter's hometown of Crowell, Texas. Socialist observers accused Hamilton of shouting "vile epithets" at Thurman. *Appeal to Reason* (Girard, Kan.), April 30, 1910.

class ministers from Massachusetts as W. D. P. Bliss, Franklin M. Sprague, and Washington Gladden, who preached a more genteel social gospel. Christian socialism in the Southwest was closer to the crusading, communitarianism of midwesterner George D. Herron. However, Texas Reds like Stanley Clark and M. A. Smith were less likely to make the careful distinction between class consciousness and "class hatred" that characterized Herron's sermons.[72] There were a few popular preachers in the southwestern movement (notably Thomas Woodrow, a Kansas-based Unitarian-Universalist) who shared Herron's liberal, intellectual approach to the Bible, but most radical revivalists adopted a more emotional form of biblical fundamentalism that resembled the "primitive" approach of holiness sects like the Campbellites. Some Methodists like M. A. Smith, Campbellites like W. S. Noble, and Pentecostals like the Reverend Ham converted to Texas socialism from the holiness wing of revivalism.

When G. G. Hamilton went over to the enemy, he created a Socialist propaganda sensation throughout the Red River valley. The *Rebel* distributed bundles of Hamilton's conversion speech, along with a class analysis of the heretic's hometown in which the former Methodist preacher of Crowell, Texas, revealed an "inter-locking" circle including corrupt courthouse politicians, absentee landlords, parasitic credit merchants, and the elders of the Methodist church. Hamilton then drew a parallel between the way he and his Socialist comrades were treated by the local ruling class and the way in which "holiness" preachers were treated by the established denominations. After being expelled by the Methodists in his Crowell congregation, Hamilton reported that when he was turned away from

72. See Howard H. Quint, *The Forging of American Socialism* (Columbia: University of South Carolina Press, 1953), 103–14. Also see James Dombrowski, *The Early Days of Christian Socialism in America* (New York: Columbia University Press, 1936). The Reverend Thomas Woodrow, a rather exceptional Unitarian-Universalist, did attempt to bring the northern Christian Socialist Fellowship to the Southwest, but without much success. See *Rebel* (Hallettsville, Tex.), April 13, 1912, and *Social Democrat* (Oklahoma City), July 16, 1913. *Woodrow's Monthly*, published in Hobart, Oklahoma, outlined a sophisticated approach to Christian socialism. Also see clippings in Woodrow's Scrapbooks, Socialist Party Collection, University of Oklahoma.

the Methodist church at Ranger, he was readily accepted as a lecturer in the local Church of Christ.[73]

This Campbellite church, which traced its origins to the "religious rednecks" who preached the holiness gospel in established Methodist churches, had split the Disciples of Christ in 1906 over the question of organ music and other forms of modernism that conflicted with the values of primitive Wesleyanism. One historian of the Campbellites explains that this split simply resulted from a growing class conflict between the prosperous, bourgeois Disciples (largely a church of the city and county seat towns) and the poor, rural members of the Christian church who resented the "aristocratic prejudices" and liturgical liberalism of their social betters. The rural Campbellite denomination was certainly a "church of the disinherited" with a class-conscious membership that was deeply disturbed by the materialism and hypocrisy it saw in more established churches. But the clergy of the Christian church was very conservative on both religious and economic questions. In fact, the Texas Church of Christ sponsored the tour of an effective anti-Socialist preacher named W. F. Lemons.[74] The radicalism of its rural preachers was directed almost entirely at rival Methodists and Disciples, not at the ruling class in general. Furthermore, the millennial quality that had characterized the early Campbellite movement had declined as the holiness sect became a poor but, nonetheless, established church. The Church of Christ converted many poor tenant farmers throughout the Southwest, and it undoubtedly contained more Socialists than the more prosperous churches of the Disciples and the Methodists, but the Campbellites' religious doctrines were not necessarily responsible for these conversions; the church just happened to be composed largely of poor people. For the same reason, the southern Baptists, who preached

73. *Rebel* (Hallettsville, Tex.), September 23, 1911.
74. D. C. Harrell, Jr., "Sectional Origins of the Churches of Christ," *Journal of Southern History*, XXX (1964), 273, 277. Also see H. Richard Niehbur, *The Social Sources of Denominationalism* (New York: Henry Holt, 1929), 30; A. W. Ricker, *The Evils of Capitalism: A Reply to W. F. Lemons' Book "The Evils of Socialism,"* National Rip-Saw Series, No. 10 (St. Louis: Rip-Saw Publishing, 1912).

a very conservative form of fundamentalism, probably included more Socialists within their far-flung rural congregations than did the town-centered Presbyterians.[75]

After the turn of the century, religious radicalism passed from the Campbellites to the Pentecostals. This new holiness sect came to the Southwest to revive the sagging spirit of primitive Wesleyanism and to attack the spiritual hypocrisy and moral lethargy of the established denominations, including the Churches of Christ. The radical asceticism and hopeful postmillennialism of the Pentecostals resembled the more secular gospel preached by propagators of socialism.[76] Indeed, there seemed to be some connection between these holiness sects and the early Socialist cadres. In 1905 Eugene Debs actually spoke in a holiness tabernacle in southern Oklahoma. A few years later, after the Pentecostals had gained many new members in the Southwest (especially during the hard times of 1907), a Socialist organizer reported that he had founded a local among the tenant farmers around Romney, Texas, and left "a holiness preacher in charge to keep them right." He concluded by stating that "holiness people make good Socialists."[77]

The enemies of socialism certainly saw a connection between economic and religious radicalism. And in truth, in many areas of the cotton country tenant farmers seemed to attend the revivals of both the Pentecostals and the Socialists. A red-baiting newspaper editor in Hollis, Oklahoma, the scene of the Reverend Hamilton's dramatic conversion, boldly equated the two movements, putting local Socialists in that "changeable class" of people who, in their "child-like simplicity, took up one enthusiasm after another." After leaving the Socialist party, they would probably "join

75. *Appeal to Reason* (Girard, Kan.), July 9, 1910; *Rebel* (Hallettsville, Tex.), June 6, 1914. On the conservatism of the Baptists, see Rufus B. Spain, *At Ease in Zion: Social History of Southern Baptists, 1865–1900* (Nashville, Tenn.: Vanderbilt University Press, 1967).

76. Nils Bloch-Howell, *The Pentecostal Movement* (Oslo, Norway: Universitets Character, 1964), 46–47, 154–55.

77. *Independent Farmer* (Durant, Ind. Terr.), March 11, 1905; *Appeal to Reason* (Girard, Kan.), January 29, 1910.

up with the Holy Rollers," he concluded, adopting the pejorative term applied to the Pentecostals.[78]

In the early 1900s the new holiness sects of the Southwest clearly represented the primitive Christianity of the oppressed. The holiness movement was a "radical opponent" of materialism and modernism in the established churches, and in that sense it was a product of the same kind of class consciousness that led poor people to socialism. The sects were led by itinerant revivalists who were, like Preacher Casey in *The Grapes of Wrath*, free to preach a social gospel that called for radical political action. Still, Pentecostal preachers of Casey's kind were probably few and far between in the early 1900s. Their postmillennialism and radical hatred for middle-class materialism resembled that of the radical political revivalists, but they were undoubtedly appalled by the Socialists' modern belief in science and their secular approach to the gospels. The Pentecostals did preach a "chiliasm of despair" that appealed to the poor, but this other worldly quietism differed from the hopeful millennialism and dedicated activism of the radical revivalists who acted very much in and of the world.[79]

In any case, the Pentecostal movement in the Southwest was not large enough before World War I to contribute to the growth of any political party. The region was fertile ground for holiness preachers in the early 1900s, but in 1911 the Pentecostals could only claim a few thousand real disciples in the area, and many of them were in the black ghettoes of Houston and other cities where the Socialist party had little influence.[80]

78. Hollis (Okla.) *Post-Herald*, July 11, 1912. On the term "Holy Rollers" see Bloch-Howell, *Pentecostal Movement*, 1. For evidence that holiness revivals occurred in the rural precincts where the Socialist party was strong, see *Marshall County News-Democrat* (Madill, Okla.), August 6, 1909.

79. Bloch-Howell, *Pentecostal Movement*, 11, 47, 154–55. For evidence of hostility to Socialists within a Texas holiness group, see the remarkable letter to T. A. Hickey from H. O. Sydow, a Pentecostal preacher who was punished for participating in the party. Sydow to Hickey, December 1, 1914, in Meitzen Exhibit No. 1, U.S. Commission on Public Relations, *Final Report and Testimony*, X, 9263–64.

80. Bloch-Howell, *Pentecostal Movement*, 57; for statistics on sect and church membership in the Southwest, see U.S. Bureau of the Census, *Religious Bodies, 1906* (Washington, D.C.: Government Printing Office, 1910),

Most of the religiously committed people in the Socialist party were probably not formally attached to any form of organized religion. They were often raised in one of the established churches and occasionally attended a holiness revival or one of the more sedate ecumenical gatherings sponsored by the Methodists or Baptists, but they were distanced, socially and geographically, from the town congregations controlled by businessmen, professionals, and well-to-do farmers. The rural poor often resented the modern forms of religion practiced in these established churches, and they hated the blatant form of discrimination they suffered there. According to one researcher, southwestern country churches had declined because class distinctions had divided rural people from wealthier townspeople and had created a "very lamentable state of social feeling" between them. Church attendance dropped markedly among tenants because the "preacher in town . . . associated with merchants . . . bankers and landlords" whom the renter somehow thought of as being different from himself.[81]

Although protestantism did tighten its hold on southerners in the early twentieth century, "a certain amount of frontier indifference to organized religion still prevailed" in Texas and Oklahoma. This indifference was accentuated by prevalence of conservative Baptist and Methodist churches in this period.[82] The revivalism of the Campbellites had died out in the nineteenth century and the holiness sects did not gain a widespread following until the 1920s. During the interval, class conflict often transformed rural indifference toward established denominations into real hostility.

The Socialist party recruited its dirt-farmer membership largely from these alienated children of the country church who were searching for something the churches and sects no longer provided: they were looking forward to salvation in an earthly millennium that they could help create. They still thought in a traditional Christian manner and for most of them biblical socialism

---

Pt. I, 293, 348–49, 357–64, and *Religious Bodies, 1916* (Washington, D.C.: Government Printing Office, 1920), Pt. I, 240–41, 299–301, 311–18.

81. Warren H. Wilson, "Social Life in the Country," *Annals of the American Academy of Social and Political Science*, XL (1912), 124–25.

82. Francis Butler Simkins, *A History of the South* (New York: Knopf, 1953), 411.

made much more sense than dialectical materialism. But they had broken with organized religion, decisively if not irrevocably, and they were searching for a new form of revivalism. As Tom Hickey pointed out in 1914, many rural folk were shifting away from "old time religion," from the camp meetings at which Baptists argued about the correct form of immersion and Campbellites fought about the propriety of organ music. For many years these revivals had inspired weary farmers after the crops were laid by, but now a change was coming over the people. "They are as religious as their fathers and mothers," Hickey wrote, "but they are not going to the camp meetings as of yore." Religious revivals no longer seemed to revive the faithful because the burden of life and labor on the farm had created a sense of despair from which there was no escape, a sense of anger for which there was no outlet. As a result, Hickey reported, the rural poor were beginning to question the "natural order of things," and they were beginning to turn to a new form of radical revivalism which involved debates over the land question rather than the questions of immersion and organ music.[83]

The ebullient editor of the *Rebel* was of course indulging in some wishful thinking. There were still plenty of Socialists who attended both holiness revivals and party picnics and there were still hundreds of thousands of poor Protestants in the Southwest who endured their suffering as part of the "natural order of things."[84] But there was, in reality, widespread disaffection from the established churches. Revivalism was on the wane. And most significantly, in the early 1910s, the Socialist party's summer camp meetings were drawing more people than either the holiness revivals or the ecumenical conclaves of the established churches. Tom Hickey was right. Times were changing.

83. *Rebel* (Hallettsville, Tex.), November 7, 1914. See also G. E. Etherton, "Why Revivals No Longer Revive," *International Socialist Review*, VI (1906), 687–88.

84. Letters to the editor of the *Rebel* revealed that the chief objection Socialist propagandists faced was that socialism was irreligious. C. E. Lawless to editor, and W. D. Samples to editor, in *Rebel* (Hallettsville, Tex.), July 12 and 22, 1911. One comrade wrote that a farmer he met, a steward of the Christian church, opposed socialism because it allegedly allowed a man to have twenty-five wives if he could take care of them!

V

Industrial Unions and the Socialist Party, 1910-1912: The Proletarian Perspective

TIMES WERE CHANGING in the countryside, and they were changing even more in the Southwest's booming cities and industrial towns. Major railroads crisscrossed the region, served by big yards and maintenance shops on the outskirts of cities like Little Rock, Ft. Worth, Texarkana, and McAlester, Oklahoma. Many of the southwestern coal mines were owned by the railroad corporations. By 1910 about thirty thousand miners toiled in the rich bituminous fields of the old Indian Territory, Sebastian County, Arkansas, north central Texas, and southeastern Kansas, and nearly all of them belonged to the United Mine Workers union (UMW) which had won a closed shop after its "long strike" ended in 1903. As we have seen, these miners were among the earliest supporters of the Socialist party, having been exposed to socialism through many of the strong locals established in the coal camps during the early 1900s. Militant miners, especially in Oklahoma and Arkansas, continued to play an important role in the party during the early 1910s.

A much larger work force of sixty-three thousand men labored in the logging camps and sawmills of the rich yellow pine belt in western Louisiana and East Texas. The timber workers conducted a number of spontaneous strikes in the early 1900s, but they did not form an industrial union until 1910, being handicapped by the lack of a national union like the UMW, by the lumber barons totalitarian control of their communities, and by the racial tensions

176

in a work force evenly divided between blacks and whites. Nonetheless, when industrial unionism did come to the piney woods, it took the revolutionary form advocated by the Industrial Workers of the World (IWW) and it rapidly opened timber workers to the appeals of socialism. The IWW not only created the strongest interracial union in the Southwest, it introduced a militant proletarian perspective into the Socialist parties of Louisiana and Texas at a time when they were dominated by neo-Populists and craft unionists who favored a segregated, "evolutionary" form of party organization.

SOCIALISM AND INDUSTRIAL UNIONISM

During the "age of industrial violence" between 1910 and 1915, industrial unionism assumed a radical and at times revolutionary posture because organizations like the UMW and the IWW engaged the strongest capitalist corporations in violent struggles. Class conflict in the Rocky Mountain mining states had rapidly produced a class-conscious ideology among the miners which contained both syndicalist and socialistic tendencies. In the West, the syndicalist tendency came to predominate, leading to the formation of the IWW. In the Southwest, the popularity and organizational ability of the Socialists allowed the socialistic tendency to predominate, even when the IWW was involved, as in the case of the timber workers' struggle.

Most Socialists in the region held to the party line and opposed the Wobblies' dual unionism and open advocacy of sabotage. Instead, they turned to the UMW (the AFL's largest affiliate) as a model union that allowed Socialists to "bore from within" the established labor movement. This position seemed to be vindicated between 1906 and 1914 when Socialist miners acceded to the leadership of both southwestern UMW districts. As John Laslett explains, the influence of Anglo-American miners with long experience as political activists disposed the midwestern UMW toward political action more strongly than the Western Federation of Miners was disposed, the latter having faced more violent resistance from employers who controlled all the important forms of political power.[1] For the midwestern miners, who had gained considerable influence through the old parties, and for the southwestern miners, who had strongly pressured the Populists in Kansas and the progressive Democrats in Oklahoma, political action could be combined effectively with direct action. Since the national UMW convention of 1909 endorsed a demand for the collective ownership and democratic management of the means of production, miners were drawn more and more to the Socialist party as the organization that most consistently claimed to defend their interests. Furthermore, the UMW's hard-fought struggle for industrial unionism created in the ranks a popular sentiment for Socialist pioneers of the "one big union" idea, notably Eugene Debs and Mother Jones, whose influence upon the southwestern miners has already been noted. As Jon Amsden and Stephen Brier argue, the creation of the United Mine Workers in the 1890s was the result of increasingly massive strikes that reflected growing solidarity between the skilled miners and other unskilled workers; in other words, the growth of the UMW was made possible by the absence of exclusive craft-union consciousness and the presence of inclusive industrial-union consciousness. Although industrial unionism did not always produce socialism, the southwestern coal miners' bitter struggle for recognition and better conditions clearly created a strong solidarity and anticapitalist proclivity which naturally benefited Socialist parties. The Socialists actually depended upon the strength of the UMW to build their party in the coal fields. As James Weinstein argues, the Debsians "saw their function in relation to unions not primarily as organizers—though Socialists were instrumental in organizing many unions—but as supporters of the existing unions." Thus, "the basis of Socialist strength within the unions was the party's public presence outside the unions, its visible intention to take power in society at large."[2]

    1. John Laslett, *Labor and the Left* (New York: Basic Books, 1970), 191–93, 241–51.
    2. Jon Amsden and Stephen Brier, "Coal Miners on Strike: The Transformation of Strike Demands and the Formation of a National Union," *Journal of Inter-Disciplinary History*, VII (1977), 583–616; James Weinstein, *Ambigu-*

In the period between 1905 and 1915 when several Socialist miners were elected not only to union offices, but to public offices, including the post of Kansas state mining inspector, the political promise of the Cooperative Commonwealth seemed very attractive to many miners, especially when progressive Democrats failed to enact promised reforms. However, as Robert Hoxie observed in 1911, the miners seemed to practice a more class-conscious form of socialism than the skilled workers who had elected the party to office in cities like Milwaukee. Although the Socialist party gained some influence among the AFL craft unions in places like Oklahoma City, Dallas, and New Orleans, socialism failed to compete effectively with the local Democratic machines that controlled the AFL. Socialism also failed to present itself as more than a politically radical form of trade unionism. "Boring from within" the "pure and simple" city craft unions limited the scope of Socialist politics in those unions far more than it did in the mine fields where collective ownership of the mines was a real issue (endorsed by the workers' national union) and where striking rather than bargaining still governed industrial relations. The difficult, protracted struggle to build an industrial union of all southwestern coal miners, black and white, native and foreign, created more than trade-union consciousness in the early twentieth century. It produced a sense of class solidarity and hostility to capitalist ownership that allowed Socialist party members to encourage Socialist consciousness among large numbers of mine workers.

This process occurred even more rapidly in the southern pine region where the class struggle was sharper and where the workers were more isolated from sources of outside support. In order to battle the powerful lumber trust, the Brotherhood of Timber Workers (BTW) had to extend industrial unionism to include not only blacks but housewives, tenant farmers, tradesmen, and other residents who sided with the workers against the companies. Be-

---

ous Legacy: The Left in American Politics (New York: New Viewpoints, 1975), 19. In other words, industrial unionism did not necessarily lead to "third party militancy" among miners. Laslett, *Labor and the Left*, 291. But in the Southwest the UMW created the kind of solidarity upon which Socialist organizers could build.

cause the BTW lacked the support of a national AFL union like the UMW and because it faced the hostility of Democratic officials at all levels of government, it tended to be more syndicalistic than socialistic. This was reinforced by the violent opposition the BTW faced—which called up a need for direct action more readily than for political action—and also by the disfranchised position of most timber workers, especially the blacks, who could not have voted even if they had wanted to. The syndicalism of the BTW seemed firmly cemented when it affiliated with the IWW in May of 1912, shortly before the Wobblies were expelled from the Socialist party for advocating sabotage.

This split affected the Louisiana Socialists more than their south-western comrades in other states because it exacerbated the conflict between the moderate Yellows who controlled the state head-quarters in New Orleans and favored segregated locals and "boring from within" the AFL, and the upland Reds who favored interracial solidarity and the dual unionism of the IWW. By the summer of 1912 the Reds had taken over the leadership of the party and were using its resources to aid the BTW. Like the Socialists in Oklahoma and Arkansas who supported the UMW and gained recruits from its locals, the Red Socialists in Louisiana actively supported the IWW and became more and more popular among the white timber workers who were able to vote. The Wobblies reciprocated by distinguishing their Red supporters in the party from the Yellow "labor fakirs" who attacked the IWW. When Bill Haywood came to the southern piney woods, he provocatively advocated sabotage, but did not reject political action. In fact, he warmly endorsed Eugene Debs's fourth presidential candidacy and praised the efforts made by Texas Socialist party comrades to form a renters' union based on the IWW industrial union model. Like all Wobblies, Haywood rejected the syndicalist label. The IWW favored Socialist political action in support of direct mass action through industrial unionism. To Haywood "industrial unionism was socialism with its working clothes on."

In fact, industrial unionism did continue to draw unskilled workers to socialism even after the IWW was purged from the Socialist

United Mine Workers of District 21 at their 1910 convention in McAlester, Oklahoma. Dan Hogan seated sixth from left, front row; Fred Holt, seventh from left; Peter Stewart, eighth from left.

Courtesy Wayne State University

Italian miners at play, Radley, Kansas, 1910.

Courtesy Pittsburg State University

Immigrant women and their children in front of company house at a coal camp in Crawford County, Kansas, 1902.

Courtesy Pittsburg State University

George D. Brewer speaking near Frontenac in Crawford County, Kansas, during his successful 1914 campaign for the state legislature.

Courtesy Wayne State University

Oscar Ameringer and the Hogan sisters (Freda on right) at the UMW convention in Ft. Smith, Arkansas, 1916.

Courtesy Freda Hogan Ameringer

Dan Hogan, as editor of the Huntington, Arkansas, *Herald*, 1904.

Courtesy Freda Hogan Ameringer

Mother Jones

Courtesy West Virginia University

Timber workers in Texas.

A. L. Emerson, president of the Brotherhood of Timber Workers.
Courtesy Wayne State University

William D. Haywood during his Idaho
trial in 1907.
Courtesy Library of Congress

One Big Union ideal symbolized on an
IWW poster.

Frank Little of the Agricultural Workers'
Organization, the prototypical Wobbly.
Courtesy Wayne State University

party. The Brotherhood of Timber Workers and the IWW also recruited some tenant farmers who "naturally sympathized" with the lumber workers, and the two groups provided a model of industrial unionism and a proletarian political perspective (of the "reddest hue") to Socialist renters who were organizing against the landlords and usurers of the cotton country. In contrast to the influence the Socialist party gained through class-conscious industrial unionism in the coal and lumber industries, the party's record of "boring from within" the city AFL craft unions seemed dismal.

The Socialist party waged its best urban campaign in Oklahoma City, where Oscar Ameringer devoted his *Pioneer* to effectively opposing the May, 1910, "good government" charter reform designed to eliminate ward representation. He also publicized the party's striking mayoral victory in Milwaukee and vowed to "Milwaukeeize" Oklahoma City. The Socialist party "made itself felt directly" in the charter reform's narrow defeat and in the actions of the Oklahoma Federation of Labor, whose representatives branded William Murray, the progressive candidate for the Democratic gubernatorial nomination, an "enemy of the masses" and later endorsed several radical resolutions introduced by Socialists. In the fall of 1910 the Socialist ticket headed by Tad Cumbie and John Wills polled 900 votes in Oklahoma County, a substantial increase of 400 over Debs's 1908 total, but still less than 8 percent of the total vote.[3]

In February, 1911, a violent strike of streetcar men was broken by armed deputies, largely businessmen, who were appointed by Democratic officials. Ameringer's *Pioneer* made the most of this situation, and the Socialists seemed to be winning more workers away from the incumbent party. But, as Garin Burbank shows, the Oklahoma Socialist party was a long way from "Milwaukeeizing"

3. *Oklahoma Pioneer* (Oklahoma City), May 11, September 3, 1910, January 14, 1911; *Daily Oklahoman* (Oklahoma City), May 6–11, April 13, 1910; *Oklahoma Labor Unit* (Oklahoma City), May 28, July 23, 1910. Ameringer and the Socialists analyzed the probusiness basis of municipal reform in terms very similar to those adopted by contemporary historians. See James Weinstein, "Organized Business and the Commissioner and Manager Movements," *Journal of Southern History*, XXVII (1962).

the new state capital. In fact, in March of 1911 a new charter installing the commission form of government was enacted through popular referendum, as working-class turnout declined and middle-class turnout surged, due to a well-coordinated business campaign for "good government." Nevertheless, the Socialists were encouraged with their progress, especially after the conversion of J. Luther Langston, secretary-treasurer of the Oklahoma Federation of Labor, who denounced the new governor, Cruce, for threatening to call out the militia against the striking streetcar workers. Langston also denounced both old parties and called upon workers to join the party of their class. This "sensational event," coupled with the workers' growing opposition to the Democrats, encouraged Oscar Ameringer to run for mayor of Oklahoma City in April, 1911. He polled 1,876 votes (23 percent) in a three-way race with two businessmen; he carried the working-class eighth ward with 47 percent but won only 8 percent in the "silk stocking" seventh ward. His overall vote correlated strongly with the vote cast a year earlier in opposition to the commission form of government.[4]

The Socialists also made noticeable gains in other cities during the spring elections of 1911, notably in McAlester, Oklahoma, and in the Texas towns of Texarkana, Dennison, and Houston where transport workers had conducted violent strikes that year. The violence produced by the 1911 Harriman railroad strike, which gave the Socialist party added votes in Dennison, also produced a crowd of thirty-five hundred to hear Debs speak in strike-torn New Orleans. In the same year the moderate Socialists who controlled the port city local won an endorsement for their policies from the city's Central Trades Council and its official newspaper, but their candidates still ran poorly in municipal elections. The Socialists held about 400 votes in Dallas where the city's labor council maintained its endorsement of George Clifton Edwards'

4. *Oklahoma Labor Unit* (Oklahoma City), April 8, 1911; *Oklahoma Pioneer* (Oklahoma City), April 18, 22, May 6, 20, 1911; *Daily Oklahoman* (Oklahoma City), April 1, 17, May 10, 1911. For a fuller account, see Garin Burbank, "Socialism in an Oklahoma Boom Town: 'Milwaukeeizing' Oklahoma City," in Bruce Stave (ed.), *Socialism and the Cities* (Port Washington, N.Y.: Kennikat, 1975), 99–115.

Socialist weekly, the *Laborer*, and they made quite substantial gains in nearby Ft. Worth where a Socialist-labor ticket polled 1,207 votes. Earlier in 1911 Texas Socialists from these major cities made a bold but unsuccessful effort to "take over" the state labor federation's newspaper. But at this point, although the party was still growing in rural areas and in the mill and mining towns, socialism had reached its highwater mark in the cities.[5]

The Oklahoma Socialists lost prestige in the labor federation when Luther Langston was removed from office for "malfeasance," and they overplayed their hand late in 1911 by packing a meeting of the Oklahoma City Labor Council and withdrawing support for the pro-Gompers paper, the *Labor Unit*. But the Socialist party's support had already been eroded. The collapse of the building boom in the capital city caused the exodus of construction workers who had been some of the party's strongest supporters. The Carpenters' Union, which claimed 1,200 dues-paying members in 1911, a good percent of them Socialists, had barely 150 members in mid-1913. "The mechanic has to follow his job," said one discouraged Socialist worker. The party's bold effort to "Milwaukeeize" Oklahoma City had failed because, as Burbank points out, this southwestern boomtown with its relatively small and poorly organized, native American work force was not at all like Milwaukee with its large, strongly unionized, immigrant working class. Even before the building boom declined, the craft union leaders in Oklahoma City were not inclined to follow Luther Langston into the Socialist party. They were not only content to follow Samuel Gompers' program of "bread and butter" unionism, they were willing to identify with the values of a business class that proved by 1912 to be much stronger and better organized than the working

5. *Appeal to Reason* (Girard, Kan.), April 15, May 20, 1911; Dallas *Morning News*, April 15, 1911; *Daily Oklahoman* (Oklahoma City), October 4, 6, 1911; *Arkansas Gazette* (Little Rock), November 5, 6, 1911; *Rebel* (Hallettsville, Tex.), June 8, 1911; Hardy to Thompson, June 10, 1911, in Socialist Party Papers, Perkins Library, Duke University; J. C. Kennedy, "Socialistic Tendencies in American Trade Unions," *International Socialist Review*, VIII (1907), 337. Also Dallas *Laborer*, April 3, 1909, May 12, 1910; C. W. Woodson to John L. Sullivan, February 2, 1911, in Labor Movement Collection, Barker Library, University of Texas, Austin.

class. The rest of the Socialist movement found little proletarian inspiration in the political activity of trade unionists in the southwestern cities.[6]

The Socialist party won more substantial and lasting support in industrial unions that recruited across lines of race, skill, and nationality. These larger unions, especially of miners and timber workers, also influenced the movement as a whole because they actively sought the support of farmers and small-town merchants. Community support, including that of women and blacks, could not be ignored in the struggles workers waged against giant corporations in isolated industrial towns. Unlike the city craft unions which remained firmly in the hands of Democrats, the industrial unions elected militant leaders who played an important role in the growth of the Socialist movement. By 1912 the United Mine Workers and the Brotherhood of Timber Workers, claiming a combined membership of forty thousand workers in the region, were controlled by Red Socialist leaders who were anxious to spread the influence of proletarian radicalism as broadly as possible through the region. In most cases this meant mobilizing support from farmers and others through the Socialist party, and in the case of the BTW, it involved actually recruiting farmers, working-class housewives, and merchants as union members.

The Knights of Labor originally brought militant industrial unionism to the Southwest in the 1880s when they conducted two major interracial strikes against Jay Gould's railroads and organized two big walkouts of black field hands in the Louisiana "sugar bowl" and the Arkansas cotton country. After winning a major victory against Gould in 1885, the Knights lost the 1886 rematch, and the strikes of the black plantation workers were brutally repressed.[7] The Knights of Labor declined rapidly in the Southwest after these defeats, but the order remained strong enough in the coal camps of the Indian Territory to lead a militant strike against

6. *Oklahoma Pioneer* (Oklahoma City), July 9, 1913; Burbank, "Socialism in an Oklahoma Boom Town," 101, 103, 109.
7. See Ruth A. Allen, *The Great Southwest Strike* (Austin: University of Texas Press, 1942); and Sidney Kessler, "The Negro in Labor Strikes," *Midwest Journal*, VI (1954), 16–18, 22–34.

the depression wage cuts that were imposed in 1894. The coal companies evicted several hundred miners from their houses and actually deported them from the Territory, but the workers returned to close down most of the mines including those operated by black "scabs," some of whom were induced to join the union. This militant 1894 strike overlapped with the nationwide railroad boycott organized by Debs's American Railway Union during the Pullman strike. In Oklahoma's Cherokee Strip where "the most alarming forms of terrorism and sabotage" hit the railroads, farmers showed their support for industrial unionism by protesting against the use of federal troops in the Territory. Meanwhile just to the north, the Populist governor of Kansas, Lorenzo Lewelling, supported Debs and the American Railway Union and denounced President Cleveland and the railroads. The governor also attacked the coal companies for using armed force to break a miners' strike organized by the Knights in Crawford and Cherokee counties. Lewelling, who later became a Socialist, denied "military aid to corporations engaged in an armed revolt against the law of the state."[8]

Although the Knights of Labor won their strikes in the Kansas and Oklahoma coal fields in 1894, the old order died out to be replaced by the young United Mine Workers. The UMW advanced industrial unionism in the coal fields by continuing to recruit blacks (including the scabs brought in during the 1898–1899 strikes) and by integrating new immigrant miners into the locals.[9] However, the American Railway Union did not advance the interracial industrial unionism practiced by the Knights in Martin Irons' era. When the Railway Union was crushed by federal action in 1894, industrial un-

8. Gene Aldrich, "A History of the Coal Mining Industry in Oklahoma to 1907" (Ph.D. dissertation, University of Oklahoma, 1952), 70–112; Federal Writers' Project, W.P.A., *Labor History of Oklahoma* (Oklahoma City: Van Horn, 1939), 6–13; Almont Lindsey, *The Pullman Strike* (Chicago: University of Chicago Press, 1964), 258. Lewelling quote in Norman Pollack, *The Populist Response to Industrial America* (Cambridge, Mass.: Harvard University Press, 1962), 56. On Lewelling's socialism see O. Gene Clanton, *Kansas Populism* (Lawrence: University of Kansas Press, 1969), 223–24.

9. Ft. Smith (Ark.) *Elevator*, July 14, 1899; Aldrich, "Coal Mining Industry in Oklahoma," 70–75, 86, 91, 219. Also see Herbert Gutman, "The Negro and the U.M.W.," in Julius Jacobsen (ed.), *The Negro and the American Labor Movement* (Garden City, N.Y.: Anchor, 1968), 49–127.

ionism died on the railroads. The four remaining railroad "brotherhoods" practiced the exclusionary "pure and simple" unionism common to most AFL craft unions of the time. They tried to purge radicals from their ranks, but Socialists were able to win control of the machinists' and small switchmen's union in the early 1900s. Southwestern socialism gained significant support from railroad workers in big cities like Little Rock and Ft. Worth, in medium-sized rail centers like Dennison and Longview, Texas, and in smaller maintenance areas like Mena and Van Buren, Arkansas. Many of these workers were old Knights and American Railway Union men recruited into the Socialist movement by Martin Irons and Gene Debs around the turn of the century. Others were more recent converts who belonged to the Socialist-led machinists' and switchmen's unions. And there were even a few silent Socialists in the four conservative railroad brotherhoods.[10] But the absence of class-conscious industrial unionism among southwestern railroad workers (who were more numerous than any other group of wage earners) prevented the Socialists from winning the kind of support among them that they achieved among coal miners and lumber workers.

In 1911 a bitter strike against the Harriman system in the Southwest and South Central states gave the Socialist party an opportunity to extend its influence among railroad laborers. The strike began when machinists and other shopmen in the Midwest struck against a number of abuses, including the introduction of scientific management. The leading union involved, the International Association of Machinists, had just elected a Socialist slate of officers in 1911. Further, the striking shopmen were dissatisfied with the traditional craft unionism that divided workers in time of trouble, and so they formed a "system federation" to speak for machinists and other shopmen who were not in the big four brotherhoods— the conservative aristocracy of railroad labor. Harriman's giant Illinois Central system refused to negotiate with the new federa-

10. Eugene Debs, "Railroad Employees and Socialism," *International Socialist Review*, IX (1908), 241–48. On socialism in the machinists' union, see Laslett, *Labor and the Left*, 144–81.

tion, and this precipitated a violent strike that raged through the Mississippi valley for four years.[11]

Bloody conflict flared in New Orleans and in Houston, Dennison, and El Paso. The *Rebel* supported angry workers by attacking the rather moderate leadership of the strike, which included a number of Socialists who opposed violent direct action. It also sponsored a Texas tour for the more militant Socialist president of the switch-men's union and allied itself with Carl Person, a left-wing Socialist from Illinois, who was leading a rank-and-file insurgency against the International Association of Machinists leadership. In fact, Hickey and Covington Hall, editor of the IWW *Lumberjack*, joined with Person to form a "Rebel Press" association that attacked bureaucratic centralization in the AFL and the IWW. In addition to the decentralizer papers edited by Hickey and Hall and Person's militant *Strike Bulletin*, the association included the influential left-wing *International Socialist Review* and the *Argus Star* published by Red Socialists close to the UMW in West Virginia. The association was rather informal, however, and it devoted most of its efforts to defending Person, who had killed a company gunman. He was finally acquitted after a nationwide defense campaign sponsored by a number of left groups, including the Syndicalist League of North America, led by William Z. Foster and the Browder brothers in Kansas City, a "storm center" during the Harriman strike. Interestingly enough, the syndicalist proponents in southwestern socialism represented by Hickey and Hall never made significant contact with the League. Indeed, the syndicalism of the militant Socialists in Texas and Louisiana seemed clearer in retrospect than it did in 1911, for at that point, Hickey and Hall were still committed to working for industrial unionism within the Socialist party, still believing that direct action in the unions and political action through the party could be combined.[12]

11. See David Montgomery, "The 'New Unionism' and the Transformation of Workers' Consciousness in America, 1909–1922," *Journal of Social History*, VII (1974), 523.

12. *Ibid.*, 523–24; *Daily Oklahoman* (Oklahoma City), October 4, 6, 1911; *Solidarity* (New Castle, Pa.), October 14, 1911; *Rebel* (Hallettsville, Tex.), October 14, 1911, March 8, 1912; U.S. Commission on Industrial Relations,

In the thick of the struggle, the *Rebel* expressed its discontent
with the AFL craft union leadership by calling for a new industrial
union, modeled after Debs's American Railway Union, which would
include every railroad worker from the Pullman conductor on
down to the "humble section hand." Since Pullman conductors
rather than porters were mentioned, it was clear that this was not
destined to be the "one big union" to advance beyond the American Railway Union and include black railroad workers. In any case,
this rather rhetorical call for a return to industrial unionism failed
to appeal to the striking Harriman workers. Most of them, including the Socialist militants, preferred the "federated system" that
allowed for some craft autonomy (without crippling craft divisions) and created the possibility of unified strike action. As David
Montgomery argues, neither wing of the Socialist party (the moderates who believed in working within AFL unions like the International Association of Machinists nor the militants who favored
the IWW's dual unionism) understood the significance of the
"new unionism" springing up in the ranks during "worker control" struggles such as the one fought against the Harriman lines
between 1911 and 1914.[13]

Unable to organize another industrial union for all workers, the
Texas Socialists bravely set out to organize the "humble section
hand." This effort to recruit unskilled trackmen was doomed from
the start. Scattered in groups of ten or fifteen across the length
and breadth of the state, these racially and ethnically divided construction and repair gangs simply could not be organized with the
resources available to the Socialists. Hickey and other party leaders
thought they could duplicate the success of the Renters' Union in
this dubiously entitled "industrial union," but when the Trackmen
Union's founder and leading organizer, George Andrews, was jailed
on a trumped-up charge, the effort collapsed.[14] Industrial unionism

---

Final Report and Testimony (Washington, D.C.: Government Printing Office,
1916), 9950–51. Also see Covington Hall, "Labor Struggles in the Deep South"
(Typescript in Howard-Tilton Library, Tulane University), 224–30, on the
syndicalist tendencies in southwestern radicalism.

13. *Rebel* (Hallettsville, Tex.), March 8, 1912; Montgomery, "The 'New
Unionism'," 510–11, 521–24.

14. The Socialist Trackmen's Union did, however, attempt to organize

capable of bringing all railroad workers into "one big union" had suffered a fatal blow when Martin Irons and his Knights of Labor lost the Great Southwestern Strike in 1886. It had recovered briefly in 1894 when Debs's American Railway Union organized in Texas and other parts of the region. But by 1895 it was dead. It received its official funeral when Martin Irons was buried in Bruceville, Texas, in 1900, shortly after the old Knight had completed a Socialist speaking tour with his younger admirer, Gene Debs.[15] The Texas Socialist party's brief effort to resurrect industrial unionism for the unskilled railroaders was hardly more than an apparition.

SOCIALISM AND THE SOUTHWESTERN COAL MINERS

The Socialist party gained a strong foothold in the Southwest's most powerful labor organization, the United Mine Workers of America. Party locals developed almost spontaneously in many coal camps during the "long strike" that ended in 1903. John Chase, Gene Debs, Mother Jones, and early Socialist party organizers won their first loyal supporters from these coal miners whose struggles went back past the UMW organizing drive to the Knights' big strike of 1894 and, in some cases, back to the Molly Maguire mine wars of Pennsylvania and the Illinois battles of the 1870s. After the "long strike" the UMW in the Southwest in two years increased its membership from 1,745 in 1902 to 11,492. In 1908 District 21 (eastern Oklahoma, western Arkansas and north central Texas)

across racial lines, mainly because the gangs were mixed and included Mexican and Chinese workers and new immigrants from Italy, Poland, and Greece, as well as older Irish and American workers. In other words, like many industrial unions, this one simply had to organize all races in order to survive in an industry where workers were mixed. Like Father Thomas Hagerty, who tried to help organize Mexican railroad workers around the turn of the century, Andrews found that the brown workers were often more class conscious than the whites. *Rebel* (Hallettsville, Tex.), March 8, 23, 1912, June 28, April 19, 1913. On the militancy of Mexican workers in the Southwest see Juan Gómez-Quiñonez, "Chicano Labor Organizing, 1900–1920," *Aztlán*, III (1973), 13–49.

15. Interestingly, it was not until 1911 that southwestern labor commemorated Martin Irons' death. A monument, sponsored chiefly by Missouri railroad men and Arkansas miners, was erected at his grave in Bruceville, Texas, at that time. *Liberator* (Sedalia, Mo.), May 27, 1911.

claimed 16,005 members amounting to 87 percent of the work force. District 14 in southeastern Kansas increased its membership to over 9,000 (about 75 percent of the work force) under the militant leadership of Alex Howat, a Scotch Socialist who fought through the bitter Braidwood lockout during the Illinois mine wars. When District 21 of the UMW reached its peak in 1908, rank-and-file miners elected Socialists like Howat to replace Pete Hanraty's administration of Democratic party loyalists. Fred Holt, a Red from McAlester, Oklahoma, became secretary-treasurer of the district and Peter R. Stewart, a Socialist miner from Hartford, Arkansas, replaced Hanraty as president. Under the able administration of Stewart and Holt, which lasted over the next six years, the southwestern coal miners "gained in power and prestige."[16]

During these years Socialists often traveled through the Oklahoma coal fields speaking in opera houses and at encampments. They enjoyed a large following among the miners of District 21 who eagerly read the *Appeal* and the writings of Oscar Ameringer. In fact, during the early years party organizers used these coal camps as enclaves from which to recruit support tenants and dirt farmers who had been largely unorganized by the Populists.[17] Next to Mother Jones, Gene Debs continued to be the most popular speaker in southwestern coal communities. These two notorious agitators were the only Socialist speakers who could credibly criticize important UMW officials like John Mitchell. For example, on

16. *Report of the U.S. Coal Commission* (Washington, D.C.: Government Printing Office, 1922), Pt. III, 1052, 1387. On Howat, see Gary M. Fink (ed.), *Biographical Dictionary of American Labor Leaders* (Westport, Conn.: Greenwood, 1974), 164; on Stewart and Holt, see Frederick L. Ryan, *The Rehabilitation of Oklahoma Coal Mining Communities* (Norman: University of Oklahoma Press, 1935), 35. Also see Aldrich, "Coal Mining Industry in Oklahoma," *passim*; Stanley Clark, "Immigrants in the Choctaw Coal Industry," *Chronicles of Oklahoma*, XXXIII (1955–56), 440–55; and Oscar Ameringer, *If You Don't Weaken: The Autobiography of Oscar Ameringer* (New York: Henry Holt, 1940), 236, 240–42.

17. Ryan, *Oklahoma Coal Mining Communities*, 87. For a study of a similar relationship in Chile through which militant, class-conscious miners helped to radicalize the "inquilinos" or tenant farm workers in the surrounding countryside, see James Petras and Maurice Zeitlin, "Miners and Agrarian Radicalism," *American Sociological Review*, XXXII (1967), 578–86.

July 4, 1908, Debs received an enthusiastic response from a crowd of five thousand at Coalgate, Oklahoma, when he attacked Mitchell and Gompers for cooperating with big capitalists in the National Civic Federation.[18]

Socialism grew within the UMW on the national as well as district and local levels. In 1909 miner delegates to the union's national convention passed a Socialist party resolution favoring "the public ownership and democratic management of all those means of production and exchange that are collectively used." An Illinois party member, Frank Hayes, was elected international vice-president at the same time; he carried District 21 by a three-to-two margin as did his Illinois comrade J. H. Walker, who lost narrowly to a Mitchell supporter in the presidential contest. The Socialist candidates carried all but a few locals in Oklahoma and swept all the largest ones in Arkansas.[19]

The miners of District 21 remained militant even after the "long strike" ended, and mine operators in Oklahoma and Arkansas reported the highest number of working days lost on account of strikes between 1905 and 1914, the year Socialist leadership ended. When the UMW's contract with the Southwestern Coal Operators' Association expired in April, 1910, thirty thousand miners in Districts 21 and 14 launched a violent five-month strike that helped make union men more receptive to Socialist appeals. Near the strike's end terrible suffering and near starvation in some of the coal communities led to attacks on scabs and company property.[20]

Reminding their rural members that the UMW endorsed the party's demands, in 1909 Socialist officials made appeals to farm

18. *Appeal to Reason* (Girard, Kan.), July 8, 1908. See also Ray Ginger, *Eugene V. Debs: The Making of an American Radical* (New York: Colliers, 1966), 234–35, 287; Mary Field Parton (ed.), *Autobiography of Mother Jones* (Chicago: Charles Kerr, 1925), 56–62, 96–102.

19. *Appeal to Reason* (Girard, Kan.), February 6, 1909. See also Frank Hayes, "Why a Union Man Should Be a Socialist," *Industrial Democrat* (Oklahoma City), October 29, 1910. Also see *Proceedings of the Twentieth Annual Convention of the United Mine Workers of America, 1909* (2 vols.; Indianapolis: n.p., 1909), II, 1140–43, 1470.

20. *Report of U.S. Coal Commission*, Pt. I, 226–27; *Daily Oklahoman* (Oklahoma City), May 6, 9, August 14, 1910.

locals for contributions to a relief fund for the starving miners. Fred Holt, Socialist secretary-treasurer of District 21, told coal-town merchants to support the strikers, because if the corporations destroyed the UMW, as they just had in Alabama, the workers would become "peons" and the independent businessmen would be driven away.[21]

In September of 1910 Pete Stewart, whose leadership during the strike was widely praised, retired to South Texas to recover from exhaustion. His union had won a victory over the operators and his party made gains at the polls. The Socialist party polled over 1,000 votes in Oklahoma's two leading coal-producing counties, and one quarter of the vote in the coal town of Krebs, where it already controlled the municipal government. In the nearby city of McAlester, however, the party made a poor showing. In fact, its nemesis, Pete Hanraty, leader of the Catholic Democratic faction in the UMW, was elected mayor, the recent disfranchisement of black voters under the grandfather clause giving him a narrow margin of victory over his Republican opponent.[22] A comparison of the elections in these two Pittsburg County coal towns reveals a good deal about the strengths and weaknesses of socialism among the Oklahoma miners.

In 1911 Robert Hoxie cited the Socialist party victory in Krebs as an example of a more "class conscious type of socialism" than he had found in other cities like Milwaukee where the party won power. The UMW's leaders were experienced miners of "old English stock" who placed a good deal of emphasis on "ultimate Socialist ideals."[23] This older group of skilled miners undoubtedly

21. *Oklahoma Pioneer* (Oklahoma City), September 30, 1910; *Industrial Democrat* (Oklahoma City), August 20, 1910.
22. Harthshorne (Okla.) *Sun*, September 22, November 3, 1910; McAlester (Okla.) *News-Capital*, December 10, 1910; Aldrich, "Coal Mining Industry in Oklahoma," 28–33. Oliver Benson, *et al.*, *Oklahoma Votes, 1907–1962* (Norman: University of Oklahoma Press, 1964), 77. Local returns are from the Oklahoma State Election Board, Capitol Building, Oklahoma City.
23. Robert F. Hoxie, "The Rising Tide of Socialism," *Journal of Political Economy*, XIX (October, 1911), 618, 624. In an unpublished paper, David Montgomery argues that the "worker's control" practiced by skilled craftsmen like the iron puddlers was in fact "the American style of Socialism." Most workers imagined the Cooperative Commonwealth "simply as the

played an important role in Socialist politics at Krebs as well, but we should note that this town claimed the highest percentage of new immigrants in Oklahoma. In 1910 Krebs's population of roughly three thousand could be divided into three nearly equal parts: the native born, including a large percentage whose parents had emigrated from the British Isles; new immigrants, largely from southern Italy; and residents of mixed parentage (an unusually high proportion). Only about one hundred of the blacks who had originally come to Krebs as strikebreakers during the "long strike" remained. The town also claimed a notable colony of about 150 Syrians, largely merchants and peddlers, whose presence indicated that the miners had freed themselves from the monopoly of the company store.[24]

The new immigrants from Italy played an important role in UMW and Socialist party activity in Krebs, even though they were less experienced in union and partisan activity than the older British immigrants. In 1910 over three quarters of the 450 foreign-born males over the age of twenty-one (largely Italians) were disfranchised because they were not naturalized citizens. In the fall elections the Socialist party polled only 77 votes in Krebs, but

---

world governed by union meetings." (David Montgomery, "Trade Union Practice and the Origins of Syndicalist Theory," 1969, paper in his possession.) It is certainly true, as Carter Goodrich demonstrated in *The Miner's Freedom* (Boston: Marshall Jones, 1925), that skilled mine workers exercised an unusual degree of control in the pits. It is natural to assume that the skilled workers who enjoyed this informal control over the means of production might turn to socialism as a formal means of guaranteeing their rights. Given the leadership of skilled miners of English stock in the southwestern Socialist movement, this assumption is warranted. However, their vision of the Cooperative Commonwealth was not limited to a model of the world run by union meetings.

24. United States Immigration Commission, "The Bituminous Coal Industry in the Southwest," in *Immigrants in Industries* (2 vols.; Washington, D.C.: Government Printing Office, 1911), Vol. II, Pt. IV, pp. 19–20. Freda Hogan Ameringer later commented on the significance of the UMW's closed-shop victory for workers in small company-dominated towns like Krebs: "Before they had the Union, the miners all had these company houses which were very depressing to look at, just about as plain and unattractive as you could make them. Then as the Union was organized, these miners were able to build their own little cottages with vegetable gardens in the back yard and flowers in the front yard." Interview, June 21, 1974.

earlier in the year Frank Hayes, the Illinois Socialist, won 234 votes there in his successful race for the national UMW vice-presidency.[25] Clearly, disfranchised immigrant miners voted Socialist in this union election. At Krebs, the Italians seemed either active in Socialist politics or else rather uninvolved politically. In 1910 the United States Immigration Commission surveyed the town and reported that the southern Italian miners formed highly segregated neighborhoods, participated less in civic and union affairs than other groups, and resisted "Americanization" even into the second generation. It also revealed, however, that in certain Oklahoma localities like Krebs the Italian miners were "controlled by leaders who are advocates of radical political ideas"—leaders such as Mike Tasso, a Socialist miner who was elected town alderman.[26]

The voters of Krebs, native and foreign born, resented the disfranchisement of immigrants and opposed the restriction of black suffrage rights; they cast 68 percent of their votes against the grandfather clause in the 1910 referendum. The voters of neighboring McAlester acted differently; they recorded 64 percent of their votes *for* black disfranchisement in August and only 3 percent for the Socialist party in the November election that gave Democrat Pete Hanraty the mayoralty. This town differed in many ways from the smaller coal camp a few miles to the east. In 1910 McAlester was the largest city in southeastern Oklahoma, with a total population of twelve thousand, including three thousand blacks. Two thirds of its citizens were native born and those of foreign origin were largely older immigrants from the British Isles.[27] McAlester was an important railroad and marketing center for the surround-

25. Immigration Commission, "Bituminous Coal Industry in the Southwest," 105–107, 117–22. The author would like to thank Garin Burbank for tabulating this vote and the returns from the elections of several other coal towns. Returns in UMW election are from *Proceedings of the Twentieth Annual UMW Convention, 1909*, pp. 106–1124.

26. "Bituminous Coal Industry in the Southwest," *Immigrants in Industries*, 119–22.

27. McAlester (Okla.) *News-Capital*, April 8, 1914; Clark, "Immigrants in the Choctaw Coal Industry," 443; Aldrich, "Coal Mining Industry in Oklahoma," 28–33. (Returns are from Oklahoma State Election Board, Capitol Building, Oklahoma City).

ing coal and cotton fields of the region; it contained a powerful business-professional class and a prosperous group of merchants that commerced rather differently from the Syrians and poor white tenants who peddled their goods in the streets of Krebs.

McAlester was ethnically more homogeneous than Krebs, but it was divided more clearly by class. The smaller coal community contained only a tiny middle class; most of its citizens were miners or tradesmen who had worked in the pits. Furthermore, it was a traditional union stronghold. The Knights had organized one of their first assemblies at Krebs in 1884. Ten years later it became the center of resistance in the great depression coal strike, and it was also the scene of one of the worst mining disasters in Oklahoma history. The tragedy of 1892 snuffed out the lives of ninety-six miners and united the ethnically divided village more than did the sporadic efforts of the Knights.[28] In 1898 the UMW founded its first local there and by 1910 Krebs claimed three union locals with a total membership of 507. In McAlester, however, there was no history of union militancy or of community solidarity with the workers. It was a much larger town than Krebs, but it had only 264 UMW members in 1910, most of them old miners of Anglo-American descent.[29] The Socialist party appealed far more to the

28. The Socialists focused a great deal of attention on the mine-safety issue, because after the turn of the century Oklahoma still had one of the highest fatality rates in the nation (6.83 as compared to 4.30 for the nation, *Report of U.S. Coal Commission*, Pt. III, 1266). When six miners were killed in an explosion at Wilburton, where the Socialist party had one of its largest locals, the *Appeal* reported that five of the dead men were "red card members" and the sixth a sympathizer. "Thus," the paper editorialized, "the damnable system takes the lives of the best and most progressive of the working class," and still the world insisted on erecting monuments and alloting pensions to the "veterans of military wars" rather than to the "heroes and veterans of the great army of industry." *Appeal to Reason* (Girard, Kan.), April 16, 1910, May 20, 1911; *Oklahoma Pioneer* (Oklahoma City), February 11, 1911.

29. Aldrich, "Coal Mining Industry in Oklahoma," 181–87, 195; *Third Report of Oklahoma Department of Labor, 1909–1910* (Oklahoma City: n.p., 1910), 44–45; interview with Dave Archibald, a Krebs miner, who was involved in the "long strike" that began in 1898, on tape recording dated November 12, 1974, in Archives and Record Division, Oklahoma Department of Libraries, Oklahoma City.

class-conscious miners of Krebs than it did to the citizens of Mc-Alester.

In the spring elections of 1911 the Socialists again carried Krebs, electing three of four councilmen. They also showed more strength in McAlester where one party member won an aldermanic seat representing a working-class section of the city. In the following year a violent streetcar workers' strike polarized the Pittsburg County seat just as a similar conflict had in Oklahoma City. When Mayor Hanraty appointed special deputies to protect traction company property, he was recalled by a majority of McAlester's voters, including workers who accused him of betraying union men, businessmen who blamed him for not preserving law and order, and Republicans who opposed him because he was a Democrat. In the same month that Hanraty left office in McAlester (April of 1912), his Socialist successor to the UMW district presidency, Pete Stewart, became the mayor of Hartford, Arkansas, the largest coal town in the Sebastian County fields.[30]

The Socialists had been active in the mining camps of western Arkansas since the turn of the century. After Father Hagerty and "Uncle Pat" O'Neill left the area to organize the Industrial Workers of the World, Dan Hogan, an Irish lawyer, settled down in the coal town of Huntington and started a Socialist weekly that helped Debs poll 620 votes there in 1908, just 9 less than he tallied in coal-rich Pittsburg County, the source of his largest vote in Oklahoma. After denouncing Franklin Bache and other big coal operators during the 1910 strike, Hogan was nominated by the Socialist party to run for governor of Arkansas. He polled over 500 votes in Sebastian County where the party had its most active locals in UMW strongholds like Huntington, Hartford, Bonanza, and Jenny Lind. Hogan and State Secretary Ida Callery helped popularize socialism in Arkansas by working closely with the union and by importing the Oklahoma encampment to spread the gospel to farmers in the Ozarks. In the fall of 1911 they planned a camp meeting at Huntington, billing it as the "biggest gathering of its

30. *Appeal to Reason* (Girard, Kan.), May 20, 1911; McAlester (Okla.) *News-Capital*, April 25, 1912; *Rebel* (Hallettsville, Tex.), April 6, 1912.

kind ever held" in that section. The speakers included the Hogans, the UMW district leaders Holt and Stewart, and Frank Hayes, the union's new Socialist international vice-president. The greatest attraction at the encampment was to be the singing of the Marseillaise by "a chorus of 100 voices accompanied by a socialist orchestra." Pete Stewart's mayoral victory in Hartford the following spring showed that Socialist activity in the Sebastian County coal fields of western Arkansas was just as effective as it was in the mining region across the state line in eastern Oklahoma.[31]

The Socialist miners in southeastern Kansas also enjoyed a good year in 1911. They reelected as president of District 14 Alex Howat, later known as "the stormy petrel of the Southwest miners," and voted in another comrade, Joe Variott, as secretary-treasurer. In the spring elections a third party member named Leon Besson was voted state mining inspector by a majority of his sixteen thousand fellow workers. Described by the *Appeal* as a "sturdy young Frenchman, square of jaw," Besson promised to be absolutely uncompromising on the question of mine safety. The new inspector lived and worked at the Dunkirk coal camp in Washington Township of Crawford County, a polyglot community of about three thousand miners, small merchants, and their families. In the fall of 1910 just after the violent strike ended, the Socialists had swept the entire township, polling about two thirds of the vote and electing an entire slate of local officials who promptly threw out the poll tax.[32] The Socialists were even more successful when Besson ran for mining inspector in the spring of 1911; they carried many different kinds of coal camps in Crawford County including Dunkirk, which was mixed; Franklin, 90 percent foreign born (largely Slavic); Croweberg, a predominantly black precinct where the party had an active "colored voters local"; and Mulberry, where most of the miners were of "old English stock." Socialist mayors were also elected in the mining towns of Arma and Curranville, both towns

31. Huntington (Ark.) *Herald*, September 30, 1910. *Daily Oklahoman* (Oklahoma City), September 24, 1911; interviews with Freda Hogan Ameringer, May 23, 1969, and June 21, 1974.

32. *Appeal to Reason* (Girard, Kan.), November 12, 1910, May 20, July 8, 1911, May 4, 1912.

having strong UMW locals and mixed populations. The Socialist party served as a cultural as well as a political organization in many of the Kansas coal towns. It sponsored a black choir in Croweburg, established a night school in Breezy Hill to help Austrians gain their citizenship, and staged a number of events, notably May Day parades. For example, in Dunkirk, a May Day parade was highlighted by "the Girard women's committee, in white dresses and red caps." This broad base of Socialist support indicated that the party had benefited from the solidarity generated by the 1910 strike, from the leadership ability of Alex Howat and other militant union leaders, and from its own organizing efforts among blacks and immigrants. It was not difficult to predict that the Socialists would carry Crawford County in their 1912 campaign. Debs defeated his presidential opponents in Crawford County (a very unusual occurrence), polling a plurality of 35 percent and winning his largest margins (which ranged up to 72 percent) in the precincts with the strongest UMW locals, regardless of their ethnic composition. George D. Brewer, a Kansas farm boy who joined the *Appeal to Reason* staff in 1901 after being crippled in a railroad accident, ran one of the nation's best Socialist congressional races in 1912, winning 24 percent of the vote in the southeastern Third District.[33]

The Socialists were not as powerful in Oklahoma and Arkansas mining townships where disfranchisement was a greater problem, but they did win office in smaller towns like Krebs and Hartford where the miners, despite their racial and ethnic differences, united around strong UMW locals with militant membership. Indeed, since Socialists consistently won union elections between 1908 and 1914, a majority of the miners in District 21 were probably party supporters or sympathizers if not party members. It is hard to understand how this power could have been ignored by the historian who studied socialism in the UMW. It is easier to under-

33. Precinct data on the ethnicity of Kansas coal-mining precincts is from J. N. Carman, *Foreign Language Units of Kansas* (Lawrence: University of Kansas Press, 1962), 110–14. For voting returns and evidence of Socialist work among black and immigrant miners in Kansas, see *Appeal to Reason* (Girard, Kan.), February 2, March 30, May 4, 25, June 8, December 7, 1912.

stand, however, why students of radical voting among coal miners have emphasized the importance of such variables as ethnicity, company hostility, job insecurity, and lack of safety. Neither these determinants, however, nor the isolated quality of one-industry towns, sufficiently explain the strength of socialism among the southwestern miners.[34]

In order to evaluate this unrecognized phenomenon it is necessary to look beyond the peculiarity of the industry, the ethnicity of the miners, and the quality of Socialist leaders. An examination of Socialist coal camps like Krebs, Oklahoma, Hartford, Arkansas, and Dunkirk, Kansas, reveals the importance of the party's involvement in liberating these communities from company control during the UMW's "long strike." After 1908 the development of Socialist-led mine union locals, which were racially and ethnically integrated, allowed the party to build upon the strength of the most powerful working-class institution in the region. These locals were real community institutions that broke the company's control over housing and marketing and opened up the camps for commercial and political activity. The Socialist party's own locals were organized around the interests of special groups—blacks, Italians, Slavs, the wives of Anglo-American miners; they did the important educational and agitational work during strikes and political campaigns, but they were really adjuncts to the union locals controlled by party members. As a result, the Socialist party was able to win widespread support from southwestern coal miners, regardless of race, ethnicity, or religion. In fact, as Freda

34. For an analysis of midwestern coal miners' voting that stresses ethnicity, see Paul Kleppner, *The Cross of Culture* (Glencoe, Ill.: Free Press, 1970), and for a general study stressing the unique importance of isolated one-industry towns, see S. M. Lipset, *Political Man* (Garden City, N.Y.: Doubleday Anchor, 1963), 104, 242–44, 408. The only history written on socialism in the UMW all but ignores the Southwest and states erroneously that the only "real power" the party enjoyed was in Illinois District 12. Laslett's study identifies key factors in the rise of socialism within the UMW, but since he focuses on national leaders he misses the importance of the party's work on a community level. He explains the miners' radicalism by stressing the hostility of the companies and the state rather than the solidarity of the miners' communities and the militancy of their local unions. Laslett, *Labor and the Left*, 230–31, 291.

Hogan Ameringer later recalled, the presence of black miners in her hometown UMW local at Huntington, Arkansas, made it possible for the Socialists to bring a few prominent black union men into the party local. It also won the support of coal-town merchants (who in towns like Krebs were often blacklisted "agitators" from the strikes of the 1890s) and the tenant farmers from the surrounding countryside who peddled their vegetables in the mining communities. Grass-roots socialism took deepest hold in places where independent working-class institutions were strongest.[35]

THE BROTHERHOOD OF TIMBER WORKERS AND THE IWW

The industrial unionists who started organizing the lumberjacks and mill hands of the Louisiana-Texas piney woods after the 1907 general strike adopted the UMW's approach. In fact, one of the first radical agitators to come to the "infected area" around De-Ridder, Louisiana, was "Uncle Pat" O'Neill, the militant miner from Arkansas who in 1905 had helped found the IWW along with his comrade from the Ozarks, Father Thomas Hagerty, and bigger names like Debs, DeLeon, Haywood, Vincent St. John, William Trautman of the Brewers, and Mother Jones of the UMW. O'Neill and the early lumber organizers had to win support from black workers, townspeople, and farmers in order to organize an industry dominated by powerful lumber companies that formed a monopolistic "trust." In fact, the timber workers' union depended even more upon community support than did a national organization like the UMW.

Industrial capitalism had come rapidly to the Sabine pine region of Louisiana and Texas, seriously disrupting the lives of the local people. Abusing the Homestead Act of 1862, syndicates from Britain and the North sent agents into the Southwest to buy rich stands of timber for as little as $1.25 an acre. As railroads pushed further into the Sabine River region during the nineties, lumber

---

35. James R. Green, "Socialism and the Southwestern Coal Miners," paper presented to the American Historical Association, 1971; and interviews with Freda Hogan Ameringer, May 23, 1969, and June 21, 1974. The author would also like to thank Jim Kendell for providing a copy of his unpublished paper on Kansas coal miners and socialism.

corporations "cut wide swaths through the Southern forests stripping them of timber." After 1880, timber production doubled every ten years until 1909 when 12 billion board feet of pine rolled out of the Gulf Coast mills. A handful of corporations, owned largely by railroads and other northern capitalists, monopolized the market and made enormous profits before they destroyed the rich yellow-pine forests.[36] Unlike the Oklahoma and Arkansas coal miners to the north whose powerful union won a closed shop in 1903, the unskilled lumberjacks and mill hands of Texas and Louisiana lacked experience with collective organizing and bargaining.

Although most of the southwestern coal diggers had experienced both industrial and trade union discipline in the mines of Europe and the eastern United States, nearly all the region's timber workers came directly from the Texas and Louisiana cotton fields, including thousands of blacks who comprised over half of the sixty-four thousand men who worked in the industry.

In addition to those who came from nearby plantations, some of the Afro-Americans came from as far away as the Mississippi Delta and the Alabama black belt, whereas others moved up from the Louisiana "sugar bowl" where black field gangs had allied with whites in two strikes in 1877 and 1886. Unlike many southern industrialists, the lumber operators of the Sabine region faced a shortage of white labor and readily hired blacks to do dangerous, demanding work in the mills for low wages.[37]

36. Paul W. Gates, "Federal Land Policy in the South, 1866–1888," *Journal of Southern History*, VI (1940), 318–28; C. Vann Woodward, *Origins of the New South, 1877–1913* (Baton Rouge: Louisiana State University Press, 1951), 118; U.S. Bureau of Corporations, *The Lumber Industry* (Washington, D.C.: Government Printing Office, 1914), Pt. II, pp. 132–53; U.S. Department of Commerce, *Twelfth Census of the United States, 1900*, IX, 803–10; *Thirteenth Census of the United States, 1910*, IX, 413, 416–17, 1198; and *Fourteenth Census of the United States, 1920*, X, 439 (Washington, D.C.: Government Printing Office, 1902, 1913, 1923).

37. U.S. Department of Commerce, *Thirteenth Census, 1910: Occupations*, IV, 384–85, 520–21. J. Bradford Laws, *Negroes of Cinclaire Central Factory and Calumet Plantation*, U.S. Department of Labor Bulletin No. 38 (Washington, D.C.: Government Printing Office, 1902), 111–13. See also Sidney Kessler, "Organization of Negroes in the Knights of Labor," *Journal of Negro History*, XXXVII (1952), 248–76; and Abraham Berglund, *et al.*, *Labor*

Some of the blacks had experienced gang labor and even collective union action, but the "redbones" (a people of "fighting stock" with mixed Indian and African blood and French or Spanish surnames) and other white farmers entered the industry unprepared for the changes demanded by life and labor in the lumber camps. They clung to agricultural work habits governed by sun and weather—not by the mill whistle. They were rugged individualists, harder to organize than the rambling, rootless lumber workers of the Pacific Northwest. But once they joined together in their own homegrown organization, these new proletarians proved to be determined union men, because, unlike the western "casual workers," they were "homeguards" who had families and kin nearby to sustain them during hard times.[38] At first, these "peckerwoods" had reacted to the corporate intruders by sniping at the surveyors and other company agents. During the Populist revolt they had joined the People's party's attack on the lumber "trust," which destroyed the forests and forced the small "cawn n' cotton" farmers off the land. After populism was crushed in the piney woods, these people held onto older agrarian values that justified the "squatter's natural right" to the land. The backwoods farmers and fishermen who came to work in the camps and mills retained these values just as they maintained agrarian habits and attitudes toward nature. Industrial capitalists provoked a violent resistance throughout the region by destroying the forests and displacing family farmers, then demanding new work habits and social attitudes from the indigenous people they employed. "These primitive forest people accepted the new scheme of things with misgivings," wrote one government investigator sent to report on class conflict in the pine

---

in the Industrial South (Charlottesville: University of Virginia Press, 1930), 54.

38. D. J. Saposs interview with Superintendent Tuxworth of Pickering Land and Lumber Co., August 27, 1914, in Record Group 174, Commission on Industrial Relations Papers, "Records of the Department of Labor," National Archives, hereinafter cited as CIR Records. Also see Vernon Jensen, *Lumber and Labor* (New York: Farrar and Rinehart, 1944), 77; Ruth A. Allen, *East Texas Lumber Workers: An Economic and Social Picture, 1870–1950* (Austin: University of Texas Press, 1961), 187.

region. "Deep in their hearts they nourished the grudge of the dispossessed and the conquered."[39]

The loggers out in the forests found their work difficult and dangerous, but it was somewhat irregular because of the weather and less disciplined than the routine inside the sawmills. The mill hands, predominantly blacks, often failed to report to the mill when the whistle blew, especially on "blue Monday" when they were frequently hung over from indulging in liquor and narcotics during the weekend. One Louisiana sheriff had orders from a lumber company to "be at the sawmill every day, and if enough men did not report to work to go to the colored quarters and 'drive' the required number out of their homes or even their beds if necessary." Faced with the difficult task of disciplining these workers to an industrial way of life to which they were "only partially and temporarily committed," corporation managers adopted thorough methods of social control in their company towns. Employers used sheriffs and company guards to discipline reluctant workers, harass union organizers as well as political reformers and radicals, and threaten merchants and "non-submissive professionals" who gave the workers an alternative to company stores and welfare programs. One of the main threats to order and discipline in the mill towns was "vice," which managers and sheriffs actively suppressed in the early 1900s.[40]

Operators, like John Henry Kirby who owned several mill towns in East Texas, practiced "mill village paternalism . . . cut from the same pattern of poverty and makeshift necessity that had served for plantation and crop lien paternalism." Kirby, who was especially concerned with the loyalty of his black mill hands, hired in-

39. David J. Saposs, *Left Wing Unionism: A Study in Radical Politics and Tactics* (New York: International, 1926), 168. Also see Roger W. Shugg, *Origins of Class Struggle in Louisiana* (Baton Rouge: Louisiana State University Press, 1939), 268–69.

40. David J. Saposs, "Self-Government and Freedom of Action in Isolated Industrial Communities," Report No. 1036, January 20, 1915, pp. 16–17, 22–25, 35, in CIR Records. For a discussion of the problem of disciplining rural workers to an industrial time schedule see E. P. Thompson, "Time, Work-Discipline, and Industrial Capitalism," *Past and Present*, No. 38 (1967), 92–93.

fluential Negroes like J. B. Rayner the old Populist organizer, to promote Booker Washington's accommodationist, self-help philosophy.[41] But he did not rely solely on paternalism as a method of social control. Kirby paid 90 percent of his wages in scrip, forcing his employees to depend solely on the company for goods and services; and like most lumber barons, he used guards to suppress anyone who challenged his control over what journalist George Creel called the "feudal towns" of Texas.[42] However, corporations found it more difficult to gain total control in towns that had been established in preindustrial times.

Black mill hands, the most exploited members of the work force, were the first to react against "mill village paternalism" and industrial discipline; in 1901 they struck at Lutcher, Louisiana (where strike leaders founded one of the few Negro locals of the Socialist party) and in 1904 at Groveton, Texas (where radical organizers of the American Labor Union, a forerunner of the IWW, assisted the strikers).[43] In 1907 nearly all the workers in the pine region spontaneously struck to protest a 20 percent wage cut and "stretch out" imposed during the panic. With the exception of the diehards around DeRidder, Louisiana, the strikers returned to work when the bosses promised to restore old wage levels. About this time, "Uncle Pat" O'Neill, the old Socialist organizer, came down from the Arkansas coal fields to organize for the IWW; he started a

41. Woodward, *Origins of the New South*, 223. See also George T. Morgan, "No Compromise—No Recognition: John Henry Kirby, the Southern Lumber Operators' Association, and Unionism in the Piney Woods, 1906–1916," *Labor History*, X (1969), 193–204; Jack Abromowitz, "John B. Rayner—A Grass Roots Leader," *Journal of Negro History*, XXXVI (1951), 172. Kirby also used a black school principal in Silsbee, Texas, as an antiunion speaker. See A. J. Criner to J. H. Kirby, August 10, 1911, and Kirby to Criner, August 11, 1911, in John H. Kirby Papers, University of Houston.

42. See Saposs, "Self-Government in Isolated Industrial Communities," 6; P. A. Speek, "Report on Conditions in Texas Company Towns," Folder 299, pp. 77–79, in CIR Records; and George Creel, "Feudal Towns in Texas," *Harper's Weekly*, LX (1915), 76.

43. Jenson, *Lumber and Labor*, 86–87; Eraste Vidrine, "Negro Locals," *International Socialist Review*, V (1905), 389; Ruth A. Allen, chapters in the *History of Organized Labor in Texas* (Austin: University of Texas Press, 1941), 187–88; and Allen, *East Texas Lumber Workers*, 168.

paper called the *Toiler* in Leesville, but failed to start a Wobbly chapter.[44]

In December, 1910, two southern-born lumberjacks founded the Brotherhood of Timber Workers at a damp logging camp near Carson, Louisiana. John H. Kirby described one of the founders, Arthur Lee Emerson, as a "tin-horn gambler and sawmill loafer . . . who is a rank socialist with some attainments as a scholar" and the other, Jay Smith, as a tree sawyer with twenty years of experience in southern and West Coast forests, a "desperate kind of fellow with a great deal of natural ability but little education." He was also a Socialist, Kirby warned, and "by nature a criminal."[45]

Kirby watched the new union closely and early in August of 1911 demanded action from the Southern Lumber Operators' Association, because the Brotherhood was "covering the country like a blanket." The Lumber Operators' Association responded by starting a lockout in the "infected mills," importing strikebreakers and demanding "yellow dog" contracts from new workers. But after a month of repression, the Association admittedly failed to "break the back" of the BTW.[46] Emerson and Smith adopted the rituals of the Knights of Labor and various fraternal organizations to conceal their organizing activities under an umbrella of secrecy. "When the lumber barons began their crushing operation in 1911, they found the Brotherhood everywhere and nowhere," wrote Covington Hall, who came up from New Orleans to help with the organizing. "It entered the woods and mills as a semi-secret organization with the usual passwords and grips so dear to Southerners, regardless of race." The BTW had also adopted the Knights' interracial, in-

---

44. Philip S. Foner, *Industrial Workers of the World, 1905–1917* (New York: International, 1965), 235–36; Hall, "Labor Struggles in the Deep South," 125. For a fuller account, see James R. Green, "The Brotherhood of Timber Workers, 1910–1913: A Radical Response to Industrial Capitalism in the Southern U.S.A.," *Past and Present*, No. 60 (1973), 161–200.

45. Kirby to E. P. Ripley, August 8, 1911, in Kirby Papers.

46. *Ibid.*; *Southwest: Southern Industrial and Lumber Review* (Houston), August 22, 1921, September 23, 1911, July 22, 1912; Agent E-17 to Kirby, August 7, 1912, J. H. Herndon to C. P. Meyer, May 31, 1912, and S. J. Carpenter to Kirby, September 12, 1911, all in Kirby Papers.

dustrial unionism, seeking to organize all timber workers, black and white, skilled and unskilled, into "one big union."[47]

During the hard winter of 1912, the Brotherhood went underground and almost expired. In the spring, however, its organizers and most committed members came out of the woods to hold their first official convention in Alexandria, Louisiana. "Big Bill" Haywood traveled down from IWW headquarters in Chicago to urge southern timber workers to affiliate with his revolutionary union. When Haywood discovered that black unionists were meeting in a separate hall in compliance with state segregation laws, he asked them to join the main body of white delegates. Haywood's bold appeal for more equality within the BTW was echoed in a southern drawl by "Covy" Hall, who was about to start a union paper called the *Lumberjack* at Alexandria. The red-neck membership of the Brotherhood voted to join the IWW and to accept women as well as blacks. After giving women membership rights the chairman of the Alexandria convention asked if this meant that females could vote on strikes. One member answered: "A man can go fish and hunt during a strike, but she has to stay at home listening to the babies cry and wondering where the next meal is coming from. Besides, if it weren't for the work of women, many of the men wouldn't hold down jobs. Yes, this is meant to give her a full and equal vote even as to the right to call strikes." The record indicates that this interpretation was approved by the chairman. In the Louisiana piney woods, radical industrial unionism raised fundamental questions about the role of working-class women, just as it did in the Kansas Balkans where the immigrant wives of UMW members participated actively in suffragist and Socialist organizations.[48]

47. Hall, "Labor Struggles in the Deep South," 128. On ritual and secrecy see *Constitution and Bylaws of the Brotherhood of Timber Workers* (Alexandria, La.: n.p., 1911), 4, 8. Copy obtained from Calcasieu Parish Court House, Lake Charles, La.

48. William D. Haywood, *Bill Haywood's Book* (New York: International, 1929), 241–43; Hall, "Labor Struggles in the Deep South," 136–39; Linda Deknatel, "Louisiana Lumber War," *Louisiana Worker* (New Orleans), December, 1973; *Workers' Chronicle* (Pittsburg, Kan.), December 5, 12, 1913, for examples of the Socialist activity among miners' wives.

The Wobblies' militant leadership and insistence on interracial, direct-action tactics breathed new life into the BTW, to use one employer's words. As a result, however, the Southern Lumber Operators' Association also found it easier to brand the Brotherhood as an anarchistic, race-mixing organization, in their campaign to weaken the union's public support. Shortly after affiliating with the IWW, union leaders presented a list of demands to ten companies in the DeRidder area; the Lumber Operators' Association responded with a lockout, and the second phase of the Louisiana "lumber war" began. In the course of this struggle, the Wobblies emphasized the importance of organizing black workers who held a majority of the sawmill jobs. Originally, the BTW had accepted the racial status quo; its constitution called for separate black lodges and for control of all dues by white locals. The Brotherhood actively recruited black workers from the start but it did not grant them any power in union affairs until Bill Haywood persuaded the delegates at Alexandria to join the IWW and accept its equalitarian bylaws. After this the black workers expressed affection for the BTW and supported it loyally. Union meetings and social gatherings provided the only opportunity for association available to workers in an increasingly segregated society.[49]

As the lumber war escalated, the use of black strikebreakers threatened the racial solidarity of the union. But BTW leaders tried desperately to explain that their hatred was for "scabs," regardless of race. As one Wobbly put it: "There are white *men*, there are Negro *men*, and there are Mexican *men*, but no 'niggers,' 'greasers' or 'white trash'. All *men* are on the side of the Union, and all

49. M. L. Alexander to Kirby, May 11, 1912, in Kirby Papers; Saposs, *Left Wing Unionism*, 169; New Orleans *Times-Democrat*, May 17, 1912; *Southwest: Southern Industrial and Lumber Review* (Houston), June 23, 1912; Covington Hall, "The Louisiana Lumber War," *Coming Nation* (Girard, Kan.), June 22, 1912; *Constitution of Brotherhood of Timber Workers*, 14; Hall, "Labor Struggles in the Deep South," 241–42; and Sterling D. Spero and Abram L. Harris, *The Black Worker* (New York: Columbia University Press, 1931), 325, 332. For an account of a racially mixed Brotherhood of Timber Workers' picnic held to celebrate "Negro emancipation," see *Southwest: Southern Industrial and Labor Review* (Houston), July 12, 1912, p. 33. For a detailed analysis of how industrial unionism was used to cope with racism see Green, "Brotherhoood of Timber Workers," 183–90.

greasers, niggers and white trash are on the side of the Lumber Trust." The IWW's militant equalitarianism heightened class consciousness and promoted solidarity within the Brotherhood, but it could not overcome racism entirely. At most, Covington Hall recalled, "we prevented . . . our opponents from using it against us."[50]

The BTW's allies among farmers and townspeople were almost as important as its black supporters. Wobbly leaders drew on the farmers' hatred of the "lumber barons" who had driven them off their land or forced them to become tenants and then refused to open their cut-over lands to settlement. Despite the theoretical objections of Wobbly ideologists, the BTW recruited tenant farmers as dues-paying members and cooperated with the Socialist Renters' Union in Texas. Union leaders drew upon the shared agrarian values and anticorporation sentiments of farmers and workers to broaden their base of support and to convince all poor people in the piney woods that the "lumber barons" were a "common class enemy." During the first lockout in the summer of 1911, *Southwest*, the lumber industry trade journal, reported that the BTW was successfully drawing to its meetings many farmers whose "presence and enthusiasm showed their sympathy for the new order." Despite the Lumber Association's attempt to "bring disruption between the farmers and the union," rural support for the Brotherhood actually seemed to increase after it joined the IWW. One Louisiana mill manager said that the "redbones" (who were a majority of the white workers at his plant in Cravens) were the "backbone of the 1912 strike" and that the farmers in the area, "who came from the same stock, sympathize with them."[51]

50. New Orleans *Times-Democrat*, July 30, 1912; *Southwest: Southern Industrial and Lumber Review* (Houston), August, 1911, pp. 22–24; Hall, "Labor Struggles in the Deep South," 189; Spero and Harris, *Black Worker*, 325; Hall, "Labor Struggles in the Deep South," 190–91; and Covington Hall, "Negroes Against Whites," *International Socialist Review*, XIII (1912), 349.

51. Covington Hall, "The Farmer Question," *Voice of the People* (New Orleans), August 7, 1913; New Orleans *Times-Democrat*, August 15, 1912; Saposs interviews with T. J. Pinchback and Superintendent Tuxworth, August 27, 1914, in CIR Records; Southern Lumber Operators' Association Report to R. L. Weathersby, January 13, 1912, Alexander to C. D. Johnson, June 24, 1912, both in Kirby Papers; *Southwest: Southern Industrial and Labor Review* (Houston), August, 1911, p. 24.

Merchants, professionals, and tradesmen who had commercial or social ties with the workers also gave the BTW valuable support, especially in towns that were not owned outright by the companies. In many older agricultural villages like Leesville and De-Ridder, Louisiana, both union strongholds, small businessmen contributed financially to the BTW. In Silisbee, Texas, for example, an Lumber Operators' Association agent reported that the Brotherhood's membership included "farmers, merchants, and small men of trade who naturally sympathize with the working masses." In the company towns, however, the middle class could not remain neutral, let alone support the union. If businessmen and professionals did not side with the company they were harassed and sometimes driven out of town.[52] As a result, the BTW never developed much strength in the "feudal towns" of East Texas owned by J. H. Kirby. When the lumber war heated up in the summer of 1912 the Lumber Operators' Association also began to put a good deal of pressure on prounion townspeople in relatively "open" villages like DeRidder and Oakdale, Louisiana.[53]

REDS VERSUS YELLOWS: THE IWW AND THE SOCIALIST PARTY

The BTW's struggle radicalized the Louisiana Socialist party. Before 1910 the state party had been controlled by segregationists in the New Orleans local whose candidates polled a few hundred votes in the city and a few more from old Populist strongholds like Winn Parish. In 1906 a group of Reds led by Covington Hall invited Daniel DeLeon, a founder of the IWW and leader of the rival Socialist Labor party, to speak in the city. Outraged by this left-wing

52. *Southwest: Southern Industrial and Labor Review* (Houston), August, 1911, p. 26; W. D. Haywood, "Timber Workers and Timber Wolves," *International Socialist Review*, XIII (1912), 106; Alexander to Johnson, August 5, 1912, in Kirby Papers. For examples of how Kirby's managers planned to harass independent merchants who extended credit to strikers and to put economic pressure on a prounion barber and an editor see Meyer to B. F. Bonner, August 3, 1912, P. A. Heisig to Kirby, August 11, 1911, both in Kirby Papers. See also Allen, *East Texas Lumber Workers*, 157.
53. Kirby to F. H. Waltz, May 8, 1912, Bonner to Kirby, January 12, 1912, Alexander to M. L. Fleischel, January 10, 15, 1912, Alexander to Fleischel, January 10, 1912, all in Kirby Papers; New Orleans *Times-Democrat*, August 3, 1912.

gesture the moderate trade-union leaders in the New Orleans local canceled DeLeon's invitation. This affair forced the Reds out of the party. After the 1907 New Orleans strike, Hall and the pro-IWW elements moved out to the piney woods to try to organize the angry timber workers who had launched their own general strike during the panic.[54]

Despite this "internecine strife," a new state secretary named Walter Dietz reorganized the Louisiana party and by 1908 had helped increase the number of locals to four hundred. Debs doubled his previous presidential vote after the "Red Special" campaign, but the party had obtained little support from the rebellious lumber workers of the piney woods. When J. R. Jones, a left-wing Socialist, challenged progressive Congressman A. J. Pujo for his western Louisiana seat in 1908, he lost by a ten-to-one margin.[55]

During its early organizing phase in 1911 the Brotherhood of Timber Workers remained independent of the Socialist party. In fact, Hall and the few revolutionaries involved were actually hostile to the state organization in New Orleans. When Kate Richards O'Hare toured the region for the *National Rip-Saw* later in 1911 she and her fellow left-wing Socialist, H. G. Creel, found the timber workers receptive to their propaganda, but "stolidly indifferent" to political parties. Because so many timber workers, especially the blacks, were disfranchised, and because the Socialist party tended to ignore the unorganized and unskilled, the Brotherhood

54. Much of this information is drawn from Grady McWhiney, "Louisiana Socialists in the Early Twentieth Century: A Study of Rustic Radicalism," *Journal of Southern History*, XX (1954), 315–36. A recent historian claims that the famous Longs of Winn Parish were neither Populists nor Socialists, though he grants that Huey Long, Sr., may have been sympathetic to the former. T. Harry Williams, *Huey Long: A Biography* (New York: Knopf, 1970), 23, 44–45. However, Walter Dietz, who was state secretary of the Louisiana Socialist party between 1908 and 1914, said he believed that the elder Long was a member of both parties; he knew for certain that "Old Hu" was a subscriber to the *Appeal to Reason*. H. L. Mitchell interview with Walter F. Dietz, in Socialist Party Papers, Duke University.
55. State Secretary's Record Book, 1909, in Walter F. Dietz Papers, Louisiana State University Library, Baton Rouge. Mitchell interview with Dietz, in Socialist Party Papers. McWhiney, "Louisiana Socialists," 323–24.

of Timber Workers became a syndicalistic organization and affiliated with the IWW just before the Wobblies were expelled from the Socialist party for advocating sabotage. Despite the critical attitude Hall and other BTW leaders expressed toward the Yellow party leadership in New Orleans and Chicago, these radical industrial unionists did consider themselves proletarian (*i.e.* Red) Socialists, and they did cooperate with left-wing party leaders like O'Hare, Creel, and Tom Hickey in Texas.[56]

Since the leadership of the Louisiana Socialist party remained in the hands of right-wing segregationists, the interracial union of timber workers had little contact with official party organizers. However, in Texas, where Reds controlled the state office, party recruiters were sent into the timber towns. For example, W. S. Noble, a leader of the Renters' Union, conducted a ten-day organizing tour of Angelina County in the fall of 1911, which led to the formation of seven locals with eighty-two members in the heart of the yellow-pine forest. Another organizer, Bill Lafollette, was also sent in to organize in the dangerous vicinity around Kirbyville, according to a Lumber Operators' Association "secret agent." But the workers in J. H. Kirby's "feudal towns" were not free to join a Socialist local or to vote for the party of their choice. Both union and party organizers found it very difficult to penetrate these backwoods company towns, and so most of the BTW and Socialist party support was concentrated in open communities not dominated by a company. For example, the secretary of a party local in Warren (one of the few timber towns in East Texas where the BTW built up a strong local) reported that it was very difficult to break into other sawmill towns on account of the surveillance. Kirby, who criticized his fellow Association member at Warren for not "nipping the union at the bud," used surveillance and outright repression to make sure that the bud of industrial unionism did not blossom into socialism. Kirby also contacted AFL President Samuel Gompers through the National Civic Federation in an effort to

56. *National Rip-Saw* (St. Louis), October, 1911, p. 3; New Orleans *Times-Democrat*, October 28, 1912.

bring in a craft union to rival the IWW. According to Philip S. Foner, Gompers refused to correspond about the matter, but agreed to meet secretly with Kirby in Chicago. When the lumber baron reported on the meeting at the Southern Lumber Operators' Association convention in New Orleans, southern unionists lodged strong protests with Gompers, who abandoned whatever plans he had made to cooperate with Kirby in replacing the IWW with the AFL.[57]

Although factionalism continued in the Louisiana Socialist party for some time, the Reds did capture most of the northern locals by the end of 1911 and were beginning to use the limited resources of the party to help the BTW. For example, when the Operators' Association started a lockout in the summer of 1911 (and justified it on the grounds that some of their employees were "members of the Socialist movement"), BTW and Socialist party members circulated a petition throughout the region denouncing this act of repression and demanding a state seizure of the lumber trust that would allow for the distribution of the product to the people. This cooperation bore fruit in the spring elections of 1912 when, on a combined BTW-Socialist ticket, E. F. Presley was elected mayor of DeRidder, which was in the heart of the "infected area" where, according to a New Orleans paper, "a majority of the people sympathize with the timber workers."[58] Like the party in the Kansas coal fields and in Choctaw mining towns like Krebs, the Socialist party grew in the Louisiana piney woods by mobilizing support for the industrial union movement, a movement that represented a good deal more than a trade-union challenge to management. At this point in time, industrial unionism constituted a direct and broadly political challenge to the most powerful capitalists in the

57. B. F. Evans to editor, *Rebel* (Hallettsville, Tex.), November 11, 25, 1911, and J. F. Cox to editor, *Rebel*, July 8, 1911; Agent E-17 to Fleischel, August 7, 1911, Alexander to Fleischel, January 10, 1912, and Kirby to A. J. Peavy, December 9, 1911, all in Kirby Papers. On the Kirby-Gompers meeting, see Foner, *Industrial Workers of the World*, 238–40.

58. *Rebel* (Hallettsville, Tex.), August 10, 1911; New Orleans *Times-Democrat*, July 30, 1912. Also see Charles H. McCord, "A Brief History of the Brotherhood of Timber Workers" (M.A. thesis, University of Texas, 1959), 24.

region. The struggles of the miners and timber workers in the early 1910s created more than trade-union consciousness; the industrial phase of the southwestern class conflict also created a strong anticapitalist consciousness which disposed unskilled workers toward socialism.

Shortly after the BTW voted to join the IWW in May, 1912, Socialist delegates gathered in Chicago for one of the most important conventions in the party's history. There was a growing tension between the Reds who supported the IWW's dual unionism and the moderates and right-wingers who opposed the Wobblies' direct action, favoring instead the strategy of "boring from within" the AFL. This tension was particularly strong in Louisiana, but it was also a serious matter in other states where both the Wobblies and the Socialists were active. However, when the Chicago convention opened, the differences between the Reds and their party rivals were patched over. On the fifth day of the convention the labor committee, which included Tom Hickey and Oscar Ameringer (the leaders of the opposing factions in the Southwest), astonished the delegates with a compromise report endorsing industrial unionism without actually supporting the IWW instead of the AFL. Happy that he could finally cooperate with rivals like Oscar Ameringer, Hickey shook hands with Los Angeles party leader Job Harriman, with whom he had been feuding for nineteen years. "Big Bill" Haywood then took the floor to speak in favor of the compromise and to assure the delegates that political action complemented industrial direct action. Before concluding his warmly applauded speech, the Wobbly leader remarked: "So, as Tom Hickey has shaken hands with Job Harriman for the first time in twenty years, I feel I can shake hands with every delegate in this convention and say we are a united working class." This euphoria did not last long.[59]

Shortly after Haywood finished, a right-wing delegate proposed to amend the constitution to read that "any member of the party

59. John Spargo (ed.), *Proceedings of the National Convention of the Socialist Party, 1912* (Chicago: M. A. Donahue and Socialist Party, 1912), 122–37.

who opposes political action or advocates sabotage or other means of violence . . . shall be expelled from the party." A bitter four-hour debate over this "sabotage" amendment followed, in which right-wing leader Victor Berger attacked the Reds for "using our political organization . . . as a cloak for what they call direct action, for IWW-ism, sabotage and syndicalism." Dan Hogan of Arkansas begged the delegates to avoid a vote that would split the party, but the antisabotage clause passed 191 to 90. Tom Hickey spoke out violently against the clause because he was opposed to "warning the working class against anything." He then voted against the clause along with J. R. Jones, Louisiana's lone delegate, Dan Hogan and Ida Callery of Arkansas, and four other Texas comrades who were close to the IWW. The Oklahoma delegation followed the leadership of Ameringer and Branstetter and voted for the clause, with the exception of J. G. Wills, the old American Railway Union man.[60]

The split did not seriously damage the southwestern Socialist parties. There were no IWW locals in Oklahoma and Arkansas and there were few Socialists whose loyalty to the Wobblies preceded their commitment to the party. In Texas pro-Wobbly forces led the party. Through the *Rebel*, they denounced the expulsion of the IWW as a right-wing plot, but since they maintained power within their own state organization, they remained in the party. The repercussions in Louisiana were more severe. The antisabotage clause bolstered the fortunes of the right-wing faction in New Orleans, even though the old guard had nearly lost control of the state organization to the upcountry Reds. However, left-wing Socialists had no intention of abandoning the party to the moderates on the basis of this one defeat. In fact, when Bill Haywood returned to the piney woods in the summer of 1912, he campaigned for Gene Debs (again the party's presidential nominee) and preached sabotage at the same time. Like his Louisiana comrades, Haywood was willing to live awhile longer with the contradiction of being an

60. *Ibid.*, 100, 130–31, 134, 136–37; New Orleans *Times-Democrat*, August 3, 1912.

IWW and a Socialist, for socialism and industrial unionism were still integral to the Reds.

After the BTW joined the Wobblies, the region's leading Red, Covington Hall, warned the operators that the Brotherhood had destroyed the "great bugaboo of 'nigger domination'" and was ready for a long fight. The "timber wolves" could not intimidate the union with their armed guards, "for the boys up in the forests and mills at once notified the gunmen that they could shoot just as straight and just as quick." As the lockout wore on "weird things" began happening. Guards were ambushed and company property was "mysteriously" destroyed. "The colored workers say voodoo is loose in the timber belt," Hall wrote, "while the Jacksonian Christians say God is making the lumber kings pay for their injustice to the workers."[61]

Reds like Hall believed that sabotage was "a legitimate form of guerilla warfare when used against the capitalist class," and they did not hesitate to say so. Although the IWW advocated violence against property as well as armed self-defense, it held the sabotage tactic in reserve, favoring disciplined nonviolence over armed struggle.[62] The Wobblies knew that when it came to gunplay, the bosses always had superior fire power. On July 7, 1912, a violent incident bore this out dramatically. On that sweltering Sunday BTW President A. L. Emerson led a band of one hundred strikers and their families toward Bon Ami where the huge King-Ryder mill was operating with scab labor. When they learned that Socialist agitator H. G. Creel had nearly been assassinated in that vicinity, the leaders changed directions and headed for the small Galloway mill in Grabow. When they arrived, Emerson mounted a wagon and began to speak to his followers and to a few bystanders around the town. Almost immediately company gunmen opened fire on the group from concealed positions in the company office. As the people ran for cover, several armed union men fired back at the gunmen. In the ten-minute battle that followed three hun-

61. Covington Hall, "Rebels of the New South," *Solidarity* (New Castle, Pa.), May 25, 1912.
62. Hall, "Labor Struggles in the Deep South," 120, 150, 230.

dred rounds were fired, largely by the company guards, and four men were killed—two unionists, one bystander, and one hired gunman. In addition, forty people, including several women and children, were wounded. That evening hundreds of angry farmers and workers from Calcasieu Parish armed themselves and gathered at DeRidder, many of them wanting to violently avenge the victims of what they called the Grabow "massacre." After a long night of belligerent talk, A. L. Emerson and other BTW leaders persuaded the people to disperse and "let the law take its course."[63]

Soon after the gun battle at Grabow lawmen arrested Emerson and sixty-four other union men and indicted them on charges of murdering a guard employed by the Galloway company. The defendants remained in the cramped confines of the Lake Charles jail for two months awaiting trial, using the opportunity to form a unique "branch local" of the Socialist party. Meanwhile, experienced Wobbly agitators came into the region to help organize a defense movement. The IWW press, with Covington Hall's help, began a national publicity campaign. *Southwest* denounced "this frantic effort . . . to make it appear as though it were a trial of the 'lumber barons' versus the 'workingmen,' instead of a case of the State of Louisiana against a crowd of rioters." Nevertheless, a New Orleans paper reported that a "dangerous state of opinion" existed in the pine region because so many farmers and workers were outraged by the course the law had taken following the Grabow massacre.[64] Further violence did not occur, however, largely because Wobblies and Socialists worked feverishly to channel frustration and anger into political activity—especially into legal defense work for the Grabow defendants in the Lake Charles jail.

These dramatic events even brought together the warring factions of the Louisiana Socialist party. On July 10, 1912, Reds and Yellows united in New Orleans to sponsor a protest rally in La-

63. New Orleans *Times-Democrat*, July 8, 28, 1912; Lake Charles *American Press*, July 12, 1912.
64. Lake Charles *American Press*, August 15, 1912; *Southwest: Southern Industrial and Lumber Review* (Houston), October, 1912, p. 6; Hall, "Labor Struggles in the Deep South," 150–59; W. F. Dietz, "Putting One Over on the Sawmill Operators," Socialist Party Circular, August 16, 1912, in Dietz Papers.

fayette Square where 2,500 workers heard a fiery address by Covington Hall who boldly advocated sabotage. Shortly after Hall made the French Quarter ring with revolutionary slogans, he appealed for assistance to the Socialist party's national office. If top-notch speakers and organizers "blanketed" the pine region, the party might be able to carry one or two congressional districts in the 1912 elections, Hall predicted. The national office raised three hundred dollars for the BTW, but it did not dispatch its agents to the strike-torn timber belt. The moderates who controlled the National Executive Committee had no interest in furthering the aims of the IWW, even if their party stood to gain votes as a result.[65] However, left-wing Socialists like H. G. Creel óf the *National Rip-Saw* returned to the Deep South forests and spoke to enthusiastic audiences. At the height of the lumber war the *Times-Democrat* reported that Creel was "looked upon as a modern Moses sent to the sawmill operatives out of the wilderness." In fact, the *Times* continued, agitators like Creel were winning many converts to socialism because the Grabow massacre had created an "intense bitterness" against the capitalists. "The whole lumber region as far west as the Sabine River has been generally plastered with Socialist literature of every description. It has had a demoralizing effect among many of the natives. Some of them have become imbued with the idea that the only way to remedy the evils that exist in the sawmill industry is by armed revolution."[66]

Although redadecked timber workers and the "redbone" farmers who "naturally sympathized" with them responded favorably to the revolutionary rhetoric of young "rebel rousers" like Hall and

65. *Southwest: Southern Industrial and Lumber Review* (Houston), July 20, 1912, 24–25; McWhiney, "Louisiana Socialists," 331; *Appeal to Reason* (Girard, Kan.), July 20, 1912; James Weinstein, *The Decline of Socialism in America, 1912–1925* (New York: Monthly Review Press, 1967), 38, 39*n*. This tension was also reflected in the region. Although the BTW prisoners at Lake Charles had formed a "jailhouse local" of the Socialist party, Louisiana party secretary, W. F. Dietz, quarreled privately over the politics of the defense campaign. Dietz to A. L. Emerson, August 10, 1912, in Dietz Papers.

66. New Orleans *Times-Democrat*, August 15, October 23, 1912. For a study of how class conflict created class ideology in the Rocky Mountain mining towns see Melvyn Dubofsky, "The Origins of Western Working Class Radicalism," *Labor History*, VII (1966), esp. 139.

Creel, the radical rank and file in the piney woods distrusted the national and state leadership of the Socialist party. James P. Cannon, reporting on the national IWW convention in September, 1912, wrote that the BTW delegates continued to take a somewhat contradictory position: "Despite the fact that a large percentage of the Timber Workers are Socialist Party men, and have the active cooperation and assistance of the party," they still "believe sabotage to be the most effective way of harassing the timber wolves." To Cannon, an impressionable young Kansas City Wobbly, the BTW's "splendid band of militants" seemed "uncompromising revolutionaries," untouched by the "germ of opportunism" and unconcerned with respectability. "Every man was a Red," he concluded glowingly, "and most of them with jail records too."[67]

The moderates who dominated the Socialist party's National Executive Committee took a different view. "They saw little advantage," Grady McWhiney observes, "in supporting a group of ignorant lawless lumberjacks at the expense of possibly losing votes among the respectable elements in the country in the November election." Although Bill Haywood had campaigned for Gene Debs in the summer of 1912, the Socialist presidential candidate did not reciprocate by supporting the BTW when he came through Louisiana in September. Debs, who avoided party faction fights, disappointed his supporters in the piney woods by speaking only in New Orleans in accordance with the wishes of his campaign managers.[68]

Despite the expulsion of the IWW from the Socialist party and despite the reluctance of higher party officials to support the timber workers' struggle, the BTW contributed significantly to the growth of socialism in western Louisiana and to a lesser extent in East Texas. Despite their renegade status and their bold advocacy of revolutionary tactics, including sabotage, the Wobblies "breathed new life" into the Brotherhood. And despite their insistence upon interracial solidarity, these industrial unionists helped to actually increase the support the timber workers enjoyed from farmers and

67. J. P. Cannon, "The Seventh IWW Convention," *International Socialist Review*, XIII (1912), 424.
68. McWhiney, "Louisiana Socialists," 332.

townspeople.[69] The IWW's influence in Louisiana also helped Red Socialists like Hall, Barnes, and Jones transform the party outside of New Orleans into an organization that favored interracial radicalism. This was the most important result of the Wobblies' revolutionary industrial unionism upon the Louisiana Socialist movement. The IWW also introduced a proletarian perspective to the party in Texas that affected the development of the radical tenant movement.

THE PROLETARIAN PERSPECTIVE

Thomas A. Hickey, though not a consistent left-winger, became the IWW's strongest Socialist supporter in the Southwest. Like his Louisiana comrade, Covington Hall, who ran afoul of the IWW national office for insisting on recruiting farmers into the BTW, Hickey made himself an enemy of the National Committee by attacking the party's bureaucracy. A disciple of DeLeon and an experienced industrial unionist, Hickey was moved by the BTW-IWW campaign in the pine belt; it encouraged him to introduce a more proletarian perspective into the Renters' Union he had helped found in 1911.[70] The timber workers' remarkable racial solidarity also encouraged him to modify the Renters' Union's "white only" constitution. At the Union's second annual convention in Waco, radicals of "strong socialistic sentiment" predominated, according to a disturbed *Farm and Ranch* reporter. Although the organization maintained its nonpartisan posture, "only resolutions emphasizing the bitter relations between tenants and landlords passed." After denouncing landlords who evicted tenants because they were union members or Socialists, the convention voted to strike the word "white" from its constitutional membership clause and to substitute a measure providing for "persons of African decent [*sic*] to be organized into separate locals."[71] Although the Socialists in the

69. Alexander to Kirby, May 11, 1912, in Kirby Papers.
70. *Rebel* (Hallettsville, Tex.), November 11, 1911, July 6, 27, 1912; Hall, "Labor Struggles in the Deep South," 180–830; and Thomas A. Hickey, "The Land Renters' Union in Texas," *International Socialist Review*, XIII (1912), 239–44.
71. *Farm and Ranch* (Dallas), October 28, 1912.

Renters' Union settled on a segregated form of organization, they did advance beyond the Farmers' Union to recruit some black and brown tenants. These efforts to organize nonwhite renters resulted mainly from the proletarian influence of the interracial BTW with which the Renters' Union formally identified itself in the 1912 convention. Socialist leaders like Hickey and Meitzen refused to openly recruit blacks into the party when most of them could not vote anyway, but they apparently accepted the necessity of bringing blacks into a syndicalist organization like the Renters' Union.[72]

After noting that the tenant delegates identified themselves with the BTW's "revolt against the lumber trust," *Farm and Ranch* lamented that the "only leaders who offered themselves to the convention were men committed to the militant socialistic program." It concluded: "If the wiser and saner leadership had been present, if the landlords themselves had been there to help, that convention would have assumed a far different aspect and a far superior one. It might have been a really beneficial force in solving the land tenure problem which confronts the South."

However, Hickey and the other Renters' Union leaders intended to preserve the Union's "industrial autonomy" by excluding landowners and all other bourgeois elements. Many members of the dirt-farmer majority in the Farmers' Union who had struggled unsuccessfully to keep out businessmen and Democratic politicians were now disillusioned with "business unionism" and were "ready for a class conscious organization."[73]

The Brotherhood of Timber Workers offered the Renters' Union a model of a militant industrial union broad enough to include blacks as well as whites, farmers as well as workers. When "Big Bill" Haywood toured the region in the summer of 1912 he insisted that there was a direct connection between the two movements: "The influence of the Timber Workers' Organization in the South is extending to the men who work on the plantations. In fact, many

72. See *Rebel* (Hallettsville, Tex.), August 26, 1911, May 16, 1914, April 3, 24, August 24, October 23, 1915, May 13, 1916.
73. *Ibid.*; Dallas *Laborer*, November 8, 1911; *Rebel* (Hallettsville, Tex.), January 6, 1912.

farmers and laborers work at both vocations in season. The necessity of industrial organization is recognized and communication is
being established between the farm renters of Louisiana and those
in Texas who are already organized into a union."[74]

In late 1911 and early 1912, just after the BTW's first confrontation with the Lumber Operators' Association, the Renters' Union
organized three strikes in the Texas black belt and, according to the
Rebel, won them all. These were local tenant strikes against the
landlords' demands for additional or "bonus" rents and increased
shares. In one instance, however, the renters struck to compel a
landlord to deal fairly with the widow of a fellow tenant.[75]

In Oklahoma there was less enthusiasm for the IWW because
party leaders were committed to working within the AFL. There
was very little hostility expressed toward the IWW however. In
fact, the most influential propagandist in the movement, Oscar
Ameringer, was still a close friend of Wobbly leader Covington Hall
from the days when they battled the AFL labor bosses in New
Orleans. Most of the support for the IWW in Oklahoma prior to
the organizing campaigns that began among harvest stiffs and oil
workers in 1915 came from militants who were organizing tenant
unions in southern Oklahoma along the industrial lines laid down
by Tom Hickey in Texas. But even in the western part of the state
there were a few industrial unionists like John G. Wills who supported the "Wobs." Indeed, during the height of the debate over
sabotage, Jasper Roberts, editor of the *Advocate* in Beckham
County, called Bill Haywood "the leading revolutionist in the
country," a radical who did not "believe in begging for a crumb in
the form of some political advantage." To those comrades who
criticized Haywood's IWW for being too radical Roberts said,
"Sometimes I think we are not radical enough."[76] The vanguard in-

74. Covington Hall, "Labor in the South," *Solidarity* (New Castle, Pa.),
October 12, 1912, p. 3; *Rebel* (Hallettsville, Tex.), May 25, 1912. Also see
Hickey to Bill Haywood, July 27, 1911, reprinted in *Revolt* (San Francisco),
August 19, 1911.

75. *Rebel* (Hallettsville, Tex.), March 2, 1912.

76. It is difficult to say how many blacklisted Knights and American
Railway Union men like Wills homesteaded in western Oklahoma; Amerin-

fluence of the Wobblies extended even to the most rural section of the movement in western Oklahoma.

Nearly all of the southwestern Socialists who supported the IWW were concentrated below the Red River in western Louisiana and Texas, but the United Mine Workers provided a comparable proletarian influence in the Oklahoma and Arkansas parties. Key leaders in these states like Nagle, Ameringer, and Hogan praised the radicalizing potential of the UMW's industrialism as lavishly as Hickey praised the IWW. Although the former opposed the dual unionism and violent rhetoric of the Wobblies, they were critical of the exclusionary craft unionism and were anxious (far more so than Hickey) to apply the UMW's interracial method of organization to the locals of the Socialist party and the Renters' Union. Socialist mine union leaders, especially Holt of Oklahoma, were very active in introducing a proletarian perspective to the rural movement.[77]

The Socialist movement north of the Red River was affected by the violent class struggle in the coal fields and by the solidarity the UMW achieved in its conflict with the region's biggest corporations. But most tenant farmers and small-town party members were far removed from the mining zone. Indeed, some miners resented the white tenants—derisively called "hoosiers" or "pea-

---

ger and other Socialists claimed that "old timers" of this sort were scattered all through the area. Oscar Ameringer, *If You Don't Weaken*, 259–60. Karl Pretshold, "Memo, Oklahoma Politics," 1932, pp. 6–7, in State and Local Correspondence, Socialist Party Papers, Duke; *Beckham County Advocate* (Carter, Okla.), May 15, 1912. Even the United Mine Workers, a loyal AFL affiliate, showed some respect for the rival IWW in the Southwest. In fact, a UMW local in Pittsburg, Kansas, sent a delegate to the IWW's founding convention in 1905. *Proceedings of the Founding Convention of the IWW, 1905* (New York: Pathfinder, 1969), 526. Many years later Dave Archibald, a loyal UMW member from Krebs, Oklahoma, said when asked about the Wobblies: "Don't let anybody ever tell ya' they wasn't all right too. They's good people; they done a lot a good deeds in that Western country." Archibald interview, Oklahoma Department of Libraries.

77. See Oscar Ameringer, "Where I Stand," *Social Democratic Herald* (Milwaukee), February 15, 1913; Patrick S. Nagle, "Shall the Socialist Party Help the Miner," *Oklahoma Pioneer* (Oklahoma City), September 3, 1910; and "The Farmer and Unionism," *Appeal to Reason* (Girard, Kan.), July 6, 1912.

pickers"—because some of them acted as strikebreakers in the battles of the 1890s.[78] Unlike the tenants and townspeople in the piney woods who could not escape the battle between the BTW and the Southern Lumber Operators' Association and consequently were forced to take sides, most residents of the cotton country learned about the miners' struggles largely through the Socialist press or through the speeches by militant miners and other party speakers. As a result, the Socialist movement in the piney woods took on a revolutionary fervor encouraged by Red industrial union leaders with broad support. In western Louisiana and East Texas poor farmers had direct contact with the log camps and sawmills; they frequently alternated between lumber work and farming, or sold produce in the streets of the timber towns. And even those rural folk who were far removed from the mill villages often knew a friend or relative who had left the farm to work for the big corporations. Furthermore, many small farmers had been displaced by the sawmill companies and some of them returned to the land as tenants of the lumber trust. Under these conditions, it was not surprising that the farmers and townspeople of the pine region often identified so closely with the timber workers' struggle that they actually joined the BTW.[79] And since the national and state leadership of the Socialist party refused to intervene very forcefully in the class struggle, it is not surprising that the Socialist movement in this region tended to be rather syndicalistic. Nevertheless, in the 1912 election the party reaped considerable benefits from this struggle which, as Shannon notes, took place "against a background of violence and class conflict."[80]

78. Archibald interview, November 12, 1974, Oklahoma Department of Libraries.

79. See Green, "Brotherhood of Timber Workers," 190–200.

80. David Shannon, *The Socialist Party of America, A History* (New York: Macmillan, 1955), 37.

VI

"The Swelling Minority": Patterns of Socialist Support in the Southwest 1912

EUGENE V. DEBS'S fourth presidential campaign, in 1912, climaxed the "Golden Age of American Socialism." Debs and his comrades found a national forum for their radical critique of progressive reform represented by the candidacies of Woodrow Wilson and Theodore Roosevelt. They also won their largest audiences for speeches on the Cooperative Commonwealth's many virtues. Socialism reached its peak at the polls in most states, almost a million voters expressing their desire for a Socialist alternative to capitalism. And once again the southwestern states led the way by recording surprising gains for Socialist party candidates. The hard-fought campaign of 1912 is a useful point at which to study the southwestern Socialists' electoral strategy, and the ensuing election offers an equally revealing means of examining the nature of their voting support.

The Southwestern Socialist party vote of 1912, which encompassed nearly one-tenth of Debs's national total, was concentrated in several regions: the southern Oklahoma cotton country (not the northern wheat-growing counties where the Populists had thrived); north central and northeastern Texas as well as western Louisiana (in some but not all of the old People's party's strongholds); and in southeastern Kansas and western Arkansas (especially in the coal-mining counties). The regional pattern of Socialist voting support shows that Debs registered his highest totals in the poorest farming districts, though not necessarily in the "insecure" one-crop areas as S. M. Lipset maintains in *Agrarian Socialism*.

Precinct-level voting analysis also reveals disproportionate Socialist strength in isolated industrial towns, especially coal-mining camps.

This study of the 1912 southwestern election results indicates the slight importance of "independent variables" generally associated with midwestern protest voting, that is, one-crop agriculture, ethnicity, religion, and traditional partisan loyalties (in this case, to third parties). The concentration of Debs's heaviest voting support in the poorest regions provides a rough indication of the party's electoral support among the laboring classes, but this kind of regional analysis only gives a rather static and very broad profile of the Socialist vote—a profile that could lead to specious generalizations as a result of what voting analysts call the "ecological fallacy" (*i.e.* the assumption that votes concentrated in a certain region actually tell how individuals in that region voted).

In order to find a more meaningful pattern in Socialist voting support it is necessary to look beyond the generalizations provided by county-level correlations. A precinct-level analysis of town-country tension (a traditional conflict in late nineteenth-century southwestern social, economic, and political history) reveals the class dimension in rural Socialist support, a dimension far more obvious in the case of Debs's electoral support in one-industry working-class communities.

THE CAMPAIGN OF 1912

The explosion of working-class militancy in the piney woods and the growth of socialism among union miners in the coal fields influenced the 1912 Socialist campaign. The struggles of Socialist-led industrial unions between 1910 and 1912 raised the class consciousness of rural radicals, especially those "red carders" who belonged to the tenant unions in Oklahoma and Texas. In 1912 Socialist party candidates in the Southwest insisted on the common class identity of workers and farmers who were exploited by the same class enemy. This argument seemed especially convincing in the strike-torn yellow-pine region of western Louisiana and East Texas where timber workers of both races shared with tenant farmers an "intense bitterness" toward the lumber barons. During the summer of 1912, the "massacre" of unionists at Grabow, the arrest and indictment of the Brotherhood of Timber Workers' president, Arthur Emerson, and other workers, and the extension of the operators' lockout made it easy for Red agitators to inflame the poor people of the piney woods "against all capitalists in general."[1]

In September Wobblies from all over the country flocked into Lake Charles to help Emerson and the other Grabow defendants. In the same month the Operators' Association, unsatisfied with the progress of the lockout, moved against one of its own members. The Association persuaded the Santa Fe Railroad corporation to take full control of the American Lumber Company at Merryville, forcing out part-owner Sam Park who had come to terms with the BTW. The new management promptly fired fifteen union men who had testified for Emerson and the Grabow defendants. The next day the thirteen hundred workers at the American mill, all of them BTW members and half of them black, responded with a protest strike. The Lumber Association then began a drastic effort to "knock all the fight out of the BTW."[2]

Three days after the Merryville strike began, the well-publicized trial of A. L. Emerson and the Grabow defendants came to an end. The exciting deliberations at Lake Charles had reached a climax when the star witness for the prosecution (led by progressive Congressman A. J. Pujo) admitted that the gunmen at the Galloway mill had been drinking before the BTW marchers arrived at Grabow on July 7. He testified that at one point the millowner told his storekeeper to "pour" liquor into the armed guards until the union parade arrived. Under these circumstances, Congressman Pujo, who was famous for his investigation of the "trusts" in Wash-

---

1. New Orleans *Times-Democrat*, August 15, October 28, 1912. For a fuller account, see James R. Green, "The Brotherhood of Timber Workers, 1910–1913: A Radical Response to Industrial Capitalism in the Southern U.S.A.," *Past and Present*, No. 60 (1973), 176–95.
2. Grady McWhiney, "Louisiana Socialists in the Early Twentieth Century: A Study of Rustic Radicalism," *Journal of Southern History*, XX (1954), 332–33; W. D. Haywood, "Timber Workers and Timber Wolves," *International Socialist Review*, XIII (1912), 105–10.

ington, closed his case and hoped that his clients, the "lumber barons" of Louisiana, would not be prosecuted.

It took only a few minutes for the jury (composed of seven farmers, two businessmen, and three nonunion workers) to acquit the defendants. When the judge announced the verdict, the little courtroom erupted with cheers and the audience spilled out into the streets of Lake Charles for a victory parade. That night a "jubilation meeting" took place at the Carpenters' Hall, attended by members of many unions, plus Socialists, Wobblies, and all seven farmers who had served on the jury. The IWW placed a great deal of emphasis on winning free-speech fights and fighting for workers' constitutional rights with nonviolent methods. In this case their strategy had produced a victory. In a few months, however, the results of the Merryville strike would make that victory seem quite hollow.[3]

The outcome of the Lake Charles trial, coupled with the radical propaganda campaign it generated, increased the popularity of the Socialist party and the BTW throughout the region. After starting a party local among the prisoners in the Lake Charles jail, J. H. Helton returned to DeRidder and predicted a big protest vote for Gene Debs throughout the "infected area." The excitement also spread through East Texas and out into the Socialist locals in the cotton country. Party Secretary Ed Green and *Rebel* editor Tom Hickey headed the list of speakers who had campaigned actively to win support for the BTW and the Lake Charles defendants. Both Gene Debs and "Big Bill" Haywood, who were at the peak of their popularity as working-class leaders, came to the Texas encampments and urged the members of the Renters' Union to aid the Brotherhood and to follow in its "revolutionary footsteps." Tenant organizer Hugh Moore picked up the cadence when he declared that he was "deeply indignant over the treatment meted out to his brothers in the piney woods." Members of the tenant union would

3. Haywood, "Timber Workers and Timber Wolves," 105–10; Covington Hall, "The Victory of the Lumberjacks," *International Socialist Review*, XIII (1912), 470–71. See also letters to editor from Iola Dunn and J. H. Helton, *International Socialist Review*, XIII (1912–13), 439, 511.

stand behind the BTW, Moore promised, because the "interests of the timber workers" were "identical with those of the renters."[4] These campaign speeches could not actually create solidarity between tenants and timber workers, but they reflected the confident feeling of all leftists that the BTW's struggle would help win more support for the party at the polls in November.

As the activities of the Brotherhood of Timber Workers in the piney woods and the Renters' Union in the cotton country heated up the southwestern summer, an East Texas Democrat warned Governor O. B. Colquitt that the Socialists were "getting pretty thick" in his county.[5] Indeed, as the tempo of the Socialist campaign increased, the Democrats seemed to be losing more and more tenant supporters to the radicals. In August of 1912, Nat L. Hardy, editor of the Dallas *Laborer*, reported: "In Texas alone, in great big old rack-rented Texas, there are twenty four regularly routed organizers besides a host of volunteers and over thirty big camp meetings. The *Appeal to Reason* has a circulation of nearly 40,000 and the Socialist Party has a membership of over 6,000, most of them tenants."[6] The Texas Reds organized an impressive total of 181 new locals in the winter and spring of 1912. They attributed this marked growth to the grass-roots activism stimulated by their new decentralization program, but the success of the Renters' Union (which enrolled 4,000 members in its first year) also helped the Texas Socialist party grow faster than any other state organization in the nation.[7]

In Arkansas, A. W. Ricker wrote to a New York Socialist daily that the growth of socialism occurred largely after the appointment of State Secretary Ida Callery, "a native Arkansas girl, who was raised and schooled in Oklahoma." She was brought into Ar-

4. *Rebel* (Hallettsville, Tex.), July 6, 20, 27, August 17, September 7, 14, 1912.
5. *Ibid.*, March 30, 1912. J. L. Tidemore to Oscar B. Colquitt, July 23, 1912, in Oscar Branch Colquitt Papers, Barker Library, University of Texas, Austin.
6. *Appeal to Reason* (Girard, Kan.), August 31, 1912.
7. *Rebel* (Hallettsville, Tex.), May 4, 24, June 29, 1912. Also see Nat Hardy, "The Texas Programme," *International Socialist Review*, XI (April, 1911), 622–23.

kansas by the State Executive Committee and made the organization "self-sustaining" despite the difficulties involved in "training and teaching mountaineers and cotton pickers to pay dues and keep locals alive." Ricker then told New York *Call* readers about the remarkable Socialist leadership in the Ozarks:

> Mrs. Callery was formerly a school teacher in the Indian Mission schools. She is a typical woman of the Southwest prairies, to whose native independence and courage have been added the culture and enlightenment of education. She is small and wiry, and can pound the typewriter all the day and into the night with nervous prostration. She has literally reached out into the mountains and valleys and led the people into organizing and maintaining locals. As a result there are now locals in the state reaching into nearly every county.

Ricker went on to describe the important roles played by Dan Hogan—"the best the South produces in bigness of soul, generousity, lightheartedness, and sentimentality"—and his daughter Freda, who produced the state Socialist newspaper in Huntington. Not to be forgotten for that matter were E. E. Perrin, the famous "blacksmith orator" of Little Rock—a "character of rare force and power"—or Comrade G. E. Mikel, the Socialist mayor of Hartford, Arkansas, who was elected president of the State Federation of Labor.[8]

In Oklahoma the party's dues-paying membership increased from 3,075 to 4,750, making it the largest "red-card organization" in the country. By 1912 the Oklahoma Socialists had successfully adapted the Milwaukee "system," placing corresponding committeemen in more than half of the state's 2,500 voting precincts. This kind of organization paid off handsomely when it came time to watch the polls and count votes. The Sooner Socialists placed a great deal of emphasis on local organization and stressed the importance of paying dues and exercising the democratic rights awarded to party members who met their obligations. Unlike the Texas Socialists, Otto Branstetter and his comrades were not afraid to emulate the tactics that Victor Berger and the Milwaukee Socialists had used

8. A. W. Ricker, "Arkansas Is Ripe for the Harvest," New York *Call*, April 15, 1912.

to build a successful political machine, but they were less bureaucratic and more democratic than their northern comrades because
they wanted to allow for grass-roots local development. Frontier
farmers, with their strong individualistic attitude toward liberty,
would have bridled under bureaucratic party discipline.[9]

Local organization provided the key to effective electioneering.
The locals acted as "Little Red School Houses" sponsoring everything from debates on evolution and revolution to party picnics
and Sunday schools for youthful truthseekers. These cells also
provided a collective meeting place for lonely farm families living
in a society almost as segregated by class as it was by race. Party
units varied from deep-rooted locals to fly-by-night groups of three
or four farmers and a village atheist. Party organizers were sent
out from state headquarters occasionally to keep stray locals in
line. Shortly after he arrived in Oklahoma Oscar Ameringer traveled to Hugo, capital of the Choctaw Nation, where he was met by
a comrade who drove him "to a sawmill town on the Red River
bearing the euphonious name of Frogville." Ameringer's job was
to reorganize a local that "had gone to pot." When he asked what
had happened to the Frogville local, the driver replied that it had
"gone to hell." Yes, but why, asked the organizer? "Capitalism,"
replied his companion in a solemn voice. The secretary of the local
had succumbed to the temptations of capitalism and absconded
with the local's three-dollar treasury. "Mindful of the bitter experience the membership had had with a profit-minded share cropper,
and to re-establish the confidence of the assembled ex- and prospective members in the integrity of the international socialist
movement," Ameringer recalled, "I decided the next secretary of
the Frogville local must be a genuine proletarian." Ameringer

9. *Appeal to Reason* (Girard, Kan.), January 13, 1912. David Shannon, *The Socialist Party of America, A History* (New York: Macmillan, 1955), 34–35. *Report of the Socialist State Convention, 1912*, in Socialist Party Papers, Perkins Library, Duke University. Otto Branstetter, "The Socialist Com-rade's Pledge," *National Rip-Saw* (St. Louis), October, 1911, p. 9; Patrick S. Nagle, "Organization," undated broadside in Socialist Party Papers, Duke. On Milwaukee socialism, see Sally M. Miller, *Victor Berger and the Promise of Constructive Socialism, 1910–1920* (Westport, Conn.: Greenwood, 1973).

picked a saw filer from the local mill, who had belonged to the UMW in McAlester, and rigged his election as local secretary. Some months later Ameringer met the same "pessimistic comrade from Frogville" at an encampment and learned that the local had "gone to hell" again. The pessimist told him that capitalism made crooks of the best of men, and that the proletarian secretary Ameringer had put in charge of the Frogville local "ran off with the treasury and took a comrade's wife with him." All of this proved to Ameringer that the "profit virus" had infected the American people to such an extent that "even proletarians could not be trusted."[10]

Despite the unreliability and downright dishonesty of some local secretaries, like the Frogville "proletarian," hundreds of party cells throughout the Southwest offered camaraderie as well as education and organization. For some red carders the local even served as a center of common labor. In 1910 and 1911 a number of locals in Oklahoma and Texas started cooperative cotton patches in which Socialists worked together to support their families and their party. Some local comrades even formed a cooperative bank in the town of Kansas, Oklahoma. In many of the rural sections of the Southwest the party local served as a little Socialist community, a sort of surrogate for the declining "country community."[11]

10. Frank P. O'Hare, "The Red Card Organization," *International Socialist Review*, XIII (1912), 668–69; W. T. Brown, "The Mission of the Socialist Local," *National Rip-Saw*, October, 1911, pp 8–9; Oscar Ameringer, *If You Don't Weaken: The Autobiography of Oscar Ameringer* (New York: Henry Holt, 1940), 253–56.

11. *Oklahoma Pioneer* (Oklahoma City), April 6, 1910; Dallas *Morning News*, May 14, 1911; advertisement for Kansas, Oklahoma cooperative bank, in *International Socialist Review*, X (1909–10), 180. *Constitution of the Texas Socialist Party, Adopted January 14, 1910, Amended 1911–1912*, p. 4, in Barker Library. On the decline of the "country community," see Warren H. Wilson, "Social Life in the Country," *Annals of the American Academy of Social and Political Science*, XL (1912), 120–30. A survey in southern Travis County, Texas, revealed that only 19 percent of the white tenants interviewed visited the local villages frequently and that of those who did 56 percent went for business reasons. Just 36 percent were members of lodges or clubs and "only 59 percent of the white tenants belonged to some church" as compared to 77 percent of the farm owners. "This," the investigator said, "is explained by the mobility and poverty of the tenant class and the relative stability and well-to-do character of the owning class." George S. Weherwein and R. B. Woods, "Social Life and Religious Activity in Southern

The Oklahoma party allowed for considerable autonomy within its thriving locals so that members could "advocate whatever political or economic action" they believed necessary for the "relief of their communities." All party members were required to support the national platform and the "principles of international socialism," but local members did influence the formulation of immediate demands for the state program. For example, the 1912 Oklahoma platform contained very specific locally initiated planks calling for the abolition of obscure land and game laws and for the elimination of esoteric legal language that nourished "petty law firms" and made courtroom proceedings incomprehensible to the poor and uneducated.[12]

The 1912 platform also contained "a much stronger plank concerning Negro rights." The Oklahoma Socialists denounced the racism of the old parties—the cowardice of the GOP, which refused to defend its own members, and the "viciousness" of the Democrats who defended the enslavement of blacks in order to maintain the loyalty of poor whites. Article 28 also protested against the "lawlessness, oppression, and violence" to which the blacks had been subjected and called for "class conscious solidarity" among farmers and workers of both races. And it once again warned poor whites that their own disfranchisement would certainly follow that of the blacks.[13] The article did not promise social equality for blacks, but neither did it endorse racial segregation, as some party members like H. H. Stallard demanded. An important official of the lily-white Farmers' Union, Stallard rose to an influential position in the western branch of the party after his relatively late conversion to socialism from the Democratic party.

Travis County, Texas," in N. L. Sims (ed.), *The Rural Community* (New York: Charles Scribner's Sons, 1920), 418–24, 498–508.

12. James B. Scales, "Political History of Oklahoma, 1907–1949" (Ph.D. dissertation, University of Oklahoma, 1949), 151–52; "State Platform of the Oklahoma Socialist Party, 1912," in Socialist Party Papers, Duke.

13. H. L. Meredith, "Agrarian Socialism in Oklahoma" (Ph.D. dissertation, University of Oklahoma, 1969), 124; and "State Platform of Oklahoma Socialist Party." Also see H. L. Meredith, "Agrarian Socialism and the Negro in Oklahoma, 1900–1918," *Labor History*, XI (1970), 277–86.

In endorsing segregation, Stallard spoke for those who believed that the party had lost at least ten thousand white votes as a result of its opposition to the grandfather clause. Stallard's call for an officially segregated party aroused a heated debate in the spring of 1912. John B. Porter, a black Socialist from Cogar, attacked this position as a deliberate offense to those blacks who were joining the Socialist party because it alone "stood for collectivism, democracy and equality." Stallard's blatant prejudice proved that he was "race conscious rather than class conscious" and his racist pragmatism proved that he was resorting to "the tactics of curbstone politician, putting the office above principle." Porter said he would "utterly despair" if not for his Socialist comrades whose belief in the unity and equality of all mankind could not be shaken by the need to win votes on "bread and butter" issues.[14]

Porter's "despair" was reduced by principled Oklahoma Socialists like Oscar Ameringer, Otto Branstetter, Pat Nagle, and John G. Wills, author of a hard-hitting attack on segregationists entitled "The Socialist Jim Crow Car."[15] These equalitarian leaders joined local comrades (like the coal miners at Wilburton who called for H. H. Stallard's expulsion) to win an endorsement of Article 28 at the 1912 party convention. This progressive resolution on the race question was then approved by the rank and file in a referendum, indicating that many Oklahoma Socialists still hoped to build an interracial party.

The 1912 Oklahoma platform also renewed the immediate demands first made in the 1909 farmer's program; these proposals finally won an endorsement from the national party congress in May. A. M. Simons again advocated the adoption of a farm program based on the southwestern movement's demands, but this time he deemphasized the importance of recruiting small-farm owners. Admitting that the rise of tenancy undermined his earlier

14. H. H. Stallard to editor, *Oklahoma Pioneer* (Oklahoma City), February 10, 1912; John B. Porter to the editor, *ibid.*, March 2, 1912.
15. Wills replied to Stallard that if the Socialists did lose ten thousand votes for opposing the grandfather clause, "they were well lost," because such a reactionary element had "no place in the socialist movement." *Ibid.*, March 16, 1912.

revisionism on the farm question, Simons finally turned his attention to the "class of farm tenants" swelling the ranks of the Texas and Oklahoma parties. He boldly called for a land-tax plank to attract tenants by taking the speculative advantage out of landholding. "Some of you are going to be frightened because you catch a phrase there which you may think we borrowed from the single tax program," he told the delegates. "But I hope that no one will bring that up again until he has read again the Communist Manifesto," which incorporated this kind of demand long before Henry George ever wrote *Progress and Poverty.* Simons concluded by encouraging the tenant unions organized by Texas Socialists to fight along the same lines as the working class.[16]

Simons and other advocates of the southwestern farm program convinced most delegates that the Oklahoma platform did not intend to save petty capitalists, yet some orthodox Socialists nevertheless insisted on demanding the immediate collectivization of all farmland. And some southwestern radicals, such as Pat Nagle and John G. Wills (one of the few "working farmers" at the convention), actually voted for this motion, although most agrarian Socialists agreed with Richey Alexander who argued that the demand would alienate all rural support by committing the party to nationalizing everything from corncribs to garden plots. After a spirited debate, a majority did vote to incorporate most of the Oklahoma "farmers' program" into the 1912 national platform. The key demands remained unchanged: state-sponsored cooperatives, state-owned transportation, storage and processing facilities, graduated land taxes, and expansion of the public domain for tenant use. The national platform diverged from the Oklahoma model in calling for collective or "socially operated" farms rather than "fee simple" tenant farms on public land.[17]

The passage of a farm program, Simons remarked, resulted largely from the recognition that the rise of tenancy and other

16. John Spargo (ed.), *Proceedings of National Convention of the Socialist Party, 1912* (Chicago: M. A. Donahue and Socialist Party, 1912), 62, 67–69, 74, 79.
17. *Ibid.*, 192–93. For a review of the whole debate over the farm program based upon documents of major importance see W. J. Ghent (ed.), *Socialism and the Farmer* (Girard, Kan.: *Appeal to Reason*, 1916).

developments tended to "verify Marx's position in regard to concentration in agriculture, something that had not been hitherto apparent in this country."[18] Many southwestern Socialists had understood the implications of these changes much earlier, and so, by 1912 the Texas and Oklahoma Socialists, with the help of Tom Hickey's *Rebel* and Pat Nagle's *Tenant Farmer*, made tenancy and the "concentration of land," the paramount issues in their campaigns.[19]

The Texas platform declared that capitalism divided rural society as well as industrial society into "warring groups and classes based on material interest." A notable example of capitalist oppression was the landlord who demanded contracts that interfered with the "personal and political liberty of the tenant." Shortly before the election, the *Rebel* described an example of landlord oppression in Coleman County that illustrated the nature of class conflict on a local level. In 1909 renters and others in and around Leaday, Texas, had organized a Socialist local. Many of the farmers were tenants of Tom Padgitt, a landlord who lived in Dallas. The Reds among them complained that Padgitt's manager, C. A. Rives, had organized an anti-Socialist league, publicly threatening members of the party and firing some who were tenants. When the Socialists got up a petition denouncing the overseer for "stirring up strife in the community," Rives admitted that Leaday was experiencing "a war" between the radicals and the "antis." Landlord Padgitt came out from Dallas to talk to the petitioners but refused to fire Rives. "Your community is split wide open, but the same thing is going on everywhere," he told them. "This is not only a

18. *Coming Nation* (Girard, Kan.), July 20, 27, August 3, 1912. Lenin came to the same conclusion based on empirical research in American agricultural statistics, but his work was not translated and was therefore unknown to American Socialists at the time. See V. I. Lenin, "New Data on the Laws of Development of Capitalism in Agriculture: Capitalism and Agriculture in the United States of America," in *Theory of the Agrarian Question*, Vol. XII of V. I. Lenin, *Collected Works* (12 vols.; Moscow: International, 1929), 190–282.

19. *Rebel* (Hallettsville, Tex.), February 24, October 19, 1912, and *Tenant Farmer* (Kingfisher, Okla.), September, 1912. Also see the comprehensive campaign pamphlet by Oscar Ameringer, *Socialism for the Farmer Who Farms the Farm*, in *National Rip-Saw* Series No. 15 (St. Louis: Rip-Saw Publishing, 1912).

Coleman County fight, it is a state wide fight, a nation wide fight."[20]
The *Rebel* gathered other evidence to demonstrate the widespread nature of the Coleman County "strife." A sociologist who
toured cotton-tenancy regions in 1912 corroborated these findings,
reporting that destructive "class distinctions in the country" caused
by the injection of "alien human material" (tenants) had ended the
"old warmth and intimacy of social intercourse" in these rural
communities. "The growth of class consciousness" in these regions,
he wrote, "is a factor of increasing consequence."[21]

"Class distinctions" cut through southern Oklahoma society as
clearly as they did through the Texas cotton belt. "The burden
of paying rent and trying to contend with the vagaries of land,
weather, boll weevil and the commodity markets produced a sense
of oppression among the tenants," writes Garin Burbank about
Marshall County. Absentee landlords in counties like Coleman and
Marshall exacerbated this sense of oppression and played into the
hands of Socialist campaigners who loved to attack oppressive
landlordism as a curse added to "the toil, drudgery and grind of
capitalism."[22] The local Socialist party candidates generally knew
tenants and workers as well as landlords and merchants, and they
could speak directly to the issues that divided the classes. It did
seem as though Socialist candidates in 1912 were trying to alienate
tenants and other workers against the "middle class,"[23] but they
were also giving political expression to long-standing lower-class
resentments.

When the 1910 census revealed that over half the Texas and Oklahoma farmers were tenants, some of the leading Southwest newspapers noted the serious and permanent nature of the land problem. However, since most of the Socialists' campaign opponents in
1912 were landlords, bankers, and merchants who profited from
the system, these opponents ignored the renters' problems or dis-

20. *Rebel* (Hallettsville, Tex.), June 8, 1912, October 26, 1912.
21. Wilson, "Social Life in the Country," 124.
22. Garin Burbank, "Agrarian Radicals and Their Opponents: Political
Conflict in Southern Oklahoma, 1910–1924," *Journal of American History*,
LVIII (1971), 10.
23. Meredith, "Agrarian Socialism in Oklahoma," 126.

missed them as temporary. "The reluctance of progressive Democracy to offer remedies to the rising tenancy rate" allowed the Socialists to make it the key issue in their campaign.[24] As Pat Nagle told the national office in 1912, "The phenomenal growth of Socialism in Oklahoma is due to the flocking of tenant farmers into the Socialist Party." The Socialist candidate went into the "sticks" with a land program and "something definite to offer the tenants," whereas, according to Nagle, "the Democrat has nothing to offer the renter save the admonition to 'love Joe Bailey and hate the nigger', funny stories and a five cent cigar."[25]

Southwestern Socialists took advantage of the fact that in Oklahoma and Texas conservative Democrats had followed progressives into office. Governor Lee Cruce, an Ardmore banker, personified the commercial capitalism the Sooner Socialists attacked. Cruce enjoyed the support of reform-minded townspeople, Nagle wrote, because he "strongly opposed bootlegging, Sabbath breaking, swearing, tobacco chewing, gambling, rowdyism of all kinds and hunting on Sunday without a license."[26] But the governor ignored tenant farmers, and he had alienated trade unionists by threatening to call out the militia in the 1911 Oklahoma City streetcar strike and by vetoing a full-crew bill the railroad brotherhoods had initiated.

In Texas, Socialists welcomed the candidacy of Governor Oscar Branch Colquitt, because he was "a candid reactionary" who had the "courage to attack Socialism in the open."[27] He was aware of rising tenant discontent, largely through renter petitions presented by the Socialists. But in order to do battle with his prohibitionist opponents, Colquitt entered into an alliance with conservatives like Senator Joseph Weldon Bailey and lumber "baron" John Henry Kirby. Many of the old protégés of Jim Hogg and most of the

24. Dallas *News*, May 25, 1911; Galveston *News*, November 8, 1911; and James A. Tinsley, "The Progressive Movement in Texas" (Ph.D. dissertation, University of Wisconsin, 1953), 150.

25. P. S. Nagle, memo to national office, 1912, in State and Local Correspondence, Socialist Party Papers, Duke. Senator Joe Bailey of Texas was a leading conservative Democrat.

26. *Ibid.*; Scales, "Political History of Oklahoma," 151.

27. *Rebel* (Hallettsville, Tex.), August 3, 1912.

young progressives participated in Texas politics as "evangelical prohibitionists" and opponents of "Baileyism." In 1912 old reformers like former governors Campbell and Culberson joined such newcomers as Houston's mayor, H. B. Rice, Congressman Albert S. Burleson, and attorney Thomas W. Gregory, in E. M. House's campaign to elect Woodrow Wilson president. During the campaign, one "militant old liberal" complained: "It looks like the leading Democrats of Texas are abundantly content with saving the nation by the election of Wilson and that they are perfectly willing now that the state should go to hell." The progressive Democrats of Texas may have been "rising" in 1912, but their activities on behalf of Wilson did not prevent the Red Socialists from raising hell among the tenants.[28]

The Wilson campaign in Oklahoma was led by two men who were more concerned about agrarian issues like tenancy than most progressives; they were Senator Thomas Gore, an old Texas Populist, and William Murray, who returned to politics in 1912, became an important Wilson floor leader at the Democratic national convention, and easily won his party's nomination for congressman-at-large after receiving a personal endorsement from Bryan. Oklahoma Senator Robert L. Owen, a progressive landlord like Murray, also campaigned for reelection as a Wilsonian, but he used the Great Commoner's terms to describe the political conflict emerging on a state and local level. "There is no question in my mind," the senator said, "but that Socialism is spreading at a phenomenal rate and that a fight between individualism and Socialism is not very remote."[29]

To the southwestern Socialist, however, the election of 1912 was a fight between progressivism and socialism. The progressive ad-

28. Tinsley, "Progressive Movement in Texas," 270; Lewis L. Gould, *Progressives and Prohibitionists: Texas Democrats in the Wilson Era* (Austin: University of Texas Press, 1973), 26, 32, 42; and Arthur S. Link, *Woodrow Wilson: The New Freedom* (Princeton, N.J.: Princeton University Press, 1956), 135.

29. Keith L. Bryant, Jr., *Alfalfa Bill Murray* (Norman: University of Oklahoma Press, 1968), 99–104; Hollis (Okla.) *Post-Herald*, May 23, 1912. See also William Jennings Bryan, "Individualism Versus Socialism," *Century Magazine*, LXXI (April, 1906), 856.

ministrations of Haskell and Campbell in Oklahoma and Texas, they argued, proved that reform Democrats really acted on behalf of businessmen and landlords, not in the interests of poor farmers and workers. The progressive presidential candidates, Wilson and Roosevelt, offered new programs, but they were like the southerners who wanted to reform slavery without abolishing the institution, Pat Nagle wrote. The New Freedom and the New Nationalism simply sought to "reform the institution of capitalism (or·wage slavery) and make it respectable." If elected, the advocates of these programs would, at best, "reduce the robbery from three fourths to two fourths."[30]

Southwestern Socialist candidates constantly tried to expose the landlord and business connections of their Wilsonian opponents and usually gained applause when they mocked the fact that the reformers were more concerned with the liquor question than the land question. For the most part, however, the candidates of the new third party were amateur campaigners, unknown outside of their own localities. They needed help badly, and Gene Debs gave it to them.

Debs was the Socialist party's star attraction, because, as the cotton tenants put it, he had "kindlin' power."[31] In September, 1912, the lanky Hoosier gave a speech at a Texas encampment that illustrates the emotionalism and millennialism of his appeal to rural audiences. "We have the richest nation in the world; a land blessed with superabundance," he told the tenants and their families, "and yet there are ten million people in this country who are virtually paupers." Debs railed against the capitalists who were responsible and promised that the people would rise up and end this terrible reign. "These are stirring days," he exclaimed. "The old order can survive but little longer. The swelling minority sounds the warning of impending change. Soon that minority will

30. *Constructive Socialist* (Altus, Okla.), October 30, 1912.
31. Oscar Ameringer, *If You Don't Weaken*, 260, 267; Callery to Debs, August 9, 1912, in Eugene V. Debs Collection, Cunningham Library, Indiana State University, Terre Haute; and Kate Richards O'Hare to Castleton, September 16, 1945, in Eugene V. Debs Collection, Castleton Papers, Tamiment Institute, New York.

become the majority and then will come the Co-operative Commonwealth."[32]

Democratic politicians worried about Debs's appeal to the giant encampment audiences, and in Oklahoma they urged William Murray to speak in "Socialist strongholds throughout the state." Campaigning as an agrarian reformer and "carrying the message of Wilson's 'New Freedom'," Murray stressed his support for a graduated land tax that "could eliminate large landholdings without recourse to socialism." However, "Alfalfa Bill's" efforts to "cut the Socialist vote" in 1912 were not very successful.[33]

THE SOCIALIST VOTE OF 1912

The Socialist ticket headed by Eugene V. Debs polled over 42,000 votes in Oklahoma, 16.6 percent of the total. This was, coincidentally, about the same number as the *Appeal to Reason*'s state-wide circulation. Although these gains were not as great as some had predicted, Debs did poll twice as many votes in 1912 as he had received in Oklahoma four years earlier.[34]

Debs received over 25 percent of the vote in twenty-three Oklahoma counties. These strong Socialist counties were the least urbanized in the state, with only 7.5 percent of their populations living in towns over 2,500. They were also among the least dynamic counties in the state, recording an average population growth of only 16 percent between 1910 and 1920, compared to a growth rate of 42 percent in the twenty-four counties where Socialist candidates polled their lowest totals. The counties in which the party won more than one quarter of the vote also had very high tenancy rates (63 percent) and very low valuations per farm ($3,244 per

32. *Rebel* (Hallettsville, Tex.), September 14, 1912.
33. Bryant, *Alfalfa Bill Murray*, 53, 105.
34. All county and state voting returns, unless cited otherwise, were drawn from Oliver Benson, *et al.*, *Oklahoma Votes, 1907–1962* (Norman: University of Oklahoma Press, 1964); *Tribune Almanac, 1913* (New York: Herald Tribune, 1913); and from the files of the Inter-University Consortium for Political Research, Ann Arbor, Michigan. Precinct returns, unless cited otherwise, are from the records of the Oklahoma State Election Board, Capitol Building, Oklahoma City. The author would like to thank Garin Burbank for sharing various precinct statistics.

farm including buildings as well as land). By contrast, only 48 percent of the farmers were tenants in the counties where Debs and the Socialists received less than 10 percent of the vote. Total farm values averaged $5,552 in these old-party strongholds.[35]

Socialist votes clearly clustered the poorest sections of the state, and the party's electoral support continued to shift from the northern wheat-growing counties, where the movement was born out of populism, to the poorer southern cotton-growing counties. As Figure 1 indicates, Debs received his largest vote in the south central and southeastern cotton-producing counties where share tenants represented 78.5 percent of all farmers (the highest rate of tenancy in the nation). Fred Holt, secretary-treasurer of the UMW, actually ran ahead of Debs in this area (the Fourth Congressional District), polling votes from coal miners, railroad workers, and small-town businessmen as well as from tenant farmers. Holt averaged 24 percent of the vote in his congressional race while the Farmers' Union official, H. H. Stallard, polled 21 percent in the corn, wheat, and cotton counties comprising the Fifth Congressional District to the southwest. Stallard's vote correlated with high mortgage rates and low land values.[36]

Debs gained 20,000 more votes in Oklahoma than he had received four years before, whereas President-elect Woodrow Wilson ran about 3,000 votes behind Bryan's 1908 total. Despite the efforts of Bill Murray and other Wilsonians, the New Freedom campaign failed to recoup all the losses Oklahoma Democrats had suffered after their popular 1907 canvass on behalf of the state's progressive constitution. They had lost votes in the 1910 election while the Socialist party gained (despite its dangerous defense of black voting rights), and some of those lost votes had undoubtedly gone to the Socialists, since Lee Cruce's conservative, moralistic gubernatorial campaign left the tenancy issue entirely to the Socialist candidate J. T. Cumbie. Wilson's presidential campaign two years later

35. All economic and demographic statistics, unless otherwise noted, are from U.S. Department of Commerce, *Thirteenth Census of the United States, 1910* (Washington, D.C.: Government Printing Office, 1912).
36. Meredith, "Agrarian Socialism in Oklahoma," 130–31.

Figure 1
SECTIONAL PATTERNS OF SOCIALIST SUPPORT
IN KANSAS, OKLAHOMA, AND ARKANSAS, 1912

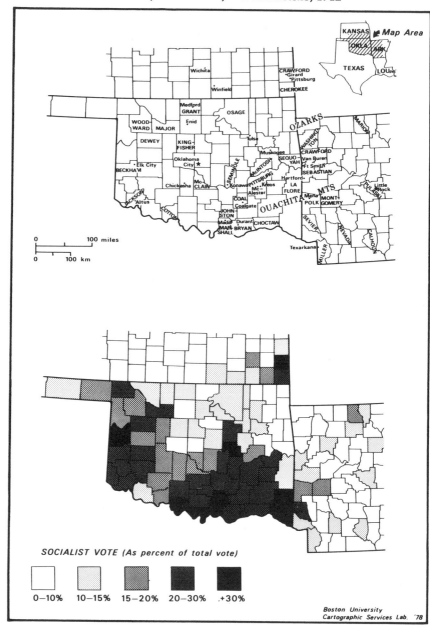

SOCIALIST VOTE (As percent of total vote)

0–10%   10–15%   15–20%   20–30%   .+30%

Boston University
Cartographic Services Lab. '78

reduced the decline of the Democratic vote largely by bringing out lazy party loyalists rather than by winning back Socialist defectors. Concurrently, the Socialist party's grass-roots campaign for Debs's candidacy pulled out new voters. The party's vote increased by 14,518 between 1910 and 1912. Some of these votes came from Democrats who continued to abandon "the party of their fathers," but not all of them, for Wilson's campaign regained almost all the voters who had failed to turn out for the 1910 election. It is also unlikely that the new voters came from the Republican party; the GOP did suffer a big loss of votes between 1910 and 1912, due almost entirely to the effects of the grandfather clause on its black supporters, but of course, disfranchised blacks could not shift votes to the Socialist party even though it had renewed its strong stand on civil rights. In short, the Sooner Socialists' grass-roots organization activated hundreds, perhaps even thousands of new voters in 1912, including a large number of tenant farmers who had dropped out of politics or had never before participated.

Debs also doubled his 1908 total in Louisiana by polling 5,249 votes (6.7 percent of the total). Most of his support came from the piney woods where the Grabow "massacre," the Lake Charles trial, and the Reds' active propaganda campaign politicized hundreds of tenants and timber workers. In fact, about 70 percent of the Louisiana Socialist vote came from the upland hill parishes. Debs polled 39 percent in Vernon Parish, in the heart of the yellow-pine region, and 29 percent in nearby Grant Parish. In addition, he won 35 percent of the vote in Winn Parish, an old Unionist, Populist stronghold, where the stubbornly independent voters also elected two Socialist parish officials. And in Winnfield, Huey Long's hometown, the citizens snubbed the courthouse "ring" by electing Reds to fill all of the municipal offices.[37]

In Arkansas Debs increased the Socialist vote to over 8,000, a substantial gain over his 1908 tally. Unlike their Louisiana comrades, the Arkansas Socialists were thoroughly united behind their gubernatorial candidate, G. E. Mikel, a UMW member from Jenny Lind who had been elected president of the State Federation of

37. McWhiney, "Louisiana Socialists," 316–17.

Labor. Mikel was one of the few state Socialist candidates who actually ran ahead of Debs, outdistancing the party's presidential candidate by over 5,000 votes. Using his influence in the labor movement and the party's growing organization among hill-country farmers in the Ozarks, Mikel won 13,384 votes in his race against Representative Joseph Robinson, a belated supporter of the New Freedom and a spokesman for the big Delta planters. Debs's campaign in Arkansas relied a good deal upon industrial union support just as it did in Louisiana and, to an even greater extent, in West Virginia and Florida where the Socialist vote came almost entirely from organized labor. (These two states were the only southern states where Socialist party voting strength compared to that of the southwestern states.) Debs ran slightly behind Mikel in Sebastian County, where UMW members cast most of the 558 votes for their union brother, but in Pulaski County, where the party polled over half of its vote in Argenta, center of the biggest rail yards in the Southwest, the beloved leader of the Pullman strike polled 40 percent and ran ahead of the party's gubernatorial candidate. A majority of the Socialist vote came from "hillbilly" dirt farmers in and around the Ozarks, but labor support in Arkansas accounted for a bigger percentage of the party's total than it did in Oklahoma or Texas.[38]

The Socialist party registered its most impressive southwestern gains in the Lone Star state, where the new locals organized earlier in the year helped Debs triple his 1908 vote. He received 25,743 votes in 1912 (8.5 percent), an increase of over 10,000 from 1908. However, Wilson's campaign was stronger in Texas than it was in any other southwestern state, and while the Democratic candidate ran behind Bryan's 1908 totals in Arkansas and Oklahoma, Colonel E. M. House's smooth-running organization pulled out more votes for Wilson in Texas than any candidate had ever received. The Socialists' gains were still impressive, but they failed to make the kind of dent in Democratic support that they made north of the Red River.

38. *Tribune Almanac, 1913,* 668. Vote totals for Argenta, Arkansas, supplied by Raymond O. Arsenault.

Figure 2 shows that Socialist support in Texas varied by region here just as it did in other southwestern states. Debs received his highest average percentage of the vote (17 percent) in the strike-torn piney-woods counties of the East Texas Sabine region. He also made his greatest advances over the 1908 vote in these old Populist strongholds. Tenancy was relatively low in this area (41 percent compared to 54 percent in the black prairie), but the quality of land was poor ($10 per acre compared to $31 per acre in the black waxy).[39] Debs received some support from the timber workers in East Texas, but the Socialists were less successful in J. H. Kirby's "feudal towns" than they were in the more open Louisiana lumber towns across the Sabine River. Consequently, most of the party's tally came from voters living in rural areas, small farmers eking out a living on the sandy land, earning their winter income by cutting ties, hauling scrap wood, or working for brief spells in the log camps.

Debs ran well in the marginal farming counties on the edge of the piney woods, notably Leon, Henderson, Rains, and Van Zandt (home of the big Grand Saline encampments). He also polled over 20 percent of the vote in Lavaca County, where Hickey and the Meitzens published the *Rebel* and several foreign-language papers. But, with the exception of Milam County, where the Renters' Union was active, the Socialists polled relatively low percentages (7 percent on the average) in the black-prairie counties just to the west. This differed from the Oklahoma cotton country where Debs polled his largest percentages in the high tenancy counties.

There were some important differences between the two regions. Tenancy had spread quickly north of the Red River and had rapidly become more exploitative. The Texas black belt was a more stable, more properous region where large landlords retained some of the old planter paternalism. But tenant discontent was growing

---

39. There was a saying that "you could make a better living on the black land by accident" than you could by trying on the sandy land, but stubborn East Texas yeomen refused to give up their farms to become tenants or cotton pickers on the black prairie. William A. Owens, *This Stubborn Soil* (New York: Charles Scribner's Sons, 1966), 39–40. Texas vote totals are from *World Almanac, 1913*, p. 763, and *World Almanac, 1909*, p. 617.

Figure 2
SECTIONAL PATTERNS OF SOCIALIST SUPPORT
IN TEXAS AND LOUISIANA, 1912

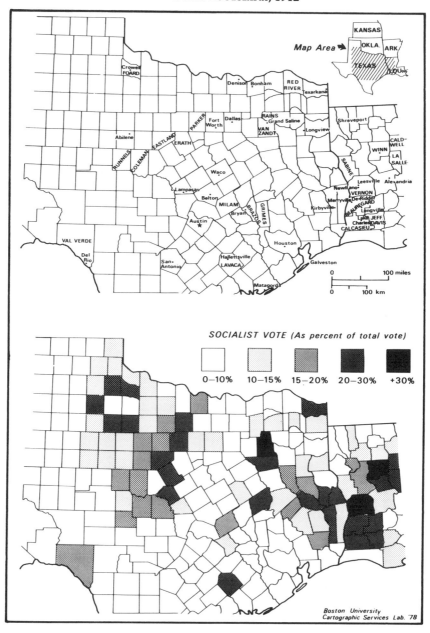

in the black waxy and was marked by a sizeable Socialist vote. In fact, Debs's absolute vote in these Texas cotton counties exceeded his statewide county average by a considerable margin, but he polled a low percentage in the black waxy because his rural vote was offset by a large Wilson vote in the prosperous cotton towns and in the larger cities like Dallas, Ft. Worth, Corsicana, Cleburne, Temple, Dennison, and Sherman (all with populations over ten thousand). For example, in Grayson County, the location of the two last cities, Debs polled 378 votes in 1912, including about 100 votes in Dennison where the party had a strong local of railroad workers. This represented only 7 percent of the total vote, however, because the Democrats ran up big totals in the four principal towns, which included 720 absentee landlords owning one quarter of the county's farmland of which 63 percent was worked by tenants.[40]

The Socialists averaged lower totals but higher percentages in the plains counties of north central Texas (9.4 percent overall). Debs ran especially well in the old Populist counties of the Western Cross Timbers region and in the newly settled area north of Abilene where land values and tenancy rates had increased dramatically after the turn of the century.[41] The Socialists also polled close to 20 percent in Runnels, Coleman, and surrounding counties where the "nesters" had battled the "cattle barons" in the fence-cutting wars of the 1880s, initiating the southwestern class struggle.[42]

40. Charles W. Holman, "Preliminary Investigation of the Causes of the Southwestern Land Struggle," in Record Group 174, Commission on Industrial Relations Records, "Records of the Department of Labor," National Archives.

41. Statistics on voting are from *World Almanac, 1913*, pp. 762–63. Statistics on population are from U.S. Department of Commerce, *Thirteenth Census of the United States* (Washington, D.C.: Government Printing Office, 1913) III, 795–96. Statistics on tenancy and land values are from University of Texas, Department of Extension, Division of Public Welfare, *Farm Tenancy in Texas*, University of Texas Bulletin No. 21 (Austin, 1915), 18–21, and W. E. Leonard and E. B. Naugle, "The Recent Increase in Tenancy, Its Causes and Some Suggestions as to Remedies," in Lewis H. Haney (ed.), *Studies in the Land Problem in Texas*, University of Texas Bulletin No. 39 (Austin, 1915), 14.

42. Debs carried Leaday in Coleman County where some Socialist tenants had been dismissed from Tom Padgitt's 12,000-acre plantation by his over-

The Socialist party recorded very low totals on the vast West Texas plains, where the population was sparse and visits from organizers were rare. The Socialists had few poll watchers in these remote counties and after the election of 1912 they charged that many of their votes were not counted. Debs was also very unsuccessful in South Texas where most Mexican-American voters were disfranchised or controlled by Democratic bosses.[43] In many counties of the Rio Grande Valley Debs received only four or five votes, and no Socialist votes were recorded in Brooks, McMullen, Willacy, and Zapata counties. Val Verde County, however, returned a significant Socialist vote, most of it coming from Del Rio, a union town across the Rio Grande from Ciudad Acuna—a center of Mexican revolutionary activity.

THE SOCIAL BASES OF THE SOUTHWESTERN SOCIALIST VOTE

One interpretation of agrarian socialism emphasizes its strength in one-crop farming areas that suffer from unpredictable weather and market fluctuations.[44] When the Socialist tide was rising in Oklahoma, some commentators attributed the party's vote simply to hard times, a result of "too much drought this year and too much rain last year," as Oscar Ameringer put it. This "excursion into the realm of causology culminates in the new discovery that 'Socialism grows when every other crop fails'." If this thesis were correct, Oscar mocked, opponents of socialism would "destroy the cause by praying for more rain as the occasion demanded."[45]

---

seer. But the local Socialists charged that their county candidates lost because many tenants had been intimidated by Padgitt's men and stayed away from the polls while Democratic election officials counted out many of their votes. *Rebel* (Hallettsville, Tex.), November 9, 1912. On the violent conflict in this area pitting "nesters," rustlers, and unemployed cowboys against the large cattlemen, their mounted riders, and the Texas Rangers, see R. D. Holt, "The Introduction of Barbed Wire into Texas and the Fence Cutting War," *West Texas Historical Association Yearbook*, VI (1930), 70–75.

43. E. E. McKee to Ethelwyn Mills, March 12, 1913, in Socialist Party Papers, Duke; O. Douglas Weeks, "The Texas Mexicans in the Politics of Texas," *American Political Science Review*, XXIV (1930), 606–27.

44. Seymour Martin Lipset, *Agrarian Socialism* (Rev. ed.; Garden City, N.Y.: Doubleday Anchor, 1968), 24–25, 213.

45. *Oklahoma Pioneer* (Oklahoma City), January 26, 1910.

Ameringer of course had political reasons for debunking those who viewed the Oklahoma Socialist vote as simply an ephemeral reaction to hard times. The steady growth of red-card members in Texas and Oklahoma and the unusually high ratio of dues-paying members to voters indicated a stable hard core of supporters, but it is possible that Socialist voters who did not pay dues responded mainly to market conditions by casting protest votes against hard times.

The price of Oklahoma wheat dropped from $1.04 per bushel in January of 1910 to $.77 per bushel in the election month of November, 1912.[46] Thus, S. M. Lipset's one-crop thesis may have some validity for the northwestern Oklahoma wheat-growing counties. Lipset is wrong, however, when he writes that "virtually all" of the Sooner Socialist vote came from this area.[47] Debs polled far more votes in the southern cotton counties, though the one-crop thesis could also apply to this high tenancy area.

The cotton market was just as capricious as the wheat market and the boll weevil was as destructive as the grasshopper. The cotton tenants, however, viewed their plight differently than did the wheat farmers. They were not property-owning entrepreneurs who could escape indebtedness with a few good crops. Cotton renters were not only the victims of an unpredictable commodity market, they were also the victims of landlords and credit merchants who demanded a big share of their hard-earned income in good season and bad. Like the wheat farmers, the cotton growers resented the middlemen, railroad men, and market "manipulators" who reduced the price they received for their crop; but the "surplus value" these "parasites" extracted from the tenant farmer seemed less obvious than the big rent taken by the landlord and the huge interest rates charged by the creditors. Cotton renters worried about the price their commodity brought on the market, but they also had to worry about how much credit the plantation

46. T. R. Hodges and K. D. Blood, *Oklahoma Farm Price Statistics*, Agricultural Experiment Station Bulletin No. 258 (Stillwater: Oklahoma A & M College, 1939), 18.
47. Lipset, *Agrarian Socialism*, 27.

store would charge and how much rent the landlord would demand.

Table I shows clearly that middlemen and manufacturers, as well as landlords and merchants, benefited at the cotton farmer's expense; it also shows that the price of cotton fluctuated a good deal during the early 1900s.[48] It does not indicate, however, a correlation between the increases in Socialist voting strength in the cotton counties and the decreases in the price of cotton. In fact, these statistics show that the Socialist party in Texas and Oklahoma registered its largest gains in 1910 and 1912, two years that showed an increase in the price of cotton.[49] As Robert L. Hunt observed, farmer protest movements developed in the Southwest between 1900 and 1914 without regard to cotton price fluctuations. "It is doubtful," he wrote, that cotton farmers ever "enjoyed greater economic security" than they did in these years; price fluctuations did not "enkindle the wrath of farmers" as much as the "disparity between prices received and prices paid by farmers."[50]

According to the one-crop thesis, natural disasters may be as important as market fluctuations in producing a farmer protest vote. The greatest scourge of the southwestern cotton growers, the boll weevil, was fading as a destructive element by 1908. The insect made its deepest penetration into the Oklahoma cotton country (just across the Canadian River) in the following year, and the last serious blight caused by the weevil hit the 1911 cotton crop in Oklahoma, destroying 27 percent of the harvest.[51] The losses incurred during this growing season were not, however, correlated with the size of the Socialist vote on a county level. The correlation between the percentage of the 1911 cotton crop lost and the

48. J. E. Pool, "The Farmer's Loss on Cotton," *Farm and Ranch* article reprinted in Harthshorne (Okla.) *Sun*, October 9, 1913.

49. In Oklahoma, for example, the Socialists' strongest performance to date came in the fall of 1912 when the price of cotton had risen steadily from eight to eleven cents per pound in the course of a year. Hodges and Blood, *Oklahoma Farm Price Statistics*, 24.

50. Robert Lee Hunt, *A History of Farmer Movements in the Southwest, 1873–1925* (College Station: Texas A & M Press, 1935), 41–42.

51. G. E. Sanborn, *Boll Weevil in Oklahoma*, Agricultural Experiment Station Bulletin No. 157 (Stillwater: Oklahoma A & M College, 1926), 20; *Daily Oklahoman* (Oklahoma City), November 1, 1911.

Table I
COTTON PRICES AND SOCIALIST VOTING
IN TEXAS AND OKLAHOMA, 1904–1912

Year	Avg. Cotton Prices Paid (cents per lb.)		Percent SP Vote in Leading Southwestern Cotton-Growing Counties	
	Farmer's	Manufacturer's	23 Texas Black Belt Counties	7 Southern Oklahoma Counties
1904	6.8	17.2	2.1	3.2
1905	7.0	12.6		
1906	9.6	12.2	1.8	2.6
1907	10.6	13.5		3.5
1908	9.0	12.2	2.7	10.2
1909	9.2	16.1		
1910	13.6	19.7	6.2	11.8
1911	8.0	15.0		
1912	13.6	19.7	10.3	22.0

percentage of the 1912 vote won by the Socialist party was -.00.

After 1910, drought was a more serious problem for southwestern farmers than insect blight, but the Socialists gained most of their votes in the cotton-growing areas east of the 30-inch rain line where long dry spells were uncommon.[52] There was a bad drought in West Texas and southwestern Oklahoma during the summer of 1911, and the *Rebel* made an issue of this disaster, circulating a petition that demanded relief and public works projects from the state. But by the time the 1912 Socialist campaign cranked up, the drought had ended, and in the end Debs did not do particularly well in the drought-stricken counties.[53]

The most significant pattern in the distribution of the southwestern Socialist vote can be traced to the class conflict between the towns and the countryside which became especially pronounced

52. O. A. Churchill, *Cotton Culture*, Agricultural Experiment Station Bulletin No. 93 (Stillwater: Oklahoma A & M College, 1912), 20.
53. *Rebel* (Hallettsville, Tex.), July 8, 1911.

in the early 1910s. Although many tenants remained loyal "brass collar" Democrats because of family traditions, religious fears of socialism, patronage ties to the landlords and county ring politicians, to name a few important reasons, some renters in high tenancy areas turned to the Socialist party as the party of their class and viewed the Democrats as the party of "the OTHER class"— of landlords, merchants, and professionals in the "electric light" towns.

For example, in the rack-rented Oklahoma cotton country Debs polled an average of 31.8 percent in 173 randomly selected urban and rural precincts in the southern part of the state. In the rural areas Debs averaged 39.5 percent and actually achieved a plurality in a number of dirt-farmer districts, whereas in the incorporated townships he received an average of 24.1 percent of the vote.[54]

The Oklahoma Socialist vote of 1912 varied in the incorporated townships according to the size, social structure, and economic function of the various towns involved. Debs won an average of 25.8 percent in the eight villages with a population of less than 1,000; these were crossroads trading centers that frequently served as polling places for the rural districts. They often contained no more than a few hundred residents (mostly small merchants and retired farmers) and supported little more than a general store, a post office, a cotton gin, a few churches, and, rarely, a railroad depot. In twelve southern Oklahoma towns over 1,000 in population (excluding coal mining communities) Debs received an average of only 8.7 percent. In the two largest and most prosperous county seat towns, McAlester (with a population of almost 13,000) and Ardmore (about 8,600) voters gave the Socialist party candidate only 5.3 and 3.8 percent respectively. These twelve commercial towns generally had railroad connections and what Veblen called a "virtual monopoly" on the farm trade.[55] Many cotton

54. All precinct returns are from records of Oklahoma State Election Board, Capitol Building, Oklahoma City.
55. Thorstein Veblen, *Absentee Ownership and Private Enterprise in Recent Times* (New York: B. W. Huebsch, 1923), 145–47; also see Robert Dykstra, "Town-Country Conflict: A Hidden Dimension in American Social History," *Agricultural History*, XXXVIII (1964), 196–99 for nineteenth-century background.

towns of this sort in the Old South were stagnating as the soil eroded and the one-crop economy collapsed, but in the Southwest such communities were still rather young and aggressive, with leaders who advocated various kinds of moral and "scientific" reforms for the backward tenants in the countryside. Many of the businessmen cooperated with the Farmers' Union to promote prosperity and supported progressive Democrats in order to promote social harmony and moral as well as economic reform. In the early 1900s these small-town reformers also tolerated radicals, but after 1910 when tenant discontent was increasing in tandem with Socialist activity, they tried to "conceal conditions from the general public" through both civic and private institutions. In 1915 a government commission studying the social and political unrest in the Southwest reported "suppression" in the form of "attempts to discredit statements . . . from the discontented side" and "booster" campaigns designed "to give the appearance that everything was all right." These repressive efforts only seemed to "intensify the bitter attitude of the radicals."[56]

The growing tension between the discontented rural poor and the prosperous property owners in the towns appeared clearly in Marshall County, Oklahoma, during and after the heated campaign of 1912. Located in the heart of the cotton country along the Red River, this county had a remarkable tenancy rate of 81 percent in 1910 and gave Debs his highest percent (35) in the presidential election two years later. Marshall County had only four incorporated towns, but they contained roughly a quarter of the county's total population; these townspeople, especially the residents of the county seat at Madill, dominated social, economic, and political affairs. They gave Debs a polite reception when he toured the area in the summer of 1912, and in the November election they gave him 15 percent of their vote. The tenants in the rural precincts, however, cast 45 percent of their vote in his favor, a clear plurality.[57]

56. Charles W. Holman, "Probing the Causes of Unrest: The Tenant Farmer," *Survey*, XXXIV (April 17, 1916), 62–63.

57. See Burbank, "Agrarian Radicals and Their Opponents," 9–10; *Marshall County News-Democrat* (Madill, Okla.), March 6, November 8, 1912.

The significance of urban-rural voting differences may seem questionable in a state where only 20 percent of the people lived in urban areas, but the definition of "urban" used to calculate this percentage did not include towns of less than 2,500 persons. If all incorporated areas had been included, one third of Oklahoma's population lived in some kind of city, town, or settled township. Furthermore, the urban population of the state increased much faster than the rural population in the first decade of the twentieth century—260 percent in towns over 2,500 as compared to 91 percent in the rural sections.[58] Most significantly, townspeople voted in much larger proportions than country folk, who were often disfranchised because of their transiency or their poverty.

For example, in Marshall County the four incorporated towns included just 24 percent of the population in 1910, but their citizens cast 48 percent of the total county vote in the 1912 election. This pattern of skewed participation holds for farming counties throughout the Southwest. On the average, twice as many white, adult townsmen voted as countrymen. Therefore, despite the predominantly rural population of the Southwest, elections in strong Socialist counties pitted propertied townspeople against rural tenants on a fairly even basis. Debs equaled or exceeded the Democratic vote in rural tenant precincts of the Oklahoma cotton counties, but he lost badly in the towns where middle-class white men cast a disproportionate percentage of the vote.

The class basis of urban-rural voting divisions in southern Oklahoma can be clearly illustrated by examining the ownership of property and the nature of social relations in Marshall County. In 1911 the total assessment of property amounted to $2,859,546. Of this total, $2,122,580 belonged to townspeople. And so, one quarter of the county's population (the town dwellers) owned at least three quarters of the property, and undoubtedly controlled a good deal more than that since retired farmers, businessmen, and lawyers, like Madill's progressive political leader William Franklin,

58. U.S. Department of Commerce, *Thirteenth Census of the United States, 1910: Statistics for Oklahoma* (Washington, D.C.: Government Printing Office, 1913), 569–72.

owned tenant plantations in the countryside. The 1,200 renters in the county (44 percent of the total adult male population) owned virtually no real property and very little personal property.[59]

This disparity in the ownership of property was of course reflected in the county's social and institutional life as well as in its politics. Madill proclaimed itself a "progressive church town" that had left behind "country town habits and ways." It had a new high school for its youth and an active commercial club for its businessmen, plus lodges, associations, well-attended churches, and even a country club for citizens with leisure time. The rural people of Marshall County had very little organized social life; they attended town functions and religious services infrequently. Most of the tenants' spiritual activity took place at irregular meetings held by itinerant preachers, frequently taking the form of "brush arbor" summer revivals.

Tenant children in cotton areas like Marshall County attended one-room schoolhouses, sometimes converted from a local church or tabernacle, while the townspeople's children attended a new high school. When the renters did send their barefooted kids into town to attend school, the children were often treated badly by their "social betters." One cotton renter's son who grew up in the Southwest remembered that class distinctions between "rich and poor children" were particularly evident in the schools. The economic gap, wrote G. L. Vaughan, who was lucky enough to attend school in town, was "16 to 1" because "a landlord with sixteen renters, who paid each one half of all crops, had sixteen times as much income as a renter family." Poor children in the cotton country could not only sense class distinctions, they could measure them.[60]

These distinctions were also reflected in the staffing of the schools. In Marshall County, where the vast majority of people lived in the country, the town schools employed all but ten of the

59. Madill (Okla.) *Times*, January 5, 1911; U.S. Department of Commerce, *Thirteenth Census*, 647.

60. G. L. Vaughan, *The Cotton Renter's Son* (Wolfe City, Tex.: Henington Publishing, 1967), 41–42.

county's seventy-one teachers. Tenants who lived in remote sections, like the sand hills along the Canadian River, complained about this inequitable distribution of resources, but to no avail. As one study of Oklahoma farm children concluded, the school system merely reinforced the "evils of poverty and ignorance" resulting from the tenant system. Nothing had been done to bridge the gap between "two well defined groups of people—the banker-merchant-landlord class and the tenant-small landowner class."[61]

Debs polled 35 percent of the vote in Marshall County despite the efforts of progressive Democrat William Franklin, an absentee landlord and lawyer from Madill, who campaigned for Wilson and his own congressional candidacy as a "sincere friend of the farmer and laborer" and an enemy of socialism and alcoholism.[62] In Johnston County, just to the north, "Alfalfa Bill" Murray's effort to cut down the Socialist vote was equally unsuccessful; Debs polled 35 percent of the vote in this county as well. He received only 14 percent in Tishomingo, the county seat where Murray practiced law, but he polled 36 percent at Emet, the polling place nearest Murray's estate. The Socialists also did well in the small towns of Johnston County that served as trading centers as well as polling places for the tenants (who comprised 80 percent of the farm population). At Ravia, where Murray had done some legal work and drew up the town charter, the people elected a Socialist administration in 1911 and gave Debs over a third of their vote in 1912. The party also polled a significant vote in the small town of Wapanucka on the Coal County border. When the Socialist district chairman spoke there before the election, he was received by a "good crowd" and met a merchant named Riley, an active party member who sold "everything from Socialist red cards to thrashing machines" at his store.[63]

Socialists won more support from merchants and professionals in small agricultural communities further west in the old Okla-

61. *Marshall County News-Democrat* (Madill, Okla.), September 26, 1913; Charles E. Gibson, "Farm Children in Oklahoma," *Child Labor Bulletin*, VII (1918), 50–51.

62. *Marshall County News-Democrat* (Madill, Okla.), June 27, 1913.

63. *New Century* (Sulphur, Okla.), March 22, 1912. On Murray's early career as a lawyer and landlord, see Bryant, *Alfalfa Bill Murray*, 25–44.

homa Territory, where tenancy was not as deeply entrenched and where town-country tension was not so intense. In the eleven towns studied in this southwestern section, the Socialist party received an average of 23 percent, compared to 36 percent in the rural precincts. Again, Debs's town vote varied according to the size and economic function of the community: he averaged 30 percent in the small trading centers with populations of less than 1,000 and only 15 percent in the county seat towns of larger size.

For example, in Beckham County, a mixed grain and cotton area on the state's western border, Debs won 16 percent in the county seat and 22 percent in the larger town of Elk City (population 3,200) where a Socialist party parade had been welcomed by merchants who displayed red flags in their windows and even helped the party finance a 1910 summer encampment. A few years later, however, the town council passed an ordinance banning party orators from the streets. A boycott against Elk City merchants by Socialist farmers in the area soon restored the right to free speech, but this turn of events indicated that the support of small-town businessmen could be very fickle indeed. At a much smaller town named Carter (population 265) Debs polled an impressive 63 percent in 1912, with the help of farmers who cast their votes in the village. Jasper Roberts, who published his Socialist newspaper, the *Beckham County Advocate*, in Carter, also learned the hard way about the unreliability of support offered by middle-class townspeople. At first, Roberts received advertising from merchants, professionals, and even from one banker, but when he began to praise "Big Bill" Haywood and criticize accepted standards of religion, marriage, and obscenity after the election of 1912, he lost their patronage and had to close up shop.[64]

Although the Socialists received some reliable assistance from small towners in western Oklahoma, most of their rural votes came from heavily indebted farm owners who dreaded mortgage foreclosures and the plunge into transient tenancy. Unlike the cotton tenants in the old Indian Territory, these yeomen were usually

64. Ameringer, *If You Don't Weaken*, 264; *Harlow's Weekly* (Oklahoma City), November 20, 1915; *Beckham County Advocate* (Carter, Okla.), April 24, May 8, 15, 29, September 25, 1913.

older farmers, often experienced from having been part of the
Populist movement, who felt roughly equal to their creditors in the
country towns.[65] Many of them had been members of the Farmers'
Alliance and later the Farmers' Union; they were not averse to cooperating with small merchants in the nearby villages who needed
their support and shared their resentment of bigger businessmen
in county seat towns and cities. Unlike the tenants, they did not
identify their interests very closely with those of the working class;
they saw themselves as honest members of the "producing classes"
who were, in classic Populist terms, being robbed of part of their
toil by middlemen, money lenders, and monopolists. But contrary
to most members of their class, these small property owners were
not convinced that the Democratic party of Bryan and Wilson represented them, even in Oklahoma where the Democrats were relatively progressive.

Socialism in the old Populist counties in north central Texas also
developed through the leadership of small, mortgaged farmers,
many of them migrants from Kansas. As Socialist organizer E. E.
McKee reported from this region after the 1912 election, the "long-
wiskered Pops" were as "wizened" and rebellious as ever. "Some
of this class of farmers own their own farms, or at least have the
use of them under mortgage," he added, "and they are the ones
who are doing the pioneer work of today." McKee used to spot
these Reds by going down to the crossroads post office to see which
farmers came out with a copy of the "Little Old" *Appeal* "tucked
down deep in their hip pockets."[66]

65. For a profile of western Oklahoma Socialist candidates who portrayed
themselves as successful farmers see *Constructive Socialist* (Alva, Okla.),
July 31, August 1, 14, September 4, 11, 1912. However, even in the wheat
country third-party candidates rarely measured up to the Democrats in
wealth, the main criterion of respectability. And in less prosperous regions,
like the Arkansas Ozarks, the disparity was even greater. For example, in
Washington County, Arkansas, which happened to be one of the fertile
agricultural areas, the Democratic candidates who were part of the Jeff
Davis machine recorded an average assessed wealth of $472.32, four times
the average wealth of the Socialist candidates in that county. Statistics fur-
nished by Raymond O. Arsenault.
66. McKee to Mills, March 13, 1913, in Socialist Party Papers, Duke.

Debs ran well in the small post office polling places where these dirt farmers voted, but he did not win many votes in the county seat towns of west central Texas, like Weatherford in Parker County, where the *Rebel* reported that 378 merchants and clerks did business in one square mile, or like Crowell in Foard County, where the "court house ring" barred the Reverend G. G. Hamilton from town after his "sensational conversion to Socialism." The reverend's new party polled about 10 percent in the Foard County seat and an average of about 45 percent in the surrounding rural precincts.[67] This country-town split in the Socialist party vote was, according to Roscoe Martin, a continuation of the "imbroglio" between farmers and townspeople that had motivated Populist voting in the nineties. He found a few rural precincts in the Western Cross Timbers area of north central Texas that gave a large vote to both the People's and Socialist parties. This correlation is interesting, but it does not "indicate beyond question the affinity" between the two constituencies.[68]

In fact, the overall statewide correlation between Debs's Texas vote and General Weaver's Populist vote 20 years before remained insignificant as a result of the important economic and demographic changes that swept the state after 1900. Many of the "old long-whiskered Pops" voted Socialist in 1912, especially in the north central counties, but many young tenant farmers in East Texas joined lumber workers (who had not voted in the 1890s) to build a new radical voting coalition.

Most of the 1912 Socialist vote came from the poor tenant districts, but Debs also won significant support in various proletarian enclaves—in urban railroad centers like Argenta, just north of Little Rock, and in small maintenance centers like Van Buren, Arkansas, where Father Thomas Hagerty had ministered his last parish. The Socialist vote dropped precipitously in Oklahoma City after Oscar Ameringer ran his spirited race for mayor in 1911 and the construction boom collapsed. But the Socialist ticket received

67. *Rebel* (Hallettsville, Tex.), September 23, December 23, 1911.
68. Roscoe C. Martin, *The People's Party in Texas* (Austin: University of Texas Press, 1933), 60, 81, 185–86.

several hundred votes in port cities like New Orleans, Galveston, and Houston, and in commercial cities like Dallas, Fort Worth, Texarkana, and San Antonio where organized labor was strong. Workers in the Socialist-led Brewer's union, the building trades, and the newer organizations of transportation workers and meat-packers seemed most inclined to support the Socialist ticket. However, the party still polled its largest working-class vote in isolated mine and sawmill localities.

The Socialists swept several coal-camp precincts in the southeast Kansas "Balkans" including the Slavic community at Breezy Hill where Debs won 82 percent, the black camp at Croweburg where a Socialist "colored voters' local" had been established, and the town of Franklin where Anglo-Americans, Franco-Belgians, and Italians belonged to the same party local. In fact, Debs won a clear plurality in Crawford County, Kansas, where Socialist voters also elected a state senator and representative. This was the home of the *Appeal* and Alex Howat's militant UMW District 14, and in this one county Debs received 3,573 votes, more than he received in some entire states of the Deep South. Commenting later on the Socialist organization in Crawford County, the Kansas City *Star* reported that the "coal camps" produced a "vast Socialistic strength," because "foreign miners had joined the party by the hundreds" and voted Socialist "in the same numbers." The Socialists also carried Cherokee County to the south, where they elected a Red state legislator. Debs carried the coal town of Mineral with 61 percent of the vote. Reds did not win this kind of support in the Oklahoma coal communities, but Fred Holt ran a strong congressional race and helped the presidential candidate poll 30 percent at Coalgate, 35 percent at Lehigh, and 40 percent at Krebs. Debs and Holt actually carried two smaller camps at Dow and Savanna, Oklahoma, where the UMW had built strong locals. Like their Kansas comrades, the Oklahoma Socialists received their highest totals in the smaller coal communities with big union locals, regardless of their ethnic and religious composition.[69]

69. The author would like to thank Neil Basen and Garin Burbank for supplying voting returns for coal-town precincts. Kansas City *Star*, November 1, 1914.

Debs also received strong support in Louisiana lumber towns like DeRidder which were relatively free from company control, and where workers and various townspeople were free to join the farmers in exercising their right to vote. However, the 5,249 votes Debs gained in Louisiana "represented only a small percentage of the potential Socialist vote," because nearly all the black workers, many of whom were in the Brotherhood of Timber Workers, were disfranchised. For example, in the town of Longville, Louisiana, the Socialist party was accorded 8 of the 64 votes cast in 1912, even though the Long-Bell lumber company employed over a thousand men there, half of them black. Unlike the Oklahoma Socialists, the Louisiana party leaders used disfranchisement as an excuse not "to organize the negroes."[70]

After issuing a civil rights appeal in its 1912 campaign, the Oklahoma Socialist party hired a black agitator from Kansas, W. T. Lane. But most militant blacks in Oklahoma were turning away from political parties controlled by white men and back toward black nationalism. Small groups of separatists left Oklahoma for Canada and for Liberia in 1911, and in 1913 a remarkable African nationalist named Chief Alfred Charles Sam appeared among the angry blacks of Oklahoma and began organizing an ambitious back-to-Africa movement. In 1914 over seven hundred Oklahoma blacks gathered at various points to prepare for a voyage to the Gold Coast on Sam's ship *Liberia*, but only half that many made it to the port of Galveston and only 60 "delegates" actually took the voyage. It proved to be the first and last "hegira" Chief Sam would sponsor, but it revealed a deep discontent among Oklahoma's disfranchised blacks, who were not much interested in the political battles between socialism and Democratic progressivism.[71]

70. McWhiney, "Louisiana Socialists," 319–20; *Rebel* (Hallettsville, Tex.), December 21, 1912.

71. *Rebel* (Hallettsville, Tex.), March 8, 1913. On Chief Sam, see William Biddle and Gilbert Geis, *The Long Way Home* (Detroit: Wayne State University Press, 1964); and Edwin S. Redkey, *Black Exodus: Black Nationalist and Back-to-Africa Movements, 1896–1910* (New Haven, Conn.: Yale University Press, 1969), 292. See Meredith, "Agrarian Socialism and the Negro in Oklahoma," for a somewhat exaggerated estimate of black support for the Socialist party.

For similar reasons, the Socialist party failed to win significant support from Oklahoma Indians or from Mexicans in South Texas, both of whom were about as thoroughly disfranchised or controlled by Democratic bosses as the blacks. The Sooner Socialists did make some efforts to agitate among the Choctaws and the Texas Renters' Union recruited a number of Mexican tenants, but these efforts could not be translated into protest votes because the red men and the brown men were either disfranchised or disinterested in the politics of white men.

The party was more successful in winning support within various European colonies in the Southwest, especially in immigrant coal-mining towns. In fact, a survey of Socialist voting in the Kansas coal towns of Crawford County shows that the party did better in areas with Slavic, Franco-Belgian, and Italian populations than it did in areas where old Anglo-Americans predominated. The Socialists won control of many of these towns in the Balkans, where they set up foreign-language locals and cut down the poll tax and other inhibitions to the franchise. In Oklahoma, where new immigrant coal miners were more frequently disfranchised, there is evidence that the Italians, the largest group, supported Socialist candidates in union elections even though they could not vote in regular elections.[72]

The Socialists did not run nearly as well in immigrant communities of farmers. The German brewers and craftsmen in the cities built some active Socialist locals, but the German farmers who settled in southern Texas around San Antonio and the Mennonites who colonized in western Oklahoma remained staunchly Republican. The party did win the support of poor German farmers in Major County, Oklahoma, where the organization was unusually

72. For example, in Krebs, Oklahoma, where less than half the foreign males were voting citizens, Debs received 105 votes (40 percent) in 1912, but a year before the UMW local had cast 238 votes for a Socialist union candidate (68 percent). On Socialist strength among immigrant miners in Kansas see *Appeal to Reason* (Girard, Kan.), March 30, May 4, June 8, December 7, 1912. Data on ethnicity by precinct are from J. N. Carman, *Foreign Language Units of Kansas* (Lawrence: University of Kansas Press, 1962), 110–14. The author also relied upon Jim Kendell's unpublished paper on Kansas miners and socialism.

strong in marginal farming precincts, and in Lavaca County, Texas, where E. O. Meitzen's publishing and electioneering machine won the support of some old forty-eighters living in the poorer sections and also of some of the newer Czech immigrants.[73] The Socialist party faced strong opposition from the Catholic church in these areas, but this was of relatively slight concern compared to the hostility of the Protestant churches which claimed dominion over thousands of poor white souls throughout the Southwest.

The Socialists took advantage of what the Presbyterian Home Board of Missions called the "decline of the country church" in high tenancy areas and of a growing feeling among poor farmers that the established denominations represented the "exploiter's church."[74] The decline of middle-class churches in county districts did not mean, however, that poor whites were becoming less religious. Most of the tenant people still read the Bible at home, sang spirituals, and flocked to the summer revivals. Revivalism reached a low point during the growth of southwestern socialism, but party leaders exaggerated when they boasted that their summer encampment carnivals replaced the "religious camp meetings of yore." They also exaggerated in arguing that socialism had replaced religion in the hearts and minds of rural party members. It would be more accurate to say that the poor working people integrated socialism into a religious world view.

At any rate, there is no significant correlation between the size of certain religious denominations in Texas and Oklahoma counties and the size of the 1912 Socialist vote. A disproportionate membership in fundamentalist denominations like the Church of Christ

73. Voting returns on Major County are from Ames (Okla.) *Enterprise*, November 15, 1912. The strength of the Debs vote in poor precincts of Mennonite farmers contrasts with the tiny Socialist vote in the prosperous Mennonite community at Okarche in Kingfisher County. The German-Russian Mennonites in Oklahoma took an interest in the Socialist party after 1914 when it led the antiwar movement. Voting and demographic statistics for Lavaca County from Hallettsville (Tex.) *Herald*, August 1, 1913, are for a special election in which E. O. Meitzen ran for state senate; also see P. C. Boethel, *History of Lavaca County* (Austin: University of Texas Press, 1936), 116–33.

74. Quoted in A. M. Simons, "The Farmer and the Church," *Coming Nation* (Girard, Kan.), March 30, 1912.

appears in the strong Socialist counties, but the prevalence of these poorer, evangelical churches is intercorrelated with various socio-economic indexes like low tenancy, low population density, and low per capita tax valuation. In other words, the correlation between Socialist support and fundamentalist protestantism in Oklahoma results largely from the fact that the sects and churches found in strong Socialist counties tended to be a part of life in most poor tenant-farming areas.[75]

In fact, Debs's support in the Southwest was primarily a class phenomenon, not a religious or ethnic one. That is, Socialist votes came largely from counties with poor cotton tenants, indebted dirt farmers, and isolated communities of miners, sawmill workers, and railroad hands. Debs's supporters included some small-town shopkeepers, country doctors and lawyers, radical clergymen, and former Populist landowners, but the majority of the people who put their "X" by Gene's name came from the southwestern laboring class; they were tenant farmers and industrial workers who belonged to what the Socialists called the "exploited class."[76]

75. Debs's 1912 vote correlated positively at +.39 with the average percentage of persons per county who belonged to Oklahoma's most fundamentalist churches and sects. However, the percentage of fundamentalists in each county also correlated at +.35 with the percent of tenancy, −.35 with per capita tax valuation, and −.42 with percent urban and average value of farm property. Statistics from U.S. Bureau of the Census, *Religious Bodies: 1906* (Washington, D.C.: Government Printing Office, 1910), Pt. I, pp. 293, 348–49. An index of fundamentalist churches and sects was compiled with the expert assistance of Sydney Ahlstrom, Department of Religious Studies, Yale University. This index includes the following religious groups: Baptist, Southern Convention, Pentecostal Church of the Nazarene, Seventh Day Adventist, Church of Christ, Presbyterian in the U.S., Cumberland Presbyterian, Lutheran Synodical Conference, and Jehovah's Witness.

76. Although the analysis of aggregate election statistics and socioeconomic data does not allow a precise statement of the proportion of the Socialist vote comprised by certain classes or groups, there is survey evidence, based upon individual responses, supporting the above generalizations. Of the 103 top *Appeal* salesmen from the Southwest listed in the 1914 *Who's Who in Socialist America*, 43 percent were farmers (unfortunately, there is no breakdown between tenants and owners), 28 percent were industrial workers, 12 percent were professionals, 10 percent were businessmen, and 7 percent were clerks or salesmen. Farmers probably comprised a larger percentage of the Socialist party voting bloc and industrial workers a smaller percentage, but these two groups undoubtedly formed the bulk of the Debs vote.

Members of certain churches and sects undoubtedly opposed socialism on religious grounds while others found its millennial gospel congenial to their own spiritual orientation, but religious preferences were much less important in explaining the 1912 Socialist vote than class identifications. The Socialists found that the poor tenants tended to be most receptive to party propaganda regardless of their religious preference, just as, regardless of their own national background, coal miners in strong union locals tended to be most willing to support Socialist candidates.

In any case, the dynamics of class relationships in southwestern society cannot be empirically measured with any more accuracy than the traditions of religion and culture to which these relationships were intimately related. Voting analysis can provide a statistical impression of patterns in Socialist electoral support, but this kind of quantitative examination only measures one kind of response to the southwestern class struggle—a political response by a registered minority of the region's poor folk. The 1912 election results do show that Eugene Debs's class-conscious campaign elicited a class-oriented response from those southwesterners who were most directly involved in the region's intense social and economic struggles. However, in order to understand the changing nature of the southwestern class struggle and to appreciate the variety of responses it called forth, we must examine a wider range of political activity and social protest than voting analysis allows us to measure.

VII

Socialism and the Southwestern Class Struggle 1913-1915

A FEW MONTHS AFTER the election of 1912, John Thacker, editor of the *Oklahoma Democrat* in Altus, wrote to President Wilson: "There is a force which is gaining currency in the country districts which is becoming sufficiently voluminous to alarm some of us Democrats, and that is Socialism." Debs polled only 3 percent of the vote in Altus, but he won an average of 25 percent in the rural precincts of Jackson County where 53 percent of the farmers were tenants. Thacker told the president that the Socialists were gaining recruits by persuading many working people "that our own system of government will not permit any radical reforms lest the great financial interests rebel." He said that most small-property owners were still resisting socialism, but, given the "extortionate" prices charged by the industrial monopolies and the "pittance" they paid in wages, it was becoming more difficult to refute the Socialists' arguments. Like most small-town progressives, Thacker hated "divisions between classes," and so he urged President Wilson to encourage more radical reforms to prevent the Socialists and larger capitalists from raising class tensions higher.[1] Other Democrats responded differently to the growth of this new force.

As socialism and industrial unionism developed grass-roots strength, they became more threatening to the southwestern ruling class. By 1914 lumber operators and planters had destroyed the Brotherhood of Timber Workers and the original Renters' Union

---

1. John Riley Thacker to Woodrow Wilson, April 6, 1913, in Woodrow Wilson Papers, Library of Congress.

270

in Louisiana and Texas. Socialists in the southwestern UMW districts also suffered setbacks in the same year, partly as a result of violent antiunion repression. Although the Socialist party vote declined in most states in the 1914 elections, it grew in Oklahoma and Arkansas and remained strong in Texas. In Louisiana, repression directed against the radical labor movement all but destroyed the Socialist party as well, but in the other states of the region the Socialists seemed to benefit politically from the intensification of the class struggle.

A TASTE OF REPRESSION

As the Socialist tide rose higher in 1912, more conservative opponents of the party emerged than ever before. Before 1910, when the progressive impulse was still strong in the Southwest, radicals were treated with relative tolerance; but when conservative Democrats won control in Oklahoma and Texas, the Socialists could no longer count on the open, optimistic political atmosphere in which regional progressivism had thrived during the 1900s. The party's "frontal assault on capitalism was far more radical than the most tolerant western states had accepted," writes one historian of Oklahoma politics, "and the politicians of both old line parties viewed the movement with alarm."[2]

After the 1912 election, A. A. Veatch started publishing the "only anti-Socialist magazine in the Southwest" at Tishomingo, Oklahoma, in order to "exploit" rising fears of radicalism. At about the same time, in Okemah, Oklahoma, C. E. Guthrie began another anti-Socialist paper called *The Kumrid*. Unlike the reactionary Veatch, Guthrie considered himself a progressive Democrat. In 1912 he named his newborn son after Woodrow Wilson. Ironically, Woody Guthrie later became the bard and radical spokesman of the Oklahoma tenant farmers.[3]

2. James B. Scales, "Political History of Oklahoma, 1907–1949" (Ph.D. dissertation, University of Oklahoma, 1949), 151.
3. *Ibid.*; A. A. Veatch to R. L. Williams, November 14, 1912, in Robert L. Williams Papers, Oklahoma Historical Society, Oklahoma City; *Social Democrat* (Oklahoma City), May 28, 1913. One historian erroneously states that the elder Guthrie was a Socialist. See R. S. Denisoff, "The Proletarian Ren-

Veatch and Guthrie quickly saw their attempts to exploit the "conservative fears of the Socialist menace which would 'soon engulf Oklahoma' . . . taken over by the editorial columns of the commercial newspapers, which began to question even the mildly progressive ideas which heretofore had earned a respectful hearing."[4] For example, Luther Roberts, editor of the Hollis *Post-Herald* in southwestern Oklahoma, praised Billy Sunday and condemned the Socialists for criticizing the churches; their attack on "our present standard of morals," he wrote, "is endorsed by every bootlegger, horse thief, train robber, murderer, and convict in the nation." Roberts clearly identified the Socialists with outlaws because they were usually members of that "changeable class" who, in their "childlike simplicity," cast off one toy after another. When they grew tired of socialism, he predicted, they might "join the Holy Rollers."[5]

The Socialists' attitude toward race angered Luther Roberts more than their views on religion. He was enraged at Tom Hickey and his "scavenger sheet *The Rebel*" for suggesting that southern Democrats, like himself, were responsible for mulattoes—"a wilful, milicious [*sic*], and unmitigated lie," Roberts retorted.

> The mulatto is a disgrace to the civilization of the South and the good people of that section acknowledge it . . . but when the socialist agitator states that the best men of the South are fathers of 'ginger cake' negroes, he vilifies the good people of our country. He will never make thinking people believe that economic determinism made the negro's skin black and the Caucasian's white or that it causes the negro, when he sweats, to smell like a peck of mashed green bugs.

The *Post-Herald* was even more emotional in its denunciation of Oscar Ameringer. "The nigger-loving Dutchman is the chief attraction at the socialist encampment in Hollis," it announced. "It is the

---

aissance," *Journal of American Folklore*, LXXXII (1969), 59. In his autobiography Woody makes no mention of his father's politics and describes him only as an aggressive man frustrated by his business failures and his wife's insanity. Woody Guthrie, *Bound for Glory* (New York: Putnam, 1968), 38–41.
4. Scales, "Political History of Oklahoma," 152.
5. Hollis (Okla.) *Post-Herald*, February 23, 1911, June 20, July 11, 1912.

first opportunity many of our people have ever had of seeing this freak who has been imported to tell the people of Oklahoma that the negro is their equal."[6]

The *Appeal to Reason*, which had a much larger circulation than any of the commercial weeklies in the area, received much abuse from small-town editors. One Oklahoma paper, emphasizing the Socialists' outlaw status, attacked Wayland of the "Appeal to Treason" for publishing "more rot per square inch in his paper than any other." And, the diatribe continued, "he calculated to poison and influence the minds of the vicious and ignorant class of people more than any other person alive—with the possible exception of Eugene V. Debbs [*sic*]."[7] When Wayland committed suicide shortly after the 1912 election, he left a note which read: "The struggle under the competitive system isn't worth the effort." Crushed at the loss of their greatest "socialist maker," Wayland's southwestern comrades explained that the *Appeal* editor had been depressed by his wife's death a few months before and by a pending lawsuit resulting from exposés he had published about prison conditions at Leavenworth. Wayland's journalistic competitors and opponents did not mourn his untimely passing.

The anti-Socialist crusade was less active in Texas, because the party was not as large and threatening as it was north of the Red River. The Christian church did, however, try to warn its large flock against the Socialist "menace" through a special publication called the *Bandsaw* and through the well-advertised speaking tours of the Reverend W. A. Lemons, author of a pamphlet called "The Evils of Socialism" to which party propagandists were forced to make detailed replies.[8]

The anxieties raised by the campaign of 1912 led to more direct attacks on socialism as well. At Cordell, Oklahoma, several party speakers were "shouted down" by Wilson supporters who had just

6. *Ibid.*, October 24, August 15, 1912.
7. Harthshorne (Okla.) *Sun*, September 12, 1912.
8. *Rebel* (Hallettsville, Tex.), April 6, 1912. See also Henry M. Tichenor, *The Evils of Capitalism: A Reply to W. F. Lemons' Book, "The Evils of Socialism," National Rip-Saw* Series No. 10 (St. Louis: Rip-Saw Publishing, 1912).

listened to a speech by Bryan and "did not come to listen to any Socialist rot." Socialist agitators and candidates were used to this kind of treatment, but it became more frequent and more bothersome during and after the 1912 campaign. More serious forms of opposition emerged in the Texas black belt where Socialist tenants were dismissed for participating in party and Renters' Union activity. But the most serious attacks on Socialists came in the pine region where the election of 1912 took place "against a background of violence and class conflict."[9]

The attempt to assassinate H. G. Creel of the *Rip-Saw* and the Grabow massacre the next day were examples of this conflict. In the following months Socialist candidates like J. R. Jones were prevented from speaking by company guards in several lumber towns. In Jasper, Texas, for example, E. I. Kellie, a Democratic candidate for Congress, wrote to John H. Kirby that he and a few of the "boys" had prevented two Wobblies from speaking. "Kellie's Old Ku Klux Klan" was not dead, he told Kirby, who commended him for his "thoughtfulness and patriotism." The "new Klan," with its emphasis on "100 percent Americanism," developed earlier in the piney woods than in many sections of the South.[10] In August, 1912, the *Rebel* made a desperate appeal to Texas Socialists to help their comrades in the timber region where the Brotherhood of Timber Workers was "engaged in a life and death struggle" and the "secretaries of the rank and file Socialist locals" were being "intimidated, shot at, and ordered to leave their communities."[11]

9. Bonham (Tex.) *News*, November 8, 1912; *Rebel* (Hallettsville, Tex.), November 2, 1912. (These charges were later documented by the U.S. Commission on Industrial Relations.) Also see David Shannon, *The Socialist Party of America, A History* (New York: Macmillan, 1955), 37.

10. Lake Charles *American Press*, July 12, 1912; H. G. Creel, "The Timber Trust Answered the Ripsaw with Bullets," *National Rip-Saw*, IX (July, 1912), 10, 12–14; *Rebel* (Hallettsville, Tex.), November 2, 1912; and E. I. Kellie to Kirby, August 18, 1912, Kirby to Kellie, August 20, 1912, both in John H. Kirby Papers, University of Houston.

The historian of the Klan in the Southwest correctly places its origins in World War I, but he misses the earlier precedents in the antilabor citizens' leagues. Charles C. Alexander, *The Ku Klux Klan in the Southwest* (Lexington: University of Kentucky Press, 1965), 12.

11. *Rebel* (Hallettsville, Tex.), August 7, 1912.

Repression increased in the fall after the BTW struck at Merry-ville. The operators used force more openly to isolate the workers from their allies among farmers and townspeople. The Merryville Good Citizen's League asked the governor to send in the militia early in February of 1913; he answered their call, but the strikers maintained their discipline and the soldiers withdrew. Shortly thereafter the League took matters into its own hands. Organized by the "leading citizens" in town, led by the company doctor, and staffed by Santa Fe gunmen, this "homespun Shutzstaffel" destroyed the union headquarters, "deported" several Wobbly organizers from the parish, and burned a soup kitchen that was staffed by female BTW members. After this battle in the "Class War at Merryville," Covington Hall said that about three hundred armed men paraded up and down the Santa Fe tracks to demonstrate their victory.[12]

By March of 1913 the Santa Fe Railroad Company had destroyed the BTW in Merryville, the last center of resistance. The strike leaders had been deported and union president, A. L. Emerson, who had led the Brotherhood from the start, was severely beaten and incapacitated by Santa Fe guards at Singer. About the same time Covington Hall's militant newspaper the *Lumberjack* was forced to move out of Alexandria. As the general lockout from the previous summer wore on and the costly Merryville strike sapped the BTW's strength, thousands of blacklisted union men left the pine region in search of work. Some went back to picking cotton and others joined the army of casual workers who followed the harvests across the great plains; others moved on to the booming oil fields of Texas and Oklahoma. By the spring of 1913, the Brotherhood, stripped of its civil rights, deprived of its leadership, and isolated from its community support, had lost a struggle that federal investigator David Saposs called "one of the most violent in the history of the American Labor Movement."[13]

12. *Lumberjack* (Alexandria, La.), February 20, 1913; Lake Charles *American Press*, February 18, 1913. See affidavits in Merl E. Reed, "The I.W.W. and Individual Freedom in Western Louisiana, 1913," *Louisiana History*, X (1969), 61–69.
13. Covington Hall, "Labor Struggles in the Deep South" (Typescript in Howard-Tilton Library, Tulane University), 184–85; David J. Saposs, *Left*

THE RISE OF THE REDS

At about the same time the IWW was being driven out of Louisiana, Bill Haywood was being recalled from the Socialist party's National Executive Committee. As a result, many of the Wobblies left the party for good. This split was not very important in the Southwest, however, because the IWW all but disappeared after its defeat at Merryville. Covington Hall and other Wobblies moved to New Orleans where they organized dockworkers and continued their feud with the Yellows in AFL locals, but by this time, the Reds had lost their influence in the decimated Louisiana Socialist party, a fact reflected in the small number of Louisiana votes cast against Haywood's recall from the National Executive Committee.

However, in Texas the party rank and file voted to retain Haywood on the National Committee by a margin of almost four to one, partly as a result of Big Bill's popular image as the hero of the West who had come to the piney woods to challenge John Henry Kirby.[14] Texas Socialists also voted against Haywood's recall because they were swayed by the pro-IWW propaganda of the *Rebel*. Hickey and the Meitzens continued to advocate the Wobblies' brand of unionism and continued to attack the "reactionary clique" of centralizers in the executive committee who wanted Haywood purged. After their unsuccessful effort to oppose the recall, the Texas Reds joined with Covington Hall's *Voice of the People*, Charles H. Kerr's left-wing *International Socialist Review*, and other semi-syndicalist publications in an effort to promote decentralization across the nation.[15]

Wing Unionism: A Study in Radical Politics and Tactics (New York: International, 1926), 170. The Brotherhood's bitter struggle had not been waged in vain. Although the union was destroyed, "some of the most obnoxious causes of dissatisfaction, such as payment in scrip, forced use of company stores, and monthly payments were modified and small wage increases and shorter hours were granted." Vernon Jensen, *Lumber and Labor* (New York: Farrar and Rinehart, 1944), 88–89.

14. Merl E. Reed, "Lumberjacks and Longshoremen: The I.W.W. in Louisiana," *Labor History*, XIII (1972), 51, 59.

15. *Socialist Party Monthly Bulletin*, IX (March, 1913); *Rebel* (Hallettsville, Tex.), January 11, March 8, 1913; Hall, "Labor Struggles in the Deep South," 234–38; *Voice of the People* (New Orleans), June 30, July 31, August

Although Oklahoma Socialists voted to recall Haywood, several papers spoke up in his defense, notably H. Grady Milner's *New Century* in Sulphur, a publication that provided a rallying point for the Oklahoma decentralizers led by Stanley Clark and Tad Cumbie.[16] The established Oklahoma leadership remained firmly in the driver's seat throughout 1912, because no one could argue with the success achieved by the party under Otto Branstetter. But the state headquarters suffered a blow to its prestige when party membership declined following the 1912 election, as it did throughout the country. A new wave of dissident opposition surfaced when the state "ex comm" decided to expel Stanley Clark for playing fast and loose with party funds. The *New Century* defended Clark and renewed its attack on the Oklahoma City leaders as pawns of Victor Berger and the right-wing National Executive Committee. Otto Branstetter and other state officials did maintain close ties with Berger, but they were not really "bosses," as their opponents charged. The Branstetter administration copied the Milwaukee form of precinct organization, but it could not recreate Berger's machine because party members rebelled against bureaucratic oligarchies.[17]

7, 24, 1913. The Texas Reds claimed that their new decentralized program helped the party grow while enhancing democracy and harmony. A letter from a right-wing Socialist challenged the *Rebel*'s claim that there was not an "atom of discord" in the Texas party. "Hickey holds the state organization by the throat," J. B. Gay wrote the national office, "and is out to capture Oklahoma for the 'Texas Programme'. I hope the national organization is not blind to this. Direct Action will get us into a bloody revolution." J. B. Gay to Thompson, January 23, 1913, in Socialist Party Papers, Perkins Library, Duke University. Also see Covington Hall's defense of the "democratic" Texas leader, in *International Socialist Review*, XVI (1915), 379.

16. *Social Democrat* (Oklahoma City), January 15, 1913; *Southern Worker* (Huntington, Ark.), April-May, 1913; *Beckham County Advocate* (Carter, Okla.), May 15, 1913; *Grant County Socialist* (Medford, Okla.), January 15, 1913.

17. *New Century* (Sulphur, Okla.), May 10, 1912; H. L. Meredith, "Agrarian Socialism in Oklahoma" (Ph.D. dissertation, University of Oklahoma, 1969), 78–82; Robert Michels, *Political Parties: A Sociological Study of the Oligarchical Tendencies of Modern Democracy* (New York: Colliers, 1962). On the Milwaukee machine and its oligarchical tendencies, see Sally M. Miller, "Milwaukee: Labor and Ethnicity," in Bruce Stave (ed.), *Socialism and the Cities* (Port Washington, N.Y.: Kennikat, 1975), 47. Also see Shannon, *So-*

The Oklahoma insurgents struck their first blow at the state convention late in 1912 when they persuaded the delegates to deny a seat to State Secretary Branstetter because he was legally a resident of Chicago not Oklahoma City. They also convinced the convention to repudiate Stanley Clark's expulsion from the party and to abolish the official party-owned press, the *Oklahoma Pioneer* edited by Ameringer and Hagel. After this show of strength by their comrades across the Red River, the *Rebel* editors boasted: "Two years ago the Oklahoma convention was controlled by such men as Oscar Ameringer, Otto Branstetter, and Jack Hagel, all of them Germans and advocates of the German centralized form of authority." But now "genuine Oklahomans" ran the party insisting upon grass-roots control and local autonomy.[18]

In 1913 the fortunes of the "so-called foreign element" in the Oklahoma party declined further. H. M. Sinclair, a boyish-looking Red from McAlester, replaced Branstetter as state secretary. The insurgents also initiated a move to recall Ameringer from his seat on the National Executive Committee because he was not a legal resident of Oklahoma, the state he claimed to represent. In June, 1913, Ameringer wrote from Milwaukee (his legal residence) that he would resign from the committee in order to preserve party harmony.[19]

When "Heck" Sinclair took over as state secretary in February of 1913, a group of indigenous leaders, including lawyer-editor Pat Nagle and UMW leader Fred Holt, replaced the professionals from the North who had contributed so much to the growth of the Oklahoma movement between 1908 and 1912. Most of the new party chiefs were left-wingers. Some also supported the decentralized program of the Texas Reds and sympathized with the direct-action

---

cialist Party of America, 21–25. In Neil Basen's interview with him, Frank P. O'Hare, who knew the Oklahoma organization as well as anyone, indicated that Branstetter was quite familiar with frontier traditions of democracy and autonomy and never intended to create a bureaucratic oligarchy based in Oklahoma City. Neil Basen to author, June 21, 1976.

18. Meredith, "Agrarian Socialism in Oklahoma," 138; *Rebel* (Hallettsville, Tex.), January 11, 1913.

19. *Social Democrat* (Oklahoma City), May 14, June 25, 1913.

approach advocated by the IWW. Thus, at the same time that hundreds of radicals left the party with Haywood, a group which included Reds with similar beliefs assumed control in Oklahoma and continued to hold power in Texas. In short, the expulsion of the Wobblies did not seriously weaken the southwestern parties, even in Louisiana where the decline of socialism resulted from external repression rather than internal factionalism.[20] Indeed the growing violence of the class struggle advanced the fortunes of Reds and semi-syndicalist elements in the party just as it did in West Virginia where a violent miners' strike created a "direct action" faction in the Socialist party.[21]

THE MINERS' MILITANCY

With the influx of new leadership in the Oklahoma party headquarters, the influence of coal miners seemed to grow; this suited the Reds who wanted to increase the influence of proletarians over neo-Populist agrarians. In 1913 miners in Oklahoma enhanced their prestige by leading a popular campaign against an amendment proposed to the state mining law requiring more expensive, but allegedly safer, underground operating rules. The Socialists claimed that the "coal trust" initiated this law in order to raise the price of coal and to force its smaller competitors out of business by enacting regulations demanding more elaborate and expensive mining equipment. Illegal diggings on unleased Indian land did in fact "honeycomb" the Krebs-McAlester vein; these "wagon mines" were operated cooperatively by farmers, tradesmen, and irregularly employed miners who produced coal at very cheap prices for the sur-

20. For two studies that emphasize the importance of the 1912 split as a cause of the Socialist party's decline see Daniel Bell, *Marxian Socialism in the United States* (Princeton, N.J.: Princeton University Press, 1967), 75–77, 79; and Ira Kipnis, *The American Socialist Movement, 1897–1912* (New York: Columbia University Press, 1952), 391–420. For a general critique of this thesis see James Weinstein, *The Decline of Socialism in America, 1912–1925* (New York: Monthly Review Press, 1967).

21. On the rise of the syndicalistic Reds in the West Virginia Socialist party, see Frederick A. Barkey, "The Socialist Party in West Virginia, 1898–1920: A Study in Working Class Radicalism" (Ph.D. dissertation, University of Pittsburg, 1971), 108–63.

rounding domestic market. The UMW militants, led by district official Fred Holt, attacked the monopoly capitalists who owned the large coal companies for proposing a fake reform to drive the cooperative miners out of business because they charged lower, "honest" prices. The Socialists united miners, farmers, and many townspeople around this issue. In August of 1913 Oklahomans rejected the "coal trust" amendment by a margin of nearly four-to-one. After assisting in the campaign, Adolph Germer, an important Socialist UMW leader from Illinois, told Debs that the coal corporations' defeat resulted largely from the farmer opposition mustered by the party. The Oklahoma miners considered it a great victory because it gave "them renewed confidence in themselves."[22]

The cooperation between farmers and miners promoted by Fred Holt and other Socialists in 1913 indicated an increasingly reciprocal relationship between industrial unionism and agrarian socialism. After 1910 Socialist activity in the coal camps did not influence the growth of rural radicalism as directly as it had in the early years, but the successful Socialist party campaign against the "coal trust" amendment in 1913 demonstrated the continuing importance of the militant miners' leadership.

By 1912 Socialist party propaganda had been publicizing workers' struggles and recruiting farmer support for labor for over a decade. In 1913 the Socialist press reported extensively on violent UMW campaigns in West Virginia and southern Colorado. After traveling west with Adolph Germer to lend a hand with organizing in the Trinidad, Colorado, mining district, Fred Holt returned to Oklahoma with news of Mother Jones's imprisonment and of the desperate condition of the western coal miners. He persuaded the Socialist state convention, composed largely of farmer delegates, to make a generous relief contribution. A month later at the UMW district convention in Ft. Smith, Arkansas, Holt and Pete Stewart asked their members to increase dues five cents a month in order

22. *Social Democrat* (Oklahoma City), March 5, 26, April 2, 9, July 16, 23, August 27, 1913; Adolph Germer to Debs, September 13, 1913, in Eugene V. Debs Collection, Castleton Papers, Tamiment Institute, New York; Frederick L. Ryan, *The Rehabilitation of Oklahoma Coal Mining Communities* (Norman: University of Oklahoma Press, 1935), 56–57, 59.

LEADING OKLAHOMA SOCIALISTS

JOHN G. WILLS,

J. T. CUMBIE,

PATRICK S. NAGLE,

FRED W. HOLT,

GEORGE G. HAMILTON,

THOS. W. WOODROW,

Courtesy Wayne State University

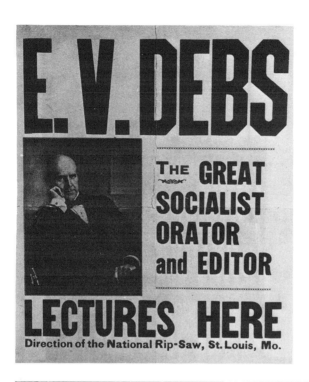

Socialists at a Socialist encampment. Left to right: James H. Maurer, chairman Socialist party, Irving Ameringer, Mrs. O. A. (Lula) Woods, Oscar Ameringer, Sigfried Ameringer, Carl Ameringer.

Courtesy Wayne State University

to give a $50,000 loan to their Colorado comrades. The rank-and-file miners of District 21 agreed. To reciprocate for the relief support offered by farmer Socialists from Oklahoma, the union leaders introduced a resolution "deploring landlordism in the rural communities" and pledging aid to the tenant union movement; it passed "unanimously and uproariously," suggesting that the party was creating a greater sense of solidarity among the miners and renters of the region.[23]

After following events in the bitter Colorado coal strike during the winter of 1914, in April southwestern Socialists heard the shocking news of the Ludlow massacre. The brutal killing of members of miners' families convinced many workers that it was necessary to buy rifles to defend themselves, as the "direct actionists" like "Covy" Hall insisted, and it persuaded some farmer Socialists that the class struggle would have to be fought with bullets as well as ballots. Party leaders like Oscar Ameringer still insisted that political action was more effective than direct action, but Eugene Debs and other militant Socialists urged the workers to arm themselves for self defense.[24]

Shortly after the Ludlow massacre, Stewart and Holt announced a strike at the Mammouth Vein in Sebastian County, Arkansas, where the Bache-Denman Company had opened several mines with scab labor in violation of the 1903 contract, because, as the owner put it, the union had "terrorized the operators into signing." On April 6, 1914, Stewart and other union leaders, along with Dan Hogan and his daughter Freda, who were prominent Socialists in the area, addressed a large meeting of miners and their supporters.

23. *Rebel* (Hallettsville, Tex.), January 17, 1914; *Appeal to Reason* (Girard, Kan.), January 31, 1914; McAlester (Okla.) *News-Capital*, February 20, 1914.
24. *Rebel* (Hallettsville, Tex.), May 9, 1914; Hall, "Labor Struggles in the Deep South," 185. After the massacre, George Moore, an Oklahoma miner from Henryetta declared that "a bitter lesson has been written in blood of the innocents at Ludlow: Labor must use every weapon at its command, even unto the high powered rifle and machine gun, to win its battles. And so we are going over to the direct actionists by the hundreds now." Letter to the editor, *United Mine Workers' Journal* (Indianapolis), April 30, July 30, 1914. Also see, Oscar Ameringer, "Ballots and Bullets," *National Rip-Saw* (St. Louis), July, 1914, pp. 12–13.

At that time the district president allegedly said that "he would rather die than see a mine run open shop" and that he would "arm every miner in the Hartford Valley if necessary to prevent it." Stewart and his Socialist comrades then led a crowd of one thousand to a nearby open-shop mine where they tried to "persuade" the nonunion miners to quit work. A pro-UMW sheriff accompanied the crowd and when the company guards at the mine refused his order to disarm, "several clashes" occurred in which the Bache-Denman employees were "routed." An American flag was then hoisted over the mine tipple along with a banner which read: "This Is Union Man's Country."[25]

A week later the UMW, which had over five thousand members in Sebastian County, organized a "mammouth march," including many farmers and townspeople, to protest a federal injunction Franklin Bache had obtained to open his mines. Community support for the miners was so strong that county and township law officers refused to protect Bache's property and the district court was forced to assign federal marshals to enforce its restraining order and to guard company property and employees. Checked by the injunction, Socialist union leaders called a temporary halt to their actions against Bache and turned their attention to other pressing matters.[26]

The president of the Southwestern Operators' Association testified in district court that Fred Holt and Alex Howat, Socialist president of UMW District 14 in Kansas, had accepted money from an owners' "slush fund" in order to secure certain arbitration procedures as part of interstate contracts in 1910 and 1912. The Socialist union leaders angrily denied the charge and expressed outrage when national UMW president John P. White "exploded a bomb" and agreed to investigate the case against them. "Extraordinary" conventions of the miners in Districts 14 and 21 exonerated

25. *National Rip-Saw* (St. Louis), April 16, 1914; McAlester (Okla.) *News-Capital*, April 7, 1914. See also Samuel A. Sizer, "This Is Union Man's Country," *Arkansas Historical Quarterly*, XVII (1968), 310–26.

26. McAlester (Okla.) *News-Capital*, April 16, May 15, 1914; Freda Hogan, "The Arkansas Miners' Struggle," *Solidarity* (New Castle, Pa.), December 19, 1914.

Howat and Holt in May, 1914, increasing tension between the Socialist leadership in the Southwest and the Democratic leadership in the national office. In addition to these troubles, a defense had to be prepared for District 21 President Pete Stewart, who was put on trial in July along with several other miners and the prounion sheriff, for leading the attack on Bache's open-shop mines at Midland in April. The trial was postponed, however, when Stewart became ill.[27]

Shortly after the April "riot," allegedly precipitated by Stewart, the federal marshals withdrew from the Bache property. The owner replaced them with a large force of hired guards because local authorities were "in sympathy" with the UMW and "refused to furnish protection." On the night of July 16, just two years after the bloody battle at Grabow, Louisiana, a "fierce riot" erupted in the Hartford Valley when Arkansas miners armed themselves and attacked Bache's mine at Prairie Creek because they were enraged by company guards who reportedly insulted their women and fired into their tent camp. Determined to strike out before they became the victims of another Ludlow massacre, the miners fired upon company guards, killing two; they also attacked six open-shop mines with explosives, leveling $100,000 worth of buildings. On July 18 armed union miners were "in complete control of the Bache-Denman coal properties."[28]

Gene Debs congratulated the Arkansas coal diggers for routing the company gunmen and saluted Fred Holt, who admitted shipping rifles across the state line from McAlester to Hartford in order to "protect wives and children from the outrages of private armed guards" and to prevent another Ludlow massacre. After being indicted for numerous crimes in August along with Pete Stewart, Holt declared that the "Arkansas miners, like their brothers in

27. *Solidarity* (New Castle, Pa.), May 23, 1914; Harthshorne (Okla.) *Sun*, May 29, 1914; McAlester (Okla.) *News-Capital*, July 3, 7, 1914.
28. Franklin Bache to commission, August 5, 1914, in Record Group 174, Commission on Industrial Relations Papers, "Records of the Department of Labor," National Archives, hereinafter cited as CIR Records; McAlester (Okla.) *News-Capital*, July 17, 1914; *Arkansas Gazette* (Little Rock), July 18, 1914.

Colorado, are in open rebellion against their masters; they have armed themselves and are determined that there shall not be any more Ludlows."[29] The Oklahoma Socialists, farmers and workers alike, apparently admired Holt's militancy, for they nominated him for governor by a wide margin in their August primary.

In September of 1914 the UMW's Socialist leadership in the Southwest was in deep trouble. President Stewart was convicted of inciting to riot and violating a federal injunction, receiving a four-month sentence in Leavenworth. At about the same time, national UMW President White decided to reopen the Holt-Howat bribery case, even though both Socialist officials had been exonerated by the rank and file of their districts. When White demanded the militants' resignation, Howat reluctantly stepped aside, vowing to take his case to court and then back to the loyal Kansas miners. Holt refused to quit. He said he was being framed by the national leadership in concert with Pete Hanraty's local Catholic-Democrats who wanted to resume control of District 21 after he and Stewart were eliminated. A few weeks after he attacked his UMW opponents, Holt did resign his union office in order to devote full time to his gubernatorial campaign.[30]

HARD TIMES AND THE 1914 ELECTION

Holt's nomination gave the Oklahoma Socialists an indigenous working-class leader whose popularity with union men no Democratic candidate could rival. And Pat Nagle's senatorial nomination gave them a candidate with grass-roots appeal to the farmers. His legal defense of night riders and his slashing attacks on influential landlords in the *Tenant Farmer* made the Kingfisher lawyer a champion of the Oklahoma renters. His articles on numerous sheriffs' sales in the drought-stricken western counties also raised the ire of small-farm owners. Therefore, Nagle's candidacy was ex-

29. Eugene V. Debs, "Bravo, Arkansas Coal Diggers," *United Mine Workers Journal* (Indianapolis), August 1, 1914; *Rebel* (Hallettsville, Tex.), September 7, 1914.

30. *United Mine Workers Journal* (Indianapolis), September 3, 1914; Mc-Alester (Okla.), *News-Capital*, September 26, 1914; Fred Holt, *An Address to the Workers*, Bulletin No. 4 (Oklahoma City: Socialist Party of Oklahoma, 1914).

pected to cut into some of Senator Thomas Gore's support in the old Oklahoma Territory.[31] The Socialist campaign in 1914 seemed especially threatening because of the class-conscious resentment generated among miners and other workers by the Ludlow and Prairie Creek incidents and because of the suffering among cotton farmers caused by the collapse of the market that came with the outbreak of World War I.

State Secretary H. M. Sinclair wanted more than a protest vote in the November elections; he counted on an increase in the number of committed "red card" members in Oklahoma. To promote grass-roots organization, local Socialists stood as precinct committeemen throughout the state and were elected in all but 200 of the 2,565 precincts; Sinclair promptly asked them to take a poll of all qualified voters in order to make canvassing more effective. These tactics increased the Socialist party's primary vote in August by 100 percent. Thousands of new members joined up, raising the party's dues-paying membership to eleven thousand. Oklahoma was clearly the party's "best organized state."[32] The Sooner Socialists also conducted their most extensive encampment tour in 1914. In August, crowds of about ten thousand heard Debs, Holt, and other Socialist orators at Sulphur and Otter Valley. The *National Rip-Saw* sponsored an ambitious series of encampments in southwestern Oklahoma, ably organized and advertised by congressional candidate Oles Stofer. Attendance at 32 four-day camp meetings in July and August varied from one thousand to sixteen thousand, according to Kate Richards O'Hare who addressed the gatherings along with Caroline Lowe, her sister Socialist from Kansas. O'Hare also reported that the *Rip-Saw* staff sold 10,800 yearly subscriptions to these "militant Socialists of western Oklahoma."[33]

31. Scales, "Political History of Oklahoma," 164.
32. H. M. Sinclair to Thompson, August 20, 1914, in Socialist Party Papers, Duke; *Appeal to Reason* (Girard, Kan.), June 22, 1914; Shannon, *Socialist Party of America*, 35. The party had also raised a $15,000 campaign chest from local dues and the contributions of the cooperative cotton patches. *Harlow's Weekly* (Oklahoma City), June 20, 1914, p. 9.
33. *Rebel* (Hallettsville, Tex.), August 22, 1914; Oles Stofer, "Conducting Socialist Encampments," memo to national office, 1914, in Socialist Party Papers; *National Rip-Saw* (St. Louis), July and August, 1914, 7, 16.

Socialist candidates blamed the current cotton crisis on the Democrats and warned the tenants that by the end of the year "everything they have in the world will be taken from them by the capitalist landlord class." They criticized the emergency measures offered by Murray and Gore and other southwestern agrarians. Like President Wilson's "ridiculous buy-a-bale campaign," these piecemeal reforms would not repay the tenants for the losses already suffered during the "crisis" or alter the fundamentally exploitative system.[34]

"Heck" Sinclair wrote a widely circulated pamphlet attacking the Wilson administration's farm legislation, contending that the landlords, bankers, and merchants got the lion's share of federal money just as the "interlocked parasites" got their "fair share of rent, interest and profit." Sinclair's tract declared, "The real producer's share enables him to exist in a rented shack, the parasite's share enables him to live in a fine house, wear good clothes and send his children to the best schools and colleges."[35] The Democrats' emergency measures could not meet the crisis because cyclical depressions were a part of capitalism that could not be regulated.

Pat Nagle's "interlocking parasites" bulletin was also widely circulated, as it used the economic crisis to expose the "absentee landlords" or "so-called retired farmers" who "came to town to die, but forgot what they came for," the "village usurers," "the grafting politicians," and other "creatures of the bank and landlord interests." These petty capitalists were of course controlled by the "greater capitalists" who owned the banks, railroads, and factories. All of these "parasites" were united—interlocked—in "defense of their right to exploit" the "honest labor" of farmers and workers. As a result, Nagle said, rural producers, especially renters, were being "drawn into reciprocal solidarity with wage workers from

---

34. *Appeal to Reason* (Girard, Kan.), October 3, 1914. See also Keith L. Bryant, Jr., *Alfalfa Bill Murray* (Norman: University of Oklahoma Press, 1968), 123–24; and Thomas P. Gore, "The Cotton Situation in the South," *Congressional Record*, 63rd Congress, 2nd Sess., No. 6.

35. H. M. Sinclair, *The Cotton Situation*, Bulletin No. 3 (Oklahoma City: Socialist Party of Oklahoma, 1914).

industry in an attack on the exploiting interests." In the rural Southwest, these class lines "ran fairly clear between the interlocked parasites in the electric light towns and the surrounding tenant population," the party's senatorial candidate continued. "The fact that the geographical and economic lines are the same makes for a clear cut fight."[36] The increase in tenancy and absentee ownership in the Southwest had transformed traditional town-country tension into class conflict. The Socialist vote of 1912 was a political expression of that conflict. It is not surprising, then, that during the party's militant campaign in 1914 "Democrats all over Oklahoma listened with increasing anxiety to 'class' appeals and," as Garin Burbank notes, "feared for their political dominance."[37]

"The size of the Socialist vote in 1912 haunted the Democrats," one historian observes, and "gubernatorial nominee R. L. Williams and the entire Democratic ticket in Oklahoma were running scared in 1914."[38] During the summer Williams, chief justice of the state supreme court, faced a difficult primary campaign against a number of strong candidates including Al Jennings, a reformed outlaw, who brazenly toured the state showing a movie of his train robbing exploits to full houses. Because he attacked the Democratic party establishment and "church and business elements" who were scandalized by his candidacy, Jennings was expected to garner a "large percentage of the Socialist vote" in the Democratic primary. He was not able to do so, however, because the energetic work of Socialist precinct committeemen doubled the level of rank-and-file participation in the Socialist primary and kept nearly all "red carders" out of the Democratic contest.[39]

36. Patrick S. Nagle, *The Interlocked Parasites*, Bulletin No. 1 (Oklahoma City: Oklahoma Socialist Party, 1914).
37. Garin Burbank, "Agrarian Radicals and Their Opponents: Political Conflict in Southern Oklahoma, *1910–1924*," *Journal of American History*, LVIII (1971), 10.
38. Bryant, *Alfalfa Bill Murray*, 126–27.
39. McAlester (Okla.) *News-Capital*, May 8, June 3, 1914; *Harlow's Weekly* (Oklahoma City), June 24, 1914, pp. 9–10; *Beckham County Agitator*, (Sayre, Okla.), July 24, 1914; *Oklahoma Democrat* (Altus), April 9, 1914. On Jennings' notorious career see O. Henry (William Sidney Porter), *Sixes and Sevens* (Garden City, N.Y.: Doubleday, 1920), 46–63.

As the 1914 campaign heated up, R. L. Williams wrote to his old ally from the Constitutional Convention, Congressman Bill Murray, begging him to return from Washington to campaign against the judge's opponents, Fred Holt of the Socialist party and progressive farm editor John Fields of the GOP. Although they were both lawyer-landlords from adjoining counties in southern Oklahoma who had cooperated closely as Bryanites in 1907 and 1908, Murray and Williams felt differently about the campaign of 1914. "Alfalfa Bill" refused to return home for the canvass. He told the alarmed judge to simply "support the President by name, praise the tariff and the Federal Reserve, and call for rural credits legislation." Williams, who was a good deal more concerned about the recent growth of socialism than was Murray, followed this advice and added emphasis to moral reform; this approach appealed to small towners and many farmers, as the incumbent governor, Lee Cruce, had illustrated in his successful campaigns.[40] But moral appeals did not increase the popularity of the Democrats in the rural districts where cotton farmers were still in great distress. In the weeks just preceeding the election Williams received several letters warning him of the growing spectre of socialism in the cotton country.

John Humphreys wrote that the "stress of hard times" was "breeding discontent" and that the Democrats would "bear the brunt" of it. "Even President Wilson is losing popularity here," he said.[41] From the cotton counties in the south, where some angry tenants were "night riding," Williams learned that the cotton crisis had "taken the starch out of the Democratic farmers" who were "sore." The Socialists, who were filling the schoolhouses for their speakers and attracting thousands of tenants to their encampments, might carry most of the rural precincts in Seminole, Cleveland, and Commanche counties. After going out among the people

40. Bryant, *Alfalfa Bill Murray*, 126–27; Scales, "Political History of Oklahoma," 171–72. For an excellent portrait of R. L. Williams and his "faction," which exposes the class fears and hatreds of this group, see Garin Burbank, *When Farmers Voted Red: The Gospel of Socialism in the Oklahoma Countryside, 1910–1924* (Westport, Conn.: Greenwood, 1976), 93–105.

41. John Humphreys to R. L. Williams, October 18, 1914, in Williams Papers.

a few days before the election, Jefferson Lee Bice of Indiahoma reported: "Everybody seems to have gone Socialist."[42] From Cheyenne in western Oklahoma, one Democrat wrote that socialism in Roger Mills County was "a protest against hard times and indirectly an assault on the party in power."[43] But the intensity of radical feeling in the south, where the cotton crisis struck most severely, seemed to be more permanent and class conscious. As G. W. Crosser, a renter from Stephens County, told Williams after receiving a Democratic appeal for contributions: "I have been a member of the Socialist Party for years; it is the only party that will ever save this world from chaos, so you need not expect any support from me or my class."[44]

In November Fred Holt and the Oklahoma Socialists polled 52,703 votes or 21 percent of the total; this represented a remarkable increase of over 10,000 votes in an off-year election when the Socialist party was suffering losses throughout the nation. Judge Williams ran 20,000 votes behind Wilson's 1912 total as a result of defections to the Socialists and a poor Democratic turnout. Elected with less than 40 percent of the vote, Williams was thereafter "rankled" by his status as a minority governor.[45]

Holt received his best response in southeastern Oklahoma where his congressional candidacy in 1912, his leadership in the fight against the "coal trust" amendment in 1913, and his bold actions in the Prairie Creek "mine war" made him a hero to thousands of miners and tenants. Although only 50 percent of the adult males in the Third Congressional District voted in 1914, Holt averaged 34 percent of the vote in these counties of the old Choctaw and Chickasaw nations; he received 30 percent in Bryan, Judge Williams' home county, and 41 percent in Marshall County where the Socialists came within 37 votes of winning and "threw a basement

42. J. H. Cobb to R. L. Williams, October 24, 1914, John Allen to R. L. Williams, October 27, 1914, J. L. Bice to R. L. Williams, November 1, 1914, *ibid.*
43. E. L. Mitchell to R. L. Williams, *ibid.*, October 29, 1914.
44. G. W. Crosser to R. L. Williams, *ibid.*, October 29, 1914.
45. *World Almanac, 1916*, p. 761; Scales, "Political History of Oklahoma," 172.

scare into the Democrats."[46] The class-conscious response of farmers and workers to the Hartford Valley struggle and the cotton crisis also helped Dan Hogan, the coal town lawyer-editor, who polled 10,434 votes in his race for Arkansas governor. Holt and Hogan were probably the only Socialist gubernatorial candidates in the country to poll more votes in 1914 than Debs polled in 1912. In the southeastern Kansas "Balkans" Socialist George D. Brewer was elected state representative from Crawford County. Brewer, who edited the *Workers Chronicle*, an excellent Socialist labor paper in Pittsburg, Kansas, took advantage of an endorsement by UMW District 14 to poll 44 percent of the vote, defeating a Democrat and a Progressive. The Kansas Socialists made a bold appeal for the black vote in this election, running black miner G. W. Reid for county coroner and appealing for white votes this way: "The sooner the white comrades of the state make up their mind to sacrifice some things to win the colored vote of Kansas, the sooner the party will take . . . power." This appeal did not yield results for the state ticket, but in Crawford County, where Reid polled 4,863 votes, the Socialist party seemed to benefit from the racial solidarity created by the UMW.[47]

The Oklahoma Socialists ran a very strong race in the southeastern cotton and mining counties of the old Indian Territory, but their greatest gains in 1914 came from the western part of the state, especially the southwestern counties where H. H. Stallard, running in his third race for Congress, polled 9,121 votes (33 percent) to 11,861 (or 43 percent) for Jim McClintic, his victorious Democratic opponent. John Thacker's influential *Oklahoma Democrat* led the commercial weeklies of the region in praising McClintic's candidacy; he was a successful businessman and booster, in contrast to

46. Oliver Benson, *et al.*, *Oklahoma Votes, 1907–1962* (Norman: University of Oklahoma Press, 1964), 142–43; *Marshall County News-Democrat* (Madill, Okla.), November 6, 1914.

47. *World Almanac, 1916*, p. 750. *Worker's Chronicle* (Pittsburg, Kan.), October 31, November 6, 1914. For example, in West Virginia, where Debs recorded his greatest increases in 1912 as a result of a "mine war," the Socialist vote dropped in 1914, except in the mining precincts. Barkey, "The Socialist Party in West Virginia, 1898–1920," 163–64.

Stallard, who was a failure as a farmer, a politician, and an editor. But many of the heavily mortgaged farmers of western Oklahoma resented rather than admired the success of small-town business-men. Stallard, like many of the rural radicals who supported him, had failed in many things, but in 1914 he did succeed in polling enough votes to become one of the strongest Socialist congressional candidates in the country. Pat Nagle's aggressive senatorial candidacy also helped the party in the west, where local candidates ran ahead of the Democrats in many poor farming areas and carried two counties, Major and Roger Mills. As a result, six Socialists were elected to the state legislature and scores to town and county offices.[48] The hard times in the west brought on by drought and low crop prices undoubtedly boosted Socialist party totals. However, Stallard and Nagle also gained from the extensive *Rip-Saw* encampment tour which covered nearly every county in the region and the grass-roots activity of party committeemen who covered nearly every precinct.[49]

The Sooner Socialists' success impressed the editors of the *Appeal* so much that they decided to focus even more of their attention on farm problems. The "marvellous" results in Oklahoma proved that farmers could be brought to socialism and as class-conscious "red carders" they would support the struggles of workers in the mines, mills, and factories.[50]

The Texas Socialists also entered the 1914 campaign with a strong ticket and an ambitious encampment program. The market

---

48. *World Almanac, 1916*, p. 761; *Oklahoma Democrat* (Altus) October 29, 1914; Boswell (Okla.) *Submarine*, November 13, 1914. The Socialists elected at least one hundred county and local officials including two county sheriffs. See report on the election results in forty-nine of seventy-six counties compiled by the state office in Oklahoma City, in Socialist Party Papers, Duke.

49. The effects of Sinclair's organizing campaign were evidenced by the fact that in the strong Socialist counties (over 25 percent) an average of 90 percent of the precincts had committeemen whereas in the weak counties (under 10 percent Socialist) an average of 54 percent of the precincts had committeemen. Calculated from figures in *Socialist Party, Proceedings of the State Convention of Oklahoma, 1915* (Oklahoma City: Socialist Party of Oklahoma, 1915), 29–30.

50. *Appeal to Reason* (Girard, Kan.), November 21, 1914.

crisis was naturally a big issue in the largest cotton-producing state in the nation. "Agrarian radicals" like Joe Eagle and Robert Henry joined "Alfalfa Bill" Murray in criticizing the Wilson administration's inadequate response to the crisis and in proposing more extensive credit and currency legislation to Congress.[51] Less adventurous Texans, Secretary of Agriculture David Houston for example, urged cotton farmers to hold their crop and to cooperate with businessmen in the "buy-a-bale" campaign. But these efforts did not seem to quell the "wonderful unrest" one Texas Democrat observed among the people of the cotton country.[52]

The Texas political situation changed in 1914 when a Democratic candidate made tenancy a campaign issue. James E. Ferguson, a small landlord and country banker from Bell County, beat the favored candidate in the primary by running on a "land plank" that pledged to enact a law limiting the amount of rent tenants paid. For the first time in many years prohibition became a secondary issue in Texas politics. As a result, Ferguson won the support of the brewery interests as well as the Farmers' Union, an organization kept alive since 1908 with funds from merchant and banker organizations. Ferguson ran as a "friend of the farmer" and openly appealed to the tenants, but he also received the support of country merchants and bankers, as well as smaller landlords who blamed the large absentee owners for stirring up tenant unrest by charging

---

51. Arthur Link has suggested that a group of agrarian radicals, led by Congressman Henry and largely including old Bryanites from the Southwest, pushed steadily for more liberal legislation and helped make President Wilson an "advanced progressive." See his "The South and the New Freedom: An Interpretation," *American Scholar*, XX (1951), 314–24. Another historian has questioned this interpretation, pointing out that with the exception of Murray, these southern congressmen took conservative stands on many issues. See Richard M. Abrams, "Woodrow Wilson and the Southern Congressmen, 1913–1916," *Journal of Southern History*, XXII (1956), 417–37.

52. President Wilson prevented the passage of rural credits legislation proposed by southwestern congressmen in the spring of 1914 because it would have amounted to "special legislation" for farmers who wanted money at lower interest rates than other classes. Arthur S. Link, *Woodrow Wilson: The New Freedom* (Princeton, N.J.: Princeton University Press, 1956), 262. Quote on "unrest" is from Sam H. Acheson, *Joe Bailey: The Last Democrat* (New York: Macmillan, 1932), 376.

excessive rents and blamed city bankers and cotton buyers for helping create the cotton surplus.[53]

During the runoff primary the Socialists attacked both Ferguson ("a landlord, a banker, and a notorious usurer") and his more conservative opponent (a corporation lawyer who defended the interests of "capitalist criminals" like John Henry Kirby). Although reactionaries criticized Ferguson's land plank for being socialistic, the Socialist candidates dismissed it as a fake reform calculated to "take the discontented tenants away from the Socialist Party." Farmers should not be confused because the "right men," like "lumber baron" Kirby, opposed Ferguson, since the progressives belonged to the same political party—"the court house square party, the landlord party, the party of privilege in Texas." The Socialist party also attacked Peter Radford, president of the once powerful Texas Farmers' Union, who supported Ferguson, calling Radford a "lackey" for county seat bankers and businessmen. The Socialist press publicized an attorney general's report exposing Radford's Farm Life Commission as a front for the Texas Businessmen's Association, an organization "indicted for defrauding and misleading the public" and for "acquiring control of bona fide agricultural movements and farm organizations."[54]

The Socialists nominated a ticket headed by E. R. Meitzen, who helped his father publish the *Rebel* and acted as an organizer for the Renters' and Typographers' unions. Meitzen's running mate was W. S. Noble, a farmer who had migrated from Kansas at the age of 16. After starting a career as a minister for the Church of Christ, Noble had settled down in Eastland County where he was elected as Populist sheriff in the 1890s and during the early 1900s built one of the strongest Socialist locals in the state.

The Texas Socialists adopted a platform by referendum that called for the "industrial" organization of farmers and workers

53. Seth S. McKay, *Texas Politics, 1906–1944* (Lubbock: Texas Tech University Press, 1952), 55–60; Robert Lee Hunt, *A History of Farmer Movements in the Southwest, 1873–1925* (College Station: Texas A & M Press, 1935), 138–40.

54. *Rebel* (Hallettsville, Tex.), April 14, July 8, 1914; Carl Blasig, *Building Texas: A History of the Commercial Organization Movement and Its Impact on Texas Progress*, (Brownsville, Tex.: Springman-King, 1963), 100–101, 109–10.

and condemned the "crimes against humanity" committed at Grabow, Merryville, and Ludlow. They also claimed credit for making tenancy the central issue in the campaign. Meitzen and Noble touted their own land program with its emphasis on the confiscatory land tax and exposed Ferguson's "land plank" as a plan to permanently legalize the exploitative rent of one-third grain and one-fourth cotton. Even if rent regulation could be enacted, the radicals argued, the law would not be enforced any more strictly than was the dormant antiusury statute which Ferguson's own bank in Belton allegedly violated. Furthermore, this "land reform" simply promised to force large plantation owners to displace tenants and hire cheap wage laborers, as Ferguson himself had done on his 1000-acre farm in Bell County. Tenants would thus be driven into "abject peonage"; they would become more "enslaved" than the Mexican peasants who had been forced to launch a "bloody revolution" to liberate their land.[55]

The Texas Socialists countered "Farmer Jim's" colorful "one-gallus" campaign with their most extensive encampment program. The Grand Saline encampment, managed professionally by Richey Alexander, attracted more East Texas farmers than ever before. And the big *Rip-Saw* tour, featuring Debs and Kate O'Hare, attracted thousands more as it swung through the central and western counties in July and August. Accustomed as he was to "great crowds and intense enthusiasm," Debs confessed that "these remarkable demonstrations were something of a revelation" to him. He was amazed to see eight thousand farmers and their families pour into a grove near a little village in West Texas. "They came in procession and all the highways were filled with their wagons. Every man, woman and child carried a red flag. It was the first time I had ever seen a parade in the country and it was a sight not to be forgotten. Far as the eye could reach along the roads there was a stream of farmers' wagons, filled with their families, and all of them waving red flags. It looked as if the march to the Socialist Republic had actually begun." Despite withering heat and drought,

55. "Platform of the Socialist Party of Texas," May, 1914, in Barker Library, University of Texas, Austin.

the crowds were "without exception large and full of enthusiasm." Debs exclaimed, "These farmers have the true Socialist spirit. Many of them have scarcely a crop between themselves and destitution and yet they are the most generous, wholehearted people on earth, and for Socialism they would give the last of their scant possessions."[56]

As a consequence of this electoral support generated by Debs, O'Hare, Meitzen, and other Socialist speakers and by the *Rebel*'s relentless efforts to expose "Farmer Jim's" connections with banking, brewing, and other business interests, Ferguson failed to match Wilson's 1912 totals. The Texas Socialists lost only a few hundred votes from 1912 but their performance compared unfavorably with the great gains the party made in Oklahoma. As one historian remarked, Ferguson's "demagogic appeal to the tenant farmer" apparently "bled" the Socialist party by co-opting the land question and shifting attention away from the radicals' plan to abolish the whole system through a confiscatory land tax. "Ferguson stole the Socialist Party's thunder," Tom Hickey wrote after the election, "but he is in hopeless error if he thinks his election will do anything more than emphasize the class character of the Democratic party."[57]

Although the Texas Socialist party vote declined by a few hundred votes between 1912 and 1914, the party's percentage of the vote increased from 8.5 to 11.7 as a result of a decline in Democratic turnout.[58] Furthermore, the Socialists' raw vote actually grew in sections where the class struggle was growing more intense. They gained votes in Lavaca County where Judge E. O. Meitzen's campaign for the state senate in August, 1913, had mobilized indebted dirt farmers (including many newer Czech and German immigrants). And the party also made gains in Van Zandt and Rains counties where tenants had launched a "widespread move-

56. *National Rip-Saw* (St. Louis), July, 1914, p. 9, and Eugene V. Debs, "Revolutionary Encampments," *ibid.*, September, 1914, p. 12.
57. *World Almanac, 1916*, pp. 761–66; James A. Tinsley, "The Progressive Movement in Texas" (Ph.D. dissertation, University of Wisconsin, 1953), 173; *Rebel* (Hallettsville, Tex.), November 28, 1914.
58. *World Almanac, 1916*, p. 766, and *World Almanac, 1919*, p. 763.

ment" to sue usurious bankers. In fact, a Socialist party congressional candidate actually picked up votes on Representative Sam Rayburn in the north central black belt district that included these two troubled counties. The Reds also advanced in several piney woods counties where farmers and timber workers nourished their anger against the repressive antiunion tactics employed by lumber barons like John Kirby. Despite the hostile atmosphere reigning in East Texas, Socialist Arch Lingan increased the party's vote in his campaign against conservative Congressman Martin Dies in the heart of the piney woods. Dies was supported by Kirby, who not only outraged the lumber workers but also angered tenants by his practice of holding his cut-over lands for speculation and oil development. In the Third Congressional District, a marginal cotton-farming area between the black prairie and the piney woods in northeast Texas, R. T. Bryant polled 25 percent of the vote against the incumbent Democratic congressman, Jim Young.[59] Bryant, a novice in electoral politics, thought this was a significant accomplishment "when you take into consideration the fact that Mr. Young is already a member of Congress and has all the money and influence the capitalist press can provide and I am only a little country physician known only in the radius of my own county."[60]

And so despite Ferguson's demagoguery, the Texas Socialist movement gained strength in areas where the class struggle had intensified. After the 1914 campaign, Debs praised the Texas tenants' "class conscious enthusiasm" and proclaimed them fully eligible as members of the "revolutionary movement of the working class." He declared them "real Socialists" who were "ready for action, and if the time comes when men are needed at the front to fight and die for the cause the farmers of Texas and Oklahoma will be found there."[61]

---

59. Hallettsville (Tex.) *Herald*, August 8, 1913; *Rebel* (Hallettsville, Tex.), August 16, 1913, August 29, 1914, January 9, 1915; *World Almanac, 1916*, p. 766.
60. *Rebel* (Hallettsville, Tex.), December 12, 1914.
61. Debs, "Revolutionary Encampments," 12.

CLASS CONFLICT AND VIOLENT PROTEST

Radical renters became more militant in 1914 because the ruling Democrats failed to relieve the suffering caused by the cotton crisis; they also became angrier as harassment of Socialist speakers and voters increased. For example, when E. O. Meitzen was wounded by an unknown assailant in the summer, Tom Hickey said that he took calls for hours at the *Rebel* office telling agitated supporters not to come to Hallettsville to seek revenge against the courthouse "ring" thought to be responsible for the shooting.[62]

Socialist voters, especially on the tenant plantations and in the company-owned lumber towns, faced more intimidation than ever before. As W. L. Thurman, a leading party organizer, explained: "The election was held in the midst of a panic. Almost everything was mortgaged. There was no price for cotton. Foreclosure and ruin lay just ahead. Taking advantage of the situation, the 'interlocked parasites' used every opportunity to intimidate those indebted to them and to compel them to vote 'right.' Many were whipped into shape this way. Others were so intimidated that they didn't vote at all."[63]

Several studies by federal investigators and university researchers documented this intimidation in the Texas cotton country. The Commission on Industrial Relations' chief researcher concluded that the region's "deeply rooted and widely spread discontent" resulted partly from landlords who threatened to raise rents on tenants who voted for increased land taxes or to "keep tenants on the move" if they joined the Socialist party.[64]

Political repression had spread to the cotton country from the piney woods of Louisiana where radicalism had been virtually

62. Hickey claimed that the shooting of Meitzen created a sensation unlike anything since the "shooting of the immortal Brann," an iconoclastic editor from Waco whom the *Rebel* group idolized. *Rebel* (Hallettsville, Tex.), July 25, 1914.
63. *Ibid.*, January 9, 1915.
64. Charles W. Holman, "Probing the Causes of Unrest: The Tenant Farmer," *Survey*, XXXIV (April 17, 1916), 63.

suppressed by 1914. Federal investigator David J. Saposs reported that BTW men and Socialist party members were constantly harassed by company agents. The lumber companies' control of the election machinery was now so complete that the "secret ballot was a farce."[65] J. R. Jones, leader of the defeated Red faction, joined party secretary Walter Deitz in contesting two piney woods congressional seats in 1914, but the Socialist candidates polled only a few thousand votes between them. The violent class struggle in western Louisiana had produced a class-conscious Socialist movement, but it had also provoked powerful reactionary forces that destroyed the movement.[66]

Neither the BTW nor the Socialist party ever gained a foothold in Kirby's East Texas "feudal towns," but radicals were active in other mill villages. Even in these previously "open" towns, however, repression soon increased. Just after the 1914 campaign, Socialist agitator H. L. A. Holman was beaten to death for trying to address workers in Groveton, the mill town where black workers had launched one of the region's first strikes in 1904. "Cawn n' cotton" farmers in the backwoods remained relatively safe, but it was increasingly dangerous for Texas lumber workers to engage in Socialist activity.[67]

The powerful Oklahoma Socialist party suffered less repression, though renters in the state's southern party strongholds were starting to be blacklisted. Party officials had to launch Wobbly-style "free speech" fights in Muskogee and Tulsa, plus a consumer boycott in Elk City, to regain speaking rights for their "soap boxers."[68] The Arkansas Socialists also suffered far less than their Louisiana comrades, but the imprisonment of Socialist UMW officers Stewart

65. David J. Saposs, "Self-Government and Freedom of Action in Isolated Industrial Communities," Report No. 1036, January 20, 1915, in CIR Records.
66. Grady McWhiney, "Louisiana Socialists in the Early Twentieth Century: A Study of Rustic Radicalism," *Journal of Southern History*, XX (1954), 333–35.
67. Saposs, "Self-Government in Isolated Industrial Communities," *passim*; *Rebel* (Hallettsville, Tex.), November 28, 1914.
68. *Harlow's Weekly* (Oklahoma City), November 20, 1915; *Rebel* (Hallettsville, Tex.), January 9, 1915.

and Holt after the Prairie Creek "mine war" did deprive them of their most effective leaders.[69] The arrest of Stewart and Holt, combined with the destruction of the BTW, reduced the proletarian influence within the southwestern Socialist parties just at a time when the militant Reds were adopting a more radical posture and turning more toward the direct action practiced by Wobblies and UMW militants. Although the Oklahoma and Texas Socialist parties retained a programmatic emphasis on land-tax reform, Reds devoted more attention to tenant members who called for direct action in response to increased economic exploitation and political repression.

During the early months of the 1914 cotton crisis, some militant renters used violence to try forcing certain growers to withhold their crops from the market. Night riders continued after the crisis had passed, as tenants directed their attacks against certain landlords who charged "bonus" rents (often cash payments levied by absentees over and above the customary shares) and certain bankers who charged usurious interest rates.

Even before the cotton crisis developed, the usury issue had agitated southwestern farmers. In the spring of 1914 tenants in Choctaw County, Oklahoma, formed a Growers' Protective Association and asked a radical lawyer named W. T. Banks, the Socialist candidate for attorney general, to sue banks violating the state antiusury law. This organization grew rapidly in the summer until it claimed nine thousand members in southern Oklahoma, 95 percent

69. Freda Hogan, "The Miners of Arkansas," *International Socialist Review*, XV (January, 1915), 38–39; and "The Prairie Creek Mine War," *Woodrow's Monthly* (Hobart, Okla.), May, 1915, 24–25; *Rebel* (Hallettsville, Tex.), January 30, 1915; *Appeal to Reason* (Girard, Kan.), March 13, 1915, *Arkansas Gazette* (Little Rock), October 30, 1915; Theodore Debs to Germer, April 20, June 30, 1915, in Debs Papers, Tamiment.

As Fred Holt languished in prison, he kept busy by organizing a Socialist local, but, he told Debs, his enemies in District 21 were busy breaking down the organization he had helped build in the UMW. After his release Holt went to campaign in West Virginia to try to help maintain the loyalty of Socialist coal miners who were attracted to a new Democratic-labor party. Fred Holt to Eugene Debs, February 23, 1915, in Eugene V. Debs Collection, Cunningham Library, Indiana State University, Terre Haute.

of them tenants. In some of the court cases Banks initiated, defense lawyers pre-emptorily challenged all Socialist jurors on the "grounds that they were all bitterly opposed to the assessment of all interest."[70]

After the election of 1914 when the Protective Association's legal actions against usurious bankers had proved frustrating, more militant, secret organizations were founded that drew members from the old Renters' Union. The Farmers' Emancipation League, formed by Red Socialists in Pittsburg County, Oklahoma, drew up a program that was "entirely revolutionary," according to H. Grady Milner, a left-wing editor who served as secretary. The League proposed to act "en masse" to secure the money owed by various banks to its members under the antiusury law and to force rent reductions from landlords who demanded more than their "customary" share. Like the Working Class Union, founded at about the same time by Wells LeFevre in "Hobo's Hollow" near Van Buren, Arkansas, the League vowed ultimately to abolish rent, interest, and profit-taking—by revolutionary means if necessary. Meeting in secret to avoid the landlord blacklists that had decimated the original Renters' Union, these radical sects recruited hundreds of tenants in the old Indian Territory and the Arkansas Ozarks after the 1914 election. The Red Socialists who organized the Emancipation League and the Working Class Union pledged to act through legal channels first, but some of their members quite likely engaged in night riding expeditions against "oppressive landlords" from the start. In one well-publicized case, party lawyer Pat Nagle successfully defended Sam and Luke Spencer of McClain County, the original founders of the Oklahoma Renters' Union in 1909, who were charged with night riding. Nagle criticized night riding as a futile tactic, but explained: "Men ride not because they are 'bad men' or 'good men', but because they are desperate men. And the desperation that incites them to ride is not born of in-

---

70. *Appeal to Reason* (Girard, Kan.), April 18, 1914; U.S. Commission on Industrial Relations, *Final Report and Testimony* (Washington, D.C.: Government Printing Office, 1916), IX, 9095, hereinafter cited as *CIR Testimony*. Hartshorne (Okla.) *Sun*, December 17, 1914.

herent wickedness—it is the child of exploitation. I have known night riders to pray before they saddled their horses and reached for their Winchesters."[71]

The rapid growth of tenancy and absentee landlordism in southern and eastern Oklahoma, coupled with the suffering caused by six cent cotton and the anger caused by evictions, foreclosures, bonus rents, and usury, "generated a widespread and dangerous unrest," according to one labor history.[72] And in Texas the unrest spread from the cotton country through other regions. Although the Renters' Union helped channel some tenant unrest into Socialist political action, the tenant organizations lost some of their militancy after the BTW's demise and the repressive antiunion actions of landlords and ranch managers.

Late in 1914 Tom Hickey formed a new organization called the Land League (named after Michael Davitt's Irish tenant organization); it focused on the single-tax demand, but rejected a tactical alliance with small landowners proposed by non-Socialist members.[73] The League lacked the proletarian perspective of the original Union, but it did send two organizers, the Hernandez brothers, into the tense South Texas country to recruit Mexican-American tenants and attempt to tap the sympathies they had with the revolution in progress across the Rio Grande. At about the same time more militant members of the old Texas Renters' Union formed a secret, oath-bound branch of the Oklahoma Protective League in order "to avoid the widespread evictions and blacklists" that had

---

71. *New Century* (Sulphur, Okla.), January 16, 30, 1915; Federal Writers' Project, W.P.A., *Labor History of Oklahoma* (Oklahoma City: Van Horn, 1939), 40–41; *CIR Testimony*, X, 9076–77; Nagle quote is from *Tenant Farmer* (Kingfisher, Okla.), May, 1915.
72. W.P.A., *Labor History of Oklahoma*, 40–41.
73. *Rebel* (Hallettsville, Tex.), November 28, 1914. By this time a number of non-Socialist politicians had become advocates of the single tax. D. A. Paulus, a state senator for Lavaca County, introduced a land-tax measure in Austin, and J. J. Pastoriza, a well-known follower of Henry George, was elected tax and land commissioner in Houston on a single-tax platform. *CIR Testimony*, X, 9194–200; Harthshorne (Okla.) *Sun*, March 25, 1915; *Rebel* (Hallettsville, Tex.), January 1, 1916. Earlier in 1914 federal investigator P. A. Speek reported: "The single tax sentiment is very strong among the masses of Texas." Folder 299, CIR Records.

all but destroyed the old organization. Like the tenants who had joined the secret Socialist unions organized by Martin Irons and G. B. Harris in the late 1890s, these "direct actionists" took to night riding, threatening merchants and buyers who refused to accept tenant-dictated prices and farmers who refused to hold their crop and destroying the property of landlords who charged bonus rents. The night riders, for example, sowed a noxious weed called Johnson grass on the property of offending landlords and threatened the tenants who accepted rent increases.[74]

The most effective action taken by Texas tenants after 1914, however, occurred in legal, political channels. During the Ferguson-Meitzen campaign, Socialist tenants in Rains County, the birthplace of the Farmers' Union in 1902 and a "hotbed of political radicals," brought suit under the state antiusury law against a county seat bank that had generated "very intense feeling in the community" by foreclosing on farmers at the height of the cotton crisis.[75] The first Socialist who pressed his case declared: "The banks have robbed and squeezed the people as long as they can stand it and they are not going to stand it any longer." When the bank's threats failed to intimidate this tenant and five other Socialists, including a black renter, its officers settled out of court. The news spread rapidly and "set the county wild." The credit problem in Texas, a Texas A & M study concluded, was provoked by violations of customary lending practices (some interest rates were reportedly as high as 35 percent). But the discontent of debtors also reflected the long-standing grievances of cotton tenants who were unable to climb the "agricultural ladder" because of the high cost of land and credit.[76]

Most bankers in the troubled area blamed the Socialists for provoking the agitation, although a few thought that their competi-

---

74. *Rebel* (Hallettsville, Tex.), September 19, November 28, 1914; Holman, "Probing the Causes of Unrest," 63; University of Texas, Department of Extension, Division of Public Welfare, *Farm Tenancy in Texas*, University of Texas Bulletin No. 21 (Austin, 1915), 90–94.
75. Hunt, *Farmer Movements in the Southwest*, 46.
76. Walton Peteet, *Farming Credit in Texas*, Texas A & M Bulletin No. 34 (College Station, Tex., 1917), 33–34, 37–38, 40–42.

tors, the credit merchants, had encouraged it. Some storekeepers criticized the "hard-nosed" methods of the bankers, but they did not go so far as to condone the wave of suits initiated under the antiusury law. The credit and supply merchants were often more flexible in dealing with their customers than the banks, but they also charged "extortionate" interest rates and kept farmers permanently in debt through the crop lien system. Furthermore, they often shared the bankers' fear that the tenants, especially the "lazy and unreliable" members of that class, were being imbued with dangerous ideas by the Socialists. As one credit merchant from Emory, Texas, put it: "The farmers of Rains County are backward and nonprogressive; they are indolent, thriftless and ignorant. There are signs of improvement as the 'nesters' die off, but the change is very slow. Our firm was established as a cash house but we soon found that we had to do a credit business. We had to deal with our farmer customers just as we do with children. When they come in for credit we have to decide how much money they should have and then dole it out to them month by month."[77]

Landlords, bankers, merchants, newspaper editors, and university professors still insisted that only lazy tenants failed to climb the "agricultural ladder" to ownership. A few members of the propertied class, however, admitted that rising land values and the "curse" of absentee ownership created the "dangerous conditions" existing in rural Texas. A banker-landlord from the Panhandle knew a surprising number of farmers who were "imbued with Socialism and anarchy." He warned that an increasingly "dangerous state of opinion" existed in that region, especially among the young tenants.[78]

Conditions were rapidly growing worse in West Texas at the start of 1915, but class tensions rose much higher in the black waxy cotton belt to the east where tenancy rooted itself deeply and where bankers actually admitted charging usurious interest rates while landlords openly charged bonus rents and discharged radical renters. The tenants' fears and anxieties increased when

77. *Ibid.*, 43–50.
78. *Ibid.*, 73; *CIR Testimony*, IX, 9051.

many lost their jobs during the cotton crisis and had to work for wages as field hands, tie cutters, and sawmill laborers. The crisis presented large plantation owners and bonanza farm managers with the opportunity to replace tenants with wage workers, especially cheap Afro-American or Mexican laborers. Even smaller landlords like Jim Ferguson followed suit, because, as one black belt planter explained it: "White tenants are the least desirable; they are ignorant and lazy and seem to do as little work as possible to get along. None of them ever accumulates anything. They move frequently and are very unreliable, rebellious, resentful, suspicious and unthrifty."[79]

Some landlords accused the Socialists of instilling these attitudes in the farmers. For example, one Brazos-bottom landlord living in Waco who charged the Socialists with stirring up "class hatred," reflected the bitter feeling of his own class when he declared: "White tenants are a worthless, lazy, lying anarchist lot. I have kicked every one of them off my farm except one and replaced them with negro laborers, who I can boss and will do what I tell them. My experience with white tenants was disastrous. They will lie, steal, and cannot be depended on to take care of the property entrusted to them. I do not know what is to become of this country so long as this class continues to increase, for they are socialists at heart—every one of them." However, another large landowner from the Brazos Valley blamed property owners themselves for the "dangerous feeling among tenants toward the landlords." Many black and white tenants in the valley were ready to arm themselves to get food because their credit was cut off at the height of the cotton crisis. If landlords did not treat their renters better, "serious harm" would come to the cotton country. But many property owners remained hostile to discussing land reform because it would "put devilment into the heads of the tenants."[80]

The class struggle in the cotton country became more intense after the 1914 election because the promises of Governor Ferguson, "agrarian" congressmen, and the Wilson administration failed to develop into real reforms. When the U.S. Commission on Indus-

79. Peteet, *Farming Credit in Texas*, 55, 73, 79.
80. *Ibid.*, 71, 54–55.

trial Relations scheduled hearings on the southwestern land question in Dallas, the *Rebel* solicited letters from Texas tenants as evidence to present to the commission. These letters, written in late 1914 and early 1915, expressed the farmers' mood of anger, frustration, and increasing radicalism. Some renters said they were near starvation and had had to leave the farm to cut railroad ties and work in the sawmills they hated and feared. Others talked of "moving on" to escape the hard times. And some vowed to take armed action against their oppressors. They were all skeptical of Ferguson's land plank and Wilson's emergency legislation, but they retained their faith in the Socialists who had finally made tenancy the "paramount issue" in the state.

G. W. Walston, who worked the shares in a big clearing on the Trinity River, told Hickey that the tenants there were subsisting on nothing but bread cooked in water and salt. "We have to live like dogs," he exclaimed, "and if something is not done soon something is going to happen." The farmers who "went around braying and bawling for Ferguson," Walston reported, were "now near starvation." Young mothers in Harrison County worked cutting ties to get bread while others fell to begging, said Mrs. Dote McCarthy. "This is a beautiful country," she wrote, "full of poverty and starvation."[81]

A tenant from El Campo recorded land values "so high that we renters have about given up hope of ever becoming owners." This tenant believed that "this country is in bad, not because we have a Democratic administration, but because capitalism is getting ready to be harvested." J. A. Chapman of Lomasco talked to "lots of men of the renting class" who said "that never in their life have they been in such a distressing condition." The landlords "are trying to soothe our minds by telling us that Woodrow is going to see that we don't suffer, and 80-percent Ferguson is soon going to take charge at Austin, and things are going to get better."[82] But these

81. G. W. Walston to Hickey, December 13, 1914, and Mrs. Dote McCarthy to Hickey, February 3, 1915, in *CIR Testimony*, 9277.

82. J. C. Smith to E. O. Meitzen, March 7, 1915; and J. A. Chapman to Hickey, November 27, 1914, *ibid.*, 9276, 9279. "Eighty percent" is a reference to the rate of interest allegedly charged to some farmers by Ferguson's bank at Belton.

promises seemed hollow to tenants who reported "all kinds of oppression" from their landlords. A renter from Leon County expressed his desperation: "We people are starving. We cannot get work at any price. We can't buy winter clothes. We gathered our cotton on nothing but cotton-seed lard made into gravy; no hope for meat. It is trouble." Writing to Hickey, he added, "I want to tell you I have lived honestly all my life, never committed a crime, but I am ready to do something that will help my starving family; if it takes my life, let it be."[83]

But these depressed people still maintained an almost religious faith in socialism and expressed frustration with farmers who did not join the movement. To one West Texas tenant socialism was "the only hope for deliverance from peonage. May the great God of heaven help us to secure our liberty and freedom. He has promised to help those who help themselves. So we must work together to help our brethren see the light. Give us Socialism and the religion of our Lord and Savior Jesus Christ."[84]

Since the *Rebel* editors solicited these letters as documentary evidence for the Commission on Industrial Relations, some tenants expressed cautious optimism that the federal hearings would draw national attention to their problems. J. R. Goodgame, a renter from Jones County, told Meitzen that he and his tenant neighbors all agreed that "the Washington government is not for us" and that the Farmers' Union petition to Congress would be useless. "We are looking for relief from this investigation that is going to take place in Dallas, but perhaps the fight may be turned down." Goodgame said he was pessimistic because "there is a class struggle; one class owns the government and rules the other class."[85]

After hearing testimony in Dallas for four days in March of 1915, the U.S. Commission on Industrial Relations concluded that "a state of acute unrest" existed in the Southwest as a result of usurious interest rates, bonus rents, blacklists, and other forms of "op-

83. S. S. White to Hickey, December 11, 1914, C. C. Irwin to Hickey, December 6, 1914, T. A. Davis to Hickey, December 17, 1914, and G. W. Walston to Hickey, December 5, 1914, *ibid.*, 9266, 9270.
84. A. C. Walker to Hickey, February 7, 1915, *ibid.*, 9266–67.
85. J. R. Goodgame to Meitzen, November 28, 1914, *ibid.*, 9262.

pression" inflicted on tenants; in fact, an "organized resistance" had already appeared which could produce civil disturbances of "a serious character."[86] Significantly the investigators had chosen to include the southwestern land struggle in their nationwide inquiry into the causes of industrial violence. Striking similarities did appear in the conflicts between landlords and tenants and the more violent industrial struggles in Colorado, Arkansas, and Louisiana.[87]

Indeed, the commission's chief field investigator, Charles Holman, testified at the start of the hearings: "A very large percent of tenant farmers have slipped away from the old feudal conception of being tenants of the soil, and have dropped into the modern condition of being laborers in fact." The southwestern renters were "very closely akin" to the casual laborers who worked in the extractive industries. The "transformations" caused by the speculative increase in land values and the concentration of land ownership in the cotton region had produced a "rising absentee landlord class and a descending tenant farmer class," Holman stated.[88]

In making his investigation, Holman and his assistants had cooperated with the Socialists, whom they considered to be experts on the land question. The witnesses who testified included more landlords, bankers, Democratic politicians, and academic experts than tenants or their radical champions, but the hearings nevertheless resulted in a significant propaganda coup for the Socialist party.

Holman asked W. S. Noble of the Land League to bring a representative tenant family to the hearings so that the renters could have their say. The appearance of Levi and Beulah Stewart made a great impression on the commissioners and the press. Chairman Frank Walsh questioned Stewart at length about his "wanderings and perennial hard luck" at working the shares throughout the

86. U.S. Commission on Industrial Relations *Final Report* (Washington, D.C.: Government Printing Office, 1915), 130.
87. Graham Adams, Jr., *Age of Industrial Violence, 1910–1915: The Activities and Findings of the U.S. Commission on Industrial Relations* (New York: Columbia University Press, 1966), 198–302.
88. *CIR Testimony*, IX, 8952–54. See also Holman's comprehensive "Preliminary Report on the Land Question," February 17, 1915, in CIR Records.

Southwest. The tenant said he had subscribed to the *Appeal to Reason* for a time, but was not a Socialist; his testimony was concerned entirely with his back-breaking labor and depressing life as a tenant. His wife, "a shrinking little woman with faded eyes and a broken body," also testified at some length in a low drawl which "quivered with nervous tension." Mrs. J. Borden Harriman, "a prominent society woman" on the commission, asked to question Mrs. Stewart. Appearing before the commissioners in a blue sunbonnet and a faded gingham dress, accompanied by a two-year-old child, Beulah Stewart described her work in the fields from sunup to sundown, a routine she had begun at the age of fifteen, and continued when she was pregnant. Commissioner Harriman naively asked this farm woman if she did all the cooking, sewing, milking, and housework as well; Mrs. Stewart replied: "There ain't no one else to do it."[89]

Leading newspapers and commercial associations angrily denied that the Stewarts were representative tenants, but their straightforward testimony made an impact nonetheless. The *Appeal* reprinted most of it along side that of a wealthy landlord-banker from Ellis County under the title: "Are There Classes in America? U.S. Commission Offers Proof."[90] The Dallas hearing showed, as one historian noted, that "militant class consciousness" was not "limited only to industrial communities"; it "now threatened sweeping social change in one of the most exclusively agrarian regions in America." The recorded testimony "lent little comfort to those who envisioned their nation as a community of harmonious classes."[91]

The commission's investigations in the Southwest gave the Socialists and their cause a great deal of publicity in 1915 and embarrassed some of the most powerful men in Texas, notably Governor Ferguson and Postmaster General Burleson.[92] However,

89. Holman, "Probing the Causes of Unrest," 62–63.
90. *Rebel* (Hallettsville, Tex.), April 17, 1915; *Appeal to Reason* (Girard, Kan.), April 17, 1915.
91. Adams, *Age of Industrial Violence*, 203.
92. In his testimony, Judge Meitzen, who had been in the muckraking business for a long time, presented evidence to show that in previous years Governor Ferguson's bank in Belton had charged usurious interest rates

its recommendations on the land question, including a single-tax plan, were all but ignored by the Wilson administration. By the summer of 1915, the rise of cotton prices and the enactment of some state and federal "emergency" legislation convinced many businessmen, editors, and politicians that socialism and class conflict would decline. The president of the Texas Bankers' Association attacked the Commission on Industrial Relations and its findings on usury. Affirming the honesty of his banking colleagues, he blamed the failure of the Texas tenants on their own thriftlessness; there was nothing "radically wrong" with the system. He urged the bankers to wage an advertising campaign to "encourage saving and teach thrift," just as President Wilson had suggested when he said that "the greatest need of the American banker is to find a shorter road to the minds of the American people." Although some might accuse bankers of "selfish motives in their efforts to stimulate a spirit of thrift," it was clear that the psychological moment for the campaign had arrived, because the "great war" had sobered people up: the "spirit of doing without" was "in vogue."[93]

In Marshall County, Oklahoma, where the Socialists had come within 37 votes of victory in 1914, the newspaper reported improved conditions in the following spring. "Harmony" would again prevail. Bankers from several southeastern counties gathered in Madill to promote better relations with farmers and to have "a great time at the country club." In a nearby county another commercial weekly explained that "wild-eyed radicals" had exploited a "political revolt" of the tenants who fell into the borrowing class as a result of the cotton crisis. But a recent state supreme court decision sustaining the antiusury law would surely "spike the Socialist guns."[94]

The aura of harmony the bankers promoted was shattered in the fall of 1915 when the *Appeal* published a speech by J. S. Williams,

---

and Postmaster General Burleson's plantation in the Steiner valley had used convict labor to force the old tenants off the land. *CIR Testimony*, IX, 8958, 8965, and X, 9144–45; Meitzen Exhibit No. 2, 9288–89, in CIR Records.

93. *Texas Bankers' Record*, IV (June, 1915), 92.

94. *Marshall County News-Democrat* (Madill, Okla.), May 21, June 9, 1915; Harthshorne (Okla.) *Sun*, August 5, 1915.

comptroller of currency, to the Kentucky Bankers' Association revealing that 455 bankers in Texas and Oklahoma had admitted charging usurious interest rates.[95] A month later the "capitalist press" began to comment on the speech in which the comptroller had read "blood curdling" reports from the southwestern farming districts "like the stories from darkest Russia about the oppression inflicted on the peasantry." Williams said, "Here in the country, we find bankers, men of business, who should be respectable, literally crushing in the faces of their neighbors. They have fertilized the soil for a fearful crop of disaster." The *Daily Oklahoman*, heretofore "ultra-conservative in its attitude toward the usury question," observed that Texas and Oklahoma enjoyed "the questionable distinction of having more money sharks in the banking business than any other region." "Is it any wonder," its editorial asked, "that Oklahoma is a veritable spawning bed of Socialism?"[96]

Following this "revelation," *Harlow's Weekly* predicted that a special session of the state legislature would enact stronger anti-usury laws with the criminal penalties that Socialist legislators demanded. Pat Nagle in his *Tenant Farmer* had forced the issue on the public with "fiery vehemence," said *Harlow's*. "With unanswerable logic, fortified by appeals to prejudice and emotion, he is depicting the suffering and practically hopeless fate of a large submerged class." The tenancy and usury issues were "cognates," because both grew out of "the abuse of power by those who have of those who have not." Reforms were necessary, but they would be difficult to enact because many of the most powerful men in Oklahoma politics were "thoroughly identified with the present tenant system." Leading progressives, like Congressman William Murray and Senator Robert Owen, were landlords; they treated their tenants fairly and tried to work for credit and currency reforms in Washington, but the editors thought "it would be difficult to presume" that the representatives would use their influence to "secure legislation which looks primarily to the interest of the ten-

95. *Appeal to Reason* (Girard, Kan.), October 16, 1915.
96. *Ibid.*, November 13, 1915; *Harlow's Weekly* (Oklahoma City), October 30, 1915, p. 331; *Daily Oklahoman* (Oklahoma City), October 27, 1915.

ant even though it may be contradictory to that of the landlord."[97] Tom Hickey duplicated the tactics of his Fenian comrade north of the Red River and exposed the capitalist interests of the Texas "farmer governor" in the same way that Pat Nagle had revealed the landed interests of progressive Senator Robert Owen and the exploitative practices of planter Governor R. L. Williams.[98] The *Rebel* drummed away Governor Ferguson's unenforceable rent regulation law and his probanker stand on the usury question. During the spring and summer of 1915, the "socialistic element" in the Red area of Rains and Van Zandt counties launched another widespread movement to sue local banks for the recovery of usurious interest rates.[99] This campaign added force to the *Rebel's* attack on "Farmer Jim" Ferguson, who owned part of the bank in Belton that had been accused of charging illegal interest rates.

The destruction of the Brotherhood of Timber Workers, the decline of the old Renters' Union, and the party's loss of votes to Ferguson discouraged Texas Socialists, but in 1915 their movement was still "alive and kicking." And at the end of the year the following editorial in Governor Ferguson's hometown newspaper indicated that the issues raised by the Reds were still very pertinent: "The Socialist Party of Texas will make a campaign this year on usury and the land question. They want usurers sent to the state penitentiary and they desire that use and occupancy be the only title to the land. It may be said in passing that their propaganda is winning converts everyday."[100]

97. *Harlow's Weekly* (Oklahoma City), October 30, 1915, p. 33.
98. Senator Owen eventually became worried enough about Nagle's charges to cut up his large tenant farm and to sell it off in small parcels. *Ibid.*, October 18, 1916, p. 3. Unlike other planter-politicians, notably progressive landlords like Owen and Bill Murray, Governor Williams regarded himself as an old-fashioned, "benevolent" land owner. Consequently, he was "shocked" to learn that his tenants were discontented. Edward Everett Dale and James D. Morrison, *Pioneer Judge: The Life of Robert L. Williams* (Cedar Rapids, Iowa: Torch Press, 1958), 381–83.
99. The new outbreak of protest against the bankers was caused not only by the continuation of usurious interest charges, but by the retaliatory actions of creditors who cut off radical renters, forcing some of them off their land. Peteet, *Farming Credit in Texas*, 32–35.
100. Temple (Tex.) *Telegram* quoted in *Rebel* (Hallettsville, Tex.), January 29, 1916.

The Oklahoma Socialist party remained much livelier than its southwestern counterparts in early 1915, but dues-paying membership declined to about seven thousand partly as a result of tenant poverty increased by the cotton crisis. However, this lapse soon ended, and by the close of 1915, State Secretary Sinclair reported a remarkable doubling of the Oklahoma party's membership. This encouraging growth combined with a fund-raising drive that netted ten thousand dollars (twice the amount collected in the previous nonelection year of 1913) caused the progressive editors of *Harlow's Weekly* to warn its sleepy readers of socialism's "Menace to the Present Political Order."[101]

The Sooner Socialist party had not only doubled its membership to fifteen thousand, it planned a 1916 encampment program covering two hundred sites and reported a circulation of forty thousand for the Oklahoma City edition of the *Appeal*, edited by J. O. Welday, "one of the brightest minds in Oklahoma politics." Furthermore, Pat Nagle's *Tenant Farmer* continued to embarrass leading Democratic politicians by revealing their land holdings and business practices. *Harlow's* warned the state establishment that Oklahoma socialism was much more than a protest against hard times. The Socialist party was a well-organized political force which had already recruited a majority of the state's 110,000 tenants and had "gained a strong foothold in organized labor" where "the percent of union laborers carrying socialist cards" was "surprising." In addition to its growing support among the "lower classes," the Socialist party had converted some merchants and professionals in country districts and had even started a Young People's Socialist League at the state university in Norman which attracted some bright young men from good homes.

"With these elements at work in and outside of campaign times, there is reason to give attention to the question of socialism," *Harlow's* concluded. "With an organization that is unparalleled both in financial backing and methods of effectiveness, with a membership

101. *Socialist Party, Proceedings of the State Convention of Oklahoma, 1915*, 28–31; McAlester (Okla.) *News-Capital*, December 29, 1915; *Harlow's Weekly* (Oklahoma City), September 25, 1915, p. 31.

whose belief in socialism approaches the religious, it is difficult to measure the danger of socialism to other political institutions."[102] This assessment accurately reported on the Oklahoma party's continued growth, but it exaggerated the menace of socialism, conveniently ignoring the losses the Socialists had suffered in the southeastern cotton country as a result of the anti-Red blacklist and the internal problems the party faced over the rising tide of vigilante violence practiced by the tenant movement's militant minority.

102. *Harlow's Weekly* (Oklahoma City), September 25, 1915, pp. 31–32.

VIII

From Socialist Activity to Social Banditry: The Politics of Frustration 1915-1916

BY 1915 THE Louisiana Socialist party had been virtually destroyed by repression. The parties in Texas, Arkansas, and, to a lesser extent, Oklahoma also suffered from increased harassment and intimidation, but these organizations maintained their strength by continuing to represent the farmers and workers most directly involved in the class struggle and by mobilizing maximum resources to meet the repressive challenge of their opponents. This involved continuing agitation for land-tax reform and continuing litigation against disfranchisement and other forms of intimidation, but party leaders also had to support militant members who followed the Arkansas miners by turning to violent direct action. Most left-wing officials found direct-action politics to their taste, and they responded, especially in Texas, with increasingly revolutionary rhetoric based on the slogans of the Mexican land revolution. The Reds also continued to reflect the syndicalist influence of the IWW, whose direct-action approach appealed more and more to the militant minority of workers and tenants frustrated with repression and other provocative measures taken against them by property owners. The increasing frustration of militant rank and filers who grew doubtful about the efficacy of the Socialist party's electoral strategy created confusion within the movement's leadership, particularly in Texas, where left-wingers supported insurrectionary activity in Mexico and direct-action politics within the party without questioning the Socialist party's electoral strategy, which had begun to reach the limits imposed by disfranchisement.

DISFRANCHISEMENT

Suffrage restriction and election reforms enacted around the turn of the century helped eliminate the potential for an interracial Populist revival.[1] Of course, these restrictive laws also limited the Socialist party's electoral potential. Disfranchisement took several forms in the Southwest. Grandfather clauses amended to the state constitutions of Louisiana and Oklahoma in 1898 and 1910 respectively acted as an effective barrier to black participation at the polls, and poll taxes in Arkansas and Texas disfranchised poor whites as well as blacks. These taxes required cash payment nine months prior to the election, at a time when farmers' loans were due and political interest was at a low ebb; they were especially discouraging to poor voters because they were cumulative taxes. Residency requirements also eliminated many potential voters who were transient tenants or migratory laborers. "Travelling cotton pickers" were "disfranchised *en masse*," reported Tom Hickey, just like the harvest stiffs and migratory industrial workers in the lumber and construction industries. As a result of the Terrell election "reforms" (enacted in 1903 and 1905), the poll tax, and such other "iniquitous provisions" as residency requirements, participation in Texas elections was reduced to one in every seventeen qualified male voters, compared to one in every seven qualified midwestern male voters.[2]

Furthermore, election laws in the Southwest gave the incumbent Democrats control over the registration and election machinery. Local registrars could disfranchise (and even blacklist) insurgent voters in a number of ways both legal and illegal and election officials could easily defraud the Socialists in areas where they

1. See J. Morgan Kousser, *The Shaping of Southern Politics: Suffrage Restriction and the Establishment of a One-Party South, 1880–1920* (New Haven, Conn.: Yale University Press, 1974).
2. On the grandfather clause, see C. Vann Woodward, *Origins of the New South, 1877–1913* (Baton Rouge: Louisiana State University Press, 1951), 342–46; and Hickey to Thompson, May 26, 1913, in Socialist Party Papers, Perkins Library, Duke University. See *Rebel* (Hallettsville, Tex.), November 9, 1912, on Texas disfranchisement laws.

lacked poll watchers.[3] This was a real problem for the party in a large state like Texas where Democratic courthouse "rings" enjoyed unchallenged control of the electoral process in most of the remote southern and western counties. In Oklahoma, however, extensive Socialist precinct organization prevented a good deal of fraud and helped neutralize some of the influence the Democrats had gained through their control over the registration and election machinery.[4] Residency requirements made it impossible for the Sooner Socialists to register all transient laborers and renters, but since state disfranchisement laws were aimed solely at Afro-Americans, Oklahoma's voter turnout was consistently higher than it was in other southern states. For example, in 1912, 54 percent of the adult males of Oklahoma voted whereas in Texas only 33 percent of those qualified actually participated. This difference undoubtedly helps to explain why Debs's percentage of the Oklahoma vote was double that of Texas.

After the Oklahoma Socialist party failed in its campaign to defeat the grandfather clause in 1910, the party turned away from the suffrage issue and concentrated on recruiting white tenants. Disfranchisement once again became an important issue when the Supreme Court declared the clause unconstitutional in 1915 (*Guinn* vs. *U.S.*), and the Democrats searched anxiously for new ways of limiting the black vote. The Williams administration proposed a poll tax to the legislature in the spring, but the proposal lost by a narrow margin because Socialist and Republican legislators convinced some of the more independent Democrats that blacks and poor whites might be violently provoked by such a blatant disfranchisement law. The Democrats may also have been persuaded to vote against the poll tax by a GOP lawmaker who warned them that the measure would only antagonize the Socialists and increase their "agitation"; the Socialist party would make sure its members paid the tax whereas the poor whites and blacks who continued to

3. See P. S. Nagle, "The Oklahoma Election Laws," *Harlow's Weekly* (Oklahoma City), February 5, 1916, pp. 10–11.
4. However, socialists complained of fraud in Oklahoma as well. R. E. Dooley to John M. Work, November 21, 1912, in Socialist Party Papers, Duke.

vote for the old parties would be disfranchised in large number.[5]

After the defeat of the poll tax bill, the Oklahoma Democrats proposed another suffrage reform designed to strengthen the incumbent party's control over the registration process by adding a literacy test requirement specifically directed toward the "illiterate negro." The Socialists responded by drafting their own "fair" election law to outlaw literacy tests and poll taxes along with other standard disfranchisement measures and to reduce the control of the election machinery granted the party in power under the Goebel election law. The Socialists campaigned hard during the summer of 1915 to counter Democratic propaganda that labeled the "fair" election law a "bid for the negro vote." In September party leaders claimed a "tremendous victory" after securing a record number of signatures (seventy thousand) on their initiative election law.[6]

In March, 1916, Governor Williams called a special session of the legislature to consider his party's new disfranchisement proposals. Charities and Corrections Commissioner Kate Barnard warned her fellow Democrats that their "mad" attempts to deprive the masses of their political rights invited "red riot and bloody revolution," but administration representatives ignored this warning and forced their reforms through the legislature amidst threats, fistfights, flying ink wells, and some distinctly unparliamentary procedures.[7] In addition to a substitute for the grandfather clause, the Democrats

5. Republican legislator quoted in *Appeal to Reason* (Girard, Kan.), April 17, 1915.
6. *Ibid.*, September 25, October 16, 1915, March 11 and 15, 1916; *Harlow's Weekly* (Oklahoma City), April 8, 1916, pp. 14–19. The literacy test was to be applied specifically to blacks by exempting voters whose relatives served any nation in military service prior to 1860. Indian tribes qualified as "nations" but African tribes did not.
7. Quoted in *Appeal to Reason* (Girard, Kan.), March 11, 1916; *Harlow's Weekly* (Oklahoma City), April 8, 1916, pp. 14–19. When editors of the most powerful paper in the state first heard about the Democrats' proposed disfranchisement legislation they commented: "50,000 Socialists scattered throughout the rural regions are incomparably more of a menace than 40,000 blacks confined to comparatively few counties." *Daily Oklahoman* (Oklahoma City), quoted in the *Appeal to Reason* (Girard, Kan.), November 13, 1915.

gained more control over the electoral process through an amendment to the Goebel law requiring all voters to register and declare their party affiliation several months before each election to officials appointed by the incumbent administration. Democratic election officers could now compile convenient registration lists of the Socialist voters in each precinct; in the hands of cooperative landlords and creditors, they could be used as blacklists.[8]

Before 1915 political discrimination against Socialists in Oklahoma was not as widespread as it was in Louisiana and Texas. But after the election of 1914 in which Fred Holt and the Reds swept most of the rural precincts below the Canadian River, landlords, merchants, and bankers, and their political representatives began to take reactionary measures. In the fall of 1915 some of the leading businessmen in Tishomingo, Congressman Murray's hometown, threatened "drastic measures against the Socialists" after the Reds boycotted the town merchants for refusing to contribute to the financing of a summer encampment that brought everyone a great deal of business. The reactionaries proposed a "retaliatory measure to rid Johnston County of Socialists"—landlords were urged to ask all prospective tenants about their "political affiliations" and "to decline to rent their land to Socialists." A similar blacklist had already been initiated in McIntosh County where party members were allegedly stirring up trouble in the schools; it was said to have reduced the number of Socialists.[9]

After the special session of the Oklahoma legislature amended the Goebel election law in March of 1916, landlords could easily weed out Socialist tenants simply by asking the local Democratic registrar for his list. Emboldened by this advantage, the Democrats in Johnston County publicly announced their retaliatory measure against the Socialists, and in May, 1916, the editor of the Tishomingo *Capital-Democrat* threatened to publish the "name of every varmint who registered that way [Socialist]." Despite threats against his life, he did publish a few names. The Democrats "openly alleged" that this list would "be used as a blacklist for

8. *Harlow's Weekly* (Oklahoma City), May 20, 1916, pp. 5–6.
9. *Ibid.*, September 25, 1915, pp. 4–5.

credit and renters," *Harlow's Weekly* revealed. This "open boycott against the socialists that has been conducted by landlords, bankers and business institutions generally," the report continued, "has undoubtedly resulted in many socialists having been driven out of southeastern Oklahoma."[10]

Registration statistics from the spring of 1916 confirmed this evaluation by showing a dramatic reversal of the Socialist party's growth in the Red counties of the southeast. Significantly, the party's biggest drop in registration came in Marshall County where Fred Holt had made his strongest showing in the 1914 election.[11] The class anxieties aroused by the Socialists of Marshall County were reflected in the increasingly hysterical tone of local journalists and politicians who attacked their radical opponents as "vicious atheists who would destroy home, family, church and the white race." Consciously identifying Socialists with immorality, respectable opinion-makers declared that the Socialist party's "class" doctrines only accentuated the vices of the "inferior" poor whites to whom it appealed. As the anti-Socialist offensive progressed during the summer of 1916, the Democrats used their increased control over the registration process to gain 488 voters in Marshall County. At the same time the Socialists lost 238 men from their rolls.[12] Local Democrats admitted disfranchising Socialist party members under the new registration law, a statute aimed directly at that "floating class of people" who contributed nothing to the county but trouble. In the fall of 1916 the Marshall County *News-Democrat* reported that 113 Socialists and their families had actually left the county during the year. "This blows up the socialist party in so far as winning any county offices is concerned," the editor noted with some relief.[13]

10. *Ibid.*, May 20, 1916, pp. 5–6.
11. *Ibid.*; Oliver Benson, *et al.*, *Oklahoma Votes, 1907–1962* (Norman: University of Oklahoma Press, 1964), 62.
12. Garin Burbank, "Agrarian Radicals and Their Opponents: Political Conflict in Southern Oklahoma, 1910–1924," *Journal of American History*, LVIII (1971), 10. For articles and editorials expressing a growing concern with the Socialist "menace," see *Marshall County News-Democrat* (Madill, Okla.), May 25, June 1, 8, 18, 22, 1916; *Harlow's Weekly* (Oklahoma City), May 20, 1916, pp. 5–7.
13. *Marshall County News-Democrat* (Madill, Okla.), October 19, 1916.

The exodus of Socialist tenants from the over-populated, over-cropped counties of the old Indian Territory began with the depression of 1914 and accelerated with the repression of 1915–1916.[14] The party suffered as a result of this forced migration but its overly optimistic leaders ignored these reversals and emphasized registration gains in central and western counties and growing support in the State Federation of Labor. And on August 1, 1916, they claimed a "great victory" when the literacy test requirement passed by a Democratic legislature in March failed by a margin of 42,000 votes in a special referendum conducted along with the party primaries. Despite its newly increased control over registration, the Democratic party's primary vote dropped by 25 percent whereas the Socialists showed a remarkable statewide increase of 100 percent over 1914. This increased Socialist party growth undoubtedly contributed to the defeat of the Democrats' literacy test amendment.[15]

Although the law specifically applied to blacks, the Socialists still convinced most of their poor white supporters to vote against it. Some may have voted against disfranchisement in principle; others (including some who had voted for the grandfather clause six years earlier) may have been persuaded that a literacy test for blacks was only the first step toward more sweeping suffrage restrictions. At any rate, *Harlow's* declared, the referendum results represented a "clear repudiation of the Democratic administration." After the setback, Governor Williams, who hoped to make Oklahoma a Democratic stronghold like his native Alabama, denounced the Socialists for insinuating that he was "trying to perpetuate something crooked on the voters of the state" and vowed to defend his party's control over the election machinery with the militia if necessary.[16]

After the defeat of the literacy test amendment most Democratic leaders continued to raise the old spectre of "nigger domination"; some progressives, however, revealed a more dangerous "menace"

14. Carter Goodrich, *et al.*, *Migration and Economic Opportunity* (Philadelphia: University of Pennsylvania Press, 1936), 693–99.
15. *Harlow's Weekly* (Oklahoma City), May 20, 1916, p. 7; *ibid.*, August 12, 1916, p. 3; *Appeal to Reason* (Girard, Kan.), July 29, August 12, 1916.
16. *Harlow's Weekly* (Oklahoma City), September 6, 27, 1916, pp. 3, 5.

than black voters—Red Socialist voters. According to *Harlow's Weekly*, politicians saw socialism merely as a protest against the Democratic "machine" and the abuses of landlords and bankers. Most "utterly failed to realize" that it was a class movement led by men and women who had "revolutionary purposes" and frankly admitted that they were pledged to "aid the working class in obtaining its mastery over the capitalist class."[17]

This publication still ignored the Socialist party's internal weaknesses and failed to recognize the limits imposed on the party's electoral strategy by disfranchisement, but its editors did understand the revolutionary purposes of the Socialist leadership and the class consciousness of the rank and file. They quoted at length from a "carefully written and lucid explanation" of the party's radical goals by L. D. Gillespie, editor of the Oklahoma *Appeal*, who said: "The class struggle in this state is vividly portrayed by the marked contrasts between the luxurious lives of the master class in its arrogant possession of wealth and the melancholy condition of the working class, whose incessant toil leaves them hungry in the midst of plenty." The growing bitterness of this struggle, he added, resulted from the increased exploitation of working farmers by landlords and bankers charging bonus rents and usurious interest rates and from the blatant restriction of popular suffrage attempted by the Democrats' "sordid" machine. "But the day of reckoning is at hand," the *Appeal* editor concluded in a dramatic fashion: "A new revolutionary organization, known as the Working Class Union, is being formed among the tenant farmers and wage workers of the state. This organization is growing with the marvellous rapidity that characterized the formation of the revolutionary clubs that battered down the Bastille in Paris and overthrew the feudal lords of France."[18]

THE WORKING CLASS UNION AND THE RURAL PROLETARIAT

The Working Class Union (WCU) did indeed aim to overthrow the capitalist landlords of America. Founded late in 1914 by Dr. Wells

17. *Ibid.*
18. *Ibid.*, October 18, 1916, p. 5; L. D. Gillespie, "Hunger in the Midst of Plenty," *International Socialist Review*, XVII (November, 1916), 282–85.

LeFevre, an old Arkansas Socialist, the Union initially put pressure on landlords and usurious creditors through legal channels. Like the Farmers' Protective Association, organized by H. Grady Milner and the southeast Oklahoma Reds, the WCU endorsed the principles and program of the Socialist party, but the party did not officially endorse the Union because it was a secret organization.[19] Red party officials sympathized, however, because the Renters' Union experience told them how vulnerable open tenant organizations were to the sanctions of landlords and creditors. They also accepted the validity of the WCU's direct-action approach, because they knew the Renters' Union had failed to implement regular trade union tactics.

After LeFevre organized the Working Class Union in "Hobo's Hollow" near Van Buren, Arkansas (where the radical priest, Thomas Hagerty, had his parish before moving on to help found the IWW in 1905), its members joined with the Farmers' Protective Association in taking legal action against usurious bankers in eastern Oklahoma. Although both secret tenant unions promised to first use legal methods against their employers and creditors, they also pledged to take "direct actions" if their grievances were not redressed. Unlike the original Renters' Union, which opened its membership to all tenants regardless of political affiliation, the WCU and the Protective Association required of all members a solemn oath that pledged them to secrecy (under the pain of death) and to an ultimate goal—the abolition of rent, interest, and profit-taking "by any means necessary." When the Protection Association's suits against bankers under the Oklahoma antiusury law failed in 1915, some militant tenants on Oklahoma's "eastside" joined the Arkansas-based WCU whose Wobbly-influenced leaders urged renters to join wage laborers and to take violent direct action against their "oppressors."

Between 1915 and 1917 the Working Class Union grew powerful in eastern and southern Oklahoma, recruiting several thousand

19. Federal Writers' Project, WPA, *Labor History of Oklahoma* (Oklahoma City: Van Horn, 1939), 40–41.

members.[20] During these troubled years, its members engaged in a series of direct actions ranging from strikes and boycotts to barn burning, bank robbing, and night riding. The WCU's tactics resembled those of a long and notorious line of southwestern vigilantes and outlaws more than those of industrial unionists, but its leaders and most of its members were not "primitive rebels" of the kind E. J. Hobsbawm has described in "prepolitical" peasant societies.[21] They were influenced by agrarian Socialist ideology, even though their tactics reflected frustration with the Socialist party's legal, electoral approach. In fact, as this militant minority in the Socialist tenant movement engaged more in direct action, its leaders gravitated toward the southern Wobblies' homegrown brand of "syndicalism," though they never adopted the IWW's disciplined, nonviolent approach to the class struggle.[22]

Late in 1915 *Harlow's Weekly* warned its readers of the WCU's growth among the tenants on the "eastside" and of the appearance of the IWW's Agricultural Workers' Organization in the northwestern wheat counties. These two "analagous organizations" would open "new phases of economic warfare" in Oklahoma. The IWW and the WCU were "flaming warning signals" that "no shrewd politician can afford to ignore." The Workers' Organization had al-

20. *New Century* (Sulphur, Okla.), January 16, 30, 1915; Stuart Jamieson, *Labor Unionism in American Agriculture*, Bureau of Labor Statistics Bulletin No. 836 (Washington, D.C.: Government Printing Office, 1945), 262; *Daily Oklahoman* (Oklahoma City), August 11, 1917; Shawnee (Okla.) *Daily News-Herald*, September 25, 1917. Between eighteen thousand and thirty-five thousand members were recruited, according to the exaggerated estimates of these two newspapers.
21. E. J. Hobsbawm, *Primitive Rebels: Studies in Archaic Forms of Social Movement in the 19th and 20th Centuries* (New York: W. W. Norton, 1965), 1–29.
22. In fact, in his memoirs of the southwestern radical movement, Covington Hall stressed the syndicalism, especially after 1914, of Socialists in the Louisiana-Texas piney woods and the hill county on the Oklahoma-Arkansas border. He also linked the IWW directly to the Working Class Union, whose charter was influenced by blacklisted members of the Brotherhood of Timber Workers. These men formed a terrorist Clan of Toil in Louisiana in 1913, before their 1914 move to the eastern Oklahoma oil fields where they made contact with the secret tenant union. Covington Hall, "Labor Struggles in the Deep South" (Typescript in Howard-Tilton Library, Tulane University), 183, 205–206.

ready created turmoil by organizing harvest hands around towns like Enid while the WCU was causing "concern among business interests" in some eastern cotton counties by "making open contest in such matters as usury" and by threatening to use violence and arson.[23]

The Agricultural Workers' Organization became the Wobblies' most successful union by using experienced organizers who moved efficiently through the familiar terrain of skid rows and jungle camps where thousands of unorganized, marginal workers responded to their "rough and ready" appeal. Eventually the IWW grew strong enough to effectively ban liquor and drugs from many camps and to make the red card of the One Big Union the only ticket to safe passage on the freight trains. After 1914 they were able to take advantage of a labor shortage in the Midwest and the increased price of wheat caused by the war in Europe to win wage increases and better working conditions for harvest "stiffs" throughout the grain belt.[24]

Most of the field hands organized by the Wobblies in northwestern Oklahoma and other wheat-growing areas were "casual workers" whose "contempt for most of the conventions of bourgeois society" made them especially receptive to "the iconoclastic doctrines of revolutionary syndicalism." They were, as *Solidarity* boasted, "the *franc tireurs* of the class struggle." Frank Little, leading organizer of the Agricultural Workers' Organization, "personified the IWW's rebelliousness" and the toughness of Wobbly harvest hands. "A tall, spare, muscular man with a weatherbeaten face . . . Little looked the complete proletarian." He also practiced proletarian politics.[25] When Little, a native Oklahoman of Cherokee ancestry, was asked to bring the tenant-based Working Class Union into the Workers' Organization, the one-eyed organizer re-

23. *Harlow's Weekly* (Oklahoma City), December 11, 1915, pp. 431–32, and June 5, 1915, pp. 376–77; *Solidarity* (New Castle, Pa.), June 26, July 10, August 28, 1915. See also E. F. Doree, "Gathering the Grain," *International Socialist Review*, XV (June, 1915), 740–43.

24. Melvyn Dubofsky, *We Shall Be All: A History of the Industrial Workers of the World* (Chicago: Quadrangle, 1969), 313–21.

25. *Ibid.*, 186, 313.

fused. The IWW restricted its membership to wage-earning laborers. This decision rankled Covington Hall who had argued unsuccessfully for the inclusion of tenant farmers in the IWW. But Hall's fight for a decentralized organization that would include proletarianized farmers ran counter to the IWW's centralized reorganization, which seemed to bear fruits in the rapid growth of the Agricultural Workers' Organization.[26]

Although the WCU did not affiliate formally with the IWW, it continued to reflect the Wobblies' influence. The presence of a few former Brotherhood of Timber Workers members in the Oklahoma oil fields and a few pro-IWW miners in the coal fields provided the Working Class Union with proletarian advisors having a syndicalist bent. Furthermore, some of the displaced tenants and their sons returning to cotton country after the wheat harvest brought IWW doctrines back to the Oklahoma Ozark hill country as a result of their experiences as Agricultural Workers' Organization members in the west. The proletarian influence of the IWW upon the WCU was reflected in the expansion of the secret organization's base beyond the old Socialist Renters' Union to include wage laborers as well as tenants and blacks as well as whites. In fact, on May Day of 1916, the Working Class Union organized a strike of field hands around Moffatt, Oklahoma, just across the state line from Ft. Smith, Arkansas, because employers refused to increase wages from $1 to $1.25 a day. "The number of strikers cannot be learned," said one report, "but it is understood that the movement has affected many. Several farmers and planters from the Moffatt region declared that their employees were not in sympathy with the strike, but refused to work for fear of being dealt with violently."[27] Char-

---

26. Hall, "Labor Struggles in the Deep South," 218–20, 230. Also see Hall's articles on the farmer question in *Voice of the People* (New Orleans), May 28, June 20, 1914, and the IWW's official response, "The Working Farmer and the IWW?" in *Solidarity* (New Castle, Pa.), March 6, 1915. On Hall's fight for decentralization in the IWW, see Paul Brissenden, *The IWW: A Study in American Syndicalism* (New York: Columbia University Press, 1919), 305.

27. See Carey McWilliams, *Ill Fares the Land: Migrants and Migratory Labor in the United States* (Boston: Little Brown, 1942), 93; and Jamieson, *Labor Unionism in American Agriculture*, 262.

acteristically, the WCU revealed its vigilante heritage even as it attempted to emulate the Wobblies' industrial union tactics. However, this strike of southwestern cotton pickers did not advance the unionization of the rural proletariat any further than had the strike of black Arkansas cotton pickers organized by the Knights thirty years before. And except for the WCU, which was hampered by its terrorist reputation, other radical groups failed to unionize the rural proletariat. The Socialist party devoted its limited resources to organizing tenant unions, and its one effort at mobilizing casual workers, the Texas Trackmen's Union, was crushed immediately. Socialist leaders saw no advantages in trying to recruit more disfranchised migratories.[28] Outside of the Agricultural Workers' highly successful organization of scarce wheat field workers in northwestern Oklahoma and Kansas, the IWW rarely sent organizers into the Southwest. In the piney woods the BTW had signed up a surprisingly large number of tenant farmers who supported the lumber workers, but the Wobblies lacked the organizers to tackle the enormous task of unionizing the migratory army of southwestern cotton pickers who worked for wages. The IWW's experience in building interracial unions like the BTW and organizations for migratory field workers like the Agricultural Workers' Organization, made it the only labor union capable of unionizing the racially divided proletariat that picked the region's enormous cotton crop.[29] But experience could not compensate for

28. After interviewing casual laborers around Texas in 1914, federal investigator, P. A. Speek wrote, "They have no right to vote on account of their migration; they cannot become steady members of any organization and seemingly do not have much interest in Socialism." P. A. Speek, "Notes on Interviews in Texas," October 14, 1914, in Record Group 174, Commission on Industrial Relations Records, "Records of the Department of Labor," National Archives. On the disfranchisement of Mexican migrants, see W. W. Panell, "Mexican Workers in the Southwest," *International Socialist Review*, XVI (1915), 250–51.

29. Over half of the wage-earning farm laborers in the Southwest were still white in 1910, but the proportion of Mexican-American and Afro-American workers was growing steadily. Although landlords and ranchers feared that the Mexican Revolution would cause industrial unrest among immigrant workers from Mexico, no strike actions were reported. The migratory Mexican field hand, especially the immigrant who could quickly be deported, was difficult to organize. One spontaneous strike of black cotton

the lack of human and financial resources. The IWW's only action in this area came in 1912 when Wobbly organizers intervened in a spontaneous strike of Mexican onion pickers in South Texas. Although the One Big Union enjoyed some success in the Tampico oil fields of Mexico, it failed to build any locals among the Mexican workers north of the Rio Grande.[30] In fact, its intervention in the onion-pickers strike ended in defeat. Following this debacle, one of the IWW organizers, Charles Cline, a BTW veteran, was arrested and sentenced to ninety-nine years in prison for allegedly killing a deputy sheriff in a skirmish while leading a young band of Chicanos across the Rio Grande to join the revolution. The speedy Texas "justice" that dispatched Cline, Jesús Rangel, and their comrades aroused a joint IWW-Socialist party defense committee in 1915 which succeeded in winning a reduction in the prisoners' sentences.[31]

THE MEXICAN REVOLUTION AND SOUTHWESTERN SOCIALISM

Following the destruction of the Brotherhood of Timber Workers, the IWW's influence declined below the Red River. Even the Wobblies' warmest southwestern supporters, Covington Hall and Tom Hickey, became disenchanted as the One Big Union centralized more control in its Chicago headquarters and turned more toward building stable unions like the Agricultural Workers' Organization. Hall, who tried briefly to combine his proletarian and agrarian interests in his Farm and Forest Workers' Union, left the IWW after losing his decentralization fight in 1913. While helping

---

pickers was reported in Ellis County, Texas, but no union organizing followed. See U.S. Commission on Industrial Relations, *Final Report and Testimony* (Washington, D.C.: Government Printing Office, 1916), IX, 9001–9004, hereinafter cited as *CIR Testimony*.

30. On the onion-pickers' strike and the general problems of organizing Mexican labor in South Texas, see Paul S. Taylor, *Mexican Labor in the United States* (2 vols.; Berkeley: University of California Press, 1930), II, 325–52; on the IWW in Tampico, see Harvey Levenstein, *Labor Organizations in the United States and Mexico: A History of Their Relations* (Westport, Conn.: Greenwood, 1971), 66, 70.

31. See letters from Charles Cline, *International Socialist Review*, XV (1914), 316–17, 635, and XVI (1915), 383.

to organize the clandestine Clan of Toil, an underground group of blacklisted timberworkers bent on settling scores with sheriffs and company guards, Hall was drawn to the Mexican revolutionaries through his work on the Rangel-Cline Defense Committee. In 1916 he started a small anarcho-syndicalist journal in New Orleans called *Rebellion* which praised the armed insurrection below the Rio Grande. Tom Hickey, though remaining at the top of the Texas Socialist party, followed a course similar to Hall's. After the decline of the Renters' Union, which had been based directly on the IWW model, Hickey formed his new Land League with a more reformist emphasis on the single tax. At the same time, as if to balance this slide toward reformism, the Irish agitator adopted more insurrectionary rhetoric, borrowing the revolutionary slogans of Emiliano Zapata's Morelos Land Revolution. While Hall devoted his considerable efforts to the Rangel-Cline defense, Hickey was helping mobilize Socialists on behalf of the anarcho-syndicalist Magon brothers who were imprisoned in the United States after the failure of their invasion of Baja California. This unsuccessful revolutionary adventure, which involved one southwestern Socialist, Tex Reilly, won the admiration of Hall and Hickey who became leading figures in the substantial Socialist campaign to free Ricardo Flores Magon.[32]

Magon's anarchist newspaper *La Regeneración*, published in Los Angeles, enjoyed a significant readership among Texas Mexicans, according to Emelio Flores, head of the moderate Mexican Protective Association, who blamed the Magonistas for inciting "revolutionary inclined" refugees from below the border. In testifying

32. *Rebel* (Hallettsville, Tex.), December 26, 1914, and *Voice of the People* (New Orleans), May 28, 1914. On the Socialist party defense committees for the Magons, see *Daily Oklahoman* (Oklahoma City), February 25, 1910, *Appeal to Reason* (Girard, Kan.), March 13, 1909, and W. W. Anderson, "The Nature of the Mexican Revolution as Viewed from the United States" (Ph.D. dissertation, University of Texas, 1967), 34–41, 45, 105. On the Magons' Baja Revolution and the IWW's participation, including that of Tex Reilly who returned to Texas afterward to publish the *Rio Grande Coyote*, see Lowell L. Blaisdell, *The Desert Revolution: Baja California, 1911* (Madison: University of Wisconsin Press, 1962). Also see Juan Gómez-Quiñones, *Sembradores: Ricardo Flores Magon y el Partido Liberal Mexicano* (Los Angeles: Aztlan Monograph No. 5, 1973).

before the Industrial Relations Commission in 1915, Flores accused the Magon brothers of provoking several border clashes including the Dimmitt County affair in which the Rangel-Cline party had been arrested and charged with the murder of a law officer. He also warned the commission that the Texas Magonistas had organized "grupos" throughout the Southwest and were "prepared to take up arms" against Anglos who failed to "respect their rights."[33]

Mexican revolutionary activity in Texas did not necessarily win many recruits for the Socialist party. In 1910 the party organized two fairly large Chicano locals, one among miners at Bridgeport and another among fishermen on Matagorda Bay, but the Renters' Union failed to recruit many brown tenants in South Texas over the next two years. In 1912 Socialist tenant organizer Antonio Valdez reported that revolutionary activity north of the Rio Grande made his job more difficult, because landlords, alarmed by border raids and the restless sentiment among their immigrant workers, threatened to fire and deport any renters or laborers who talked of "revolution or socialism." For example, German landlords from southern Travis County just below Austin, harassed the Renters' Union organizer and frightened Mexican employees with various threats. "These counties are infested with the worst kind of tenants," Valdez wrote, "all cowards [are] scared on account of the Mexican war."[34]

After the failure of their trackmen's "industrial union," which aimed its organizing partly at migrant Mexican railroad workers, the Texas Socialists concentrated on recruiting Chicano tenants through the Renters' Union and then in 1914 through the new

33. Flores quoted in *CIR Testimony*, X, 9200–9203. Also see letters from Mexicans throughout the Southwest, including farm laborers in Texas and miners in Oklahoma, in *La Regeneración* (Los Angeles), December 4, 1911.

34. *Appeal to Reason* (Girard, Kan.), March 13, 1909, and December 10, 1910; *Rebel* (Hallettsville, Tex.), June 29, 1912. The Socialists averaged only 4 percent of the vote in Travis County in the elections of 1912 and 1914. On the conservative opinions of the racially divided tenants of this county see the interesting survey in George S. Weherwein and R. B. Woods, "Social Life and Religious Activity in Southern Travis County, Texas," in N. L. Sims (ed.), *The Rural Community* (New York: Charles Scribner's Sons, 1920), 504.

Land League. Through the tenacity of the Hernández brothers, who were converted to socialism by working with the Rangel-Cline Defense Committee, the League recruited about one thousand Mexican renters in South Texas in 1914 and 1915. However, in the summer and fall of 1915 raids by "bandits" from Mexico on towns in the Lower Rio Grande Valley created a wave of hysteria which led to the lynching of twenty-three Chicanos in a four-month period. This situation made tenant organizing among Mexican-Americans even more difficult. In fact, while the lynching hysteria was running wild in Brownsville, authorities in San Antonio arrested F. A. Hernández of the Land League for allegedly "inciting rebellion against the United States." The incarceration of this resourceful organizer stymied the recruitment of Mexican renters. While Hernández languished in prison his Socialist comrades established a defense committee on his behalf; these efforts helped the Mexican organizer win an acquittal late in 1915. Although the Texas Socialist party actively supported Hernández, its leaders made many mistakes in their efforts to recruit Mexican-American tenants. As Emilio Zamora, Jr., points out, the party's official newspaper, the *Rebel*, never published articles in Spanish, but it did print letters by Anglo members that revealed anti-Mexican attitudes. Therefore, the Socialist effort to recruit Chicano farmers through the Land League was hampered not only by external repression, but by internal discrimination by Anglo Socialists.[35]

As repression increased, the Texas Reds adopted more revolutionary rhetoric. After Ricardo Flores Magon's imprisonment at Leavenworth following the abortive Baja Revolution, the *Rebel* turned to new resurrectionary heroes. Hickey lionized Pancho Villa and Emiliano Zapata as "class conscious revolutionists," redeeming the land from the church and the aristocracy and pre-

35. *Rebel* (Hallettsville, Tex.), June 28, 1913, January 31, July 18, 1914, October 23, 1915; Emilio Zamora, Jr., "Chicano Socialist Labor Activity in Texas, 1900–1920," *Aztlán*, VI (1975), 221–36; Charles C. Cumberland, "Mexican Revolutionary Movements in Texas," *Southwestern Historical Quarterly*, LII (1949), 301–24. At the time, a Mexican agent of the so-called "Texas revolution" was reportedly recruiting north of the Rio Grande. *Daily Oklahoman* (Oklahoma City), October 19, 1915.

venting counterfeits like Francisco Madero, Victoriano Huerta, and Venustiano Carranza from compromising the revolution. To Tom Hickey Pancho Villa was a Socialist who had been forced to become a bandit by the "system." Like Sam Bass, the legendary "social bandit" of Texas, "he never robbed a poor man and always paid for his lodging."[36] In 1914 Hickey declared the columns of the *Rebel* open to Zapata and exclaimed: "For all of us who struggle for land and liberty in Texas, Oklahoma, and in all portions of the cotton kingdom, I say, God speed Zapata." In the same issue the *Rebel* printed Zapata's "plan de Ayala," drawn largely from Flores Magon's "land and liberty" program, and declared southwestern tenants to be struggling for the same principles. "If you do not accept this solution," Hickey warned the landlords, "then look for another Zapata to arise on this side of the Rio Grande."[37]

The Texas Reds defended their heroes even as most United States newspapers were judging Villa and Zapata as nothing more than murderous bandits. During the height of the hysteria caused by border raids on the lower Rio Grande in the fall of 1915, E. R. Meitzen boldly spoke at Kingsville, not far from the troubled valley. He denounced the King family, who owned the town, its bank, and most of the surrounding ranchland, for calling out the militia to protect its own interests. The owners of Kingsville were "bank bandits who robbed the poor" and they had good reason to fear the Mexican bandits who robbed mainly from the rich. And in 1916 when the Socialist press condemned Villa for his notorious raid on Columbus, New Mexico, the *Rebel* again refused to turn on its hero. Covington Hall, who loved to romanticize rebels and desperados of all kinds, said no one had proved Pancho's presence at the raid, and he thought the whole affair seemed "fishy." Hall

36. *Daily Oklahoman* (Oklahoma City), March 8, 1913. For a discussion of "social banditry" see E. J. Hobsbawm, *Bandits* (New York: Delacorte, 1969), esp. 14. On Sam Bass, who was known as a "knight of the road, a generous, open-handed highwayman" who shared the loot he stole from the Southern Pacific Railroad with the farmers who sheltered him, see Walter Prescott Webb, *The Texas Rangers: A Century of Frontier Defense* (Austin: University of Texas Press, 1965), 371; and J. Frank Dobie, "The Robin Hooding of Sam Bass," *Montana*, IV (1955), 38.
37. *Rebel* (Hallettsville, Tex.), January 31, March 14, November 7, 1914.

warned *Rebel* readers not to succumb to the interventionist sentiment that was being whipped up by the Wilson administration to
justify the destruction of the Mexican land revolution.[38] Pershing's
invasion soon followed, however, putting an end to revolutionary
activity in South Texas and increasing racist attitudes toward Mexicans on the part of most Anglos north of the border.

As their commitment to the Mexican Revolution grew, the Texas
Reds adopted a more apocalyptic view of their own "land struggle." As early as 1913 Hickey warned that unless the southwestern
land question was settled on the Socialists' terms, the landless
masses would "seek a solution at the muzzle of a gun" just like
the "Mexican patriots." Three years later he concluded, along with
the Meitzens, that the Commission on Industrial Relations had
raised false expectations of meaningful change and that the time
had come for a "social revolution" in the United States. Exploitation and repression had actually increased in the Southwest, making that region the "ripest" for upheaval. Though Hickey and Hall
nourished illusions about the "rebel" farmers of the South rising
again, the Texas Reds equivocated, because they undoubtedly realized that an armed uprising north of the Rio Grande would be
immediately crushed.

The *Rebel* still told tenants to join the Land League and to support the Socialist party in order to end landlordism and usury, but
for the first time its editors openly doubted the possibility of winning power in an electoral system controlled by the Democratic
party. Without abandoning the Socialist party's approach, Hickey
suggested that tenants consider the path taken by their Irish and
Mexican comrades who were overthrowing the landlord class by
force of arms.[39] The political dilemma of the Texas Reds grew
deeper as the party and the League emphasized land reform (the
single tax) more than ever before while their newspaper adopted
more revolutionary rhetoric. The Mexican Revolution clearly height-

38. *Ibid.*, November 6, 1915. Also see Charles C. Cumberland, "Border
Raids on the Lower Rio Grande Valley, 1915," *Southwestern Historical
Quarterly*, LVII (1954), 285–311; Anderson, "The Nature of the Mexican
Revolution," 87–88; *Rebel* (Hallettsville, Tex.), March 18, 25, 1916.
39. *Rebel* (Hallettsville, Tex.), March 8, 1913, May 20, 1916.

ened this tension by forcing Reds like Hickey, Hall, and the Meitzens to follow their political convictions to a revolutionary conclusion at a time when the party and the League needed to reach new, but less adventurous constituents. "Insurgent Mexico" undoubtedly influenced some rank-and-file Texas Socialists, especially the militant minority already inclined toward direct action. The revolution also converted a small number of Chicanos to socialism, but, despite the Reds' rhetoric about the rebellion spreading north of the Rio Grande, the mass of Texas tenants were not moved to action by the insurrectionary events below the border.

SOCIAL BANDITRY AND BANK ROBBERY

While Mexican revolutionary activity in Texas increased political repression and social tension after 1915, the Working Class Union's direct actions provoked a reaction in eastern Oklahoma and western Arkansas. WCU activity, especially "social banditry," roughly paralleled that of Mexican revolutionaries like Villa and clearly revealed the influence of the IWW, but the Union's actions also resembled the earlier exploits of southwestern night riders and outlaws.

The WCU's most "primitive" sort of protest erupted in late 1915 when its members began dynamiting vats used to dip cattle in arsenic in order to prevent the spread of "Texas fever," a disease carried over the Rio Grande by Mexican steers infected with ticks.[40] The small farmers and tenants of eastern Oklahoma objected to the tick eradication law because it killed some of their cattle and benefited only the large ranchers who could afford to lose a few head. Furthermore, the big cattlemen's herds were responsible for bringing the disease up from Texas in the first place. As the resistance to the dipping law spread throughout the eastern part of the state in 1916, it took on characteristics similar to the range wars fought between "nesters" and cattlemen in Texas during the 1880s and in the Oklahoma territories in the 1890s and early 1900s.[41]

40. Stanley J. Clark, "Texas Fever in Oklahoma," *Chronicles of Oklahoma,* XXIX (1952), 429–44.
41. *Harlow's Weekly* (Oklahoma City), September 25, 1915; *Marshall County News-Democrat* (Madill, Okla.), October 28, 1915.

Tension between large ranchers and small farmers had produced violence in Osage County, Oklahoma, a few years before when the homesteaders had protested against the cattlemen's monopoly on Indian lands and the destruction and disease spread by their large herds. Despite threats by "cowboy desperados" hired by the ranchers, the small farmers organized around Socialist candidates who campaigned for school and road construction in the county and imparted some political content to the "last of the cattle wars."[42]

When the WCU also began to attack some of the county officials and federal demonstration agents who administered the tick eradication program,[43] the resistance movement resembled other traditional patterns of hill country intransigence—especially in the recurring hostility of poor white hillbillies toward government officers who tried to prevent them from making moonshine whiskey or to force them to pay federal excise tax. The dirt farmers of eastern Oklahoma and the Arkansas Ozarks insisted on regulating their own lives even if it meant resorting to violence. One old "Arkie" interviewed in the 1930s explained that despite the violent reputation of the Ozarks, his people acted tolerantly in regulating life within their own rural communities. "I don't reckon we was what you mought call narrer-minded—not 'bout most things anyhow," he declared. Religious and political deviance, including catholicism and socialism, could be tolerated, and most disputes were family affairs not concerning the whole community, let alone the law. If a man went and lived on another's land or took his stock, however, the community had to take action. "We never done nothin' hasty, but if a feller . . . kept on a stealin', he'd find a letter

42. Nat L. Hardy, "The Last of the Cattle Wars," *Coming Nation* (Girard, Kan.), June 22, 1912; *Arkansas Gazette* (Little Rock), April 30, 1915. See also R. D. Holt, "The Introduction of Barbed Wire into Texas and the Fence Cutting War," *West Texas Historical Association Yearbook*, VI (1930), 65–79; and Glenn Smith, "Fence Cutting and Stage Robbing in Runnels County," *West Texas Historical Association Yearbook*, XLI (1965), 42–50.

43. In Pontotoc County the barns of county officials administering the tick eradication program were burned and an attempt was made to assassinate the county attorney who was prosecuting the Working Class Union for dynamiting dipping vats and terrorizing federal demonstration agents who supervised the program. Muskogee (Okla.) *Daily Phoenix*, January 6, 1916; *Harlow's Weekly* (Oklahoma City), January 15, 1916, pp. 37–38.

on his door some mornin' sayin' how folks was gettin' sick an' tired o' sich goins'-on, and advisin' him t' git plumb out o'th district afore the moon changed. Some called us bald-knobbers, some called us white cappers, an' some called us night-riders, but 'mongst th' home folks we was jest th' committee."[44] The "committee" insisted on its right to regulate the community and if law officers intervened from the outside, it warned intruders that they were apt to leave the district in a pine box.

As the Socialists gained more influence in the poor rural districts after 1910, they began to politicize the dirt farmers' hostility toward the propertied classes of the towns and cities who passed laws telling them not to make corn whiskey, to dip their stock in arsenic, and not to hunt game. These "interlocked parasites," argued the Socialists, violated the farmers' "natural rights" to "full value labor" and to just rents and interest rates. This political propaganda helped shift the attention of rural regulators in and around the Ozarks from rustlers to landlords and from "revenooers" to usurers. Agrarian Socialist propaganda about the "crimes" of avaricious bankers and landlords helped legitimize vigilante activity against property owners and creditors, especially if the victims were absentee landlords or relatively new financial men who would be viewed as outside intruders as well as "oppressors."[45]

The Working Class Union's attack on the dipping vats (which inaugurated ten years of intermittent warfare against the tick eradication program) represented a rather traditional effort to regulate the obnoxious practices of outsiders (in this case, government agricultural authorities). But there were enough Socialists among the antidippers to convince many night riders that the tick eradication program was a conspiracy between government officials and the big cattlemen. It is not surprising then that the WCU in 1916

44. Quoted in Vance Randolph, *Ozark Mountain Folks* (New York: Vanguard Press, 1932), 89, 91.
45. For a study of how poor Protestants in another historical context legitimized the use of violence in defense of traditional rights and customs, see E. P. Thompson, "The Moral Economy of the English Crowd in the Eighteenth Century," *Past and Present*, No. 50 (1971), 76–136.

turned to a more violent campaign against offensive landlords who charged bonus rents and county seat bankers who charged usurious interest rates.[46]

The campaign against the oppressive credit system began with the Oklahoma Emancipation League's suit against certain bankers for charging usurious interest. The WCU joined in this legal campaign, but its members quickly adopted more militant tactics when their attorney, L. C. McNabb, was removed from his post as a judge in Sequoyah County, where the Union allegedly enjoyed the sympathy of an "actual majority" of the voters. After pledging to continue the WCU's "bitter fight against usury and landlordism," McNabb was placed on trial at Sallisaw, the county seat, for malfeasance in office. Outraged by this "conspiracy" against a sympathetic local official, the Union threatened to bring in a thousand "rampaging" men to stop the trial. The situation grew so threatening that authorities moved McNabb's trial to Muskogee. When the proceedings began, a party of WCU members paraded through the city wearing red shirts. This "Red Shirt Brigade," *Harlow's* editorialized, depicted an "open defiance" of authority that would have been unbelievable a few years before. In March, 1916, with McNabb's case on its way to the supreme court on appeal, a special session of the state legislature enacted a tougher antiusury law, and WCU violence receded.[47]

The southwestern Socialists criticized the Missouri night riders who had murdered several landlords and merchants in 1915, but they did not oppose the WCU's violent tactics because its members included class-conscious farmers involved in a union struggle; indeed many card-carrying Socialists rode with the Oklahoma "regulators" who sabotaged property and terrorized tenants for cooperating with offensive landlords. The Socialist party opposed these tactics but it could not dismiss WCU activists as frustrated Demo-

46. The Working Class Union began to blacklist landlords "obnoxious to the organization" and to enforce their boycotts by terrorizing tenants (usually by whipping) who refused to cooperate. *Harlow's Weekly* (Oklahoma City), January 1, 1916, pp. 3–5, February 26, 1916, p. 3.
47. Clark, "Texas Fever in Oklahoma," 432–34; *Harlow's Weekly* (Oklahoma City), February 26, 1916, p. 3, March 11, 1916, p. 11.

crats who turned to "anarchistic" violence and murder like the rebellious renters of the Missouri "boot heel."[48] Oddly enough, one of the few critical comments on the WCU's violent tactics came from Covington Hall, the most revolutionary southwestern Red, whose paradoxical writings for the *Rebel* in 1915 and 1916 reflected the dilemma political violence presented for radical Socialists. He said that attempts to coerce tenants into joining the movement would divide the ranks of the rural proletariat, and like Pat Nagle, who had capably defended several Oklahoma night riders in court, Hall argued that "lawless methods" tended to provoke violent reactions from lawmen. This was the position IWW leaders had advocated during the Louisiana "lumber war." Nevertheless, Hall concluded, the WCU had conveyed an "effective warning" to landlords and bankers whose "extreme provocations" (in the form of bonus rents, usurious interest rates, and blacklisting) forced "peaceable, law-abiding farmers" to adopt "criminal ways."[49]

After the Union's attempts to sue bankers under the state antiusury laws had come to naught, some frustrated farmers had indeed adopted "criminal ways" to redress their grievances against the finance capitalists of the region. The "epidemic of bank robberies" that swept the old Indian Territory (an area with a larcenous history) after the hard times of 1914 was blamed mainly on professional "yeggmen" and old-time outlaws like Henry Starr, who was captured for the last time in eastern Oklahoma at the height of the antiusury movement in 1915. The infamous train robber, who was known by lawmen as the "bravest and kindest"

48. Although the press, because the party was fairly strong in the area, charged that the Missouri night riders were Socialists, the *Rebel* pointed out that all but two of the sixty-six offenders first arrested were Democrats. *Rebel* (Hallettsville, Tex.), April 29, 1916. On the night riders of the southeast Missouri lowlands see *Daily Oklahoman* (Oklahoma City), November 25, 1915, and *Arkansas Gazette* (Little Rock), April 21, 25, 1915. See also L. P. Ogilvie, "Populism and Socialism in the Southeast Missouri Lowlands," *Missouri Historical Quarterly*, LXV (1971), 159–83. The *Rebel* criticized the night riders' violent tactics and even sent W. S. Noble of the Land League to try to organize the incendiaries. *Rebel* (Hallettsville, Tex.), February 26, April 29, 1916.

49. *Rebel* (Hallettsville, Tex.), April 29, 1916; *Tenant Farmer* (Kingfisher, Okla.), May, 1915.

of the Oklahoma outlaws, proclaimed, via the *Appeal to Reason*, that many of the bankers he victimized were in the "robbery business too."[50] Others blamed the "epidemic" of hold-ups on Al Jennings, another famous train robber from territorial days, who had run a strong populist campaign for the 1914 Democratic gubernatorial nomination, showing a film depicting his outlaw exploits to full houses across the state.[51]

Harlow's Weekly doubted, however, that the influence of these bad men fully explained the increase of bank robberies in Oklahoma. The depression of 1914 made many poor people "desperate" enough "to take up violent means to secure what they want." And though professionals still performed most of the big robberies, the wave of store lootings in 1914, as well as many of the small-town bank robberies (including most of the unsuccessful ones), were the work of amateurs, largely impoverished, indebted dirt farmers.[52]

By 1917 most of the inmates in the state prison at McAlester (80 percent of the total being tenants or common laborers) were serving time for crimes against property, even though a large number of arrests were made in the state every year for assault and battery, vagrancy, and violation of state laws, especially those prohibiting gambling and bootlegging.[53] Whether these crimes against property were politically motivated by the Socialists' active campaign against bankers and other "parasites" who "robbed" the

50. *Harlow's Weekly* (Oklahoma City), December 13, 1916, pp. 3–4. On Starr's arrest and early career see McAlester (Okla.) *News-Capital*, November 19, 1915, and Harthshorne (Okla.) *Sun*, April 1, 1915. *Appeal to Reason* (Girard, Kan.), April 17, 1915. For background see Glenn Shirley, *Law West of Ft. Smith: Frontier Justice in the Indian Territory, 1834–1896* (New York: Henry Holt, 1957).

51. *Harlow's Weekly* (Oklahoma City), January 9, 1915, p. 23. When the Oklahoma state legislature criticized Jennings and passed a special law to suppress bank robbers, the Socialists complained that no attention was paid to the "bank robbers who work on the other side of the window and rob the tenant or mortgaged farmer with usurious interest." *Rebel* (Hallettsville, Tex.), March 13, 1915.

52. *Harlow's Weekly* (Oklahoma City), January 9, 1915, p. 23; see also *Oklahoma Democrat* (Altus), March 6, 1913, June 17, 1915.

53. McAlester (Okla.) *News-Capital*, February 10, 1912.

"honest producers" or were encouraged by the favorable publicity the party press gave to "social bandits" on both sides of the Rio Grande can be determined, in part, by looking at the degree of contact between the prisoners at McAlester and the Socialist movement.

In 1912, a year Oklahoma led the nation in bank robberies,[54] the warden of the state "pen" at McAlester took a poll of the prisoners' political preferences just before the party nominating conventions; it showed that Gene Debs was by far the most popular candidate among the white inmates. The man who had himself been converted to socialism in prison received 204 votes from this group of convicts, with Roosevelt winning 139, Bryan 132, Champ Clark 93, and Woodrow Wilson 24. By contrast, the prison guards and other employees gave the Democrats 69 straw votes whereas the Republicans received only 3 and the Socialists none. Debs was also popular among the black inmates who gave him 139 votes. Nearly all Afro-Americans in Oklahoma considered themselves Republicans to some degree and so Roosevelt, the most progressive of the GOP candidates, led among the blacks with 253 votes. All of the Democrats combined received only 70 votes from black prisoners. Wilson, who went on to win the nomination and to carry the state of Oklahoma with 47 percent of the vote, received only 1 percent of the total convict vote whereas Debs, who polled 16 percent in the general election, won 32 percent of the total prison poll.[55]

These contrasts should not be surprising since the McAlester prison poll represented the political preferences of lower-class whites and blacks who were disfranchised or "counted out" almost as thoroughly when they were free men as when they were in chains. And the poll does show that a disproportionate percentage of the convicts in eastern Oklahoma considered themselves Socialists. Their politics probably did not motivate their criminal activity, but it undoubtedly served to legitimize their actions, espe-

54. An average of 12.6 bank robberies per year were reported in Oklahoma between 1905 and 1917, quadruple the average of 3.6 per state across the nation. Figures compiled from the *Annual Proceedings* of the American Bankers' Association, 1912.
55. McAlester (Okla.) *News-Capital*, February 10, 1912.

cially if the offenses they committed were directed against the people and institutions that many in their class had come to see as sources of oppression and exploitation.

In late 1916, as the number of bank robberies in eastern Oklahoma reached "epidemic" proportions, *Harlow's* reported that the people being arrested as suspects included a larger number of local people than ever before. In one case a dozen local people, mostly tenants, were arrested and charged with robbing a bank in Vian, Sequoyah County, an area in which the Working Class Union reputedly had fifteen hundred members. L. C. McNabb, the Union's attorney, defended the suspects, who were widely believed to be members of the secret order. Indeed, some bankers and businessmen charged that the WCU was responsible for many of the robberies in the troubled section, because the banks that were sued and boycotted for charging usurious interest rates seemed to suffer more than others. At any rate, the Socialists and the WCU had stirred up a "strong prejudice" against the banks in this part of the state, the *Weekly* observed, so strong that insurance companies had canceled their policies on the grounds that "public sentiment against the banks was so severe as to encourage robberies." The progressive journal concluded: "There is no doubt of a most dangerous sentiment among a large element of the people that there is little crime in robbing a bank." The bankers of eastern Oklahoma could not rely upon the protection of insurance company guards or local law officers who were viewed as incompetents or actual WCU sympathizers; the bankers therefore hired their own guards and provided them with special cars that had mounted machine guns. This was the same course adopted by the managers of the Taft Ranch in South Texas when they thought Mexican revolutionaries might raid their property or cause an uprising among their workers.[56]

But by this time state and county lawmen were launching a concerted effort to destroy the WCU, because of its expansion to the west and its increased terroristic activities against farmers who

56. *Harlow's Weekly* (Oklahoma City), December 13, 1916, pp. 3–4; McAlester (Okla.), *News-Capital*, January 3, 1916; A. Ray Stephens, *The Taft Ranch: A Texas Principality* (Austin: University of Texas Press, 1965), 198–99.

did not support its boycotts. It was quite difficult, however, for authorities to uproot a well-organized secret union that threatened death to members who broke their oaths of secrecy. The popularity and political influence of the WCU in the eastern counties where most of the "depredations" occurred made some law officers reluctant to arrest the night riders. "Drastic actions" taken by local authorities "to suppress WCU violence" in mid-1916 had little effect. Pat Nagle, for example, successfully defended eight men charged with riot in a whipping case near Stigler. But in September the union members were finally convicted on another whipping charge and sentenced to two years in Leavenworth, a conviction hailed by the press and by harassed bankers, landlords, and county officials. In the next month thirty-three men from McCurtain County received stiff prison sentences for complicity in "outrages committed by the WCU." By January, 1917, the Union was said to be in decline, these convictions having lifted the "stonewall of secrecy behind which the white cappers have been hiding."[57]

The Working Class Union's violent activities provoked more repression against Socialists in southeastern Oklahoma where the party had already suffered serious losses as a result of a blacklisting campaign organized by Democratic businessmen, landlords, and politicians.[58] Night riding (a perfect expression of the politics of frustration) also contributed to an increasingly hysterical response to crime and disorder on the part of propertied townspeople. Political and social unrest, *Harlow's Weekly* warned in the fall of 1916, had awakened a "mob spirit" not only in rural areas of WCU activity but in the more civilized towns and cities where vigilante action was on the rise. Lynching became more common in 1916, as recently enfranchised blacks participated more in politics and began arming themselves to resist white lynch mobs in cities like Muskogee. And for the first time since the territorial days of the Anti-Horse Thief Association, white men were lynched. On October 4, 1916, a mob "presumed to be composed of the city's best

57. *Harlow's Weekly* (Oklahoma City), August 19, 1916, pp. 9–10, September 27, 1916, and January 31, 1917, pp. 3–4.
58. *Ibid.*, May 20, 1916, pp. 6–7.

citizens" took four white Oklahomans from a jail at Ada, the seat of Hughes County, and hanged them.[59]

The vigilantes who appeared in the county seat towns of Oklahoma in 1915 reacted to disorder and dissent with the same kind of repression citizens' leagues had used to destroy interracial industrial unionism in the piney woods. The opponents of socialism had always identified the party with crime, and when Working Class Union violence erupted in areas of Socialist influence, vigilante reactionaries argued for the destruction of all opposition movements in order to preserve law and order. The seeds of wartime repression were planted long before the United States actually entered the European war.

59. *Ibid.*, June 3, 1916, pp. 8–9, October 4, 1916, pp. 5–6.

IX

War and Repression
1917-1920

The Socialists maintained leadership of the southwestern land struggle in 1916, even though a militant minority of tenants, represented by the Working Class Union, had broken party discipline by adopting violent tactics. And despite the increasing turn toward agrarian radicalism by Congressman Murray, Governor Ferguson, and other reform Democrats, the Socialist party could still make the land question their "paramount issue" in the 1916 campaign. The enactment of progressive farm legislation on the eve of this campaign did not win many Socialist farmers over to Wilson's New Freedom. However, the popularity of the president's neutrality pledge, combined with Debs's absence from the presidential race, cost the Socialist party votes. The party's poor performance in the 1916 election increased discontent with "politics as usual" and played into the hands of the WCU and other secret organizations.

Even in Oklahoma, the only state where the Socialists made significant electoral gains in this election, the Working Class Union continued to win converts. The failure of the Sooner Socialists' spirited fight against Democratic disfranchisement legislation increased the sense of futility the militant minority felt toward electioneering. Although the Socialists in Oklahoma and other southwestern states immediately assumed the leadership of the fight against military preparedness and finally against intervention and conscription, they could not control the actions of the secretly organized "direct actionists" who planned violent resistance to the draft as soon as the United States declared war.

The unsuccessful efforts made by the WCU and other groups to oppose the draft led to widespread repression of the Socialist party and the IWW, organizations that did not advocate violent opposition to the war. And these abortive direct actions hastened the repression of the entire left in the Southwest, though armed draft resisters did not actually cause the widespread suppression of all forms of radical activity. Even without a sensational event like the 1917 Green Corn Rebellion against the draft, government officials possessed the legal authority to suppress radicalism. They used this authority quite effectively in 1917 and 1918 to destroy the Socialist movement throughout the West and Midwest in states without insurrectionary events. The passage of criminal syndicalism laws and the raids connected with the 1919 Red Scare wiped out the last pockets of radical resistance organized by UMW and IWW militants in the coal and oil fields.

Official government suppression of southwestern radical movements, combined with vigilante repression, allowed the opponents of socialism to use patriotism as a pretext for destroying a domestic enemy with tactics that would have been difficult to employ in peacetime. The dynamics of the southwestern class struggle created a situation in which Socialists were viewed not just as the irrepressible political rivals of the dominant Democrats, but also as the class enemies of the region's ruling class.

By 1919 the southwestern Socialist movement, including the powerful Oklahoma Socialist party, had been virtually destroyed. Its most militant newspapers had been suppressed, its party locals disbanded, its boldest leaders imprisoned. More important, Socialist rank and filers had been intimidated and demoralized by the possibility as well as the reality of government or vigilante repression. The Democratic landlords, merchants, and lawyers who took a leading hand in organizing the repression had every reason to believe that the "class issues" the Socialists injected into southwestern politics would now disappear. But the Socialists had not created the southwestern class struggle; they had simply politicized it. Therefore, the destruction of the Socialist party did not put an end to class conflict or remove class issues from the region's politics.

PREPAREDNESS AND THE 1916 CAMPAIGN

The southwestern Socialists entered the 1916 campaign in an optimistic mood. In Oklahoma the state legislature passed a stronger antiusury law, and in Texas it enacted Governor Ferguson's rent regulation proposal. Thus it seemed that Socialist protest had been fairly effective. Furthermore, the enactment of reforms to regulate rent and interest rates did not diminish tenant militancy. Commodity prices improved somewhat after the crisis of 1914, but the rural Southwest remained a depressed area. Many cotton farmers, Democrats as well as Socialists, still criticized President Wilson and Secretary of Agriculture Houston for opposing the rural credits legislation southwestern congressmen proposed.[1] In addition, the Democratic administration's preparedness program and "neutrality" policy rankled many isolationist farmers and met with open opposition from staunch supporters like Senator Thomas Gore of Oklahoma.

In Texas, Jim Ferguson campaigned for reelection as the "friend of the farmer," but in 1916 the governor turned his attention from the land question to the perennial issue in state politics, liquor.[2] With this return to normalcy, the Socialists resumed the initiative in their land struggle. They lashed out at the ineffectiveness of rent regulation and antiusury laws and reemphasized the land tax as a "sure fire" way to destroy landlordism.

Although the Texas Reds praised the "land revolution" in Mexico, for their own constituency they continued to stress the im-

1. For a direct complaint by a Democratic tenant to the president see T. M. Smith to Woodrow Wilson, August 7, 1915, in Series 4, Case File 1720, Woodrow Wilson Papers, Library of Congress.
2. Ferguson's own paper, the *National Optimist*, blamed Democratic factionalism over the liquor question for "promoting" socialism. Quoted in *Rebel* (Hallettsville, Tex.), February 5, 1916. See Seth S. McKay, *Texas Politics, 1905–1944* (Lubbock: Texas Tech University Press, 1952), 61, on the failure to enforce rent regulation.

portance of land reform based on confiscatory taxes. After the Walsh Commission recommended the graduated land tax as a necessary reform in 1915, newspapers in the cotton country began to comment favorably on the idea. Then the *Rebel* decided that the Socialist party had to adopt a more "radical and scientific" land program by switching from a graduated land tax, exempting improvements, to a single tax on the full value of land, regardless of improvements, in order to force large landlords to actually abandon their holdings.[3] The paper consistently criticized Henry George and his followers for failing to see that equality depended on the collective ownership of all means of production and not simply on the redistribution of land. Although they criticized the political naiveté of the single taxers, the Socialists recognized the value of their proposal as an immediate demand and popularized it a good deal "among the masses of Texas."[4] At the beginning of the 1916 campaign, the *Rebel* inaugurated a "land petition" asking the state legislature to enact the single tax; it was written by J. J. Pastoriza, the controversial tax commissioner of Houston who had gone as far as the law would allow in taxing real estate at full value. The Socialists could not support Pastoriza's impending mayoral candidacy because he was a Democrat, but they were pleased to have his help in circulating the land petition.[5]

"Alfalfa Bill" Murray, the leading agrarian among the southwestern Democrats, responded to this growing single-tax sentiment

3. *Rebel* (Hallettsville, Tex.), September 18, 1915; U.S. Commission on Industrial Relations, *Final Report and Testimony* (Washington, D.C.: Government Printing Office, 1916), 23–79. For press comment on the growing attention given to the single tax see *Oklahoma Democrat* (Altus), April 6, 1915, *Marshall County News-Democrat* (Madill, Okla.), April 30, August 9, 1915; Harthshorne (Okla.) *Sun*, March 25, 1915. See also L. H. Haney, "The Single Tax," in *Studies in the Land Problem in Texas*, University of Texas Bulletin No. 39 (Austin, 1915), 197–202.

4. Harthshorne (Okla.) *Sun*, March 11, 1916. On the popularity of the single tax among the masses in Texas see P. A. Speek, "Notes on Interviews in Texas," October 14, 1914, in Record Group 174, Commission on Industrial Relations Records, "Records of the Department of Labor," National Archives, hereinafter cited as CIR Records.

5. Harthshorne (Okla.) *Sun*, April 1, May 6, 1916. The Texas Socialists were also impressed by the fact that the State Federation of Labor endorsed the single-tax amendment.

by recommending a "severely graduated land tax which could be used to break up large landholdings." Congressman Murray, who faced a difficult campaign for renomination in a factionalized Democratic party, also worried about the unpopularity of his vociferous defense of President Wilson's preparedness program. After being received with thunderous applause at his party's state convention in April, 1916, Murray gave a speech on preparedness which "simply sizzled with good, old-fashioned patriotism"; this "dismayed" the delegates, who booed at his remarks. Oklahoma was still William Jennings Bryan country at this point, isolationist to the core.[6]

Most other Democrats in the Southwest sensed the unpopularity of the preparedness program and refused to speak out in support of the president. Others, principally Senator Gore of Oklahoma and Congressmen Jeff McLemore and Oscar Calloway of Texas, led the opposition forces on Capitol Hill. Isolationist, antipreparedness sentiment spread throughout the South and West, growing especially strong in the Southwest where the Socialists and their *Appeal to Reason* played an important role in mobilizing public opinion against the country's entry into the European war.[7]

The Reds adopted an uncompromising antiwar position from the very beginning. At their state convention in 1914 the Texas Socialists declared that the war was being waged to see which "capitalists would control certain lands and markets to the detriment of their competitors." After vowing unanimously to oppose any attempts to bring the United States into the conflict, they organized antiwar demonstrations in Houston and other cities.[8] The Oklahoma Socialists went even further. In December, 1914, their state convention adopted the following resolution unanimously: "If War is declared, the Socialists of Oklahoma shall refuse to en-

6. Keith L. Bryant, Jr., *Alfalfa Bill Murray* (Norman: University of Oklahoma Press, 1968), 135, 138.
7. Ralph Easley to Joseph Tumulty, January 24, 1916, in Series 4, Box 134, Woodrow Wilson Papers, Library of Congress. See also Monroe Billington, "Thomas P. Gore and Oklahoma Public Opinion, 1917–1918," *Journal of Southern History*, XXVII (1961), 344–53; and T. L. Miller, "Oscar Calloway and Preparedness," *West Texas Historical Association Yearbook*, XLIII (1967), 80–93.
8. *Rebel* (Hallettsville, Tex.), August 15, 22, 29, September 19, 1914.

list: but if forced to enter military service to murder fellow workers, we shall choose to die fighting the enemies of humanity in our
ranks rather than to perish fighting our fellow workers."[9] This
"revolutionary stand," widely interpreted as a pledge by Socialists
to "turn their guns on their officers," may have been the "most disastrous ever made by the party in Oklahoma."[10] However, in the
three years prior to America's entry into World War I, this militant
position received widespread support in the Southwest among Socialists and non-Socialists alike.

As usual, Debs and the *Appeal to Reason* took the lead. In December of 1915, the Socialist leader told 700,000 *Appeal* readers
that the only war he would fight in was a working-class revolution:
"I have no country to fight for; my country is the earth; I am a
citizen of the world. I am a proletarian revolutionist. I will refuse
to obey any order to fight for the ruling class, but I will not wait
for a command to fight for the working class."[11] In the same
month, however, Debs withdrew his name from consideration as
the Socialist party's presidential nominee for 1916. The *Rebel* expressed its deep regrets and proposed a leftist national ticket led
by Arthur LeSeur, a North Dakota lawyer and head of the People's
College in Ft. Scott, Kansas, and Kate Richards O'Hare. However,
since neither LeSeur nor O'Hare were well known outside of the
Midwest and Southwest, they lost out in a party nominating referendum to Allan Benson and George Kirkpatrick of the Rand
School in New York, who achieved national reputations in a matter of months by writing popular antiwar articles.[12]

Although they were absorbed in a difficult campaign for election
reforms in 1916, the Oklahoma Socialists also worked zealously
against preparedness, which they declared "a menace to the working class." In February party members in the state legislature in-

9. *Socialist Party, Proceedings of the State Convention of Oklahoma,
1914* (Oklahoma City: Socialist Party of Oklahoma, 1914), 14.
10. H. L. Meredith, "Agrarian Socialism in Oklahoma" (Ph.D. dissertation,
University of Oklahoma, 1969), 164–65. See also H. G. Creel, "Oklahoma Socialists Take Drastic Action to Prevent War in This Country," *Appeal to
Reason* (Girard, Kan.), January 9, 1915.
11. *Appeal to Reason* (Girard, Kan.), December 25, 1915.
12. *Rebel* (Hallettsville, Tex.), February 19, 1916; David Shannon, *The Socialist Party of America, A History* (New York: Macmillan, 1955), 91.

troduced a resolution attacking increased military appropriations; it lost by a margin of 65 to 23, with some Democrats who supported Senator Gore's attempts to "preserve American neutrality" favoring the resolution.[13]

When Congressman Murray lost the Democratic nomination to a candidate who criticized Wilson's domestic and foreign policy and attacked the incumbent congressman's jingoism, other politicians took notice. Oklahoma Democrats were especially concerned at the 100 percent increase in registered voters the Socialist party recorded in the spring of 1916, despite the loss of support from blacklisted tenants in the southeast. The Socialists' campaign for their fair election law also picked up widespread support during the summer. On the eve of the election, *Harlow's* urged the Williams administration to shift its focus from new disfranchisement legislation to land reform. Regular Democrats should follow the progressive example of Senator R. L. Owen who responded to Socialist criticism by selling off his tenant farm in parcels and joining other reformers in calling for a graduated land tax. It was about time, the *Weekly* concluded a few weeks before the election, that politicians recognized "the reality of the tenant problem" and responded to the "socialists and the problems raised by them."[14]

At the same time the Wilson administration finally moved to quell farmer unrest by pushing the Federal Farm Loan Act through Congress. Although the act did not contain the "radical" rural credits proposals advocated by southwestern congressmen like Murray and Gore of Oklahoma and R. L. Henry of Texas, it was a popular piece of legislation that promised to reduce Democratic defections in the farm country. More important, as the presidential election approached Wilson altered his position on foreign policy, deemphasizing military preparedness and promising to keep the United States out of the European war.[15]

13. *Appeal to Reason* (Girard, Kan.), January 8, February 15, 1916.

14. Bryant, *Alfalfa Bill Murray*, 134–35, 140–41; *Appeal to Reason* (Girard, Kan.), May 27, 1916; *Harlow's Weekly* (Oklahoma City), October 18, 1916, p. 3.

15. Monroe Billington, *Thomas P. Gore: The Blind Senator from Oklahoma* (Lawrence: University of Kansas Press, 1967), 60–63; *Rebel* (Hallettsville, Tex.), August 9, 1916.

The southwestern Socialists became more disenchanted with Benson's lacklustre campaign the closer the election came, and party leaders prepared for the losses they would surely suffer at the polls. " 'He kept us out of war' is a powerful slogan," admitted the *Rebel*; it would probably capture many "radically minded voters" for the Democratic party. The "red card core" would remain loyal but the new converts would probably return to the party of their fathers. "These radical voters are not real Socialists," the Hallettsville weekly pointed out, "but they are the element we always depend upon for our converts and gains."[16]

The *Rebel*'s prediction proved accurate. Alan Benson, who ran a "miserable race," polled just 585,113 votes, about two-thirds of Debs's 1912 total. Only in Oklahoma did he improve upon his predecessor's performance. However, Benson ran 10,000 votes behind Fred Holt's 1914 total in the Sooner state and 6,000 votes behind E. R. Meitzen's 1914 total in the Lone Star state.[17] The Socialist party suffered greater set-backs in other states, but the southwestern Socialists took little comfort from the continued "strength and militancy" of their parties in the face of the appealing "peace and prosperity" campaign. For optimistic party loyalists who expected the growth of socialism to be irreversible, the 1916 election was a very discouraging experience.

Many Socialists cast their votes for Wilson to keep the country out of war rather than voting for Benson to register a protest against capitalism. "After all," Oscar Ameringer recalled, "the cooperative commonwealth was still a few years off while the war was already pounding at the gates."[18] The Socialist party also lost votes as a result of increased repression, especially in South Texas where Pancho Villa's border raids provoked a wave of reactionary hysteria and in southeastern Oklahoma where the night riding of the Working Class Union helped to produce a "mob spirit" and to justify the blacklisting of Socialist tenants. For example, in Val Verde

16. *Rebel* (Hallettsville, Tex.), November 11, 1916.
17. Shannon, *Socialist Party of America*, 91–92; *World Almanac, 1918*, p. 545.
18. Oscar Ameringer, *If You Don't Weaken: The Autobiography of Oscar Ameringer* (New York: Henry Holt, 1940), 309.

County, the only source of significant Socialist support in the Rio Grande Valley, the party's vote dropped from 75 in 1914 to 5 in 1916. And in Marshall County, Oklahoma, where Fred Holt had come within 7 votes of defeating his Democratic opponent in 1914, the Socialist vote dropped from 1,000 to 600, largely as a result of the blacklist against Red renters.[19]

Socialist leaders worried about the Democrats' discriminatory use of their new powers over the registration process but believed that Oklahoma voters would reject the unfair legislation enacted by the incumbent party in the statewide referendum held in conjunction with the 1916 presidential elections.[20] Their confidence was well placed, for the voters not only rejected the Democrats' election reforms by a 35,000-vote margin, they also endorsed the Socialist party's fair election law. The Socialists barely had time to celebrate their victory. Shortly after the referendum results were counted, the Democratic state election board nullified the Socialists' election law, because the measure received only a plurality, not a majority of the votes cast in the presidential election. The law would have won a clear majority, the Socialists protested, if the board had printed up enough ballots. Party lawyer Pat Nagle produced scores of affidavits from poll watchers documenting the shortage of referendum ballots; he also published a letter from one Democratic county chairman telling party members to come to the polls early in order to use the limited supply available. Nagle publicized this evidence in an advertisement carried by *Harlow's* and launched a joint suit with GOP lawyers to reverse the ruling of the state election board.[21] The law was on the side of the Republicans

19. *Harlow's Weekly* (Oklahoma City), May 20, 1916, pp. 5–6; *World Almanac, 1920*, p. 826; *Supplemental Report of the Secretary of State, 1916* (Austin: State of Texas Press, 1917), 47; Oliver Benson, *et al.*, *Oklahoma Votes, 1907–1962* (Norman: University of Oklahoma Press, 1964), 63, 78.

20. *Harlow's Weekly* (Oklahoma City), December 6, 1916, 5–6. Pat Nagle later charged that the Democrats' control of the election machinery in 1916 allowed them to exclude about one third of the Socialist vote. Memo to Socialist party National Executive Committee from Nagle, Oklahoma City, April 1, 1922, in Socialist Party Papers, Perkins Library, Duke University.

21. Harthshorne (Okla.) *Sun*, November 16, 1916; P. S. Nagle, "Will the People Defend Their Constitution?" *Harlow's Weekly* (Oklahoma City), November 29, 1916, pp. 12–13.

and Socialists, but the Democrats had time on their side. The case was postponed until after the war broke out. The GOP abandoned its efforts in the suit and finally in the fall of 1918 the courts ruled against the Socialists. By that time, the Socialist party needed more than a fair election law to protect its interests at the polls.

ANTI-WAR RESISTANCE AND THE GREEN CORN REBELLION

Despite the discouraging results of the 1916 election, throughout the winter of 1917 the southwestern Socialists continued their agitation against armed neutrality and preparedness. On April 7, one day after the United States declared war, the Socialist party held an emergency convention in St. Louis to respond to the crisis. Kate O'Hare of Kansas and Dan Hogan of Arkansas joined the majority on the resolutions committee in drafting a searing condemnation of militarism and national patriotism and in pledging the party to actively oppose the war.[22] Southwestern Reds began to organize antiwar opposition immediately, zeroing in on the conscription law then before Congress. In mid-April Tom Hickey used the first anniversary of the Dublin Easter Rebellion to remind the government that free men would fight to protect their rights even in wartime.[23] Some southwestern farmers who believed the draft violated their natural rights had already joined secret unions pledged to resist conscription by any means necessary. The Working Class Union sprang to life again in the spring of 1917 after having been seriously weakened by vigilant authorities during the previous fall. Early in May *Harlow's* reported that enlistments in the Oklahoma National Guard were very low in the eastern part of the state. "An organization of slackers, said to be an auxiliary of the IWW," was allegedly to blame. In fact, H. H. "Rube" Munson, an IWW member wanted by the law in Chicago, was active in the South Canadian River country recruiting WCU members pledged to resist the draft. When the Selective Service Act became law on May 18, outbursts of resistance were expected in this section, but only scattered inci-

22. Shannon, *Socialist Party of America*, 94.
23. *Rebel* (Hallettsville, Tex.), April 21, 1917.

dents occurred. In one of these incidents Claude, Ed, and Lee James of rural Pittsburg County, "who claimed to be second cousins of the late Jesse James of Missouri, created some excitement by announcing that they would not only refuse to register, but would resist any attempts to arrest them with rifles."[24]

Just before registration day on June 5, federal agents arrested thirty men in southeastern Oklahoma who signed a petition pledging to resist the draft by force. The prisoners included WCU State Secretary Homer Spence and Wobbly agitators "Rube" Munson and Cash Stephens. More dramatic events were unfolding in West Texas where the leaders of another secret group, the Farmers' and Laborers' Protective Association (FLAP), were being arrested for plotting a "seditious uprising."[25]

Red renters secretly organized the so-called FLAP in the summer of 1916 in order to prevent the landlords and bankers from destroying the movement with "the boycott and blacklist as they did in the case of the old Renters' Union." In 1917 G. T. Bryant, an Association leader with ties to the IWW, made contact with a similar group in Oklahoma. Along with other militants, he persuaded the FLAP membership to organize "armed and forcible opposition to the oppressions of the capitalist class." In February, 1917, the Association members met in Eastland County and voted to affiliate with the Oklahoma Working Class Union and to resist "any demands of the capitalist class to invade a foreign country or to shoot fellow workers." The delegates returned to their lodges and began to stockpile arms and ammunition while the leaders went across the Red River into Oklahoma to renew contact with the WCU and the IWW. After the conscription act was signed, the Association made plans for an armed uprising on registration day, June 5. Before the secret order could act, however, federal agents and Texas Rangers arrested its leaders. One member who armed himself to resist the draft on the designated day, died from twenty-three gunshot wounds inflicted by law officers who attempted to

24. *Harlow's Weekly* (Oklahoma City), May 16 and June 13, 1917.
25. *Ibid.*; *Arkansas Gazette* (Little Rock), May 21, 1917.

arrest him on his farm near Mineral Wells. Among those arrested peacefully were FLAP leader G. T. Bryant and the newly elected state secretary of the Texas Socialist party, W. P. Webb.[26]

During the roundup Tom Hickey was kidnapped from his farm near Brandenburg and held incommunicado for two days. Rangers and other lawmen arrested Hickey, but they did not attempt to indict him for conspiring with the FLAPs. The *Rebel* gave sensational coverage to the kidnapping of its famous editor and declared that it was time for the "weak-hearted" to drop out of the Socialist party, because its enemies had now served notice that they would stop at nothing until it was destroyed. That was the last issue of the *Rebel* ever published.[27]

On June 9, 1917, Postmaster General Burleson chose the Hallettsville journal as his first victim under the newly enacted, but as yet unsigned, Espionage Act. After being released because the government decided not to press conspiracy charges, Tom Hickey sent out a circular to his anxious Texas comrades explaining why he had been kidnapped and why his paper had been the first in the country to be banned from the mails. Both actions were the result of "war hysteria," but they were directed at the *Rebel* because it had exposed the mistreatment of the tenants on Burleson's Texas plantation. Hickey also charged that Attorney General Thomas W. Gregory had ordered his kidnapping because the *Rebel* exposed the business connections of the "trust-busting" lawyer from Austin. The Socialist weekly had "incurred the enmity of the large banking and landed interests in the state" whose political representatives held high positions in Washington. "The national administration has pillored [*sic*] itself before the world," Hickey declared. In singling out the *Rebel* for "persecution," it admitted being "controlled by Texas politicians of the landlord and banker stripe such as Col. E. M. House, Albert Burleson, et al.," who took "advantage of a national crisis to crucify a political opponent they could not

26. *Rebel* (Hallettsville, Tex.), August 5, 1916; *G. T. Bryant, et al.* v. *United States*, Brief for Defendants in Error, 3250, Fifth Circuit Court of Appeals, Northern District of Texas, February 6, 1919; New York *Times*, May 29, 1917; Fort Worth *Star Telegram*, June 5, 1917; Houston *Post*, June 23, 1917.
27. *Rebel* (Hallettsville, Tex.), June 2, 1917.

bribe or control."[28] Although the Socialist party had played no part in planning the FLAP uprising, Hickey's arrest and State Secretary Webb's indictment identified the party with sedition and made it easier for opponents to crush the Texas movement during the war.

Meanwhile, in Oklahoma registration day passed more quietly, but in July signs of a much larger underground draft-resistance movement appeared in the tenant districts of the old Indian Territory. In southern Pottawatomie County eight men were arrested in the Pink and Brown communities along the Canadian River for plotting "to resist the draft by force of arms"; they were allegedly members of a secret, radical group called the Jones Family, which had about three hundred members in the area.[29] This unusual organization, probably named for a family of "anti-slickers" active in Missouri during the 1840s, had some contact with Working Class Union organizers and "Rube" Munson, the Wobbly agitator, but its ideology and organization were quite "primitive."[30] Brought together hastily to resist the draft, the Jones Family had little of the class-conscious ideology the WCU had developed in the course of its militant struggles with landlords and bankers in the region. It drew less upon Socialist ideas and syndicalist tactics than it did upon the traditionally clannish resistance of southwestern "hillbillies" to government laws that violated their natural rights and to law enforcers who attempted to regulate their simple, "nonprogressive" communities. The ancestors of the Jones Family had been notorious for bushwacking federal "revenoorers" and Confederate draft recruiters. In 1917 they were simply carrying on a

28. T. A. Hickey, circular, "To the Friends of the *Rebel*," June 30, 1917, in Thomas A. Hickey Papers, Barker Library, University of Texas, Austin.

29. Shawnee (Okla.) *Daily News-Herald*, July 20, 1917. At about the same time, twenty-four men were also arrested in Rains County, Texas, for organizing "forcible resistance to the draft." This was the locale of the strong antiusury movement led by the Socialists in 1915, a movement that appealed to hundreds of farmers who thought their natural rights had been violated by the bankers. See H. C. Peterson and Gilbert Fite, *Opponents of War, 1917–1918* (Madison: University of Wisconsin Press, 1957), 38.

30. For a note on the original Jones Family see Richard Maxwell Brown, "The American Vigilante Tradition," in Hugh Davis Graham and Ted Robert Gurr (eds.), *The History of Violence in America* (New York: Bantam, 1969), 186, 92n.

long tradition of self-defense. Some members of the Family were Socialists; others were Democrats angry at President Wilson's breach of faith. And others were illiterate, nonpartisan tenants who simply thought the draft violated their rights. They were determined to resist being taken away from their families and sent far away to fight a bloody war they neither knew nor cared anything about.[31]

Although two of its leaders, "Rube" Munson and Homer Spence, had already been indicted for obstructing the draft, the Working Class Union continued to organize in eastern Oklahoma and by midsummer it had recruited a membership estimated at between eighteen thousand and thirty-five thousand.[32] On August 2, the Seminole County sheriff and some deputies set out from Wewoka to investigate mysterious radical activities in a district with WCU loyalties. The lawmen were ambushed and driven away by five black men who belonged to the secret order.[33] That night, just a day after the body of Oklahoma-born Wobbly, Frank Little, was found hanging from a trestle outside of Butte, Montana, the WCU called a secret meeting on a sandbar in the Canadian River and decided to take action.[34] Munson and Spence, who were free on bail, had been agitating in and around Seminole County for several days,

31. In other words, the Jones Family corresponds more closely than the Working Class Union to the "primitive rebel" groups which Hobsbawm describes in "pre-political" peasant societies. E. J. Hobsbawm, *Primitive Rebels: Studies in Archaic Forms of Social Movement in the 19th and 20th Centuries* (New York: W. W. Norton, 1965), 1–5. Several years later, J. Y. Sanders, former governor of Louisiana, told Covington Hall that he thought the men of the Jones Family rebelled against the draft because they had "Jeffersonian principles" that were more important than Socialist ideas. "They actually believed they had rights the government was bound to respect," Sanders said. Quoted in Covington Hall, "Labor Struggles in the Deep South" (Typescript in Howard-Tilton Library, Tulane University), 220.
32. Estimate on membership in *Daily Oklahoman* (Oklahoma City), August 11, 1917, and Shawnee (Okla.) *Daily News-Herald*, September 25, 1917.
33. Wewoka (Okla.) *Capital-Democrat*, August 9, 1917.
34. Shawnee (Okla.) *Daily News-Herald*, July 29, 1917. There is no evidence to show that Frank Little's lynching had anything to do with provoking an uprising, but the one-eyed Wobbly organizer was very popular among the Working Class Union members and his grisly death was well publicized in the local press. See, for example, *Daily Ardmorite* (Ardmore, Okla.), August 1, 1917.

urging resisters to arm themselves and to prepare for a fight. Sentiment against the war and the draft had been rising since the spring. As pressure for conscription increased, the isolated tenants of the old Indian Nations grew more determined to resist the patriotic demands of President Wilson and his agents in the county seats. They were not going to let the "Big Slick" in Washington send them off to die in France.[35]

On the morning of August 3, resisters from the WCU and the Jones Family gathered on a bluff near the farm of "old man" Spears who had raised the "red flag of rebellion" above his barn a few days before. During the night raiding parties went out to cut telegraph and telephone wires and to burn railroad bridges in the area. They also blew up some oil pipelines leading out of the Healdton fields. On the previous day, WCU agitators had been blamed for a spontaneous "political" strike at a large coal mine in Wilburton, where the Socialist party had one of its largest locals. The new secretary of District 21, a Democrat who had replaced Fred Holt, failed to persuade the militant miners to return to work. He suspended the charter of this UMW local which he said was under the influence of the IWW. Agents of resistance also moved into the poor cotton country south of the Canadian River, where they encouraged armed action against the draft. Incendiary posters like the following were found along the country roads in Marshall and Bryan counties: "Now is the time to rebel against this war with Germany boys. Get together boys and don't go. Rich mans war. Poor mans fight. If you dont go J. P. Morgan Co. is lost. Speculation is the only cause of the war. Rebel now."[36]

The main body of militants on Spears' Bluff gathered more supporters from the surrounding tenant country, including a group of black WCU sharecroppers and several Indians led by John Harjo, one of the many relatives of the Creek renegade, Crazy Snake, who

35. For more detailed accounts of these events see Charles C. Bush, "The Green Corn Rebellion" (M.A. thesis, University of Oklahoma, 1932); and John Womack, Jr., "Oklahoma's Green Corn Rebellion," typescript in his possession.

36. Harthshorne (Okla.) *Sun*, August 2, 1917; *Daily Ardmorite* (Ardmore, Okla.), August 6, 1917.

had led the last armed rebellion against white rule in the Indian Nations eight years before. A WCU organizer, W. L. Benefield, led the largest contingent, a group of about fifty well-armed tenants from the Lone Dove community near Saskawa. "Captain" Bill, wearing a sabre and a dashing red sash, took overall command of the resistance army at Spears' Bluff. Along with other revolutionaries, he railed against the "Big Slick" and the tyranny of conscription. "Rube" Munson told the men that other uprisings were occurring throughout the West. A large army of Wobblies would march on Washington to overthrow the government and put an end to the war and the draft. The Working Class Union should start its own march to the nation's capital, and link up with thousands of farmers and workers throughout the land who would also be up in arms. The Oklahoma rebels would be the vanguard of an army marching across the South to the sea, living on beef and ripe corn as it traveled. And so, this uprising came to be called the Green Corn Rebellion.

The insurgent farmers who gathered along the banks of the Canadian River on August 3 never started marching. A posse of seventy mobilized immediately after hearing about the resisters' violent activities and quickly advanced on the rebel stronghold. The undisciplined tenants disobeyed "Captain" Benefield's orders and fled when they saw the armed townsmen moving against them; the bloodless "battle" of Spears' Bluff was a rout. "The papers said we were cowards," a Green Corn rebel recalled, "but we weren't." Walter Strong explained, "Some of the men in the posse were neighbors of ours and we couldn't shoot 'em down in cold blood. That's the way we felt 'bout the Germans too. . . . We didn't have no quarrel with them at all."[37]

For the next week posses rounded up radicals, resisters, and suspected rebels. They fought several bloody skirmishes with backwoods renegades, but within a week the law enforcers had crushed

---

37. McAlester (Okla.) _News-Capital_, August 4, 18, 1917; Shawnee (Okla.) _Daily News-Herald_, August 5, 6, 7, 1917. Ned DeWitt interview with Walter Strong, Federal Writers' Project, W.P.A., in "Oil in Oklahoma," Box 43, Western History Collection, University of Oklahoma.

the organized militant antiwar movement in Oklahoma. Of the 450 men arrested for allegedly participating in the rebellion, 184 were indicted, 150 convicted, and in the fall about half that number sentenced to prison terms.[38] After the fear of lynch mobs receded, most of the men arrested in the roundup, including many Socialists who had had no part in the rebellion, were released from the state penitentiary at McAlester. The rebel leaders, including Tad Cumbie, Socialist party gubernatorial candidate in 1910, and the WCU captains, were given stiff sentences at Leavenworth, because they were responsible for "misleading" the ignorant farmers. Initially, however, patriotic Oklahomans urged severe punishment for all of those suspected of plotting or participating in the uprising, leaders and followers alike. On August 9, the editor of the commercial weekly in the Seminole County seat called for execution or life imprisonment for anyone involved in draft resistance. Former congressman William Murray, a prominent patriot, urged reserve units in every county to put down the resistance and "nip anarchy at the bud." If people did not obey the laws, Murray declared, "they should be set up against a hill and shot."[39]

Most of the county seat papers in the southeast buried news of the rebellion for fear of provoking further disturbances among the region's restless renters.[40] The city dailies commented extensively on the uprising, however. The Socialist party actively opposed armed resistance to the war and the draft, but because many of its members had been arrested in the roundup, Democratic editors and politicians assumed an intimate connection between socialism

38. *Second Report of the Provost Marshall General to the Secretary of War* (Washington, D.C.: Government Printing Office, 1919), 208–209. The first of these trials was conducted with some difficulty because the witnesses and defendants were unwilling to testify against the Working Class Union and the Jones Family. One man who belonged to both sects actually made an unsuccessful attempt to commit suicide. He said he would rather die than "tell things I knew would be against my neighbors." Shawnee (Okla.) *Daily News-Herald*, September 25, 1917.

39. Wewoka (Okla.) *Capital-Democrat*, August 9, 1917. Tulsa *Daily World* quoted in *Harlow's Weekly* (Oklahoma City), August 15, 1917, p. 6, and Murray quoted in Harthshorne (Okla.) *Sun*, August 9, 1917.

40. Virginia Pope, "The Green Corn Rebellion: A Case Study in Newspaper Self-Censorship" (M.A. thesis, Oklahoma A & M University, 1940), 25.

and the rebellion.[41] Some editors also identified the insidious influence of German agents and IWW organizers. The influential Tulsa *World* and other papers published near the oil fields worried about the Wobblies then organizing the booming petroleum industry and demanded the mobilization of "home guards" to prevent future subversion and rebellion. Governor R. L. Williams readily responded to their plea.[42]

Some of the more analytical editors blamed the uprising on "ignorance and poverty." If the tenants of southeastern Oklahoma had shared a "little of this war prosperity," the McAlester *News-Capital* remarked, the rebellion might not have occurred. The "deplorable conditions" under which these farmers lived stood as an "indictment against their more intelligent and prosperous neighbors, who have shut their eyes and permitted these people to grow up in ignorance and crime." A "good many of these farmers are the victims of landlordism," wrote State Senator John Globie in his newspaper. "These men realize that they are in no better condition than the peons of Mexico and the peasants of Russia. They revolted in the only way they knew." *Harlow's Weekly* went even further and blamed the state legislature for not heeding its repeated warnings about the "unendurable" conditions among Oklahoma tenants; when asked to relieve these conditions, the legislature had responded with a "hastily passed impotent graduated land tax, puerile anti-usury and 'home ownership' laws." The legislators had failed to pass any reforms that went to the "heart of the problem."[43]

However, none of these editors argued that "conditions" alone were responsible for the rebellion. Ignorance and poverty simply

41. *Ellis County Socialist* (Shattuck, Okla.), August 16, 1917. In addition to Tad Cumbie, other Socialist leaders arrested included Mark Reader, sheriff of McClain County; Joe Ottl, a congressional candidate from eastern Oklahoma; local leader Herman Hobbie of Coalgate; and several local office holders. McAlester (Okla.) *News-Capital*, November 24, 1917; Shawnee (Okla.), *Daily News-Herald*, August 6, 1917, Harthshorne (Okla.) *Sun*, August 14, 15, 1917; Ada (Okla.) *News Weekly*, August 9, 1917; Wewoka (Okla.) *Capital-Democrat*, August 9, 1917.
42. *Harlow's Weekly* (Oklahoma City), August 15, 1917, p. 6.
43. *Ibid.*, and August 8, 1917, p. 4.

made tenants susceptible to Socialist antiwar propaganda and the violent remedies offered by the WCU and the IWW. Since the radicals' constituents in eastern Oklahoma were largely "poor white trash," middle-class editors commented on the ignorant and lawless traits exploited by antiwar agitators. "Ignorance, inflamed by anarchistic leaders" had produced many outbursts of fanaticism in the past, observed the Shawnee *Herald*. The "gangs of hillsmen and agitators" who annoyed "the peace loving populace of the region" for years had lived like "cavemen" in the rugged woods and river bottoms of the old Indian Nations. They were violent, immoral people given to feuding and drunkenness. Few of them were church-going people and those who had religion were usually followers of the fanatical Holy Rollers.[44]

"The men who make up this element believe that all laws and conditions are against their kind," *Harlow's* remarked. "Some are descendants of the lawless element that entered the territory several decades ago while fleeing the law, and these have mingled with the migratory tenant farmers who have drifted in from Texas, Arkansas and Missouri." They owned very little, if any, property and existed by "cropping" and working as farm laborers. "Ignorant, and out of touch with the affairs of life," the Oklahoma City *Weekly* concluded, "they readily become the pliant tools of designing propagandists."[45]

44. Shawnee (Okla.) *Daily News-Herald*, August 7, 1917. The poor white tenants who took up arms in the Oklahoma cotton country were said to be "intolerant and superstitious" followers of emotional and often mystical holiness sects. A connection between their revivalism and their rebelliousness has been implied, but not clearly stated. See Bush, "Green Corn Rebellion," 3–7. Some of the holiness sects and backwoods preachers espoused pacifism, but their influence on the rebels is unclear. Most of the tenants in the Southwest participated in religious activities, including revivals, irregularly. One Working Class Union leader had been a Campbellite preacher, but he appealed to the resisters as a revolutionary, not as a revivalist. The rebellious renters undoubtedly responded to chiliastic rhetoric, but most of the ideology they absorbed was socialistic. Their motives, or the "legitimizing notions" of their rebellion, were more political than religious. For an account of armed draft resistance in the Southwest that was strictly motivated by fundamentalist faith see James F. Willis, "The Cleburne County Draft War," *Arkansas Historical Quarterly*, XXVI (1967), 24–39, an article on Jehovah's Witnesses in the Ozarks who violently opposed conscription.

45. *Harlow's Weekly* (Oklahoma City), August 8, 1917, p. 3.

Both fascinated and repelled by the poor white rebels, editors from the "electric light towns" described the "picturesque leaders of the old mountaineer type with long unkept hair and heavy beards" who appeared as "captains" with "flaming red sashes around their wastes [*sic*]" ready and willing to lead the "terrorists" into battle. The "fighting young blades" who followed these "fanatics" found out that "times had changed since the Dalton, Starr and Jennings gangs had their way in Oklahoma," one editor wrote. They found that "law-abiding Oklahomans would much rather serve in posses to enforce the law than to ride and shoot against it."[46]

This "lawless element" annoyed townspeople and authorities with their bootlegging, moonshining, and poaching. The ignorant, backward folk of the cotton country seemed contemptuous of community leaders and all that was done in the name of progress and morality. They disobeyed prohibition laws, passed for the good of the community, dynamited dipping vats, built to protect stock from Texas fever, and, in the early days, even wrecked track and fired on trains when the first railroad was built through the region in order to promote its economic development.[47] It was no coincidence that eastern Oklahoma had one of the highest bank robbery rates in the nation or that it was plagued with bootleggers, night riders, and "anarchistic agitators." The blacks and Indians of this troubled section were almost as dangerous as the poor whites. The gunfight between black United Socialists and lawmen at Muskogee in 1907, the violent attacks on Jim Crow trains and stations in 1908, and Crazy Snake's armed rebellion in 1909 made this clear enough. It was no surprise to most resident commentators that these militant minorities had also joined in the Green Corn Rebellion.[48]

46. Shawnee (Okla.) *Daily News-Herald*, August 7, 1917; McAlester (Okla.) *News-Capital*, August 13, 1917.
47. Shawnee (Okla.) *Daily News-Herald*, August 7, 1917; Wewoka (Okla.) *Capital-Democrat*, August 19, 1917.
48. Shawnee (Okla.) *Daily News-Herald*, August 7, 1917; Wewoka (Okla.) *Capital-Democrat*, August 19, 1917. On the various patterns of resistance adopted by blacks and Indians in Oklahoma see Muskogee (Okla.) *Phoenix*, March 24, 1907; Harthshorne (Okla.) *Sun*, February 20, 1918; and *Daily Oklahoman* (Oklahoma City), March 28–31, 1909. In June of 1918 rumors spread

The historian of the rebellion also emphasized the ignorance and superstition of the poor tenants. Illiterate and "dumbly enduring," they turned to socialism "as a sort of gospel of despair" even though its "finer tenets were but faintly understood." Oscar Ameringer, who attempted to persuade the WCUs to alter their suicidal course, argued that this interpretation overemphasized the ignorance of the rebel farmers. As he wrote later: "Illiterate, poorly schooled, doped with all the mental poison their 'betters' could pour into them yes; but ignorant, no. There was a great deal of native intelligence among these people. Their state of illiteracy protected them, partially at least, against the flood of lying propaganda with which their 'betters' of press pulpit and rostrum deluged the country, while their native common sense allowed them to see through the pretensions of the warmongers better than could many a Ph.D."[49] The rebels seemed ignorant because "Rube" Munson and others had "deluded" them into thinking of themselves as the vanguard of a nationwide uprising against the draft. They may have been taken in by promises of help from a chimerical Wobbly "army," but they certainly knew they were outnumbered in Oklahoma. The poor white resisters were intelligent enough "to see the irony of their situation," Ameringer thought. "Naturally given to direct action or self-help" they took up arms to defend their rights, even though they knew defeat was likely.[50]

---

that about two hundred blacks and Indians, including followers of Crazy Snake, were gathered at Hickory Ground, the scene of the first Smoked Meat Rebellion, to plot another uprising—this time against the draft. The "home guard" of Henryetta was sent out to patrol the area. *Harlow's Weekly* (Oklahoma City), June 12, 1918, 6–7.

49. Bush, "Green Corn Rebellion," 1–2; Ameringer, *If You Don't Weaken*, 350. Walter Strong, a Green Corn rebel, later described the simple motives of his comrades. "We decided we wasn't gonna fight somebody else's war for 'em and we refused to go. We didn't volunteer and we didn't answer the draft. Most of us had wives and kids and we didn't wanna leave them here to do all the work of harvestin' and have us go over to France and fight people we didn't have anything against. We didn't have any bands and uniforms and that stuff down there in the sandhills so that crap about the Germans comin' over here when they finished up the English and French didn't go over with us." DeWitt interview with Strong, Federal Writers' Project, W.P.A., in Western History Collection.

50. Ameringer, *If You Don't Weaken*, 350.

The Green Corn rebels probably did not understand the "finer tenets" of socialism or appreciate the importance of certain party practices (disciplined nonviolence, for instance), but they were not ignorant night riders or religious fanatics, and their rebellion was certainly not "apolitical." They followed Eugene Debs, Kate O'Hare, Ameringer, and the others because these popular propagandists talked about politics and economics in a simple, concrete way that tenants and workers could understand. The rebels also understood and accepted the Socialist party's analysis of the causes of World War I and its reasons for opposing intervention; they simply rejected its nonviolent tactics.[51]

The Green Corn rebels' "hazy philosophy of violence" derived not from their connections with socialism and syndicalism (both the Socialist party and the IWW opposed violent resistance to the war) or with apocalyptic religious sects (which tended to be nonviolent in an apolitical sense). The violent tactics came partly from the traditional practices of prepolitical vigilantes and outlaws and partly from the militant sections of the Socialist union movement (the blacklisted Timber Workers, the threatened miners at Prairie Creek, and the frustrated radical renters who departed from the legal tactics of Socialist party unions). In any case, these forceful methods were developed in the context of an increasingly violent class struggle. The insurrectionists of 1917 aimed their uprising at the war and military conscription, but their action was linked to a long chain of confrontations between the rural poor and the propertied townspeople of the cotton country.[52]

51. For another view, which emphasizes the parochial aspects of the rebellion, see Garin Burbank, "The Social Origins of Agrarian Socialism in Oklahoma, 1910–1920" (Ph.D. dissertation, University of California, Berkeley, 1974), 213–15.

52. Shannon, *Socialist Party of America*, 106. Despite the "anarcho-syndicalism" of the Green Corn rebels, the uprising of 1917 cannot really be called a proletarian or "red" movement. Nor can it be termed a "pre-political" peasant revolt, or "green rising." For an argument to this effect, see W. B. Bizzel, *The Green Rising: An Historical Survey of Agrarianism* (New York: Macmillan, 1926), 3. The tenants who launched the Green Corn Rebellion had more in common with the American proletariat than they did with the peasantry in countries like Mexico. Their ideology was not primarily millenarian or agrarian, though the rebels' rhetoric sometimes revealed the influ-

The capitalists of this region were aggressive entrepreneurs who succeeded in exploiting cheap leases on Indian lands and cheap labor on coal, oil, and cotton lands.[53] Unlike the smaller property owners in the old Oklahoma Territory to the west, these rugged businessmen on the "east side" included not just the prosperous bankers and landlords, like Governors Cruce and Williams who lived comfortably in the county seat towns, but also millionaire oil and real estate men who lived in McAlester, Muskogee, and Tulsa. Invariably civic leaders who "boosted" their towns and the Democratic party as aggressively as they did their own businesses, these "big men," the winners of the Oklahoma sweepstakes, turned their considerable energies to boosting the war effort (through which they made substantial profits) and to suppressing disloyalty and dissent. Hitherto divided over various issues, like prohibition, and various political candidates, these capitalists united to crush the enemies of the nation—the Socialist party, the Working Class Union, and the IWW, organizations that also happened to be the enemies of the region's landlords, bankers, and oilmen.

One Oklahoma historian who grew up on the "east side" said that the war furthered the polarization of the region's two distinct groups, the propertied "literate, urban class" and the largely dispossessed "rural illiterate class." Virginia Pope recalled "a distinct class consciousness there"; people from town did not "mix socially with the tenants."[54] They thought the poor whites were lazy and ignorant, if not immoral and dangerous. They made fun of the tenants' clothes, speech patterns, and "old time religion," but they were also afraid of the renters' radical views and violent, lawless "traits." When the war broke out, the townspeople responded enthusiastically to patriotic appeals while the country folk along the South Canadian River remained angry and cynical. When the rural poor saw that the same "comfortable commercial classes" who

---

ence of these earlier traditions of protest; rather, their ideas were secular and modern, formed by socialism and anarcho-syndicalism.

53. For an excellent analysis of capitalist development in eastern Oklahoma see Charles W. Holman, "Preliminary Report on the Land Question in the United States," February 17, 1915, CIR Records, 30–46.

54. Pope, "Green Corn Rebellion," 43.

mocked and exploited them "became the leaders of the patriotic movements, they came to hate patriotism," Peterson and Fite noted. "If those whom they regarded as their oppressors were in favor of it, it must be wrong."[55]

Throughout the South and parts of the West, however, farmers and laborers, who were treated in a similar way by propertied townspeople, responded more favorably to the patriotic demands of their social "betters" and political leaders. Rural folk reacted differently in southeastern Oklahoma, because the Socialists had politicized their resentment of the town "exploiters" and provided an analysis of the war in Europe as a conflict fought solely in the interest of the capitalist class.

The Suppression of Southwestern Socialism

The Oklahoma party officially opposed armed resistance, but since many of its members had joined the Green Corn Rebellion, authorities arrested innocent red carders along with the armed rebels. All kinds of radicals were on the "receiving end" of the "white terror" that swept the state after the uprising. "All Socialists were considered guilty until proven innocent," one historian wrote; "no distinctions" were made during the "round up." In short, opponents of socialism in Oklahoma used the wave of reaction that broke after the rebellion as an opportunity to destroy a political party that could not be as seriously weakened without adopting thoroughgoing forms of repression.[56]

Draft resistance in Oklahoma did not end with the suppression of the Green Corn Rebellion and the speedy conviction of its leaders. For weeks thereafter, *Harlow's* reported, "echoes of the rebellion were heard" in many other sections. Incendiaries committed several acts of sabotage in the southeastern "infected" region.[57] "Manifestations of trouble" were even reported in the west-

55. Peterson and Fite, *Opponents of War*, 41.
56. Ameringer, *If You Don't Weaken*, 355; Bush, "Green Corn Rebellion," 38, 40; Peterson and Fite, *Opponents of War*, 40–41.
57. *Harlow's Weekly* (Oklahoma City), August 15, 1917, pp. 3–4. One of the most dramatic incidents occurred after seven WCUs (six of them black) were rounded up around the Lone Dove community and jailed in McAlester.

ern counties where the wheat farmers supported Senator Gore's lonely battle against the war and the draft. In August, these supporters gathered at a convention of the rejuvenated Farmers' Union and passed resolutions supporting every one of the senator's antiwar votes.[58] Although the western radical agitators, including Socialist congressional candidate O. E. Enfield and William Madison Hicks of the World Peace League, were arrested for supposedly encouraging forcible resistance to the draft, these farmers were "better situated and better educated" than the Green Corn rebels in the cotton country "and saw the futility of opposing the war by force," Ameringer wrote. "However, even in that territory, I knew of many honest farmers, who, years after the armistice, still shot jack rabbits with the Marlin rifles they had purchased for entirely different reasons."[59]

Although the Socialist party suffered grave consequences as a result of its indirect association with the Green Corn Rebellion, a much smaller organization, the IWW, became the greatest spectre in the minds of patriotic Oklahomans in the late summer and fall of 1917. The Wobblies actively organized in the wheat and oil fields, but they probably recruited less than a thousand members in Oklahoma. "Rube" Munson and several of the WCU leaders who had planned the rebellion were Wobblies, but there was no proof that the IWW national office had had anything to do with encouraging, let alone financing, the uprising. Actually, the One Big Union's official position on war resistance was less militant than that of the Socialist party and it certainly did not encourage vio-

---

Fellow union members set fire to a grain elevator in McAlester and threatened to "burn the town" if their "boys" were not turned loose. McAlester (Okla.) *News-Capital*, August 6, 11, 1917. As late as October resisters burned many gins in Pontotoc County and attacked the publishing plant of the Ada (Okla.) *News Weekly*, the county's militaristic commercial weekly. *Harlow's Weekly* (Oklahoma City), October 31, 1917, p. 8.

58. *Harlow's Weekly* (Oklahoma City), August 29, 1917, p. 5. Although in the summer of 1917 Senator Gore was attacked by almost every newspaper in the state for his antiwar stands, he claimed that his constituent mail supported him twenty to one. Billington, *Thomas P. Gore*, 86.

59. Peterson and Fite, *Opponents of War*, 38; Ameringer, *If You Don't Weaken*, 351.

lent direct action like its agrarian stepchild, the Working Class Union. Nevertheless, the IWW seemed to be blamed for every crime in Oklahoma in late 1917, from wrecking trains and blowing up waterworks in Miami and Henryetta, to gunning down a deputy sheriff in Muskogee and arming black field hands in various areas. "The mere mention of the IWW seemed to bring on visions of impending revolution," wrote two Oklahoma historians.[60]

On October 29, 1917, a bomb exploded in the Tulsa home of a wealthy oilman, J. Edgar Pew. Provoked by sensational newspaper articles, some hysterical citizens immediately assumed the hated IWW responsible for the act. Hundreds of businessmen and professionals, including some of the leading oilmen in the country, responded immediately to the Tulsa *World's* dramatic call to organize a "home guard." This call to action came at the same time that federal agents were busy rounding up Wobblies in Oklahoma and Kansas (where the Agricultural Workers' Organization was strong) and it came on the same day that ten thousand oil workers in Texas and Louisiana went out on strike. Texas strike leaders pledged not to tolerate the IWW, but Oklahoma oilmen still worried about a Wobbly-led oil strike north of the Red River, a concern undoubtedly linked to their enthusiastic participation in the "home guards."[61]

On November 5, Tulsa police raided the IWW hall and arrested eleven men on vagrancy charges. No evidence connected them to the bombing of Pew's home, but three days later a jury convicted them largely on the basis of the defendants' views toward the war and the government. Six Wobbly witnesses who came forward to

60. Melvyn Dubofsky, *We Shall Be All: A History of the Industrial Workers of the World* (Chicago: Quadrangle, 1969), 357; McAlester (Okla.) *News-Capital*, August 5, 1917; Shawnee (Okla.) *Daily News-Herald*, August 18, 22, September 25, 1917; Peterson and Fite, *Opponents of War*, 64, 171.

61. See McAlester (Okla.) *News-Capital*, November 1, 1917; Houston *Daily Post*, November 1, 2, 1917; *Oil Weekly* (Houston), December 14, 1917. For an exaggerated estimation of the IWW menace in Oklahoma, given by the head of the Councils of Defense, see John B. Meserve, "I.W.W. and Pro-German Activities in Tulsa, Oklahoma," January 26, 1918, in War Record Office, "Records of the Council for National Defense," Box 730, File 278, National Archives.

testify for the defense were also arrested, tried, and convicted. "These are no ordinary times," the presiding judge explained.[62]

The Tulsa *World* called the three-day trial a waste of time, and in an editorial entitled "Get out the Rope," declared: "If the IWW . . . gets busy in your neighborhood, kindly take the occasion to decrease the supply of hemp. A knowledge of how to tie a knot that will stick may come in handy in a few days. It is no time to dally with enemies of the country. . . . The first step in the whipping of Germany is to strangle the IWW's. Kill 'em just as you would any other kind of snake. Don't scotch 'em: kill 'em! It is no time to waste money on trials and continuances and things like that."[63] On the night this editorial appeared, a mob calling itself the Knights of Liberty broke into the Tulsa jail, took the Wobbly prisoners outside of the city in autos, whipped them severely, and poured hot tar on their wounds. Pleased with the action taken by this "patriotic group," the *World* explained that the vigilante group was composed of that "sterling element of citizenship, that class of taxpaying and orderly people who are most of all committed to the observance of the law."[64]

The hysteria over the "IWW menace" spread from Tulsa to other cities in eastern Oklahoma that fall, but the Wobblies did not allow vigilante threats to drive them out of Oklahoma. Although the Knights of Liberty action at Tulsa and the militarization of the oil fields prevented the Texas strike from spreading north, the IWW still remained active in the booming Oklahoma petroleum industry.[65]

62. Peterson and Fite, *Opponents of War*, 172.
63. Tulsa *Daily World*, November 9, 1917.
64. *Ibid.*, November 12, 1917. See also National Civil Liberties Bureau, "The 'Knights of Liberty' Mob at Tulsa, Oklahoma" (New York: American Civil Liberties Union, 1918). Also see Clayton R. Koppes, "The Kansas Trial of the IWW, 1917–1919," *Labor History*, XVI (1975), 338–58. Caroline Lowe, the veteran Socialist organizer, served as assistant council for the defense in the Wobblies 1918 trial in Wichita. She found it very difficult to raise defense funds, but Alex Howat and the Kansas miners of UMW District 14 proved unusually generous; they still believed an injury to one was an injury to all.
65. Peterson and Fite, *Opponents of War*, 175–76; Tulsa *Daily World*, November 24, 1917; Healdton (Okla.) *Herald* quoted in *Harlow's Weekly* (Okla-

However, the first "red scare" in the fall of 1917 did destroy the larger but far more vulnerable Socialist party organization. The Oklahoma party was already crippled by suppression of its newspapers, by local as well as federal sedition laws which made public speaking impossible in many towns and cities, and by the arrest and constant surveillance of many of its leaders after the Green Corn Rebellion. Therefore, the party was not prepared for a renewed wave of harassment and intimidation. As Pat Nagle, "the real head of the Oklahoma socialist movement," wrote to Roger Baldwin of the American Civil Liberties Union in November, a "reign of terror," provoked by the press and the "oil barons" in order to destroy the IWW, was being used by the Democratic machine to eliminate an increasingly powerful political competitor whose influence had not been reduced with traditional appeals to reformism and racism.[66] The Democrats, who were still concerned about the joint Socialist-GOP suit that challenged their new controls over the election process, painted the Socialists with the red brush of treason and eventually forced the nervous Republicans to abandon their "disloyal" allies. State Secretary H. M. Sinclair tried to maintain some semblance of party activity in December by requesting the appointment of Socialist jury commissioners in counties where Socialist party candidates had received a significant minority of the vote. A district judge ignored the legality of the request and refused to allow the appointments because Socialists who held "revolutionary views" had been "indicted at the bar of public opinion for insubordination to their government." In 1918 the semiofficial Councils of Defense, composed largely of businessmen, editors, and landlords, took over the task of hunting down Socialists, but by this time the once-powerful Oklahoma Socialist party resembled a ghost of its former self.[67]

---

homa City), December 12, 1917, pp. 3–4; and Meserve, "I.W.W. and Pro-German Activities in Tulsa, Oklahoma."

66. P. S. Nagle to Roger Baldwin, November 24, 1917, in American Civil Liberties Union Files, XXXVI, 1, New York Public Library.

67. *Harlow's Weekly* (Oklahoma City), November 7, 1917, p. 5, December 12, 1917, p. 5. Also see Garin Burbank, "The Disruption and Decline of the Oklahoma Socialist Party," *Journal of American Studies*, VII, No. 2 (1973), 133–52.

As a result of this repression, some of the most committed Oklahoma Socialists joined their comrades from the Midwest and Southwest in a "retreat" to a utopian Socialist colony near Fallon, Nevada. Originally founded by Job Harriman in 1914, the colony was taken over by C. V. Eggleston, an energetic Oklahoma promoter who wanted to use it as a base from which to sweep Nevada for the Socialist party in 1916. H. H. Stallard, a well-known western Oklahoma Socialist, publicized Nevada City on the encampment circuit and Fred Warren, formerly the managing editor of the *Appeal to Reason*, took over the colony's newspaper and used it to advertise the settlement as a "refuge" in the growing militaristic storm.[68]

Warren and the other colonists who had grown pessimistic about the viability of Socialist political action, helped reawaken the escapist communitarian tradition in native American socialism that had been expressed in several earlier periods, notably in the late 1890s by Debs, who wanted to start a "cooperative commonwealth" in the West, and by Warren's mentor, J. A. Wayland, who had actually founded a utopian colony at Ruskin, Tennessee. Between 1900 and 1912, when the Socialists' electoral strategy seemed to be working, utopianism receded, but with the outbreak of the war, increased repression, and political reversals, it reappeared, notably in the form of colonies at New Llano, Louisiana, and Nevada City.[69]

Originally most of the settlers who came to the desert colony in Nevada were westerners, but by late 1916 and early 1917, when it was being advertised mainly as a pacifist settlement, "the Oklahoma contingent began to overshadow all other elements." When a Sooner Socialist, the rotund promoter R. E. Bray, took over as manager at the end of 1917, he launched an advertising campaign

68. See Wilbur S. Shepperson, *Retreat to Nevada: A Socialist Colony of World War I* (Reno: University of Nevada Press, 1966).

69. In 1917 about two hundred Socialists who had founded the Llano Colony near Los Angeles moved to a new site near Leesville, Louisiana, in the old "infected area" where the Brotherhood of Timber Workers had been strong five years earlier. The colony grew steadily and in 1918 attracted a new group of twenty-five Socialist families from Texas. See Bill Murrah, "Llano Cooperative Colony, Louisiana," *Southern Exposure*, I, Nos. 3 and 4 (1974), 92.

to recruit "more Oklahoma comrades," because they made the "best boosters and colonists." Although Bray and fellow promoter from western Oklahoma, H. H. Stallard, abandoned the Socialist party and endorsed the prowar position of the *New Appeal to Reason*, antiwar Sooners kept coming to the colony. When Nevada City reached its peak population in January, 1918, just after the first "red scare," fifty-eight of the two hundred residents were Oklahomans. People in the area called it an "Okie colony."[70] They could not know that this was an advance guard of the "routed armies" of Okies that would invade the West during the Great Depression.

But although a few hardcore Socialist farmers retreated to Nevada in 1917 and 1918, the vast majority remained in the Southwest, unwilling or unable to make the trip. At home they faced intimidation and repression that forced them to remain silent, but for the most part they did not follow the example of Bray, Stallard, and some *Appeal* editors who supported the war, despite the strong pressure the county Councils of Defense exerted upon known Socialists. The members of these patriotic organizations acted as spies who were on the lookout for any statements less than enthusiastic about the war; they also volunteered as enforcers who hunted down "slackers," and as boosters who pushed citizens to buy their quota of "liberty bonds." The county councils were invariably directed by the leading banker, lawyer, and editor, appointed directly by Governor Williams.[71] Often important backers of the Democratic party, these patriotic activists used their wide-ranging powers to settle old scores with their political opponents.

70. Bray's remark about boosters suggests that rather than being tenants most Oklahoma colonists were probably more prosperous farm-owning Socialists from the west. Shepperson, *Retreat to Nevada*, 75, 93.

71. O. A. Hilton, "The Oklahoma Council of Defense and the First World War," *Chronicles of Oklahoma*, XX (1942), 18–24. For example, the Oklahoma County Council of Defense was composed of sixty-eight bankers, thirty-nine editors, thirty-five lawyers, twenty-three merchants, twenty-one farmers, twenty-one businessmen (including four oilmen), four clerks and doctors, two mayors, a priest, a worker, and a lone female volunteer who listed her occupation as "club woman." Memo to assistant chief clerk, War Department, from secretary, Oklahoma County Council of Defense, October 12, 1917, "Records of the Council for National Defense," National Archives.

The Councils of Defense made coordinated efforts to suppress dissent throughout the nation, but they were especially effective in Oklahoma because of the important "part played by the state administration in encouraging or at least, countenancing hysteria." R. L. Williams, the minority governor of 1914, nursed a strong grudge against the Socialist party, exacerbated by the party's exposé of the way his tenant farmers were treated. Needless to say, Democratic politicians and property owners who staffed the county councils shared this hostility. The letters they wrote to Governor Williams in 1917 and 1918 "suggested the irresistible opportunity" the war presented "as a pretext to wreck the Socialist movement."[72]

Initially, the councils organized a massive propaganda campaign, assisted by George Creel's Committee on Public Information, to counter "German and Socialist" antiwar propaganda which had allegedly "flooded" the state systematically in 1916 and 1917. Anti-German hysteria in the Southwest caused much suffering and several deaths in the region's tiny foreign-born communities. The "socialist menace" also concerned patriotic citizens' groups. "As persuasion gave way to coercion . . . the patriotic leaders of the councils tended to add suppression of Socialism to the worthy objects of their war work," one historian of Oklahoma politics wrote. "Socialist agitators were silenced and suspected sympathizers escorted from the state with the tacit approval of duly elected county councilmen."[73]

The repression following the Green Corn Rebellion thus continued through the "red scare" in the fall of 1917 and destroyed the Socialist party in eastern Oklahoma. But some Socialist activity continued in the western part of the state, where the party was

72. James B. Scales, "Political History of Oklahoma, 1907–1949" (Ph.D. dissertation, University of Oklahoma, 1949), 192.

73. Hilton, "Oklahoma Council of Defense," 24. For evidence of the Texas councils' concern about Socialists and Germans see T. H. Postell to State Council of Defense, August 1, 1917, and J. F. Carl to R. E. L. Knight, November 27, 1918, both in Texas War Records, Barker Library, University of Texas, Austin. For a description of attacks on Germans in Oklahoma, see *Harlow's Weekly* (Oklahoma City), April 3, 1918, pp. 8–9; quote from Scales, "Political History of Oklahoma," 191–92. Also see Burbank, "Disruption and Decline of Oklahoma Socialist Party," 135–43.

not so closely associated with violent resistance. For example, Oscar Ameringer, who returned to Oklahoma from Milwaukee in 1916, actively solicited contributions in the west for a new Socialist daily he hoped to start in Oklahoma City. Ameringer and Freda Hogan of Huntington, Arkansas, actually managed to start publishing their *Oklahoma Leader* in time for the depressing 1918 campaign, with help from their Milwaukee comrades and from the Socialists of western Oklahoma who happily rid themselves of the hated "liberty bonds" the Councils of Defense had forced them to buy. The party still pursued its joint suit with the GOP to enact the fair election law, even though most Republicans, with the notable exception of State Chairman Arthur Geissler, had "practically abandoned" their allies. Organizers of the Nonpartisan League from North Dakota also made some progress among the western Oklahoma wheat farmers with the assistance of John Simpson, the militant, antiwar leader of the resurgent Farmers' Union. In 1918 the Nonpartisan League hoped to pick up recruits from the suppressed Socialist party, but, despite its secret organizing tactics and meticulous attempts to avoid making "disloyal" statements, the councils drove these new "nonpartisan" radicals from the state by breaking up their meetings.[74]

The League also recruited in Texas, especially in the western counties where it merged with the Socialist party. Hickey, Hall, and the Meitzens all endorsed the Nonpartisan League because it was not tainted with disloyalty and because it supported essentially the same immediate demands as the Texas Socialist party. They even went to North Dakota to work with the Townley movement. But the repressive political climate on the southern Great Plains prevented the growth of this organization, which was thriving in the North. The county councils were as effective in suppressing the Nonpartisan League in Texas as they were in Oklahoma.[75]

74. Ameringer, *If You Don't Weaken*, 312–13; *Harlow's Weekly* (Oklahoma City), November 7, 1917, p. 5; Gilbert Fite, "The Nonpartisan League in Oklahoma," *Chronicles of Oklahoma*, XXIV (1946), 146–57.

75. Hickey, circular to "Texas Comrades," December 22, 1917, in Hickey Papers; San Antonio *Express*, November 15, 1917. See also E. R. Meitzen, "The Nonpartisan League, Its Methods and Principles: A Speech to South-

Despite the token activity in western Oklahoma, State Secretary "Heck" Sinclair reported his party in desperate straits at the end of 1917. Membership fell from about 10,000 in 1916 to 3,500 and the number of locals dropped from 1,100 to 470. "The falling off to this extent can be attributed mainly to the intimidation used against socialist activity," Sinclair declared. "On account of the trying times as a result of the war and acts by congress we were forced to cease political activity to a large extent." Although Oklahoma Socialists were dismayed by the prowar position the *New Appeal* adopted late in 1917, no party leaders of any importance followed suit, with the exception of Bray and Stallard, the Nevada City promoters. The fearful rank and file stopped paying dues and remained silent, but they did not join enthusiastically in the war effort or join the party of the man who had broken his pledge to keep the country out of war.[76]

Yet even in the last months of the war, patriotic Democrats worried about Socialist intransigence. In the spring of 1918, *Harlow's* described "strong arm squadrons" at work in western Oklahoma ferreting out slackers and dissenters. In Pat Nagle's home county of Kingfisher, for example, where the Socialist party had made great gains in 1916, the Council of Defense "decreed that those who were able to pay for liberty bonds and have not done so shall be given punishment never before attempted in the United States." The punishment involved publishing the names of slackers, ostracizing them socially, and refusing to sell them goods or to extend them credit. The councils were also active in other strong Socialist areas in the west, like Dewey County, where O. E. Enfield, the Socialist party's militant antiwar congressional candidate, had polled 33 percent of the vote in 1916. The council removed Dewey County schoolteachers who told their students the war was being fought for the benefit of the rich, and councilmen also claimed credit for

ern Farmers" (Waco, Tex.: Nonpartisan League, 1918). On the council's reaction to the Nonpartisan League, see J. F. Carl to "Various County Councils," April 25, 1918, in Texas War Records.

76. Quoted in Alvin Rucker, "Socialism is Definitely Falling Behind in Oklahoma," *Harlow's Weekly* (Oklahoma City), January 2, 1918, pp. 8–9, July 10, 1918, p. 5.

collecting information that helped convict Enfield and other local Socialist leaders of sedition.[77]

The councils not only silenced antiwar Socialists; they insisted on forcing opponents of the war to participate fully in domestic patriotic activities, especially the liberty loan drives. In Beckham County, for example, where Enfield had polled 27 percent of the vote in 1916, the council put an end to antiwar dissent when 20 car-loads of its members tarred and feathered William Madison Hicks of the World Peace League in the summer of 1917. "From that day on our difficulties were slight," county chairman Sam Williams reported; only "a few with religious scruples and a few Redflaggers" still dared to speak out. "What a great thing it is to have a Council of Defense . . . [to] take care of the slacker, the slicker and the dissenter," Williams wrote to his superior in Oklahoma City.[78]

Council chairman Williams, a successful businessman who owned several cotton gins in the county seat, was embarrassed by the wretched performance of Beckham County in the first liberty loan drive; this reflected badly on his reputation as a booster. When the county filled only 17.5 percent of its quota on the first drive, the state director told Williams to "make every effort to round up slackers" and to forward the full details of each case to Oklahoma City so that a "government man" could be sent out to offer assistance.[79] In the summer of 1918 liberty bond salesmen, assisted by council "strong arm squadrons," launched a determined drive to see that Beckham County filled more of its quota. Tenants and poor farmers complained to Williams that they were being coerced into making pledges they could not possibly fulfill whereas absentee landlords and town merchants escaped with low

77. *Harlow's Weekly* (Oklahoma City), May 22, 1918, p. 6; Oklahoma Councils of Defense, *Sooners in the War*, 37, in Oklahoma Historical Society.

78. Oklahoma Councils of Defense, *Sooners in the War*, 28. Sam Williams to G. W. Barnes, December 31, 1917, in Western History Collection. For Williams' request for action against a troublesome Socialist candidate see Sam Williams to J. M. Aydelotte, May 21, 1918, in Western History Collection.

79. Barnes to Sam Williams, May 23, June 29, 1918, in Western History Collection.

quota assignments.[80] One complaint came from Mayfield where a farmer explained that during a "Thrift Stamp" meeting at the Friendship schoolhouse "poor people that did not own any property at all and did not have a dollar to there [*sic*] name was Bull Dozed and made to pay as much as the men that was worth 10 to 15 teen tousand [*sic*] dollars."[81] More prosperous Socialists also resisted the liberty bond drive. A local chairman reported to Williams just after the second campaign began that a widow named Hildebrand who owned "a good farm and no mortgage against it" refused to "pay money to murder anyone" and said she "could not pledge" even though she had money. She was "a Socialist of the rankest," the salesman said, and should be "looked after" by the councils "or any other means."[82] By midsummer of 1918 Sam Williams reported to his superiors that the more forceful tactics adopted by his salesmen and councilmen had allowed Beckham County to increase its quota percentage dramatically, but he was still worried at its failure to achieve 100 percent Americanism. A large number of farmers were still recalcitrant. "It is imperative that we get quick action and attend to these dissenters or all of our efforts and hard work . . . will be nullified," he wrote.[83] The councils remained frustrated by their inability to obtain full participation in the war effort, but by the summer of 1918 they had reduced the Socialist party to the status of a paper organization and had limited "dissent" to individual acts of resistance to patriotic campaigns. There was violence involved in this campaign (in which German citizens were victimized more than American Socialists),[84] but the effectiveness of the effort depended less on exercising coercion than on creating a pervasive climate of fear.

80. W. A. Sanders, *et al.*, to Sam Williams, July 1, 1918, H. W. Advis to Sam Williams, June 30, 1918, D. C. Cummings and W. A. Mayfield to Williams, June 28, 1918, *ibid.*
81. G. M. England to Sam Williams, June 29, 1918, *ibid.*
82. J. I. Breckenridge to Sam Williams, June 29, 1918, *ibid.*
83. Sam Williams to Barnes, July 1, 1918, *ibid.*
84. For examples of the numerous attacks on Germans and other foreign-born citizens in the Southwest, see Peterson and Fite, *Opponents of War*, 99, 196, 200; "Mob Spirit Sweeps Over Oklahoma," *Harlow's Weekly* (Oklahoma City), April 3, 1918, pp. 8–10.

The county councils' repressive actions seriously affected the Oklahoma Socialist party's performance in the 1918 election. In fact, under the Democratic election law, voters who registered as Socialists could be revealed to their local council or to vigilantes. In any case, the Sooner Socialists could not conduct a serious campaign in 1918. The remaining party newspapers, the Strong City *Herald*, the *Otter Valley Socialist*, and Ameringer's new *Oklahoma Leader*, maintained their mailing privileges only by refraining from antiwar commentary and by giving space to prowar Socialists like H. H. Stallard. "Heck" Sinclair, who ran at the head of the state ticket along with Pat Nagle, risked arrest by attacking war profiteers, and tried his best to rally the comrades who "held out" in the face of "indictments, arrests, and mobs."[85]

But Sinclair and the Oklahoma Socialists polled only 7,500 votes in 1918, about one-sixth of their 1916 total. As usual, the party still won more votes in Oklahoma than it did in most southern and western states, its candidates polling over 10 percent of the vote in six western counties, including 20.8 percent in Major County and 17.4 percent in Dewey County. And O. E. Enfield, who had replaced Stallard as the party's congressional candidate in the western Seventh District, ran ahead of the ticket even though he "campaigned" from his cell in Leavenworth where he was serving a twenty-year prison term for violating the federal sedition act. Overall voter turnout declined drastically from 56.8 percent in 1916 to 35.8 percent in 1918.[86] This rate of decline correlated at +.59 with the Socialist vote in 1916 and -.84 with President Wilson's vote in the same year. The dramatic decrease of voter participation in pro-Socialist areas (especially the southeastern cotton counties) was also reflected by a correlation of +.60 between the drop in turnout between 1916 and 1918 and the rate of tenancy. In 1914 this correlation had appeared at an insignificant +.10. An analysis of precinct election returns by Garin Burbank shows that in Socialist strongholds the party's vote declined much more drastically (as

85. *Oklahoma Leader* (Oklahoma City), August 22, 1918.
86. *Harlow's Weekly* (Oklahoma City), November 27, 1918, p. 6; Benson, *Oklahoma Votes*, 64, 78.

much as 80 percent in some areas) than the Democratic vote in other precincts.[87] Although some Socialist voters undoubtedly returned to the Democratic party in 1918, the magnitude of this shift was much smaller than it had been in 1916. The fact that the Democratic gubernatorial candidate polled 40,000 votes less than Wilson had in 1916 suggests that the prowar candidate won few votes from Socialists. Since they were forced to declare their political affiliation in order to register under the Goebel law, most Socialists did not participate in the 1918 election.

The effects of wartime repression were at least as severe in Texas. Even Jim Ferguson, who ran for governor again on a pro-union, anti-Wilson platform, was red-baited and accused of pro-German sympathies. The impeached governor was trounced in the 1918 primary by his appointed successor Will Hobby, who ran a super-patriotic campaign for law, order, and prohibition. Outside of the "wet" German counties, former governor Ferguson's main support came from the piney woods counties, including several Socialist strongholds where his attacks on "lumber baron" J. H. Kirby were popular. The Socialists bravely nominated a ticket for the general election headed by W. P. Simpson, who reported that antiradical "terror" was "widespread." He received only 1,600 votes, one-eleventh of the party's 1916 total. The Texas Socialist party had in fact collapsed after the suppression of the *Rebel* and the arrest of leading Socialists during the roundup of draft resisters in June, 1917. Some of the leaders who remained above ground after these events were harassed and, in some cases, imprisoned on local "breach of peace" laws.[88] After helping with the oil workers' strike in the fall of 1917 and attempting unsuccessfully to organize the Nonpartisan League, many Texas Reds left the Lone Star state. Some, like Covington Hall and E. R. Meitzen, went to

87. Burbank, "Disruption and Decline of Oklahoma Socialist Party," 151–52.
88. *World Almanac, 1920,* p. 873; Lewis L. Gould, *Progressives and Prohibitionists: Texas Democrats in the Wilson Era* (Austin: University of Texas Press, 1973), 220–48; Minutes of Joint Conference of National Executive Committee and State Secretaries, August 10–19, 1918, in Socialist Party Papers, Perkins Library, Duke University, 96–97.

North Dakota to work for the Nonpartisan League; other rank-and-file Socialist families migrated to the refuge of pacifist colonies like Nevada City and New Llano. Late in 1918 Hall and Tom Hickey made plans to publish a new paper in Dallas to be named after Hall's old *Voice of the People*, but these plans to resurrect the pre-war *Rebel* under a Populist masthead never materialized.[89]

THE STRENGTHS AND WEAKNESSES OF
DEBSIAN SOCIALISM IN THE SOUTHWEST

Wartime repression and patriotic coercion killed the Socialist party in the Southwest. The Socialists in this region had experienced internal factionalism, but the 1912 split had not caused socialism to decline in the region. Furthermore, the "incandescent appeal" of Wilson's New Freedom and the agrarianism of Bill Murray and Jim Ferguson had failed to significantly weaken the movement. The Socialist protest in the Southwest was not absorbed by the ruling party; it was suppressed. The suppression had begun as early as 1912 when corporate violence destroyed the interracial radical movement in the piney woods; it reached its climax after the antidraft uprisings in the summer of 1917 and continued during the war years through the Councils of Defense. In 1919 the federal and state governments officially prolonged the antiradical hysteria with repressive legislation. Then in the 1920s vigilante activity returned, as one of the strongest Ku Klux Klans in the country rose to power in the Southwest.

As James Weinstein points out in *The Decline of American Socialism*, the last year of the war saw the destruction of some fifteen hundred locals in rural and small-town communities throughout the Midwest and West as well as the Southwest, because Socialists in these areas "could not work anonymously," as their city comrades often could, and they "did not dare work openly." As a result, at the time of the important 1919 Communist-Socialist split,

89. San Antonio *Express*, November 18, 1917; and Nonpartisan League circular signed by Tom Hickey, December 22, 1917, in Hickey Papers; Hickey to Frank P. Walsh, December 6, 1918, in F. P. Walsh Papers, New York City Public Library.

the older party had lost most of its prewar membership in the trans-Mississippi West. These were the Socialists in small locals, "the ones most dependent on the mails and the most exposed to vigilante and government repression," and "they were also the most solidly native-born." After the war, the Socialist party lost nearly all of these people and became largely an urban organization with a large foreign-born membership. Before 1919 the party's membership had been predominantly composed of farmers and workers from the industrial states of the Midwest and the agricultural states of the trans-Mississippi West who had given Debsian socialism a strongly American flavor. After the war the Socialist movement became preoccupied with European and especially Russian ideas and the debates swirling around questions defined by the Comintern. The old southwestern Socialists found it difficult to function in this new milieu. Dan Hogan, who had moved to Oklahoma City with his daughter Freda to work on the *Leader*, voiced the feelings of many midwestern militants when he took it for granted that all of his comrades gave "unqualified support to Soviet Russia." But, he told the 1919 party convention, American workers were different from Russian workers, and so Socialists in the United States would only isolate themselves by supporting "Russian methods for America." But, as Weinstein remarks, "large sections of the Party had already done what Hogan warned against" and in the future those old Socialists who proposed American solutions to the movement would find themselves in conflict with "the imperatives of the Russian Revolution."[90]

Before the war and the Russian Revolution no one was as successful at Americanizing Marxism and popularizing socialism as Dan Hogan and his southwestern comrades. The remarkable growth of agrarian socialism in the Southwest resulted from several accomplishments. First, the Socialists in Oklahoma and neighboring states mobilized and radicalized former Populists more effectively

90. James Weinstein, *The Decline of Socialism in America, 1912–1925* (New York: Monthly Review Press, 1967), 161–62, 181–85. Of course, Weinstein's emphasis on the 1919 Communist split as a cause of the Socialist party's decline does not apply to the Southwest, because the movement there had already been destroyed.

than their comrades in other regions; they also worked closely with various working-class militants, especially in the class-conscious United Mine Workers' union, and established a proletarian base in the cities and industrial towns. Socialists in other southern states like West Virginia, Missouri, and Florida also created "red islands" among unionized workers, but they failed to successfully employ that support to recruit the rural poor. On the other hand, socialism in other agricultural states on the Great Plains remained mainly agrarian because it lacked the strong proletarian influence present in the southwestern movement.

The Socialists of the Southwest borrowed and adapted the unique propaganda tactics of Julius A. Wayland and developed the most extensive radical press in the western United States; they borrowed the idea of the protracted encampments from the revivalists and the Populists and cleverly adapted it to their own needs. No Socialists used the *Appeal to Reason* and Wayland's remarkable "*Appeal* Army" better than the southwesterners, and no one, including party organizations in the major cities, attracted as many people to their rallies as the southwesterners attracted to their week-long encampments. Under these circumstances, party leaders in Oklahoma and Texas could express what seemed to be a naïve faith in the efficacy of self-education and self-organization.

The Socialists in these states described socialism in concrete, practical terms that made sense to poor people. They compromised with Marxian orthodoxy on the land question and the nature of Christianity, but, as David Shannon writes of the Sooner Socialists, they forged a program "concerned with the real problems and issues" of the region's farmers and workers and not with the "abstract" debates that preoccupied party theorists. The Oklahoma Socialist party rooted its demands firmly in the region's Populist tradition of protest, but it did not hide its "ultimate purpose"—to seize "the powers of government" and to use them to immediately better the conditions of workers and farmers, eventually creating a "classless society."[91] The Socialists built most of

91. Shannon, *Socialist Party of America*, 35–36. In other words, the Socialists' rejection of capitalism did not necessarily make them fanatical

their electoral support around popular demands to remedy problems ignored by the ruling Democrats, but the radicals' popularity also depended upon their ability to offer more radical solutions to those problems than the agrarian reformists. Since the Oklahoma Socialist vote continued to grow after 1912 when various progressive Democrats deliberately tried to "steal their thunder" on the land and labor questions, it seems likely that the Socialists' eloquently articulated vision of a Cooperative Commonwealth attracted supporters who decided that the American creed of "democratic classlessness" and "freedom of opportunity" could never be anything but a myth under competitive capitalism. In other words, in order to grow into a mass party at the height of the "progressive era," the Socialist party had to become something more revolutionary than the left wing of reformism. As James Weinstein writes, the Socialist party's popularity "lay in its commitment to democracy and in its strategy of making socialism vs. capitalism a central question in all of its public activity. By making millions of people aware of capitalism as a class system run by capitalists in their own interests, and by convincing these millions that socialism was necessary for the development of their full human potential . . . the old Socialist Party established the basis for a genuinely revolutionary movement. The Socialists made millions of people think about making their own history."[92]

Finally, the southwestern Socialists, notably the Oklahomans, created a strong grass-roots movement by linking their demands and their critique of the ruling party to the realities of class struggle experienced by the region's laboring poor whites. This movement's class consciousness and revolutionary potential were limited by the fact that it was based on a declining farming class more than upon a growing working class. That movement's rural support was limited even further by its inability to mobilize non-

---

sectarians, or prevent them, as Bell argues, from relating to "specific problems" in "the here-and-now, give-and-take political world." Daniel Bell, *Marxian Socialism in the United States* (Princeton, N.J.: Princeton University Press, 1967), 5.

92. James Weinstein, *Ambiguous Legacy: The Left in American Politics* (New York: New Viewpoints, 1975), 4.

white sharecroppers, casual industrial workers, and migratory field hands. The Brotherhood of Timber Workers produced the movement's most class-conscious protest because its leadership and core membership were thoroughly proletarian and because it recruited across race lines and enlisted poor white farmers in a unified struggle against common exploiters. The strength of the BTW also reflected the willingness of southwestern Socialists to adopt direct action as well as political action at a time when party members in other sections had decided to exclude so-called "anarcho-syndicalists" for advocating sabotage as a necessary form of industrial action. The solidarity forged by the BTW in the heat of the piney woods "lumber war" reduced tactical and ideological differences between radicals who were forced to follow the example of the rank and file and unite in order to fight more powerful enemies and engage in an all-out class war. After 1914 this tactical unity broke down when less disciplined forms of direct action erupted within the movement, provoking increased repression. But before that time, even the most "gradualistic" Socialist party campaigners refused to separate direct action from political action.

In other words, the party's vote-getting strategy in the Southwest did not foreclose Socialist support for the struggles disfranchised workers, racial minorities, and women waged for enfranchisement and unionization. The party's primary focus on winning the support of eligible voters did tend to discourage the recruitment of nonwhite members, as did the racism of party members, especially the poor white tenants who feared Afro-Americans and Mexican-Americans as competitors or replacements. But despite these problems the southwestern Socialist parties worked much harder to win the support of racial minorities than did their progressive rivals whose reformism remained "for whites only." Most Socialists opposed social equality for blacks (*i.e.* integration and miscegenation), but they did fight black disfranchisement in Oklahoma as staunchly as they worked for female enfranchisement. And even in Texas, where Socialist propaganda was especially tinctured with racism, the party's official paper denounced the lynching of blacks when the Democratic press remained silent. Socialist party organizers also actively recruited Afro-Americans and

Mexican Americans into tenant unions. The Kansas and Oklahoma Socialists worked harder to bring blacks into the party than did most of their northern comrades who could at least hope to gain some votes in return for their efforts. After campaigning on a 1912 platform plank that vehemently denounced racial oppression, the Oklahoma Socialists actually hired a full-time black organizer to bring Afro-Americans into the party. In fact, some party locals in Oklahoma, Kansas, and Arkansas included a few blacks in coal-mining towns where the UMW had already achieved racial solidarity through its unionization drive. These same towns contained Socialist locals of "new immigrant" workers often excluded from the party in the Midwest and other parts of the country. However, the inclusion of blacks and recent immigrants depended largely upon the favorable conditions created by militant industrial union struggles which, in the case of the UMW, actually unionized the "blacklegs" imported to break the strikes of the Anglo-American miners. Native and old immigrant workers dominated the party leadership in the coal fields, but unlike Victor Berger and other "old-line" Socialists, these militant miners did not relegate the new immigrants to a subservient status.[93]

Even if the southwestern Socialists had launched a more determined effort to recreate the Populists' interracial alliance (forged at a time when blacks still represented a crucial voting bloc), it is unlikely that Afro-Americans would have responded favorably, not only because the Socialist party contained some outspoken racists (especially in Texas),[94] but because until 1913 most blacks remained wedded to the Republican federal patronage system. Furthermore, after populism disappeared and disfranchisement was completed, most blacks either dropped out of politics entirely or turned to nationalist activity.

93. For a study of how the emphasis placed by many Socialist leaders on recruiting the "real American Proletariat" limited the growth of the party, see Paul Buhle, "Debsian Socialism and the 'New Immigrant' Worker," in William O'Neill (ed.), *Insights and Parallels* (Minneapolis: Burgess, 1973), 253–67.

94. See Hubert Harrison, "Socialism and the Negro," *International Socialist Review*, XIII (July, 1912), 65–68.

In brief, the southwestern Socialists politicized the class struggle for the kind of poor white farmers and workers who in other parts of the South remained tied to the racist *status quo*, and they capitalized largely on the efforts of demagogic Democrats who promised, but rarely delivered, neo-Populist reforms. Thus, although the Socialist party in the Southwest failed to create an interracial radical movement or to eliminate racism within its own ranks, it succeeded in winning the loyalty of a large bloc of poor whites by using class appeals to effectively counter the Democrats' appeal to racist reformism. An important group of radical Populists moved directly into the southwestern Socialist camp around the turn of century and provided the party with a solid base of politicized poor whites, but the "defeated legions" of populism in the old South "wandered restlessly and homelessly" until, as Woodward remarks, Democratic "demagogues . . . usurped command and diverted them with sham battles against assorted 'menaces' "—principally the black "menace."[95]

The relatively lower proportion of blacks in the Southwest (especially in Oklahoma, Texas, and the western sections of Arkansas and Louisiana where the party was strongest) cannot account entirely for the problems Democratic demagogues faced in maintaining a solid racist coalition of poor whites and their "social betters." The southwestern class struggle began to weaken the bonds between white tenants and landlords and between white workers and bosses even before the Socialists intervened forcefully. Even initially these bonds were a bit weaker than they were in the Old South, because southwestern populism had not been as thoroughly repressed. In fact, Democratic politicians in this region found it necessary to actually enact more reform measures than their counterparts to the east because of the pressure mobilized by neo-Populist groups like the Farmers' Union. The town-country "imbroglio" politicized by the Populists did not disappear after 1900; it became more severe as a result of the increasing polarization of the rural poor folk and the propertied townspeople. The rapid development

95. C. Vann Woodward, *Origins of the New South, 1877–1913* (Baton Rouge: Louisiana State University Press, 1951), 477.

of capitalism on the southwestern frontier not only created an "orgy of speculation" which deprived homesteaders of the best land, it also disrupted customary relations between landlords and tenants, debtors and creditors, workers and industrialists—relations that tended to prevail for a longer time in the southeastern states. The sharp class conflict produced by rapid capitalist development created a breach between rich and poor whites in the New South to the West, giving the Socialists an opportunity to mobilize a strong grass-roots radical movement of poor white men and women. Unlike the racist Democratic coalitions forged by southern demagogues, the southwestern Socialist coalition oriented its protest primarily against the common oppressors above rather than against the black "menace" below.

The Southwest combined elements of the South and the West, but the conditions of the old midwestern frontier were not duplicated there any more than were the peculiar conditions of the Old South. By 1900 the frontier phase of progressive New South development had ended for a majority of the residents. And if, as Walter Prescott Webb wrote, the open frontier "promoted individualism, stimulated self-reliance, fostered equality and political democracy," then the closure of the frontier tended to "destroy those things its existence once stimulated." The abortion of the "Homestead ideal" by the "land speculator and the railroad monopolist" took place quickly on the southwestern frontier, leaving few hopes of opportunity for the poor whites who settled there and immediately became ensnared in the old crop lien credit system and the new trap of transient tenancy. Perhaps, as Carey McWilliams wrote regarding the roots of the "Okie" tragedy, "this celebrated 'last frontier' was an illusion from the beginning." At any rate, it was not fertile ground for implanting the American creed of democratic classlessness and equality of opportunity.[96]

96. Walter Prescott Webb, *Divided We Stand: The Crisis of a Frontierless Democracy* (New York: Farrar and Rinehart, 1926), 157–58; Henry Nash Smith, *Virgin Land: The American West as Symbol and Myth* (Cambridge, Mass.: Harvard University Press, 1950), 123; Carey McWilliams, *Ill Fares the Land: Migrants and Migrant Labor in the United States* (Boston: Little Brown, 1941), 188; and Seymour Martin Lipset, *Agrarian Socialism* (Rev. ed.; Garden City, N.Y.: Doubleday Anchor, 1968), 190.

"The old pioneer individualism is disappearing," Frederick Jackson Turner told the American Historical Association in 1910, "while the forces of combination are manifesting themselves as never before." The "self-made man" of the frontier epoch had become the "coal baron, the oil king, the railroad magnate"—corporate figures hated by poor southwesterners. Under these circumstances, Turner remarked, "it is not surprising that socialism shows noteworthy gains as elections continue."[97] Although the "forces of combination," notably land consolidation, undermined the promise of equal opportunity, the small farmers of the Southwest, even the radical renters, did not entirely abandon frontier individualism. They became more class conscious and recognized that "cooperation beat competition," but as small producers they had to compete with each other in the capricious cotton and credit markets. Ownership of the land, or at least freedom to use and occupy it, was essential for their survival. Furthermore, their identity—their worth as individuals—was imbedded in the land and wedded to their ability to farm the earth. Socialist farmers recognized the trend toward land concentration, but they could not embrace proletarianization, even when higher wages were involved. To be deprived of the land was not only to be illegally dispossessed, it was to be degraded, destroyed as an individual. The agrarian Socialists recognized this and guaranteed the honest producer his "natural right" to the "use and occupancy of the land" in the Cooperative Commonwealth, as long as he did not use his land for exploitation of labor or for speculation. In fact, the Socialists' campaign to restore these alienated natural rights accounted for a good deal of the movement's militancy. But as a result, the movement never transformed the "possessive individualism" of the small farmer into a "genuine socialist version" of rural collectivism. In this sense, southwestern socialism was, as Oscar Ameringer remarked, more Populist than Marxist.[98]

97. Frederick Jackson Turner, *Frontier and Section* (Englewood Cliffs, N.J.: Prentice-Hall, 1961), 160–61.
98. Burbank, "Social Origins of Agrarian Socialism," 225; Ameringer in the *Oklahoma Leader* (Oklahoma City), April 27, 1922.

The agrarian Socialists, however, looked to the future more hopefully than had their Populist predecessors who had believed that the harmony of rural society could be restored by regulating monopolies and establishing cooperatives for exchange. The militant minority of former Populists who moved to the left rather than back toward the Democratic party developed socialistic ideas during the 1890s—futuristic ideas about cooperatives for production as well as exchange, about government ownership of all industries, not just monopolies, and about the impending proletarianization of the farmer.[99] These ideas were all incorporated in the concept of a Cooperative Commonwealth which in 1901 became the ultimate goal of the Socialist party. Although the Socialists borrowed heavily from the Populists in appealing to indebted farm producers and promised land to working farmers in the new commonwealth, they nourished no illusions about returning to an "agrarian eden" in which all the classes of rural society lived in harmony. Unlike the mainstream Populists who shied away from the divisive implications of land consolidation and tenancy, the Socialists accepted the reality of class conflict in agrarian society and argued that the new cooperative society could only be born through class struggle.

In retrospect, the southwestern Socialist parties, including the powerful Oklahoma organization, appear as weak challengers to the political dominance of the Democrats and the rough-and-ready ruling class they represented. But the Socialist challenge seemed dangerous enough at the time. Aided and abetted by a federal administration that promised a "New Freedom" for America, local landlords, merchants, and lawyers joined Democratic politicians in suppressing their troublesome radical opponents. It was necessary to destroy the Socialist party because, for all its limitations, it represented far more than an organization of muckraking journalists, irascible coal diggers, renegade preachers, suffragettes, and

99. Norman Pollack has emphasized the progressive thought of the proto-Marxian Populists, notably Lorenzo Lewelling and the Kansas radicals, without pointing out that many were actually Socialists or later became Socialists. See Norman Pollack, *The Populist Response to Industrial America* (Cambridge, Mass.: Harvard University Press, 1962).

"no 'count renters"; it was the political expression of radical dis-content among thousands of farmers, workers, and small-towners whose loyalty (or apathy) was necessary for the preservation of capitalist hegemony over the New South in the West.

RED SCARE

By 1919 even the most optimistic Sooner Socialists acknowledged the devastating effects of wartime repression. For example, Freda Hogan, a particularly irrepressible young Socialist who had spent the last year of the war hustling liberty bonds to promote a new Socialist daily, surrendered to the prevailing mood of doom. Noth-ing for her was more depressing than the incarceration of Gene Debs, Kate O'Hare, and other brave leaders of the old crusade. Late in 1919 Hogan wrote Theodore Debs that she wished "Com-rade Gene" were free to write another "Rouse Ye Slaves" that might "shame" Socialists out of their "lethargy." Freda moaned, "The war was too much without the incarceration of our com-rades. When I think about it all, it would be easy to lose my Socialist faith and become a raving anarchist." She pleaded to be told what to do and concluded by noting that her father could not trust himself to write, because he was often "almost beside him-self" with despair. "If we could just do something—it's just that we feel ourselves so powerless that it's maddening," she wrote. "Of course, we have done what we could for amnesty, but that seems so little and I feel about like we were knocking our heads against a brick wall." Freda Hogan brought her father back to Ok-lahoma to help Oscar Ameringer raise money for his daily *Leader*, knowing that it would be better for her "Papa to be back in the field again." But most of the old Socialists of Dan Hogan's gen-eration would never again return to the field of battle. Many lead-ing southwestern activists remained locked in Leavenworth peni-tentiary while thousands of rank and filers remained in political hiding.[100]

100. Freda Hogan to Theodore Debs, December 26, 1919, in Eugene V. Debs Collection, Cunningham Library, Indiana State University, Terre Haute.
  Socialist prisoners still being held at Leavenworth federal penitentiary in 1920 as a result of their opposition to the war included Stanley Clark

In 1919 the Red Scare descended upon the Southwest and drove Socialists further underground. In response to militant labor insurgency, including a general strike of the coal miners, state governments moved decisively against all unions, especially those with radical members. The governor of Oklahoma declared martial law in the coal fields and in 1919 used state troops more frequently than all of his predecessors combined.[101] And in Kansas, the governor "recruited a band of strikebreakers, and gave them military protection to operate coal mines in the vicinity of Pittsburg," the center of Alex Howat's Socialist bastion. The state also moved to crack the militant miners of District 14 by enacting a compulsory arbitration bill with an Industrial Court to try cases.[102] Kansas and Oklahoma legislators joined those of Arkansas in passing "red flag laws" to prohibit any public display of radical sympathy. These antiradical laws represented a last symbolic blow to farmers and workers who loved to drive their wagons around "with the red flag flying high." The Oklahoma and Kansas legislatures then enacted criminal syndicalism laws aimed primarily at the IWW, which was still active in the wheat fields and oil fields of both states. The precipitating incident behind this "class legislation" in

---

and "old man" Tad Cumbie, leading Oklahoma Reds from the southeast; T. H. Harris and O. E. Enfield, militants from the western counties; W. P. Webb, state secretary of the Texas Socialist party; G. T. Bryant and the other founders of the Farmers' and Laborers' Protective Association; numerous "class struggle prisoners," including many captains of the Working Class Union, leaders of the Jones Family, Wobblies like Phineas Eastman and J. E. Wiggins of the Brotherhood of Timber Workers, and Earl Browder and his brothers from Kansas. Mortimer Downing to Winnie Branstetter, September 2, 1920, and T. H. Harris to Sinclair, August 17, 1920, both in Socialist Party Papers, Duke. For a fascinating glimpse of life among the radical political prisoners in Leavenworth, see Ralph Chaplin, *Wobbly: The Rough-and-Tumble Story of an American Radical* (Chicago: University of Chicago Press, 1948), 250–324.

101. Scales, "Political History of Oklahoma," 206.

102. Four hundred miners struck in protest the day the measure became law. Howat was soon arrested for refusing to appear before the new Industrial Court. When the "fighting Scotsman" was incarcerated, Kansas coal diggers reacted with a wildcat strike closing 90 percent of the state's mines. Selig Perlman and Philip Taft, *History of Labor in the United States, 1896–1932* (New York: Macmillan, 1935), 473.

Oklahoma was a telephone workers' strike in Drumright which led Governor J. B. A. Robertson to call in six companies of militia. The strikers and their sympathizers, including Wobblies and other "radical oil workers," reportedly responded by disarming the sheriff and threatening to lynch him along with the mayor. The Oklahoma governor was appalled when the "businessmen of Drumright failed to stand up to the IWW" after the "extreme radical elements" locked up the city officials and "held the town in terror." The governor warned, "The Ku Klux Klan will have to come back unless there is a change for the better."[103] Oklahoma would not have to wait long for the Klan to rise again.

In 1920 federal prisoner Eugene V. Debs once again ran for president on the Socialist ticket and received a surprisingly large total of nearly a million votes from men and women disgusted with war, repression, and the tarnished image of Wilsonian progressivism. Debs received 25,638 votes in Oklahoma, "not a bad recovery" given the fact that the Socialists had polled only one-third that number two years earlier.[104] But the surprising 1920 tally was essentially a protest vote for Debs, an imprisoned old man who personified the persecution of American radicals during the bitter end of Wilson's New Freedom. This protest against domestic repression was also a testimony to Debs and his long-suffering comrades who languished in federal prisons for opposing what had become an unpopular war. But Debs's 1920 vote did not lead to a Socialist party recovery in the Southwest, not even in Oklahoma where the Socialists made a noticeable resurgence. The pioneer Socialists lived on to fight in other causes down through the 1930s, but the old-time grass-roots movement was over.

Writing to her husband Frank from a prison cell in Jefferson City, Missouri, Kate Richards O'Hare could only dream about "the long, hard, toilsome years" when the Debsians had created the southwestern movement. "I dreamed of Oklahoma" and "the dust

103. E. F. Dowell, _A History of Criminal Syndicalism Legislation in the United States_ (Baltimore: Johns Hopkins University Press, 1939), 14, 46–47; _Harlow's Weekly_ (Oklahoma City), September 24, October 8, 1919.

104. Shannon, _Socialist Party of America_, 157–58; _Harlow's Weekly_ (Oklahoma City), November 29, 1920.

at Stigler, that sun-baked pasture at Ada, the swealtering multitudes at Harlow," but " when the morning came," she said, "the horror of my dreams was still with me and then I thought of how our wonderful movement in Oklahoma had been scattered" as though the Sooner Socialists had been a flock of sheep terrorized "by the wolves who came down in the madness of war." Bowed but not bent, Kate retained the optimism characteristic of her generation's radical revivalists. She shared a hope with Frank that "the Oklahoma socialist movement" would rise "like Phoenix from the ashes of terrorism and official despotism."[105]

105. Kate Richards O'Hare to Frank P. O'Hare, March 2, 1920, letter no. 87, in "Letters from Kate Richards O'Hare to Her Family," Missouri Historical Society, St. Louis.

X

"If You Don't Weaken" Southwestern Socialists in the Desperate Years, 1921-1943

DESPITE THE EXCITING vote Eugene Debs polled from prison in 1920, veteran activists recognized that the Socialist Party of America was finished as an organized political force in the Southwest. "The Western element of the party, which had been more squarely in the tradition of indigenous radicalism than other sections of the party . . . was now in about the same weak and disorganized condition it had been in at the turn of the century," David Shannon notes. "The days of the Socialist encampments on the Western plains were over. No longer would Oklahoma small town merchants find it commercially expedient to display the red flag in their store window." And "at Girard, Kansas, the presses of the old *Appeal* were now putting out Little Blue Books for E. Haldeman-Julius."[1]

Individual Socialists and a few cadre of "red renters," remained politically active in the Southwest after the party's destruction during the war. In the early 1920s some of the veteran Sooner Socialists took up key positions in the powerful Nonpartisan League movement which propelled a "people's governor" into the Oklahoma statehouse. They also organized for the radical new Farm-Labor Union and battled the Ku Klux Klan, but in the late twenties old Socialists found it difficult to keep the faith. For the first time since the region had been settled, political protest vir-

1. David A. Shannon, *The Socialist Party of America, A History* (New York: Macmillan, 1955), 122. E. Hadleman-Julius bought the *Appeal to Reason* from one of Julius Wayland's sons in 1919 and during the 1920s turned the press over to publishing "little blue books"—often written by radical authors. *Appeal to Reason* (Girard, Kan.), May 24, 1919.

396

tually disappeared. As the Depression hit with full force, however, old timers rallied around Oscar Ameringer's new weekly the *American Guardian* and prepared for the Socialist revival that was sure to come.

A radical revival did take place in the 1930s, creating a kind of Indian summer for the pioneer Socialist agitators of Oscar Ameringer's generation. But there were not many agitators of Oscar's generation left by this time, and the rank and filers—the old Populists and Socialists of Grandpa Joad's generation—were also becoming scarce. Thus, when the Socialist revival came, it appeared not in the old rack-rented cotton counties of the Indian Nations and the Texas black waxy, but in a newly settled region of the Arkansas Delta. The revival was led by young men who dutifully copied the party-building tactics of Ameringer and the old masters, but they soon turned from the hopeless task of recreating the old Socialist party, to the more pressing job of building an interracial industrial union for desperate sharecroppers. The Southern Tenant Farmers' Union (STFU) was a fitting tribute not only to the old Socialist Renters' Union, from which it borrowed its preamble, but to the interracial unionism of the IWW and the Working Class Union.

When the STFU declined in the late 1930s, nothing remained to keep the old movement alive save Oscar Ameringer and his newspaper, the *Guardian*. When it suspended publication in 1942 (one year before Oscar's death), the last clear voice of grass-roots Debsian socialism fell silent.

The Radical Revival and the Struggle for Survival in the 1920s

The excesses of the Red Scare gave government repression a slightly odious reputation, and the big protest vote for Gene Debs in 1920 gave the southwestern Socialists a much-needed dose of encouragement. Radicals could finally take some time to regroup their battered forces and take stock of a confusing new situation.[2]

2. Hickey to Theodore Debs, June 20, 1921, in Eugene V. Debs Collection, Cunningham Library, Indiana State University, Terre Haute.

The terrible agricultural depression of 1920–1921 created an explosive revival in the radical southwestern farm movement. The price of cotton on the New Orleans market dropped from 41.7 cents in April, 1920, to 13.5 cents in December. In Texas, where a big rise in the cost of living accompanied the cotton crisis, night riders appeared again in the fall of 1920, terrorizing growers, ginners, and merchants who were moving cotton at depressed prices. As a result, the new Farm-Labor Union recruited 45,000 members in 1921 and pushed its membership up to 150,000 in the following year when it branched out into Oklahoma and Arkansas, just as the old Farmers' Alliance had done.[3]

In Oklahoma the Farm-Labor Union appealed to the old Socialist tenants in the southern cotton country who, according to the Union's preamble, had been "slaves for years of the manufacturers, the gamblers and the speculators."[4] Meanwhile, the resurgent Farmers' Union, under the militant leadership of John A. Simpson, appealed to angry wheat farmers who received about half as much for their wheat in 1921 as they had gained two years before. And so in September of 1921 representatives of the resurgent farmers' movement and organized labor in Oklahoma returned again to Shawnee, the site of their influential 1906 convention. Here they formed the Farmer-Labor Reconstruction League and made more demands for progressive social and economic legislation, along the lines advocated by the North Dakota Nonpartisan League. "Not a few of the old socialists were present," one historian notes, "for, as in the North Dakota experiment, Socialists took a hand in shaping the League's program." In fact, John Hagel, publisher of the Oklahoma *Leader*, actually drafted the Farmer-Labor Reconstruction League's first program[5]

3. George B. Tindall, *The Emergence of the New South, 1913–1945* (Baton Rouge: Louisiana State University Press, 1967), 112; Robert Lee Hunt, *A History of Farmer Movements in the Southwest, 1873–1925* (College Station: Texas A & M Press, 1935), 147–48, 159.

4. Hunt, *Farmer Movements in the Southwest*, 147–48, 159.

5. James B. Scales, "Political History of Oklahoma, 1907–1949" (Ph.D. dissertation, University of Oklahoma, 1949), 230; Gilbert Fite, "Oklahoma's Reconstruction League: An Experiment in Farmer-Labor Politics," *Journal of Southern History*, XIII (1947), 543.

Early in 1922 the new League held its official convention at Shawnee. Over seven hundred delegates from farmer and labor unions, including a number of blacks, decided to try to capture the Democratic party for their program. The presence of a significant number of "Negro farmers and workers" at a political convention was, the *Reconstructionist* remarked, an epoch-making event in the state's political history. The League delegates nominated Mayor Jack Walton of Oklahoma City as their gubernatorial candidate.[6] The Socialists, like Dan Hogan of the *Leader* and Luther Langston of the State Federation of Labor, played a key role in the formation of the League and in Walton's campaign. Pat Nagle served as the candidate's publicity man; Jack Hagel and Oscar Ameringer devoted their *Oklahoma Leader* to the cause. These skillful Socialist organizers took the lead in securing campaign contributions from thousands of workers and farmers throughout the state. The League also won big grants from the unions, especially the UMW and the railroad brotherhoods who were involved in a bitter strike against the open-shop drive.[7]

In Texas, where the 1922 shopmen's strike was much more extensive, Governor Pat Neff invoked the state's new open-shop law in Dennison, Sherman, and fifteen other rail towns to prevent any activity by union pickets. This strike-breaking policy provoked an angry reaction from organized labor in Texas. Led by Socialists in the Farm-Labor Union and the Nonpartisan League and by other militants, the farmer-labor alliance of 1906 reconstituted itself and nominated a candidate to run against Governor Neff in the 1922 Democratic primary. Fred S. Rodgers, a radical Farmer-Labor Union member from Bonham, was chosen as the group's candidate; he polled a strikingly large total of 196,000 votes in his unsuccessful effort to unseat the incumbent governor. The Texas Socialists

6. Stuart Jamieson, *Labor Unionism in American Agriculture*, Bureau of Labor Statistics *Bulletin No. 836* (Washington, D.C.: Government Printing Office, 1945), 257; *Reconstructionist* (Oklahoma City), February 25, 1922; Fite, "Oklahoma's Reconstruction League," 538, 544–45; Scales, "Political History of Oklahoma," 231–32, 239; Federal Writers' Project, W.P.A., *Labor History of Oklahoma* (Oklahoma City: Van Horn, 1939), 47–48.

7. Scales, "Political History of Oklahoma," 239.

were encouraged by the small but influential role they played in this Nonpartisan League primary campaign.[8]

Old Socialist party members were much more active in Jack Walton's colorful crusade in Oklahoma. "Our Jack" barnstormed through the state accompanied by a jazz band and his experienced Socialist campaign advisors. Like a brash young Louisiana insurgent named Huey Long who was also running for governor in 1922, Walton won tremendous popular response when he attacked the Democratic bosses and big oil corporations with hayseed humor and "well-directed profanity." Although both of these neo-Populist politicians would become outspoken opponents of the rising Ku Klux Klan, they did not make the Klan an issue in their first campaigns.[9]

The Klan did exert a powerful influence in the Oklahoma Democratic primary of 1922, but as far as Walton was concerned, it was a positive one, because the Klan candidate, who was backed by oil money, took away votes from Senator R. L. Owen and allowed "Our Jack" to win the primary by 35,000 votes; this was a stunning blow to regular Democrats who attacked the "revolutionary platform of the socialist" Farmer-Labor Reconstruction League. In the general campaign, Walton continued his popular canvassing tactics against GOP candidate John Fields, an erstwhile progressive farm editor who was close to banking and business interests. Fields devoted his entire campaign to "red-baiting" Walton. He charged, with some accuracy, that the "reddest of the Oklahoma Socialists" brought the League's platform down from Townley's North Dakota. But the Red Scare had ended, and this negative approach was less effective.

Walton, who had generated great popular enthusiasm for his style and his platform, trounced his Republican opponent by 50,000

8. See Rupert N. Richardson, *Texas, the Lone Star State* (Englewood Cliffs, N.J.: Prentice-Hall, 1958), 314; Hunt, *Farmer Movements in the Southwest*, 184–185. On Neff's career see Lewis L. Gould, *Progressives and Prohibitionists: Texas Democrats in the Wilson Era* (Austin: University of Texas Press, 1973), 271–76, 285.

9. On the campaign styles of Walton and Long see Fite, "Oklahoma's Reconstruction League," 547; and T. Harry Williams, *Huey Long: A Biography* (New York: Knopf, 1970), Chaps. 6–9.

votes. The Socialist vote went to the Farmer-Labor Reconstruction League instead of to the regular party candidate O. E. Enfield, who won less than 4,000 votes. However, "Our Jack" also attracted some support from black Republican voters (who returned to the polls after the grandfather clause was declared unconstitutional) to make up for some of the conservative Democratic votes in the towns that went to his opponent. "Never in Oklahoma history had class lines been so sharply drawn," Gilbert Fite writes of the 1922 election. The candidate of the "downtrodden" had triumphed over the candidate of the "plutocratic special interests."[10]

The Socialists who had directed Walton's campaign were jubilant. "Without money to speak of, with virtually the entire press of the state and . . . all the financial and monopolistic interests against us," Oscar Ameringer recalled, "we had triumphantly elected Our Jack, destined to become the Andrew Jackson of the Nineteen-twenties." But Oscar and his comrades were soon disappointed when Walton tried to win conservative support by backing down from some of the Shawnee demands and by refusing to appoint radical officials. There would be no North Dakota experiment in Oklahoma. The Socialists' disappointment soon turned to disgust as their "Jack" curried the favor of various "bourgeois booster outfits and open shop chambers of commerce." To Ameringer's disgust, the new governor was even seen playing golf with wealthy oilmen from Muskogee. In order to recoup some of the popular support he was rapidly losing, Governor Walton dramatically declared "war" on Oklahoma's powerful Ku Klux Klan.[11]

The KKK had been on the rise in all of the southwestern states since 1920. In fact, Klan-like activity had occurred much earlier when vigilantes moved against the IWW in Jasper, Texas; Merryville, Louisiana; and Tulsa, Oklahoma. After the bloody Tulsa "race riot" of 1921, which pitted armed blacks against whites who had

10. Scales, "Political History of Oklahoma," 238–41; Fite, "Oklahoma's Reconstruction League," 551–52.
11. Oscar Ameringer, *If You Don't Weaken: The Autobiography of Oscar Ameringer* (New York: Henry Holt, 1940), 379, 382; Fite, "Oklahoma's Reconstruction League," 552; and Scales, "Political History of Oklahoma," 249–50.

been competing for scarce jobs, the Klan made great progress in eastern Oklahoma oil towns where bootlegging, gambling, and other kinds of "vice" ran rampant. In fact, the KKK grew tremendously powerful throughout the Southwest as an agency of terroristic moral reform. As the historian of the southwestern Klu Klux movement concluded: "The Klan became the ideal of progressivism for hundreds of thousands of middle class Protestant Southwesterners," just as trust regulation and prohibition had been before the war. Moral laxity and other forms of "lawlessness," especially in the oil towns, incensed the petty bourgeois of the towns and cities who unleashed a veritable white terror on anyone (especially on workers) who violated Victorian standards of morality.[12] Although most of the whippings, beatings, and mutilations inflicted in 1922–1923, along with several murders, were directed against bootleggers, gamblers, "loose women," and other "sinners," the Klan was not simply a moral rearmament crusade. The attacks on the IWW by Klan-like groups in the prewar years continued in the postwar years when the KKK became the terrorist arm of the open-shop drive in the Southwest.[13]

Although Ameringer and the *Leader* officially separated themselves from Governor Walton's "apostasy" in July of 1923, Socialists still supported "Jack's war" against the Klan, which now controlled both political parties. For example, in Marshall County, Oklahoma, a Socialist party stronghold before the war, party

12. Scales, "Political History of Oklahoma," 222, 227–28; Charles C. Alexander, *The Ku Klux Klan in the Southwest* (Lexington: University of Kentucky Press, 1965), 27, 44. For a colorful description of an eastern Oklahoma oil town see Woody Guthrie's reminiscences about his native Okemah in the 1920s. He describes it as "one of the singingest, drinkingest, yellingest, preachingest, laughingest, cryingist, shootingest, fist fightingest, grumblingest, and razor carryingest of our ranch and farm towns because it blossomed into one of our first Oil Boom Towns." Woody Guthrie, *American Folksong*, ed. Moses Asch (New York: Oak, 1961), 2. See also Woody Guthrie, *Bound for Glory* (New York: Putnam, 1968), 113–89.

13. Scales, "Political History of Oklahoma," 229; *Nation* (New York), September 26, 1923, p. 311; Alexander, *Ku Klux Klan in the Southwest*, 61–62, 77–79, 113, 118. In fact, one of the Klan's most notorious murders occurred in Harrison, Arkansas, where a railroad worker was lynched because he was suspected of sabotage during the 1922 shopmen's strike.

members battled the KKK through the Farmer-Labor Union. The Union boycotted the town businessmen who joined the Klan. These radical dirt farmers called the Klan a "legitimate offspring of the Facista movement originated in Italy." [14] So in places like Marshall County, local Socialists stuck by Walton, even though he had broken his popular campaign promises and even though his notorious war against the Klan led to a declaration of martial law and the suspension of civil liberties in many counties. Walton played his final card in September, 1923, when he called the troops to prevent the state legislature from meeting to consider his impeachment. This reckless move failed. The question of calling a special impeachment session was placed on a referendum and it passed overwhelmingly, but Walton still retained some strength in old Socialist districts like Marshall County where the renters in the countryside voted overwhelmingly against considering the governor's impeachment; their old class enemies in the Klan-dominated towns voted the opposite way. [15]

After the legislature finally met and removed Walton from office, Jack remained a hero among many farmers and workers. And when the Klan became more firmly ensconced in state government, Walton won surprising support in his race for the Democratic United States Senate nomination. Again he shocked the regular Democrats by winning their party's primary when two overly ambitious Klan candidates split the anti-Walton vote. This result paralleled Miriam "Ma" Ferguson's victory over a Klan candidate in the Texas Democratic gubernatorial primary. But whereas "Ma" easily defeated her Republican opponent with her resourceful husband's assistance, Walton lost the general election to GOP Klansman W. B. Pine. This 1924 Senate election again showed strong

14. Garin Burbank, "Agrarian Radicals and their Opponents: Political Conflict in Southern Oklahoma, 1910–1924," *Journal of American History*, LVIII (1971), 13–23. Quote on Klan's similarity to the Italian fascists from Madill (Okla.) *Record*, October 15, 1923. Thanks to Garin Burbank for this source.
15. Burbank, "Agrarian Radicals and Their Opponents"; Scales, "Political History of Oklahoma," 250–51. Also see Sheldon Neuringer, "Governor Walton's War on the Ku Klux Klan," *Chronicles of Oklahoma*, XLV (1967), 153–79.

support for Walton's anti-Klan candidacy in the rural sections of Marshall County and other old Socialist strongholds.[16] An analysis of this vote casts doubt on the idea of the Klan as "a latter-day expression of provincial Populism."[17] The Socialists, who were the Populists' "lineal descendants" in Oklahoma, attacked the Klan relentlessly and remained loyal followers of the notorious Klan-fighter, Jack Walton.[18] The Klan candidates' support did not come mainly from the rural regions or industrial towns, but from the county seat towns and the cities. The southwestern Klan was led by the same professional and petty bourgeois elements who had launched vigilante attacks on the Brotherhood of Timber Workers in 1913 and on the IWW and Socialist party during World War I.[19] They extended their violent approach to southwestern class strug-gle into the postwar years.

Thus, Socialist Klan fighters happily watched the hooded order destroy itself in 1925 and 1926, though the radical diehards found other events quite discouraging. The class struggle polarized by the Klan in areas like Marshall County did not produce a new

16. Scales, "Political History of Oklahoma," 263–65; Richardson, *Texas*, 316–17; Burbank, "Agrarian Radicals and Their Opponents," 20–22.

17. Quotes on the connection between the Populists and the Klan from S. M. Lipset, *Political Man* (Garden City, N.Y.: Doubleday Anchor, 1963), 169.

18. The Socialists of the Southwest took the lead in attacking the Klan through the Farmer-Labor Union and Ameringer's hard-pressed *Oklahoma Leader*. Tom Hickey started a new newspaper in 1924 called the *Calliham Caller and Three Rivers Oil News* from the South Texas oil fields. He joined Ameringer in villifying the Klan and identifying it with the region's business classes, but, as usual, Hickey's propaganda was more acerbic than Ameringer's. He declared that "scientific studies of sexual psychopaths by Havelock Ellis and others" show how certain perverts satisfied "abnormal sexual passion by the sight of physical pain." In 1924 Hickey wrote, "I will not claim for a moment that every KKK is a sexual degenerate, but in the light of the recent . . . Texas and Oklahoma lashings I dare say that every sexual degenerate in the United States is in the KKK." See McAlister Coleman to the editor, *Nation* (New York), August 22, 1923, p. 195, on the *Leader*'s prob-lems. Also see *Calliham and Three Rivers Oil News* (Calliham, Tex.), Feb-ruary 8, 15, 1924, and Calliham (Tex.) *Caller*, March 28, 1924.

19. For class analyses of the southwestern Klan see Ameringer, *If You Don't Weaken*, 370, which corresponds to modern scholarly assessments of the Ku Klux Klan's middle-class base. See Scales, "Political History of Oklahoma," 228, and Alexander, *Ku Klux Klan in the Southwest*, 27, 29, 44, 49.

class-conscious Socialist movement. Tenancy increased even more as a result of the terrible depression of 1920–1921, but farmers now seemed to accept it with resignation rather than indignation. The Farmer-Labor Union had sprung to life in early 1920s as a radical industrial union expressing the anger of the poor tenants and laborers, but after reaching its peak in 1924 with 165,000 southwestern members, the Union declined rapidly for the same reasons that the Farmers' Alliance and the Renters' Union had declined before it. In 1926 Communist organizers of the "Red Peasant International" contacted E. R. Meitzen, in an effort to keep the Farmer-Labor Union alive, but it was too late. Covington Hall explained that the old Texas Socialists were discouraged at the failure of the Union and "bemused" at the demagoguery of their old rival Jim Ferguson and his wife "Ma."[20] Huey Long's election as governor of Louisiana a year later also puzzled the Socialist faithful. Huey had learned some socialistic rhetoric from his father, who used to read the *Appeal* and the *Rip-Saw*, and from the old Reds he debated around Winn Parish, but his sensational election troubled many class-conscious radicals who saw in Long's triumph the rise of a new kind of Democratic demagogue who would steal the Socialists' thunder more effectively than had old rabble-rousers like Jim Ferguson.

Nothing seemed to be going right for the southwestern Socialists in the mid-1920s. Troubles beset one of the few "red islands" remaining in the region, the Llano Cooperative Colony which had been transplanted from California to the piney woods near Leesville, Louisiana, in 1917. When Frank and Kate O'Hare suspended publication of the old *Rip-Saw*, they started publishing a new monthly called the *American Vanguard* at New Llano and founded a Commonwealth College for radical organizers, which promised to be a nucleus for a new southwestern Socialist movement. But,

20. Tindall, *Emergence of the New South*, 124–26; Hunt, *History of Farmer Movements in the Southwest*, 159; Jamieson, *Labor Unionism in American Agriculture*, 257; Lowell K. Dyson, "The Red Peasant International in America," *Journal of American History*, LVIII (1972), 962–65. Covington Hall to William Lemke, May 9, August 2, 1925, December 5, 1926, quoted in Dyson, "Red Peasant International."

according to Covington Hall, one of the colony's "elders," the
O'Hares' revolutionary socialism conflicted with the communitar-
ianism of the colony's founders. And so in 1925 Frank and Kate
led a splinter group of about fifty radicals away to reorganize
Commonwealth College in the little Ozark community of Mena,
Arkansas, which had had an active Socialist local before the war.
This split symbolized the difficulties of survival faced by the old
Socialists of the Southwest. When Eugene Debs died in 1926, it
truly seemed the end of an era.[21]

The southwestern Socialists, now a dwindling breed, tried to
keep the faith during the late twenties by reading the *Oklahoma
Leader*, one of the last beacons of radicalism still alight on the
southern Great Plains. But the *Leader* had to struggle along without the services of its founder and leading inspiration, Oscar
Ameringer, who had moved to the southern Illinois coal field to
edit the *Illinois Miner* and assist District 12 president Frank Far-
rington in his increasingly lonely fight against the growing power
of John L. Lewis' bureaucratic machine. When the Depression
hit the Southwest, the Socialist faithful hoped hard times would
bring a radical revival, but economic collapse only brought a more
desperate struggle for survival, which focused largely on keeping
the *Leader* afloat.[22]

21. Bill Murrah, "Llano Cooperative Colony, Louisiana," *Southern Exposure*, I, Nos. 3 and 4 (1974), 18–19. Sinclair to Theodore Debs, October 23,
1926, in Debs Collection, Indiana State University.

22. Ameringer, *If You Don't Weaken*, 395–401. Len DeCaux, a former
Wobbly who had worked with Oscar on the *Illinois Miner* during the 1920s,
wrote an interesting recollection of Ameringer's politics: "The Oscar I knew
in 1926 was hard to tag politically. He wasn't a tagger himself. He was
political. Oscar was known as an 'old socialist,' a 'reformist socialist.' At
times he called himself a 'revisionist,' when it came to Marxism. He was a
pal of early socialists whose red faded to a pretty pink pale. But Oscar was
not a 'yellow socialist.'

"In his prime, Oscar was a Debs kind of socialist, a fighter for the poor
and oppressed. As early unionist, as later socialist organizer of poverty-
stricken Oklahoma farmers, he fought for reforms and preached socialism."

DeCaux, who was on his way from the IWW to the Communist party and
the editorship of the *CIO News*, captured in this description the qualities
of reformism and radicalism existing side by side in the southwestern
movement. Oscar Ameringer personified the synthesis of these qualities.
Len DeCaux, *Labor Radical, From the Wobblies to the CIO: A Personal
History* (Boston: Beacon, 1970), 130.

Hopes for a Socialist resurgence were dimmed not only by the sad state of the national organization, but by the reemergence of southwestern Democratic demagogues who moved rapidly to the left as the tide of discontent rose. In 1929 Louisiana Governor Huey Long successfully and sensationally defeated the forces of impeachment and broadened his popular base of support by defeating the "ring" candidate for United States Senator in the Democratic primary of 1930. In the same year "Ma" and "Pa" Ferguson were using their well-established demagogic tactics to try for another term in Austin; they lost in 1930, but they won back their "redneck" following and returned to office two years later. This was the same year that Huey Long put his reputation on the line and came up to Arkansas to help Hattie Caraway win her uphill battle to return to the United States Senate seat she had won when her husband died. Long's intervention gave Caraway a surprising upset victory by portraying her as a candidate of the "common people" who was running against the bankers and special interests.[23]

In Oklahoma, the old Populist Thomas P. Gore returned to the wars along with old "agrarian radical" William H. Murray, who had been colonizing in Bolivia during the 1920s. These two progressives swept to victory in the 1930 Democratic primaries by running as "poor boys" against opponents who happened to be wealthy oilmen. During Murray's "down home" campaign for governor, his small weekly, the *Blue Valley Farmer*, edited by L. N. Sheldon, a former Socialist and founder of the Oklahoma Nonpartisan League, increased its circulation from 430 subscribers to a print run of 450,000. Like Huey Long, "Alfalfa Bill" attacked the state's oil corporations and proposed new income taxes, free textbooks, and big spending on a road program to employ the jobless. Making amends with labor and renouncing his earlier racist campaign style, Murray stomped his Republican opponent in the general election while Thomas Gore regained his old Senate seat from former Klansman W. B. Pine.[24] Although some old Socialists like Sheldon and Luther Langston backed Murray, not many of the

23. Richardson, *Texas*, 323, 325; Williams, *Huey Long*, 581–93.
24. Keith L. Bryant, Jr., *Alfalfa Bill Murray* (Norman: University of Oklahoma Press, 1968), 177–88.

old party faithful turned out to support their former enemy. Voter turnout in Oklahoma dropped from about 54 percent in 1914 (the Socialist party's best year) to around 40 percent in 1930, despite the fact that women gained and blacks regained the franchise.[25] Ameringer's *Oklahoma Leader* saw the Murray-Gore triumph as a much-needed repudiation of Hooverism, but its editorship and, most probably, its growing readership refused to be seduced by the fashionable progressivism of their one-time enemies. Their suspicions were justified when Governor Murray turned reactionary and joined Senator Gore as a conservative critic of the New Deal.[26]

SOUTHWESTERN SOCIALISTS FACE THE DEPRESSION

The Democratic demagogues seemed to cut the ground completely from under the old Socialists at the onset of the Depression, but the pioneers of Ameringer's generation refused to weaken. They had weathered hard times before, and now that the people were expressing renewed anger at bankers, businessmen, and other capitalist minions, these veteran agitators could not abandon the field of action to the opportunistic Democratic demagogues.

In 1930 Mother Jones died at the age of one hundred. Her passing was publicized in a popular phonograph record by Gene Autry, a young country singer who had worked as a railroad telegrapher up and down the Frisco line that ran through the Oklahoma coal

25. See Walter D. Burnham, "The Changing Shape of the American Political Universe," *American Political Science Review*, LIX (1965), 20–21.

26. Ameringer, *If You Don't Weaken*, 393, and *Oklahoma Leader* (Oklahoma City), August 15, 1930; Bryant, *Alfalfa Bill Murray*, 273. Given the fact that Murray was a Jim Hogg Democrat who opposed populism and then a Bryanite who opposed socialism, it is misleading at best to say that "populism of a sort, won out" when "Alfalfa Bill" was elected governor of Oklahoma in 1930. And it is simply wrong to say that this "was a shriveled ending for grass-roots American radicalism." See Daniel Bell, *Marxian Socialism in the United States* (Princeton, N.J.: Princeton University Press, 1967), 96. Murray was known as an agrarian radical only to conservative Democrats. He was racist and belligerently antiunion even when he was a progressive congressman. These tendencies, which were accentuated after Murray became governor, really represented a "shriveled ending" for the Democratic progressivism of Bryan and Wilson, which fed into wartime vigilante and Ku Klux Klan activity during the 1920s.

country.[27] Old Socialists mourned the "Death of Mother Jones," but the militant spirit she aroused among the southwestern coal miners remained alive. In 1929 Oscar Ameringer and Alex Howat had helped lead a rank-and-file rebellion against John L. Lewis, who had moved to consolidate his control over the UMW by installing his own men as officers of the hitherto intransigent Illinois district. Ameringer, who still edited the anti-Lewis *Illinois Miner*, brought Howat, together with John Brophy, Powers Hapgood, and other insurgents, including Adolph Germer and J. H. Walker (two old Socialists), and in 1930 they formed the "reorganized" UMW in open revolt against the incumbent bureaucracy. While "civil war" raged in southern Illinois between the insurgents and Lewis loyalists, Alex Howat tried to revive his old district in Kansas which had been nearly destroyed in the conflict with the Industrial Court and Lewis' first administration after World War I. Although he was more bellicose than ever (largely as a result of increasing alcoholism), Howat remained "a hero and a martyr to Kansas miners," who reelected him president. The old Scotch Socialist, serving as national president of the "reorganized" UMW, concurrently aided the Arkansas miners in attempting to revive their district, a district that had been drained by the court fight following the Prairie Creek mine war (the famous Coronado cases resolved against the UMW by the Supreme Court in the mid-1920s) and then "smashed" after a 1927 strike in which several miners were killed. Howat found the center of the Arkansas rank-and-file revival in the mining town of Paris where Claude Williams, a Socialist Presbyterian preacher, was helping the miners "reorganize their local" and "fight for autonomy" against Lewis' machine. Williams thought the miners' condition in Paris was "pitiful." After crushing the union in 1927, the owners had slashed wages from $8.00 a day to $3.50 a day and thrown many miners out of work. "No sooner was the union reorganized than a strike was called for

27. Archie Green, *Only a Miner: Studies in Recorded Coal-Mining Songs* (Urbana: University of Illinois Press, 1972), 249–50; Oscar Ameringer, "Mother Jones is Dead," *Oklahoma Weekly Leader* (Oklahoma City), December 5, 1930.

recognition throughout the western Arkansas and eastern Oklahoma coal field," wrote Cedric Belfrage. "Claude gave every moment he could spare to the strike, driving by day and night from one field to another" where "he found the miners and their families enduring great privations." After leading a big demonstration of unemployed and striking miners in Ft. Smith, the Reverend Williams, inspired by the workers' "fellowship of sweat and pride," decided to erect a Proletarian Church and Labor Temple in Paris; this awakened some "dormant spirit" in Sebastian County and, "less than a month after the birth of the idea, construction began," with "miners, farmers, masons, and carpenters, white and colored" pledging "free labor."[28]

While this inspirational activity took place in Paris, the "reorganized" UMW was collapsing on a national level and the southwestern strike was deteriorating. Lewis' men negotiated for the Oklahoma and Arkansas miners a meager increase of 50 cents a day and a dues checkoff which sent levies directly to the national office, whose occupant had now "defeated all his opponents." After the failure of the reorganized UMW in Illinois, Ameringer lost his job as editor of the insurgent *Miner* and returned to Oklahoma and his floundering newspaper, the *Leader*, which his son and his new wife, Freda Hogan, were struggling to maintain.

The defeat of the insurgent miners and their veteran Socialist leaders must have been very discouraging for Ameringer, who hoped that the coal camps would be the basis of Socialist party growth just as they had been in the early 1900s. But as usual, Ameringer refused to weaken. Facing almost insurmountable debts, Oscar and Freda abandoned the *Leader*, but refused to give up the cause of Socialist journalism in the Southwest. Instead of quitting, they transformed their old paper into a new weekly called the

28. *American Guardian* (Oklahoma City), May 16, 23, 1930. Also see Mark Naison, "Claude and Joyce Williams: Pilgrims of Justice," *Southern Exposure*, I, Nos. 3 and 4 (1974), 41–43; Cedric Belfrage, *Let My People Go* (London: Victor Gollancz, 1940), 95, 106–107, 111–13, 117, 160; McAlister Coleman, *Men and Coal* (New York: Farrar & Rinehart, 1943), 105, 138–41; on Howat, see Gary M. Fink (ed.), *Biographical Dictionary of American Labor Leaders* (Westport, Conn.: Greenwood, 1974), 165.

Norman Thomas speaking to sharecroppers in the Arkansas Delta, *c.* 1936.
Courtesy University of North Carolina

Oscar Ameringer as editor of the *American
Guardian*, Oklahoma City, *c.* 1938.
Courtesy Freda Hogan Ameringer

J. R. Butler, president of the Southern
Tenant Farmers' Union, 1938.
*Photo by Dorothea Lange
Courtesy Library of Congress*

E. B. McKinney, vice-president of the Southern Tenant Farmers' Union, presiding at a meeting while H. L. Mitchell, center, and Howard Kester look on.
Courtesy University of North Carolina

Stricken farmers in town during a drought, Sallisaw, Oklahoma, August, 1936.
Photo by Dorothea Lange
Courtesy Library of Congress

Tenant farmers displaced by tractor farming, North Texas, 1937.
Photo by Dorothea Lange
Courtesy Library of Congress

American Guardian. Ameringer continued his popular column "Adam Coaldigger," rallied old-timers like Upton Sinclair (soon to be a candidate for governor of California) and Walter Thomas Mills, and hired young talents like McAlister Coleman and Tom Tippett. The *Guardian* seemed to be consciously modeled on the old *Appeal*, which had brought the Socialist movement to life in the Southwest thirty years earlier. It combined the sensational writing of Sinclair with the educational writing of "Professor" Mills, and it blended the humorous editorials of Ameringer with the skillful reportage of Coleman, Tippett, and George Shoaf, an old *Appeal* investigator. Employing Wayland's old sales tactics, Ameringer raised a "Minute Man Army" of subscription salesmen, which helped the *Guardian*'s circulation increase from about twenty thousand in 1931 (largely old readers of the *Oklahoma Leader* and the *Illinois Miner*) to over forty-five thousand in 1934 when the weekly claimed a diverse national readership. Although Ameringer lacked Wayland's extraordinary flair for sensational journalism and salesmanship, he proved a worthy successor to the "one hoss" editor of the *Appeal*.[29]

Ameringer's *Guardian* gave the Socialists the encouragement they needed to start organizing again. The Socialist party's 1932 victory in Milwaukee showed the first real sign of a revival. Old southwestern party locals started reorganizing in the same year partly as a result of the efforts made by Ameringer and Mills who, with J. C. Thompson, onetime editor of the Texarkana *Socialist*, put together a "revival crusade." Veterans of the prewar Socialist movement in southwestern Oklahoma were also heartened by the dedication of a Cooperative Hospital in Elk City (once a site of the party's biggest encampments.) This unique "community clinic" in Beckham County was supported by John Simpson of the Farmers' Union and by the *Guardian*. It was the brainchild of a "crusading doctor" named Michael S. Shadid who had joined the Socialist party in 1912, campaigned against the mistreatment of medical patients in the 1920s, and became an important figure in the party's

29. Ameringer, *If You Don't Weaken*, 390, 398. *American Guardian* (Oklahoma City), January-July issues, 1931, December 18, 1931, April 6, 1934.

national leadership during the 1930s as a result of his successful cooperative experiment. Dr. Shadid, the Syrian-born Socialist, received anti-Semitic treatment and reactionary criticism from the medical profession, but his cooperative health plan continued to serve thousands of farmers in western Oklahoma, including a number of his old party comrades who stayed in and around Beckham County.[30] It was one of the few tangible monuments left by the southwestern Socialists.

The Socialist revival of the early 1930s started with the old-timers. It aroused experienced agitators like W. T. Mills and J. C. Thompson and old-time local leaders like Charley McCoy, a machinist, who converted a Ku Klux Klan klavern in Trumann, Arkansas, into a Socialist local, and Sam Faubus, another dedicated Debsian from the Ozarks who had kept in touch with his local during the lean years of the 1920s and pulled it together in the early thirties. When Bob Reed, a young Texas tenant farmer attending Commonwealth College, heard that Faubus needed help, he hopped a freight at Mena, jumped off near Holmes, and hiked up to Greasy Creek where he met a group of old-timers whose "old Socialist local" seemed like "one of the big events in their lives." Reed recalled that "they talked about it as if it had happened a few days ago." He also remembered meeting Sam Faubus' son, Orval, a schoolteacher who helped his father reconstitute the old local. Young Orval later joined Reed as a Commonweath College student, a decision he would regret when he ran for governor.[31]

Young Socialists like Bob Reed helped old Debsians create a radical revival in the early 1930s. These were the angry young men of Tom Joad's generation who tried farming on the shares like their fathers and grandfathers, but found themselves foreclosed or "tractored out." They were more rebellious than their fathers and they lacked the old-timers' patience and semireligious vision of the

30. *American Guardian* (Oklahoma City), August 14, 1931. Also see Michael A. Shadid, *Crusading Doctor* (Boston: Meador, 1956).
31. Interview with H. L. Mitchell, February 1, 1975; H. L. Mitchell interview with Bob Reed, April 7, 1974, p. 45, both in author's possession.

Cooperative Commonwealth. They read Oscar Ameringer's *American Guardian* hoping to find a way out of the depressed, degraded condition in which they found their class of people. They were the last generation of radicals produced by the southern poor whites who had been rebelling against their social "betters" ever since the first Scotch-Irish settlers came through the Cumberland Gap.

Two of the most effective Socialist organizers of this generation started working for the party in northeastern Arkansas shortly after the Depression began. In the little town of Tyronza, a filling station operator named Clay East and a dry cleaner named H. L. Mitchell started talking about socialism during the late 1920s. East was naturally inclined toward cooperative ideas and, when Mitchell gave him a copy of Upton Sinclair's *Letters to Jud*, he decided that socialism made a lot of "sense." Mitchell then started plying the gas station man with E. Haldeman Julius' "little blue books," which had helped to convert him to socialism when he was a sharecropper in Halls, Tennessee. Before long, Clay East had become a Socialist convert in the classical "common sense" tradition of the old *Appeal*. In fact, he became an avid reader of Ameringer's *American Guardian* and one of the leading "Minute Men" subscription agents in the country. In 1931 Mitchell and East got together with a socialistic sharecropper named Alvin Nunally, a well-known English immigrant named H. G. Panes, and about ten other like-minded malcontents, to form a Socialist party local. J. C. Thompson, the veteran Texarkana Socialist, came up under the auspices of the *Guardian* to tell them inspiring stories of the encampments and to teach them the principles of grass-roots organization. By 1932 the Tyronza Socialists were attracting from 50 to 150 people to their meetings and lectures at the Odd Fellows Hall. Through the influence of Socialist professor William R. Amberson of the University of Tennessee, the Tyronza local was able to schedule a visit from Norman Thomas while he was campaigning for president in 1932. The speech drew a crowd of about 500 to the Hall. During Thomas' visit to eastern Arkansas, East took him on a tour of the plantations so the Socialist leader could observe the dreadful conditions of life and labor which the "help" endured. After this, Norman Thomas dedicated himself to the task of drawing national attention to the plight of the southern sharecropper.[32]

The Socialists hoped that Norman Thomas' 1932 presidential campaign would begin an Socialist party revival at the polls, but it proved to be the high-point of the party's electoral recovery in the 1930s instead of the starting point. For the rest of the decade, competition from the Communists and the New Dealers, combined with the devastating effects of sectarian struggle, destroyed the remains of the Socialist party.[33] Some Socialists devoted their energies to rebuilding party locals in the early years of the Depression; many others turned to union organizing instead, continuing the traditions of the Renters' Union and other prewar socialistic groups. Their efforts blended with those of Communists and other leftists who were trying to organize the unemployed.

In 1933 unemployed workers on federal relief projects around Ft. Smith, Arkansas, organized the Workingmen's Union of the World. The Working Class Union had organized in the same area twenty years before, and some of the old syndicalists undoubtedly joined this new union, whose preamble was a blend of "hill country religion" and IWW doctrines. Led by old organizers from the UMW and various farmers' unions, the Workingmen's Union spread quickly around the Ozarks of Arkansas and into eastern Oklahoma where unemployed miners and tenant farmers founded locals in a number of old coal camps and Socialist precincts; it also recruited cotton pickers and other wage-earning farm workers, black and white, in LeFlore County, Oklahoma. But like the United Workers of the World, formed around Russellville, Arkansas, by old Socialists, the Workingmen's Union found it difficult to sustain its strikes and to keep track of its transient members. These organizations reflected both syndicalistic and socialistic influence; they

32. Transcript of tape recordings with H. L. Mitchell at the Institute for Southern Studies, 1973, in author's possession, hereinafter cited as Mitchell Transcript, 10–12, 16, 18. Also see interview with Clay East, in Sue Thrasher and Leah Wise, "The Southern Tenant Farmers' Union," *Southern Exposure,* I, Nos. 3 and 4 (1974), 13–14.
33. Shannon, *Socialist Party of America,* 209–23.

demonstrated an ability to organize across class lines and to conduct strikes, but by 1934 their meager resources were exhausted.[34]

Meanwhile Communists and other leftists were successfully organizing the unemployed farmers and workers who flooded into Oklahoma City. By 1933 Oklahoma reported over 300,000 unemployed, 42 percent of all the workers in the state. They huddled together in a giant Hooverville on the banks of the Canadian River, "maybe ten-miles wide and ten-miles long" with "people living in whatever they could junk together," recalled one resident of the Oklahoma City slum, "old rusted out car bodies," and "shacks made out of orange crates." One family actually lived in a hole in the ground. "The majority of people were hit and hit hard," Mary Owsley remembered. "They were mentally disturbed you're bound to know, 'cause they didn't know when all the end of this was comin'." Her husband, a veteran who joined the Bonus March on Washington, "was very bitter" because he "was an intelligent man" who "couln't see why there . . . was so many people starving to death" in such a wealthy country.[35]

The Communist-led Unemployed Councils mobilized many of these people and organized large and violent demonstrations in Oklahoma's capital city and other places like Henryetta, the scene of a shocking food riot. By 1933 the Communists had organized about eighty locals of about thirty thousand unemployed rural and urban workers throughout the state with seven thousand members and twenty-three locals in Oklahoma City alone. But the Unemployed Councils were soon disrupted by the arrest and conviction of their most active leaders. Many workers and farmers organized by the councils and by the short-lived Workingmen's Union of the World then joined the Veterans of Industry.[36]

---

34. Jamieson, "Labor Unionism in American Agriculture," 264–68.
35. Ameringer, *If You Don't Weaken*, 267; Carey McWilliams, *Ill Fares the Land: Migrants and Migratory Labor in the United States* (Boston: Little Brown, 1942), 187ff; Jamieson, "Labor Unionism in American Agriculture," 265. Peggy Terry and Mary Owsley quoted in Studs Terkel, *Hard Times: An Oral History of the Great Depression* (New York: Pantheon, 1970), 62–63, 67–68.
36. Jamieson, "Labor Unionism in American Agriculture," 265.

Founded by Ira Finley, a Socialist and a former president of the State Federation of Labor, the Veterans of Industry was a less revolutionary organization; it was also more durable than its predecessors and acted as "an effective pressure group for the propertyless" throughout the Depression. At its peak the Veterans claimed about forty thousand paid-up members, including a large number of blacks organized into separate locals in Muskogee and the garden-crop section of eastern Oklahoma. But many more cooperated with the Veterans' efforts to boycott agricultural employers who paid "slave wages" and to assist striking unionists in other industries by providing pickets and discouraging the unemployed from strikebreaking. Most Veterans of Industry members were unemployed, but there were also many who were working tenants and casual laborers. Although the Veterans enjoyed considerable success in mobilizing the rural proletariat along the Arkansas border, they did not move across the line, where the Workers' Alliance was organizing laborers for similar reasons, with the help of some Communist party unemployed organizers and sympathetic radicals like Claude and Joyce Williams.[37]

While individual Socialists participated in the Veterans of Industry and other proletarian unions, the party used its limited resources on educational and political campaigns, like Norman Thomas' 1932 presidential canvass. But the Depression created a need for the kind of organized action the party could no longer provide. Thomas' campaign aroused some interest, but not very much enthusiasm. The Socialist party was too weak to conduct the kind of grass-roots canvass it had waged for Gene Debs twenty years earlier. Some who had once voted Socialist now cast their ballots for Franklin Roosevelt or for "Alfalfa Bill" Murray and

37. *Ibid.*, 265–66. Ira Finley to author, January 23, 1975. Finley was a Debsian Socialist who participated in the Farmer-Labor Reconstruction League and was elected to the state legislature three times from western Oklahoma. In 1922 he ran as a Walton supporter and in 1924 as a LaFollette supporter. When he organized the Veterans of Industry Finley recruited a number of "old time Socialists like Oscar Ameringer, Kate Richards O'Hare and Stanley Clark" to fill speaking engagements. On the Workers' Alliance, see Naison, "Claude and Joyce Williams," 43–44.

Huey Long, both of whom attracted a great deal of attention in 1932 by their brief candidacies for the Democratic presidential nomination.

Although he could not foresee the bitter factionalism that would totally eliminate his party as a political force in the late 1930s, Norman Thomas could see the limited future of electoral politics in the Southwest. Nearly all blacks and most poor whites had been disfranchised by various methods. The desperate needs of these sharecroppers and rural workers had to be met more directly. When Thomas returned to the Arkansas Delta in 1934, he advised Clay East and H. L. Mitchell to build an organization, perhaps a union, for the sharecroppers, instead of spending all of their time contesting elections and doing political work. This must have been difficult advice for Thomas to offer because the Socialists of Tyronza had already built the strongest new party organization in the country. Led by H. L. Mitchell, a remarkable organizer who had inherited the skills of the Debsians, these Arkansas Socialists recruited about two thousand new members in the early thirties, including a number of blacks who followed the lead of popular sharecropper-preachers like A. B. Brookins and E. B. McKinney. Norman Thomas encouraged the croppers to join the party and vote for its candidates (notably Claude Williams who ran for Arkansas governor in 1934). But after touring the Hiram Norcross plantation, where forty tenants had been evicted so that the landlord could collect the payments due those tenants under the Agricultural Adjustment Act, Thomas decided that the sharecroppers also needed the protection of a union.[38]

"WE SHALL NOT BE MOVED": SOCIALISTS AND THE SOUTHERN TENANT FARMERS' UNION

The Agricultural Adjustment Act payments issue caused a great deal of resentment among croppers and helped the Southern Tenant Farmers' Union grow in its early years. The acreage reduction called for in the act displaced thousands of sharecroppers through-

---

38. Mitchell Transcript, 42; Thrasher and Wise, "Southern Tenant Farmers' Union," 14; Belfrage, *Let My People Go*, 188.

out the South, and those tenants who remained on the land were deprived of the subsidies they were supposed to receive under the act.[39] In fact, many planters stole the payments of their renters, because, as one historian notes, they saw their tenants as "child-like, dependent, improvident persons" for whom the landlord was obligated to make decisions. Mitchell and East had already organized an "Unemployed League" through their Socialist local to fight planter control of relief payments and public works programs; thus they were primed to organize sharecroppers around the issue of Agricultural Adjustment Act benefits, which had become a matter of life and death to many poor families.[40]

At the 1934 Arkansas Socialist convention Mitchell recruited the support of J. R. Butler, a gaunt school teacher turned sawmill hand who had supported Debs before the war and claimed membership in the Working Class Union during the time of the Green Corn Rebellion. With the help of E. B. McKinney, the black preacher, and several other Socialists around Tyronza, Mitchell and Butler, with cautious enthusiasm, started organizing the Southern Tenant Farmers' Union.[41] The organizers of the STFU brought together many of the agrarian Socialist strands that had originated in the prewar movement, even adopting the constitutional preamble of the original Renters' Union charter, which Oscar Ameringer sent to them.[42]

The STFU immediately developed a more proletarian perspective than the original Renters' Union by insisting on organizing agricultural wage laborers as well as sharecroppers. This decision may have been influenced partly by the Union's first president, J. R. Butler, who had been exposed to IWW doctrines through his membership in the Working Class Union. The influence of militant in-

39. See Richard Hofstadter, "Southern Cotton Tenants under the A.A.A." (M.A. thesis, Columbia University, 1938).

40. Donald Grubbs, *Cry from the Cotton: The Southern Tenant Farmers' Union and the New Deal* (Chapel Hill: University of North Carolina Press, 1971), 20–22; and Mitchell Transcript, 12.

41. Grubbs, *Cry from the Cotton*, 28–29, 62–63.

42. Interview with Mitchell, February 1, 1975; "Constitution, By-Laws, etc., of the Southern Tenant Farmers' Union," July 26, 1934, in Southern Tenant Farmers' Union Papers, Harvard University.

dustrial unionism was particularly evident in the STFU's insistence upon interracial organization. This was also the result of changed conditions, however. By the time the Depression began, the economic differences between white share tenants and black sharecroppers in eastern Arkansas had been partially eroded. As J. R. Butler recalled:

> It wasn't long before we had an organizer or two in jail because the plantation element in that part of the country absolutely did not want them "niggers" organized, and they didn't hesitate to say it in just those words. But the whites were niggers too. There was no difference, and some of 'em was beginning to see that there was no difference. Of course, there was still a lot of prejudice among whites in those days, but hard times makes peculiar bedfellows sometimes, and so some of them were beginning to get their eyes open and see that all of them were being used. So it was easy to get a start on organizing.[43]

The STFU gained a foothold in a section of eastern Arkansas reclaimed and settled in the 1920s by black and white croppers from many areas of the South. As a result, the area around Crittenden, Cross, St. Francis, and Poinsett counties lacked an established planter oligarchy and a long-standing system of paternalistic relations. The Union started organizing with various secret tactics before the planters even knew what was happening. It adopted the same methods used by the Brotherhood of Timber Workers, the biggest interracial industrial union in the Southwest prior to the STFU. And, like the BTW, it recruited women, whose important role in the family and the community the tenant organizers recognized. As black union leader George Stith recalled, "we had a family membership." In some cases widows took out membership cards because they were the heads of the family. "But where there was a man and his wife involved, she was a member too" and "she had a voice when it come down to talking or voting."[44]

Like the old Socialist Renters' Union, the Southern Tenant Farmers' Union relied upon religious enthusiasm and Bible social-

43. Interview with Mitchell, February 1, 1975; and Thrasher and Wise, "Southern Tenant Farmers' Union," 15.
44. Mitchell Transcript, 19, 24, 29, 56.

ism to move the rural folk of the region.[45] Black preachers like
E. B. McKinney, the Union's first vice-president, made it possible
for the organization to become interracial. The STFU also used
white holiness preachers like the Reverend W. L. Blackstone to recruit "redneck" sharecroppers who had no part in the conservative
"uptown" white churches. In fact, Mitchell recalled, some holiness
people actually transformed their congregations into Union locals.
The Socialist leaders of the STFU distrusted these holiness
preachers, but admitted that they made great organizers.[46]

The STFU's blending of black and white southern revivalism was
reflected in the famous songs the movement created. Like the Populist and Socialist encampment preachers, the STFU ministers and
young folk singers like John Handcox, a black Socialist, and Lee
Hays, later of the "Weavers," adapted old religious songs to a
struggle that became increasingly violent and repressive. The most
famous song that emerged was "We Shall Not Be Moved" sung to
the tune of "Jesus Is My Captain":

> The union is a-marching.
>   We shall not be moved,
> The union is a marching,
>   We shall not be moved.
> Just like a tree that's planted by the water,
>   We shall not be moved.

"That song i Do believe sprung from our lips with the voice of
God," wrote Union member J. W. Washington. "It re[mem]bered
my mind back to the time when Moses was Leading his childrens
of Isrel." The millennial promise of agrarian socialism had been
revived.[47]

In addition to such indigenous religious radicals as E. B. Mc-
Kinney and W. L. Blackstone, the STFU benefited from the support
of several Presbyterian preachers who had moved from Tennessee
to Arkansas and from the social gospel to socialism. Howard
"Buck" Kester, a Socialist party activist, came over from the theo-

---

45. *Ibid.*, pp. 3, 36; Grubbs, *Cry from the Cotton*, 67–68.
46. Mitchell Transcript, 91–92, 336–37.
47. J. W. Washington to H. L. Mitchell, January 19, 1936, in Southern
Tenant Farmers' Union Papers.

logical school at Vanderbilt with his roommate Ward Rodgers, the product of a Socialist family from Alva, Oklahoma. These two young radicals were at the extreme left of southern protestantism in the 1930s, and unlike the "agrarians" who had come out of Nashville a decade earlier, they were not nostalgic critics of capitalism. They organized a Southern Conference of Younger Churchmen which viewed capitalism as anti-Christian and pledged to "eliminate the system's incentives and habits, the legal forms which sustain it, and the moral ideals which justify it."[48]

Kester and Rodgers both threw themselves into the STFU's organizational work despite the risks they ran as "outside agitators." Another radical Presbyterian, Claude Williams, set up a "New School of Social Action" in Little Rock and there trained some of the STFU's black and white organizers. Williams continued organizing the unemployed through the Workers' Alliance and brought together old Socialists with young Communists from Commonwealth College who were now entering the Popular Front period, which called for cooperation with other leftists. Claude Williams' school was a uniquely religious labor education program designed for the "workaday" preachers who were leading many unionization drives in the rural South. According to Mark Naison, "Claude's presentation of the Bible as a 'continuous record of revolutionary struggle' spoke directly to their need to see their political activities in religious terms, and provided a context in which they could act creatively to overcome their followers' fear of 'race mixing', physical repression, and ostracism by the local middle class." After moving to Little Rock and making contact with the STFU leaders, Williams joined McKinney, Mitchell, and Butler as one of the leading organizers in the Delta until he was offered the presidency of Commonwealth College in 1937. After this, Williams moved closer to the Communist party and developed a perspective on agricultural unionism different from that of the Socialist STFU leaders.[49]

In its first year of activity the STFU tried to win justice for the sharecroppers by petitioning the Department of Agriculture under

48. Grubbs, *Cry from the Cotton*, 70–71, 75–77; Mitchell Transcript, 23.
49. Naison, "Claude and Joyce Williams," 44–48; Belfrage, *Let My People Go*, 287–95.

Henry A. Wallace, "that great liberal" as Mitchell derisively called him, and by agitating within the Agricultural Adjustment Administration (AAA) through liberals like Gardner "Pat" Jackson. But this approach failed. In fact, in 1935 the young liberals, including Jackson, Lee Pressman, and Jerome Frank, were "purged" after pushing to provide more legal and physical protection for sharecroppers against the planters. President Roosevelt refused to risk losing the support of Senate leader Joe Robinson, a representative of the Arkansas planters, and so he agreed to the sacking of the pro-STFU people in the AAA. Henry Wallace went along with the "purge" too. After this, the leaders of the STFU became increasingly articulate Socialist critics of the New Deal's agricultural policy, a policy that helped planters and hurt sharecroppers.[50]

The STFU organizers then decided to take more direct action and to rely less upon government intervention. In 1935 union members voted overwhelmingly to strike for a pay rate of one dollar per hundred weight (most workers were getting only forty to sixty cents). The action, which took nearly five thousand cotton pickers out of the fields, caught the planters by surprise. As George Stith, a black organizer from Cotton Plant, Arkansas, recalled:

> The strike of '35 was one of the most unique things that ever happened. We decided after meeting . . . back in early plantin' season . . . what we would have to do about trying to get some better wages. . . . We had been able to get some things adjusted like commissaries. . . . But wages just wasn't going up any.
>
> So we had decided that a general strike would be the thing. But it had taken a lot of planning to figure out how we were going to do it. The executive committee . . . had all these hand bills printed up . . . and made up packages to go to each area. . . . All the representatives came in and got their strike handbills with strict instructions. And that night at eleven o clock, they was all over Arkansas. . . . It was all done at the same time and that scared the planters to death. They wouldn't agree to sign a contract with the union, but they started to

---

50. H. L. Mitchell, "The Southern Tenant Farmers' Union, 1935," in Southern Tenant Farmers' Union Papers; Grubbs, *Cry from the Cotton*, 30–60. Also see Jerold S. Auerbach, "Southern Tenant Farmers: Socialist Critics of the New Deal," *Labor History*, VII (1966), 2–22.

make concessions to labor. Well that's really what we were looking for; we was trying to make things better for people.[51]

H. L. Mitchell, the union's leading tactician, was not troubled by the lack of a contract, because "there was a kind of unofficial bargaining." The planters "wouldn't recognize the union as such, but they'd watch to see what the union was going to demand particularly after that cotton picking experience of 1935." The STFU called a "wage conference every year" so that the members could vote on what they wanted to try to get per hundred weight. "We would announce the union was demanding a dollar per hundred pounds for picking cotton" and "this had the same effect as a wage contract," recalled Mitchell—"kind of an old IWW idea." If there was no contract, then workers had to take direct action on the job.[52] This procedure made the STFU more democratic than organizations in which the leaders did all the collective bargaining.

Although the Tenant Farmers' Union had given up on New Deal bureaucrats, it continued to rely on outsiders with fund-raising connections, notably Norman Thomas, another former Presbyterian minister, who fell into the call-and-response pattern of speaking when he addressed the southern sharecroppers whose cause meant so much to him. When Thomas spoke in the Delta against the AAA in the spring of 1935, he was attacked by drunken deputies and riding bosses in a town inappropriately named Birdsong. A few months earlier Lucien Koch of Commonwealth College and Bob Reed of the Young Communist League had been beaten at a black church in Gilmore for telling a "mixed audience" how to resist evictions. The wave of violence against STFU members, mainly blacks, that followed failed to get a response from the federal government, even from liberals like Wallace and Rexford Tugwell who were "stung by continual protests" from Norman Thomas and other friends of the Union.[53]

But despite the wave of repression in 1935, the STFU's organizers gamely expanded their operations into other sections of Arkansas

51. Thrasher and Wise, "Southern Tenant Farmers' Union," 24–25.
52. *Ibid.*; Mitchell transcript, 26, 53; Grubbs, *Cry from the Cotton*, 84–85.
53. Grubbs, *Cry from the Cotton*, 72–74.

and then into Oklahoma where Odis Sweeden organized a number of locals. A remarkable character who had learned about the STFU when he found a copy of Ameringer's *American Guardian* in an outhouse, Sweeden started recruiting in the area around Muskogee where the Workingmen's Union of the World had organized a number of black field workers. The gregarious Cherokee then expanded into other parts of eastern Oklahoma, including some localities where the original Socialist Renters' Union had been organized by "Tad" Cumbie and Stanley Clark. At the same time, the STFU made contact with Communists organizing the Alabama Share-croppers' Union and publishing *The Rural Worker*, which officially endorsed the Arkansas-Oklahoma tenant farmers' union. But Mitchell and other STFU leaders were put off when Communist party leader Don Henderson of *The Rural Worker* argued that all "toiling farmers," meaning all tenants and owners who did not exploit hired labor, should join the National Farmers' Union or the Farm Holiday Association whereas all wage workers should organize AFL affiliates. Angered at this effort to impose a "new line" on the STFU, Mitchell hotly informed Henderson that "we do not look with favor upon the introduction of 'craft unionism' in the cotton fields." The STFU would continue to pursue its brand of industrial unionism which would include all classes of farm labor. Mitchell's defense of these tactics, which made sense in an area where small owners and tenants often worked as wage hands, resembled the argument Covington Hall had made thirty years earlier on behalf of tenants and other dirt farmers in the Brotherhood of Timber Workers. When the Alabama Sharecropper's Union adopted the new Communist party line, "Buck" Kester and J. R. Butler attacked it in the STFU's *Sharecroppers' Voice*. Mitchell informed Gardner Jackson, who favored unification, that a merger of the two unions was now "impossible" because he could not "trust people who change their entire program overnight on orders from a super organization."[54]

54. Grubbs, *Cry from the Cotton*, 80–83; H. L. Mitchell to Donald Henderson, August 12, 1936, H. L. Mitchell to Norman Thomas, November 17, 1936, both in Southern Tenant Farmers' Union Papers.

The STFU struggled to hold its membership while Gardner Jackson and John L. Lewis of the new Congress of Industrial Organizations helped save the Union from destruction by persuading Senator Robert LaFollette, Jr. to launch an investigation of the violence in Arkansas. During the 1936 picking season STFU leaders decided to call a strike like the one that had successfully taken the planters by surprise a year earlier. Word leaked out about this action and it was met with violent repression, but not before some militant black farmers around Colt, Arkansas, had marched out of the hills and called out the pickers in the surrounding plantations. This spontaneous marching strike was the high point of the unsuccessful 1936 action.[55]

When Roosevelt campaigned in Arkansas in 1936 he refused to see a delegation of STFU leaders. The president actually made a speech "about what a wonderful state Arkansas was, and what a wonderful Senator 'Greasy Joe' Robinson was, but he forgot to say anything about the wonderful conditions of the sharecroppers." The sharecroppers' plight threatened to become a national issue in the 1936 campaign when Frank Weems, a black organizer of a marching strike, was reported missing and was presumed dead by the national wire services. The continuing violence against the Union's black members did not arouse much attention, however. But when a young white woman from a prominent Memphis family was flogged by a mob of "fine" looking men in their "summer whites" (who were really after Claude Williams), a furor erupted across the nation.

It was not coincidental, Donald Grubbs writes, that President Roosevelt appointed his special commission on farm tenancy shortly after this well-publicized event. STFU members, led by Claude Williams, literally had to force their way onto the commission, which ultimately did nothing for the sharecroppers. As a result of these events and the deepening of the Depression, Roosevelt's New Deal was not quite as popular in Arkansas and Oklahoma as it was in other sections of the South. But the unpopu-

55. Grubbs, *Cry from the Cotton*, 91–105; interview with H. L. Mitchell, October 5, 1972.

larity of the administration among STFU members did not help
Norman Thomas, who conducted a less successful Socialist party
presidential campaign in 1936 than he had run four years before.[56]

Still isolated and exceedingly vulnerable to repression, STFU
leaders decided to affiliate with the newly formed Congress of Industrial Organizations. The Reverend Claude Williams helped persuade STFU delegates in Memphis to affiliate with the CIO when
he delivered a rousing speech about the new labor movement, closing in traditional radical revivalist style: "The Lord spake unto the
children of Moses: Go Forward: He that putteth his hands to the
plow and looketh backward is not fit for the Kingdom of God. Go
forward, FORWARD INTO THE CIO!" And so the cheering sharecroppers voted to affiliate with the new industrial union movement.
However Mitchell and other STFU leaders worried about the status
of their union in the Communist-dominated United Cannery, Agricultural, Packing and Allied Workers Union (UCAPAWA), headed
by their rival Don Henderson, who still thought the STFU was
"neither fish nor fowl" because it organized farm laborers together with farm tenants.[57]

The STFU's association with the CIO affiliate was short-lived.
Henderson and other CIO officials "smothered" the STFU with
clerical work and "crushed" it with bureaucratic and financial obligations. In any case, Mitchell, Butler, Kester, and other Socialist
STFU leaders deeply distrusted the Communists, especially upon
deciding that Claude Williams, who was close to the Communist
party, seemed to be trying to undermine their leadership. In fact,
factionalism did increase seriously in 1938 as Williams, E. B. Mc-
Kinney, W. L. Blackstone, and Odis Sweeden lined up against the
old Socialist leadership. This was certainly no Communist conspiracy; there were legitimate tactical differences between the two
camps. But the results of the faction fight hurt the STFU. Mitchell

56. Grubbs, *Cry from the Cotton*, 107–14, 116–20. See Shannon, *Socialist
Party of America*, 243–46, on the effects of the party's factional split during
Thomas' 1936 campaign.
57. Mitchell transcript, 32 ff; Grubbs, *Cry from the Cotton*, 162–69. For a
full text of Williams' amazing speech, complete with audience responses,
see Belfrage, *Let My People Go*, Chap. 17.

regained the loyalty of McKinney, the Union's most important black leader, but the organization lost some of its best organizers including Williams, Blackstone, and Sweeden. Shortly after this battle, the STFU withdrew from the United Cannery, Agricultural, Packing and Allied Workers Union and the CIO. Don Henderson forced the issue by insisting that the Arkansas affiliate pay per capita dues its members simply could not afford.[58]

When the Southern Tenant Farmers' Union affiliated with the CIO, it claimed 30,827 members in 328 locals, mostly in Arkansas—far more members than any other UCAPAWA affiliate. But after the factionalism of 1938 and the terrible effects of the recession, the STFU began to decline. Furthermore, the giant migration of Okies and Arkies along Route 66 began to undermine the Union's base. The STFU suffered another blow in 1939 when Owen Whitfield, the charismatic black leader of the Missouri "roadside demonstration," took a number of black leaders, including McKinney, back into UCAPAWA because the CIO was "the Joe Lewis of the labor movement." Disgusted with factional splits, Gardner Jackson, the Union's "guardian angel" in Washington, withdrew his support and the northern liberal backing for the STFU declined.[59]

58. Grubbs, *Cry from the Cotton*, 172–80; and Mark Naison, "The Southern Tenant Farmers' Union and the CIO," *Radical America*, II, No. 5 (1968), 36–55.

59. Jamieson, "Labor Unionism in American Agriculture," 314; interview with H. L. Mitchell, October 5, 1972; Gardner Jackson to H. L. Mitchell, March 13, 1939, March 31, 1939, in Southern Tenant Farmers' Union Papers. The STFU's democratic rank-and-file unionism appeared in other southwestern CIO affiliates as well. The Packinghouse Workers' Organizing Committee in Oklahoma City and Ft. Worth issued the following guidelines in 1940: "It takes Organizers inside the plant to Organize the plant. The Committee that organized the Oklahoma City plant was a voluntary committee established inside the plant. You cannot wait for the National Organizer to do all the work. . . . You people here can have a Union, but you will have to work to build it." According to David Brody, the Packinghouse Workers in the Southwest, like CIO unions in other areas, aimed "to avoid 'bureaucratic' rule by putting the leadership, as one [Oklahoma City] organizer put it, not in a few hands, but 'in the whole body, in one, acting as one'." David Brody, "The Emergence of Mass-Production Unionism," in John Braeman, Robert H. Bremner, and Everett Walters (eds.), *Change and Continuity in Twentieth Century America: The 1920s* (Columbus: Ohio State University Press, 1968), 239–40.

After 1939 the Tenant Farmers' Union stopped organizing and set up a program to find its members jobs in other parts of the country. This phase lasted until 1942 when a new federal law prohibited this kind of job-getting and authorized the importation of migrant laborers from the West Indies and Mexico. At this point, STFU president J. R. Butler resigned to become a machinist and H. L. Mitchell began to spend more of his time working for the National Youth Administration. "Mitch" returned to the scene, however, when a holiness preacher took over and began to organize segregated locals in Alabama. Mitchell himself was elected president of the STFU in 1945, the Union's last year. In 1946 its name was changed to the National Farm Labor Union; it was then chartered as an AFL affiliate in 1946 through the influence of Pat Gorman, a Socialist official of the Amalgamated Meat Cutters' Union. The National Farm Labor Union moved its operations to California after the war, where it led strikes of grape pickers at the DiGiorgio Fruit Corporation (largely Okie and Arkie migrants) and of cotton pickers in the San Joaquin Valley (largely Chicanos, including a "young fellow" named Cesar Chavez).[60]

Thirty years after he had retired as STFU president, J. R. Butler (who remains a Socialist because he "couldn't be anything else and be honest with" himself), evaluated the historic significance of the Union: "Most of the unions have gotten to where they're not rank and file anyway. Even the industrial unions are controlled by officials who are not elected that often. Back in the earlier days, when people thought about joining the union, it was something like joining a church." The STFU was not really a "mass movement" in Butler's view, but "it was big enough and so much out of the ordinary that it drew the attention of the world, and so in a way I think we did a lot of good." The Union not only won more AAA benefits and better wages for its black and white members, it also succeeded in organizing an industrial union that brought poor laboring people of both races together to take effective action against their common enemy. Part of the STFU's success as an

60. Mitchell Transcript, 31, 92–94, 101; Thrasher and Wise, "Southern Tenant Farmers' Union," 30–31.

interracial organization resulted from the influence of old Socialists and Wobblies who understood the weaknesses of the prewar, poor white movement. The STFU was also able to draw more attention to the plight of the sharecropper than any other organization. It was generally frustrated in its dealings with New Dealers, but it did carry on the crusade begun by agrarian Socialists thirty years earlier and finally won some official response when it influenced the formation of the Farm Security Administration.[61]

Unfortunately the Tenant Farmers' Union affected few people outside of Arkansas, eastern Oklahoma, and southern Missouri. The STFU failed to make any progress in Texas, the birthplace of the Farmers' Alliance, the Farmers' Union, and the Socialist-led Renters' Union. As a result, many tenants were cut off from the organized resistance the Southern Tenant Farmers' Union offered and from the radical tradition it represented. In 1937 Floyd Murray, the son of cotton tenants, wrote a remarkable letter to President Roosevelt, from Bryan, Texas, a place far removed from STFU organizing. The letter reveals the profound sense of class anxiety and political passivity that affected those tenant families outside the radical tradition. "I was born and reared on a tenant farm . . . in circumstances of the most stringent poverty. . . . I am fully acquainted with the hopeless misery and bleakness, the horrible mockery of civilization which is practically . . . inevitable in this life. My own childhood and youth is a haunting nightmare, utterly devoid of a single tender memory." Murray, who was still a poor man, described his childhood in detail: "I never, at any time, had even necessary clothing, not to mention such items as would allow a measure of self respect. I could win debates; I could not spell and write themes. But I could not and would not participate in any of these things, simply because I was unable to wear presentable clothing to a program." Then he told the president that, having experienced "all these things," he should probably have become a Socialist. "I don't know why I am not a radical today, but I am not." Reflecting on his youth, Murray concluded with this pessi-

61. Thrasher and Wise, "Southern Tenant Farmers' Union," 12, 32; Grubbs, *Cry from the Cotton*, 141–45.

mistic reflection: "In those days renters . . . accepted their lot, not through fortitude or honest patience, but through absolute inability to conceive a better plane of life as applicable to them." Floyd Murray, who grew up in the 1920s, was obviously not acquainted with the old radical traditions of the tenant movement or with the visions of a new society it created. To him the indignities heaped upon the poor white class were injuries to be suffered and not wrongs to be righted. It is interesting to note that in the same year Murray wrote this pathetic letter, the STFU's agitation helped bring about the Farm Security Administration, whose talented photographers—notably Dorothea Lange and Margaret Bourke-White— took hundreds of pictures, largely of sad-faced "Okies" with a hopeless look about them. There must have been many people like Floyd Murray among these faces.[62]

KEEPING THE FAITH: THE LAST YEARS OF SOUTHWESTERN SOCIALISM

The Southern Tenant Farmers' Union was the most important organizing project the Socialist party sponsored anywhere in the country after World War I. When Norman Thomas' presidential campaign of 1936 failed to win the kind of support the party had achieved four years earlier, most southwestern Socialists pinned their hopes on the expansion of the STFU. And so when internal factionalism, planter repression, and the Okie migrations caused the Union to decline in the late 1930s, many Socialists in Arkansas and Oklahoma gave up hope of reviving the big prewar movement.

Of course the epic migration of the "Okies" and "Arkies" to California in the late 1930s removed many of the discontented poor whites who had created the radical farm movements during the previous fifty years of southwestern history. The "Okie" families left their farms in the late 1930s, but like the Joad family in *The Grapes of Wrath*, they left with anger as well as sadness in their hearts. There is an old Oklahoma folk song that captures their sad feeling and reflects the stubborn "Okie" spirit of the Joad family.

---

62. Floyd Murray to Franklin D. Roosevelt, March 19, 1937, in Franklin D. Roosevelt Library, Hyde Park, N.Y.

Woody Guthrie, who loved to sing the tune, said it was one of the most popular songs in his repertoire. This is how he sang the chorus:

> I'm goin' down this road feelin' bad,
> I'm a goin' down this road feelin' bad,
> I'm goin' down this road feelin' bad Lord, Lord,
> But I ain't gone be treated this a way.

In a 1940 recording made for the Library of Congress Woody told Alan Lomax about the song's origin. "It was wrote," he said, "by a Southern slave who run up north and was treated like a dog."

Oscar Ameringer's *American Guardian* continued to preach the Socialist gospel out of the old *Leader* building in Oklahoma City. But Oscar never realized his hope of making his weekly into a new *Appeal*. The *Guardian* recruited some important Minutemen like Clay East and some active organizers like Odis Sweeden in the early 1930s, but in the latter part of the decade it moved away from party building in the Southwest and took a more international approach. In fact, Ameringer's newspaper developed an increasingly antiwar focus in the late 1930s, which may have accounted for its increasing financial difficulties. Like Norman Thomas and other Socialists who had battled so courageously against United States intervention in World War I, Oscar Ameringer found himself in a dilemma, as a second great war threatened Europe. These Socialists supported the Republic's battle against fascism in Spain, but as the threat of total war became more menacing, they adopted a stand resembling traditional midwestern isolationism, except in its emphasis on the capitalist causes of war.[63]

When Ameringer's appropriately titled autobiography *If You Don't Weaken* appeared in 1940, it received wonderful reviews throughout the country, and, much to Oscar's satisfaction, it sold well even though it presented a pacifist message in a time of rising "war hysteria." About the time his book appeared, Ameringer wrote a memorandum to his financial supporters entitled "*The*

63. See Ameringer, *If You Don't Weaken*, 461–65; and Bernard K. Johnpoll, *Pacifist's Progress: Norman Thomas and the Decline of American Socialism* (Chicago: Quadrangle, 1970), 185–88, 205–35.

American Guardian Meets a Pressing Need." The editor wrote that forty-five thousand men and women still subscribed to his weekly and that a "large number" of them were still participating in the unique "Minute Man Army." He explained that the *Guardian* was being edited in the Southwest, on "an American front where the struggle for peace, freedom, and democracy" was being "fiercely waged." His weekly was no longer a "regional paper," however; it had more readers in California than in Oklahoma, more in New York than Texas. The voice of socialism was still being heard in the Southwest, but it was no longer the distinctly radical voice of the southwestern movement. Ameringer was now a noted national figure praised by book reviewers like Clifton Fadiman and William Allen White and in newspapers ranging from the New York *Times* to the Tulsa *World*, a leading jingoist paper in World War I.[64] In 1939–1940, Oscar's *Guardian* became an antiwar weekly, like the *Appeal* of 1917; it even took up the old Socialist call for an end to "fantastic" military appropriations and for "a national referendum on the subject of war." It also demanded "a sharp curtailment of the powers of the President to put the youth of this nation onto the European and Oriental battle fields." But these efforts to revive the antiwar movement of the Debsian era and to expand the *Guardian* on a "nation-wide scale" did not succeed. As a Jewish Socialist told Norman Thomas when the Socialist party leader was considering an antiwar presidential campaign in 1940: "This is 1939 not 1917! What was correct then must not necessarily be so today." But Thomas decided to run against Roosevelt on a pacifist platform in 1940 anyway.[65]

The campaign was no more than a symbolic gesture by Socialist pacifists. The faction-rent party was not a legal entity in many big states and it was virtually barred from the ballot in Oklahoma. The *Guardian* supported Thomas' attacks on Roosevelt's "back-door-to-war" policies and his inadequate response to the Nazi refugee prob-

64. *American Guardian* (Oklahoma City), June 28, 1940. Freda Hogan Ameringer was kind enough to show me a scrapbook of scores of favorable reviews of *If You Don't Weaken.*
65. Johnpoll, *Pacifist's Progress*, 209, 214, 217–18.

lem; it proudly recalled the spirit of the old antiwar movement when the party's leading pacifist told the Senate Military Affairs Committee: "Conscription . . . is a road leading straight to militarism, imperialism, and ultimately to American fascism and war." Ameringer and Thomas tapped some of the old antiwar sentiment among radical farmers and workers in the West and Midwest along with the more conservative isolationism of that region, but their pacifist campaign alienated Jewish support in the East, which accounted for most of the Socialist party's decimated membership. As a result of this final and nearly fatal factional fight, Thomas polled an abysmal vote of 99,557, the smallest total his party had ever received. The Socialist party was no longer a significant influence in American life.[66]

The 1940 election, coupled with the rapid decline of the Southern Tenant Farmers' Union, must have convinced the old-time southwestern Socialists that they had run their final race. Oscar Ameringer, who always supported electoral action in tandem with interracial industrial unionism and Socialist pacifism, must have realized that his movement had failed on all fronts. He carried on bravely in 1941 but in 1942, as the *Guardian*'s subscribers dropped off, Ameringer took sick and closed down his last paper. Freda drove him to Dr. Shadid's cooperative clinic in Elk City, where Oscar rallied for a time. Being among his old comrades at the scene of the biggest encampments of the Debsian days seemed to give the weakened "troubador" a "new lease on life." In 1943 old comrades like Covington Hall, his friendly rival from the old days in New Orleans, wrote to cheer him up. But on November 6, 1943, the "Mark Twain of American Socialism" died.[67]

Veteran Socialists knew that Oscar's passing symbolized the death of the old movement. Ameringer was the "Oklahoma Pioneer." He had never weakened even in the face of his party's worst defeats. He had survived, indeed thrived, long after the death of the

66. *Ibid.*
67. McAlister Coleman, "Oscar Ameringer Never Weakened," *Nation* (New York), November 27, 1943, pp. 608–10. Art Young to Oscar Ameringer, June 25, 1943, and Hall to Freda Hogan Ameringer, October 27, 1943, both in Oscar Ameringer Papers, Wayne State Labor Archives, Detroit.

movement that had given him such hope and strength in the early days. Unlike many of the urban intellectuals who abandoned socialism for Wilson's war, for LaFollette's progressive crusade, or for Roosevelt's New Deal, Oscar Ameringer and his generation of "pioneers" never lost faith in the Debsian ideal of the Cooperative Commonwealth.

In his last years Ameringer was discouraged by the virulent sectarianism that accompanied the decline of the Socialist movement. "Old friends and comrades assail one another's character and bloody one another's noses over policies which only trial and error can prove or disprove," Ameringer wrote in 1939. In typically comic fashion, he wrote toward the end of *If You Don't Weaken*: "Wings over Union Square. Right wings, left wings and winglets of wings, and most of them attached to dead birds." But he did not despair over this factionalism because he believed that someday soon Socialists would again realize that the problem of capitalism cried out for an "American solution."[68]

Kate Richards O'Hare, another leading Americanizer of Marxian socialism, was also discouraged by the splits of the 1930s. She had joined Walter Thomas Mills and other California Socialists who bolted the old party to support Upton Sinclair's unsuccessful campaign to "end Poverty in California" in 1934. But like her "beloved comrade Oscar," Kate refused to despair. Instead, she looked back proudly on the old Debsian movement because it offered an American solution to people who were looking desperately for answers. "The South was hard travelling," Kate recalled of the encampment circuit. "I hated the heat, bed bugs, mosquitoes, greasy food and the constant tragedy of warped human lives, but I loved the response of the crowds and the profound gratitude for what we were trying to do for them." Reflecting on her life as a radical agitator, in 1945 she summarized the contributions of the southwestern Socialist movement she personified:

> I have no regrets for all the years and the grilling labors I gave the Socialist movement. It was well worth while. The Party served a val-

68. Ameringer, *If You Don't Weaken*, 459.

uable purpose in American life. We took light into dark places; we became the nation's conscience and prodded lawmakers into tardy action on many social problems; we were in the vanguard of all movements for social betterment and decent human relations. We were educators, "the voices crying in the wilderness" for a quarter of a century, and we left our mark on America.[69]

69. Kate Richards O'Hare to Castleton, September 16, 1945, in Eugene V. Debs Collection, Castleton Papers, Tamiment Institute, New York.

Index

439

Index